P9-CFP-830

AFTER THE FIRES

OTHER BOOKS IN ENGLISH BY PETER DEMETZ

Postwar German Literature

(EDITOR)
Marx, Engels, and the Poets
Theodor Fontane: Short Novels and Other Writings
The Disciplines of Criticism
(with Thomas Greene and Lowry Nelson, Jr.)
An Anthology of German Literature, 800-1750
(with W.T.H. Jackson)
Twentieth Century Views: Bertolt Brecht

PETER DEMETZ

AFTER THE FIRES

RECENT WRITING IN THE GERMANIES, AUSTRIA, AND SWITZERLAND

A HELEN AND KURT WOLFF BOOK
HARCOURT BRACE JOVANOVICH, PUBLISHERS
San Diego *New York* *London*

Library of Congress Cataloging-in-Publication Data
Demetz, Peter.
After the Fires.

"A Helen and Kurt Wolff book."
Bibliography: p.
1. German literature—20th century—History and criticism.
2. German literature—Austrian authors—History and criticism.
3. Swiss literature (German)—20th century—History and criticism. I. Title.
PT401.D38 1986 830'.9'00914 86-7635
ISBN 0-15-103958-5

Designed by Margaret Wagner
Printed in the United States of America

First edition

A B C D E

Contents

Preface

There is hardly anybody who does not have definite ideas about things German in general, and, in preparing to contradict a few of them, I face a special task. The past weighs heavily on studies of German affairs, and our efforts are not exactly strengthened by the rapid losses of German in public and private language instruction, and the growing distance between the educated reader and the university *Germanisten*. I fully understand why so many, some of the best among them, have been tempted to turn away from literature to teaching theories about theories, the New German Cinema, or the idiom of German industrial corporations. I do not want to give up yet, however, and while I greatly admire the New German Cinema, now going through its own midlife crisis, I should like to contribute my share to a continuing exploration of literature. I hope to consider a few well-known and many unknown books that enlighten us, in one way or other, about how people in German-speaking societies live, think, and feel thirty or forty years after Hitler. What I really want to do is to undermine our unreflecting clichés about German affairs, so satisfying at first, so boring and empty on second thought.

In the following chapters I would like to sketch a critical and selective panorama of recent imaginative writing in German in four settings: the Federal Republic of Germany, the German

Democratic Republic, Austria, and Switzerland. Since I am confronted with entire sets of unusual issues, it is perhaps not illegitimate to think of Voltaire, who said of the Holy Roman Empire that it was a "monster unique in its kind," and to believe that the monstrous complexities of contemporary writing in German still relate to ancient tensions and divisions, made more acute by the border between two power systems and between two views of literary life—a border running right through central Europe and through the minds of many people as well. Today regions, *Länder*, cantons, and even neighborhoods are far more important to the literary imagination in German-speaking countries than they have been for a long time, and the culture map is criss-crossed and marked by many lines and colors. Both Berlins and Vienna continue their functions, though in somewhat reduced circumstances, and the situation is not made easier by the recent exodus, voluntary or not, by many GDR writers who continue to live on the western side of the Wall in a kind of social abeyance and yet are not at all alienated from the spoken and written idiom of their new fellow-citizens.

Fifteen years ago, when I published my survey of *Postwar German Literature*, I had little trouble in starting my chronicle with the destruction of the Nazi Reich and the slow renascence of cultural life, often aided by the Allied military governments, each proceeding in its own way. I believe that a new stage of writing in German began in the mid-1960s which, after a distinct turn from collective to more intimate interests about ten years ago, now extends into the 1980s, a stage so far characterized by continuities rather than breaks, revolts, or intellectual discontinuities. In many ways, the mid-sixties were a time of important political and intellectual changes: in the West the student movement emerged and radically affected intellectual and literary expectations (in Austria and Switzerland as well), while in the East a new generation of writers, born and trained in the GDR, raised its voice, strident, provocative, and thoughtful, and forced the orthodoxy of Socialist Realism (at least until the Biermann affair) to defend itself more flexibly than before. By now the middle generation in West or East consists of persons born in the last years of World War II and later who rarely remember anything about the war or the dictatorship from their own experience.

I am not interested in writing a literary history in the older tradition, rich in bibliographies and poor in value judgments. While friends and colleagues concentrating on pure theory may consider my terrestrial interests rather passé, I am eager to know how good poems, plays, and novels are made, and how they relate to each other and to the kind of writing to which they belong, within the social context of their time. I cannot but accept the internal contradictions of such an approach. What is most excellent in imaginative literature is both more and less than historical, and yet—in the German case, studied by many for many reasons—any exclusive interest in literary forms (close to my fundamental inclinations) would dissatisfy many readers, including those like myself who once were Gestapo prisoners and will be unable, for the rest of their lives, to read German without trying to look beyond the text. That is why I begin my discussions with two chapters perhaps more historical than the others. In the first, about Group 47, I hope to establish an essential link between the mid-sixties and the mid-forties, and thus show the immediacy of postwar writing. In the second, on Auschwitz and some of its repercussions, I consider the difficult question of Holocaust writing in German.

After I have defined these assumptions, I advance a compromise solution by presenting the overwhelmingly rich and contradictory materials, combining some basic information about social and political matters with other sections more attentive to literary concerns and aesthetic forms. Since I should like to do justice both to the claims of social life and to the stubborn shapes of writing, I alternate descriptions of the four settings, each represented by one or two important writers, with chapters about particular genres, each again illuminated by the achievements of a few authors of particular distinction or interest. I suggest amplitude by indirection and implication, and wish to apologize if I do not account at length for my literary preferences, which favor innovation of idiom, formal intelligence, and the presence of an open and compassionate mind.

I am greatly indebted, for frank criticism and advice, to many friends and colleagues, including Johannes Anderegg (Switzerland), Marilyn S. Fries (University of Michigan), Wolfgang Kraus (Austria), Wolfgang Leonhardt (Federal Republic of Germany), Robert Liberles (Israel), Tony Niesz (Yale), Joel Schecter (Yale Drama School), Peter Stadelmayer (Federal Republic of Germany), and Theodore Ziolkowski (Princeton). I wish to express my sincere gratitude to Inter Nationes in Bonn and the Österreichische Gesellschaft für Literatur in Vienna, which enabled me to spend a few productive weeks in West Germany and Austria talking to authors, critics, publishers, and readers of the older and younger generations. In the early stage of preparing my manuscript I was valiantly helped by James Roosa, Birgit Baldwin, and Elizabeth Strenger (who was particularly helpful in editing the bibliography), and in the later, more difficult stages, by Philip Russom and Melissa Vogelsang, who checked data, untiringly gathered information about translations, and worked in the Yale University Computer Department according to a tight schedule. I am happy to acknowledge a special debt of gratitude to my editor Helen Wolff for more than the usual reasons. The little black-clad volumes of Expressionist prose and poetry, once published by her late husband Kurt Wolff, were among the first books to challenge my literary imagination when I was sixteen years old. Later, after many decades and on another continent, I felt similarly challenged and enlightened by her extraordinary and intimate knowledge of German writing, coming as it does from years of close work with Günter Grass, Uwe Johnson, Max Frisch, and others.

Acknowledgments

I have included, in a few instances, appropriate excerpts from some of my earlier publications. Permission has been granted by Ullstein Verlag of Berlin to rewrite in English a section on the younger Handke that originally appeared in *Die süße Anarchie* (1973). A few pages on Günter Grass's Danzig trilogy, Paul Celan's early poems, Martin Walser's *Halftime*, and Uwe Johnson's *The Third Book about Achim* are reprinted with permission of Macmillan Publishing Company from *Postwar German Literature: A Critical Introduction*, by Peter Demetz, copyright © 1970 by Macmillan Publishing Company. I am also thankful to AMS Press Inc. of New York for permission to reprint a few paragraphs from my contribution to "The Fisherman and His Wife," in *Günter Grass, "The Flounder" in Critical Perspective*, edited by Siegfried Mews (New York, 1983).

Abbreviations

CDU/CSU = Christlich Demokratische Union/Christlich Soziale Union (Christian Democratic Union/ Christian Social Union; the Conservatives)
DKP = Deutsche Kommunistische Partei (German Communist Party)
FDP = Freie Demokratische Partei (Free Democratic Party; the Liberals)
FU = Freie Universität/Berlin (Free University, Berlin)
GDR = German Democratic Republic (Deutsche Demokratische Republik, DDR)
KPD = Kommunistische Partei Deutschlands (Communist Party of Germany; so named during the Weimar Republic and in 1945–56)
ÖVP = Österreichische Volkspartei (Austrian People's Party)
SDS = Sozialistischer Deutscher Studentenbund (Socialist Federation of German Students)
SED = Sozialistische Einheitspartei Deutschlands (German Socialist Unity Party)
SPD = Sozialdemokratische Partei Deutschlands (German Social Democratic Party; the Socialists)
SPÖ = Sozialistische Partei Österreichs (Austrian Socialist Party)

NOTE

All nondramatic titles are given in the original German, followed in parentheses by the date of publication and an English rendering of the original title; the date after the English title, if given, refers to a published translation. In the discussions of drama, square brackets indicate the year of a first performance, while parentheses refer to publications of texts or translations, if ascertainable.

AFTER THE FIRES

1

WEST GERMAN LITERATURE AFTER THE WAR: GROUP 47

THE AGE OF THE FOUNDING FATHERS

The Federal Republic of Germany was originally conceived as an administrative improvisation to solve the economic problems of the three Western zones of occupation. In the era of Chancellor Konrad Adenauer, a sly tactician and sturdy old man of true vision, the conservative CDU/CSU pleaded for a free market society, full collaboration with the Western allies, a somewhat rigid anticommunism, and the new house and the little car. From 31 percent in 1949, it increased its vote to an absolute majority of 50.2 percent in 1957. It defended the German "economic miracle" (impossible without the productive efforts of all working people), which advanced industrial production within ten years by nearly 165 percent, quadrupled incomes (except those of old-age pensioners and large families), and gave twenty million Germans the opportunity to move into new homes. Unfortunately, the Conservatives never excelled in developing a finer sensibility for the attitudes and needs of intellectuals, writers, and artists. These fragile groups felt closer in some instances to the small party of the Liberals (FDP) or, in far greater numbers, to the traditional Social Democratic Party (SPD).

The SPD was one of the first parties to organize again nationwide after the destruction of Hitler's Reich, yet under the chairmanship of Kurt Schumacher, a loyal and stern Socialist who had spent the Nazi years in prisons and concentration camps, it was unwilling to let go of its traditional Marxist orientation and therefore was incapable, in the 1950s, of attracting more than 30 percent of the electorate. (The traditional centers of the Protestant elite of the working class were in the German Democratic Republic, and the strongly Catholic population in the German south and southwest had come to industrialization rather late.) In contrast to Italy and France, the Communist Party, reestablished in the Western occupation zones early in 1946, did not attract overwhelming voter suport (5.7 percent in 1949, 2.2 percent in 1953). When the Supreme Court of the republic declared its activities unconstitutional in 1956, it was in full decay as an effective political organization, being barely represented in the diets of Lower Saxony and the city of Bremen. The Deutsche Reichspartei (DRP) or German Reich Party, an early conglomerate of nationalists and neofascists, was briefly represented in the first parliament, and the activities of the Sozialistische Reichspartei (SRP) or Socialist Reich Party were, after some local successes, terminated by the Supreme Court.

In the late 1940s and the 1950s, now remembered with a good deal of nostalgia, the traditionalists and the intellectuals moved in a rather simple pattern, at least as seen from today's perspective. With slight differences, this pattern recalled Thomas Mann's tension between the "burghers," now members of the CDU/CSU in dark suits and silver ties, and the "artists," now busily writing for the well-funded radio station but clad programmatically in plebeian corduroy. Group 47 satisfied the vague intellectual needs of many talented writers of the middle and younger generations, eager to stand a little apart, but not too radically, from the economic miracle. As politically conscious citizens, the intellectuals occasionally joined radical Christians, pacifists, and old Socialists in protesting rearmament (1951–55), America's offer to provide its European allies with tactical atomic weapons (1957–58), and the conservative media's habit of reporting on the other German republic as if it were located on the moon. Material advances and the new prosperity (first food, then new furniture, cars, and the yearly trip to Majorca) did not silence the arts but challenged them. After Kafka and Hemingway had been imported (or rather reimported), Böll, Grass, Uwe Johnson, and Gabriele Wohmann began publishing their stories and novels. The lyric poem, the dominant genre of the decade, was admirably strengthened by Nelly Sachs, Ingeborg Bachmann, distant Paul Celan, Günter Eich, and Wilhelm Lehmann, while adventurous younger intellectuals rediscovered in the Brecht of the 1920s and 1930s a strident countervoice to what they called—though not yet in terms of Marxist theory—the stifling West German "restoration."

The virtues and limitations of much of postwar German writing emerged from the meetings of Group 47, which, despite its timely demise in the late 1960s, continues to be discussed by nearly everybody with awe, loving sympathy, or irritated suspicion. It was characteristic of the group to insist that it was not a group at all, at least not in the traditional sense of the term. Although it never bothered to define a program, issue manifestos, establish a firm organization, or settle in a definite place, the group functioned as if it had done all these things. In the late 1950s and early 1960s it prospered miraculously and attracted to its ever-changing meeting places more literary talent, including Heinrich Böll and Günter Grass, than any other institution or organization, West or East. The original meeting in 1947 of about fifteen starving writers, for whom a friendly French occupation officer who loved German literature had written a travel order to use on trains, was a modest affair, but later meetings turned into a kind of Cannes festival for the literary stars and starlets, male rather than female, closely watched by TV cameras and the heads of all important publishing houses. But there were some basic if vague left-of-center attitudes that did not change, a group ritual that persisted, and above all a fine and unerring sense for literary quality, rarely dulled or paralyzed, least of all by partisan political ideas and demands.

Walter Kolbenhoff, Hans Werner Richter, and Alfred Andersch, whom I want to single out as the intellectual fathers of Group 47, had shared fundamental hopes and disappointments in the 1930s and 1940s. They understood each other viscerally when, early in 1945, they met in an American POW camp organized on General Eisenhower's orders to prepare an elite of German antifascist writers, teachers, and administrators for future jobs in liberated Germany. Walter Kolbenhoff (b. 1908) had grown up in Berlin as a genuine proletarian who worked in factories, tramped for years through Europe, North Africa, and the Near East, and returned to Berlin to write articles for left-wing newspapers before 1933. After Hitler came to power, he emigrated to Copenhagen, where he was ordered by his local Communist Party cell to join the Wehrmacht so as to undermine it from within. He discovered too late that, after so many years abroad, he spoke a language that his new comrades-in-arms, all German working people, no longer understood. He fought at Sevastopol, El Alamein, and Monte Cassino. He had published a novel before he went to Copenhagen, wrote poems in Danish, and after his return from the war, briefly worked for the Munich *Neue Zeitung*, the voice of the U.S. military government. He wrote *Von unserem Fleisch und Blut* (1947; *Of Our Flesh and Blood*), a novel about a Hitler Youth Werewolf who did not want to give up, and the autobiographical narrative *Heimkehr in die Fremde* (1949; *Return to a Foreign Land*). Thereafter he produced lively reportage, radio plays, and novels (whodunits and others) for many years to come, but was out of the literary limelight.

Hans Werner Richter (b. 1908) devoted the best years of his life to guiding and sustaining Group 47, and it was only fair that the West German Federation of Trade Unions publicly honored him on his seventieth birthday for what he had done to strengthen the politically committed literature of our time. Born in Bansin, a little village on the Pomeranian coast, Richter for some time did not know what to do with himself, until his mother gently forced him to accept an apprentice job in a bookstore in Stettin and later in Berlin. Finding himself unemployed along with millions of others, in 1933 he emigrated to Paris, where he went hungry, then returned to Berlin. One year after Germany invaded Poland, he was ordered to join the Wehrmacht. He too had done his stint in the German Communist Party in the early 1930s but had been formally expelled for his Trotskyist leanings. In his reminiscences and novels, which he began publishing after the war, I find a strong feeling for the German people, for whom he wants to write in an understandable, clear, and realistic way, not necessarily in consonance with recent narrative experiments. In his early novel *Die Geschlagenen* (1947; *Beyond Defeat*, 1950) he tells us, from his own experience and in the language of an infantryman, how a group of weary Germans confront the advancing Americans in southern Italy, give up, and are interrogated before being transferred to POW camps. In his reminiscences *Spuren im Sand (*1953; *Traces in the Sand*), which sketch the political anatomy of North German provincial life, his plebeian mother emerges as a quietly heroic figure who works hard to keep the family together. When Group 47 flourished, Richter's fortunes as a writer declined, but in the 1970s he returned to the sources of his strength. In *Blinder Alarm* (1970; *False Alarm*) he tells the moving story of his Pomeranian childhood and the life of his weak yet loyal and tenacious father. His *Briefe an einen jungen Sozialisten* (1974; *Letters to a Young Socialist*) plead in an age of new orthodoxies and increasing violence for a measure of pragmatism without which socialism, in practice or in theory, cannot achieve significant changes in the everyday life of the people. Richter is an author who certainly has done more for others than he has done for himself.

Alfred Andersch (1914–80) was the most gifted intellectual among the founders of Group 47, but he felt increasingly disappointed by the mercurial attitudes that emerged from the gathering of his friends and by developments in Germany at large. He was born in Munich of lower-middle-class parentage, joined the Communist Party to emancipate himself from his conservative father, and headed the Bavarian youth branch of the Communist Party when the Nazis came to power. He was held at Dachau concentration camp twice, and his final release coincided with his decision to withdraw from the Party, which in his view had lacked incisive fighting spirit. He responded to total power by "total inversion," withdrawing into the invisibility of a Hamburg office job, traveling to Italy, reading Rilke (as did so many others), and writing for himself. A manuscript of short prose pieces was rejected by a respectable publishing house during the war, but Andersch's real life as a writer began when he deserted from the Wehrmacht. His stories and reflective novels of the 1950s, *Die Kirschen der Freiheit* (1952; *The Cherries of Freedom*, 1978), *Sansibar; oder, Der letzte Grund* (1957; *Flight to Afar*, 1958), and *Die Rote* (1960; *The Redhead,* 1961), seize the timeless moment in time when people, torn between fear and resolution, assert their freedom by an irreversible choice that goes against history, political power, and social convention. They do so by crossing the front lines, as he did himself; by helping others to escape from Nazi Germany while they themselves stay to resist (Gregor in *Sansibar*); or by deciding to live among the Venetian working people rather than to go on living in rich and meretricious Germany, as does the redhead Franziska.

In 1958 Andersch left his job in broadcasting to settle in the Swiss Ticino not far from Max Frisch; by 1962 he had ceased to participate in the life of the group. The younger Left of the sixties, committed to complex theories of utopia, did not really sympathize with the anti-Stalinist Andersch, who was more interested in discussing Sartre, Elio Vittorini, and Herman Melville than in quoting Lenin; his later novels were welcomed with respect but not read widely. *Efraim* (1967; *Efraim's Book*, 1970), the story of a German Jew who returns as a British journalist to his native Berlin, seemed too self-centered for an age of collective concerns: Efraim rediscovers himself as a lonely individual, "a Jew among the Goyim," and some of his most important observations touch on the full implications of brutal new daily German idioms that he had never heard in his youth. *Winterspelt* (1974; *Winterspelt*, 1978), possibly more welcome to American reviewers than to their German colleagues (as happened often in Andersch's case), returns to the last year of the war and a quiet corner of the Western front behind which the Germans are preparing furiously for their murderous Ardennes offensive. It tells how a German major plans to turn his unit and himself over to the U.S. army, only to cancel his plan at the last minute, but independently of an order for his division to move to Italy and be replaced by the SS. An "ambitious novel" (as Ernst Pawel said in the *New York Times Book Review* of July 30, 1978), it includes portraits of a Berlin schoolteacher, an old Communist, a U.S. army captain, and a hapless German émigré acting as go-between, and elegantly and deftly comments on its own narrative process of toying with possibilities rather than recapitulating real events. In his poems of the late 1970s Andersch protests against the danger that a "nation of ex-Nazis," while pretending to fight terrorists, might again indulge in its "favorite sport" of persecuting anybody on the Left indiscriminately. In an interview a few weeks before he died, he said proudly that he fully accepted the reproach that he always went back into the German past in his books. In his stories, essays, and important novels, Andersch was one of the defeated revolutionaries of the European Left who went on writing loyally and courageously in order to prevent German history from repeating itself.

EARLY HISTORY

The early chronicle of Group 47, or rather its prehistory, begins with Kolbenhoff, Richter, and Andersch in various foxholes in southern Italy in 1944, ready to be taken prisoner or to cross over to the other side. Andersch deserted, and Richter was willingly taken prisoner. It is more difficult to say what Kolbenhoff did, because he broke into an Italian farmhouse and ordered an astonished peasant girl to get some English soldiers to take him away (when they arrived they were rather nervous, fearing a trap). After working in different POW camps in Illinois and Louisiana, the three were transferred to Fort Kearney, Rhode Island, and there joined the erudite Gustav René Hocke, a German news correspondent in Rome who had been gently persuaded by the Americans to change sides, in editing *Der Ruf (The Call)*, a newspaper distributed by the U.S. army to the nearly 400,000 German prisoners in American camps who were still disoriented and terrorized within the camp compounds by young intransigents of the Africa Corps and old Nazis. They also edited a series of educational books for prisoners, and while Wendell Willkie and Stephen Vincent Benét were eagerly read, it was Hemingway's *For Whom the Bell Tolls* that left an ineradicable mark on everybody who wanted to describe the experience of the war. The prose written by Kolbenhoff, Richter, and Andersch at that time, and the first narratives of Group 47, are unthinkable without Hemingway's parataxis, understatement, and tough idiom.

The POW *Der Ruf* was distributed in the camps from March 1, 1945, to April 1, 1946, confining itself to factual reporting of the news. After the capitulation in Germany, the periodical (now under the editorship of Hocke) turned to a systematic political analysis of the Nazi Reich and shocked the POWs by publishing photos of the concentration camp of Buchenwald taken by the American army. In October 1945, when Hocke went back to Germany, Hans Werner Richter and a friend assumed the editorship. Stressing Franklin Delano Roosevelt's liberal ideas, they irritated army authorities inclined to more conservative views by advocating a new union of democracy and socialism, German unity, total freedom of the press, and the strong belief that, for political as well as philosophical reasons, it was wrong to declare the entire German nation guilty of what had happened under the "Third Reich."

Alfred Andersch, who had taken the Rhode Island training courses (often given by Harvard professors) with great enthusiasm, returned to Germany earlier than his friends and convinced a Munich publisher that it was high time to publish an intellectual periodical that would continue *Der Ruf* in Germany. Andersch and Richter, who returned to Germany that spring, together began editing another *Ruf*, which turned out to be one of the most avidly read German magazines from August 1946 to April 1947, when permission to publish was withdrawn by the U.S. military government, which cited what it called the "nihilism" of the editors. It was, to say the least, a rather strange argument against people who, after their experiences in the Communist Party, were Social Democrats by instinct (in Andersch's case, with a dash of French existentialism added). Though they all were admittedly skeptical about American reeducation by rote and appalled by the way the American army handed German prisoners over to the French to work in the coal mines, they were enthusiastic supporters of a future Europe of politically spontaneous individuals in the liberal tradition. They had attacked the Stalinists in the Soviet zone of occupation and elsewhere (for instance, in the French Communist Party), and it was not impossible that the U.S. military government acted on a Soviet request. Richter suggests as much in his memoirs.

The legacy of the war, the POW camps, and the ideas of *Der Ruf* was intensely felt in the early gatherings of the group in the late 1940s and characterized much of its tone and procedures. Most of the invited were returning soldiers (men above the rank of sergeant were suspect), and there was a strong disinclination to work with authors of the self-proclaimed "inner emigration" (those who had published much without actively supporting the Nazis under Hitler) and not much intense interest in the émigrés, whose writings were largely unknown to a younger generation.

From the early gatherings, a kind of third literary force clearly emerged, keeping its distance from the inner emigration and from the exiles abroad. The group cultivated an almost studied attitude of shirt-sleeved professionalism, and the ritual of the meetings was tough. Richter issued invitations by handwritten postcards, relying on his own judgment or that of his friends. Authors had to sit in the so-called "electric chair" to read from their manuscripts, and the audience had the privilege of ending any performance at any moment by a gesture of thumbs-down. Even if authors were fortunate enough to read through an entire text, they faced the uncompromising criticism of the listeners and were not allowed to talk back (those who did so were automatically excluded from future invitations). One of the abused authors complained to Thomas Mann, who, from a safe distance, alluded to the "vulgar" (*pöbelhaft*) attitude of that "gang of riffraff" (*Rasselbande*); Heinrich Böll, later a member of the in-group for some time, did not like the merciless procedure either.

There was, for a long time, little sympathy for the refined and overeducated, for university professors (an attitude later selectively revised), or for any kind of complex political or literary theory. Most of the literary preferences were defined by Gustav René Hocke in a remarkable essay in the Munich *Ruf* in which he separated bad "calligraphy," or the art of writing beautifully in the service of political obfuscation, from a down-to-earth mode close to the content of experience. In the early meetings this mode involved a basic vocabulary of 300 to 400 words that, as Wolfgang Weyrauch suggested, cut a clearing (*Kahlschlag*) through the old thicket of aesthetic pretensions, lies, and illusions. The language of the future would be realistic, Richter maintained somewhat prematurely. Rilke and Hölderlin were definitely out, but Günter Eich's basic though cryptic lyrical language was very much admired. Among the short-story writers those close to Hemingway prevailed, at least temporarily, over the others who preferred what was called the "magic realism" of reimported Franz Kafka. An independent observer remarked at the time that the typical prose piece of the group was sustained by the word "shit" on every page, in conformity with the speech habits of the *Landser*, the German equivalent of the GI.

THE RISE AND FALL OF A LITERARY GROUP

If, in the late 1940s, Richter usually convened his authors in the house of some friend fortunate enough to have a roof over his head, in the early 1950s the group went irreversibly public. It gathered in cafés, hospitable children's homes, or town halls in the friendly provinces and for many years showed a rather surprisingly Gothic propensity for monasteries, castles, and ancient towns, aesthetically attractive but not entirely consonant with professional austerity. Only once were the premises of a trade union training school used. After a demonstrative gathering in West Berlin (immediately after the Wall had been erected by the GDR), it turned out that, after all, old country inns with excellent cuisine, distinguished local wines, and large parking lots offered welcome comfort to older and younger writers who in their books agreed how awful it was to live in an affluent society.

The gatherings clearly reflected the changing situation of literature and the other media in a consolidating postwar economy. From 1951 on, radio producers regularly attended, first as talent scouts and later with their trucks and crews. For many years before the advent of TV, most group members—like everybody else in literature—made a living by writing radio essays, features, and short plays for the broadcasting corporations. (Young Martin Walser, hanging around outside a meeting hall as a radio crew member, sent a message to Richter that he was writing much better than everybody else inside, and was promptly invited to read.) Publishers, who in the immediate postwar years concentrated on publishing for eager readers the great books by exiles and writers abroad that had long been proscribed by the Nazis, in the early 1950s began turning again to contemporary German writing and discovered that the gatherings of the group were a convenient marketplace for new commodities. Soon the first honest voices were heard complaining that the meetings were functioning as a literary stock exchange. From the early 1950s on, a literary prize was awarded by the group. In 1951, when Heinrich Böll, who had made his first appearance looking like a "friendly neighborhood plumber," was chosen to receive the award—at that time one thousand marks donated by an American PR firm—he dashed to the local post office to cable the money home to feed his children, but also offered a small loan to the Yugoslav-Viennese writer Milo Dor, an unsuccessful competitor. The initial list of winners included Günter Eich (1950), Heinrich Böll (1951), Ingeborg Bachmann (1953), and Günter Grass (1958), which shows that the members of the gathering, who voted by placing a piece of paper with a name in an old cigar box, did know a good text when they heard one.

The group may have been established by people who believed in simple language, Hemingway, and the sober rediscovery of social experience, but they fought a losing battle. In the 1950s and early 1960s realism—in spite of Heinrich Böll—was increasingly repudiated and finally pushed out of the group, to be taken up later by the radicals or those young Austrians who wanted to protest against overrated experimentation. In the 1950s, lyric poems and prose parables were favored more and more, and even the older realists could not but admire the work of Ilse Aichinger and Ingeborg Bachmann, two Austrian women writers of poetic tales and meditative verse. (Yet at one point, the original realists were close to staging an exodus in protest against too much metaphor.) Discussion once again centered on the slogans of pure poetry versus *engagé* writing, but by 1960 a new style of radical experimental writing had made itself energetically felt in Uwe Johnson's Faulknerian prose and Helmut Heissenbüttel's Concrete Poetry, and an entire new generation of writers appeared who preferred to test language itself rather than to explore nonlinguistic experience. Andersch withdrew from group activities, and even Richter gave up reading his own prose but, with unshakable humor and wonderful tact, continued loyally to conduct the expansive meetings, now often attracting a hundred or more writers and critics. Literary criticism within the group consolidated its own considerable strength. Walter Jens, professor of classical philology at Tübingen, had long attended the gatherings (as a writer rather than critic), and Joachim Kaiser, of high musical and literary erudition, had usually been present. But by 1960 at the latest, a phalanx of critical experts had constituted itself, including Walter Höllerer, who with a smile bridged the gap between semiotics and his own writing; Marcel Reich-Ranicki, a cunning master of harshly incisive analysis; and last but not least Hans Mayer, an erudite Marxist and connoisseur of world literature. These critics—in one body, so to speak—usually took their seats in the front and debated with so much skill, exuberance, and erudition that at least one witness remarked that their intellectual ping-pong game would have been equally brilliant if there had been no readings at all. It is also true, however, that the ritual of criticism by professorial luminaries strengthened the inclination of many writers to read compact poems, somewhat anemic stories, and chapters of novels complete in themselves and making an epigrammatic point, because they felt that the critics would respond more easily to short rather than long texts. Thus the ritual itself favored particular genres and forms over others.

In the final years (1963–67) the group wavered between the sweet temptation of nationally and internationally representing German writing at its best, and a distinct hankering after its modest and austere origins. For the meeting at Saalgau (1963), Richter intended to keep down the number of invited authors and to concentrate on strictly professional matters, but the subsequent meetings at Sigtuna in Sweden (1964) and above all at Princeton (1966) produced more internal tension and media noise than new and convincing writing. In his report about the Princeton meeting, the critic Joachim Kaiser suggested that the end was near because he could feel that the group was falling apart. He was not alone in perceiving that the American gathering revealed the rapidly widening gap between the generations, and a striking absence of lively, courageous, and juicy writing. All the signs of worldly success were there—the grants from the Ford Foundation; the neon letters "Welcome Group 47" on U.S. 1; the Princeton invitation to convene the meeting in the hall of the Whig Society, the oldest literary group in the United States. Yet there was also increasing frustration over the actual readings, including Walter Jens's scenes from a somewhat desiccated Rosa Luxemburg play and Reinhold Lettau's perfect yet minute prose pieces, and more than twenty other unexciting texts. Joseph P. Bauke, writing in the *New York Times Book Review* of May 15, 1966, confessed that he was not at all surprised that German audiences actually preferred reading Norman Mailer and James Baldwin to a native writing that lacked life. The literary sensation, at least in the polemical sphere, was provided by fragile Peter Handke, who, attending for the first time (and the last), was roughly handled for his insipid excerpts from a whodunit to end all whodunits, and who in careful Wittgensteinian prose protested against the impotence of talents and the descriptive mania of new writing (except his own). Some of the latent political issues emerged somewhat later when two younger writers and Peter Weiss, the author of the Auschwitz oratorio *The Investigation,* attended a student teach-in on Vietnam and carefully stressed that, according to group tradition, they were speaking for themselves and not for the collective at large. Questions of commitment versus aesthetic experience also dominated the public encounter of some of the German writers with Allen Ginsberg, Susan Sontag, and Leslie Fiedler. While the Germans, including Grass and Weiss, were adamant about the necessary commitment, they were astonished to hear that some of their American colleagues were more inclined to discuss an "explosion of happiness," LSD, or, like Susan Sontag, the grand joy of creating aesthetically satisfying forms.

The inevitable end had come when the group, gathering in 1967 at the Pulvermühle, an ancient Franconian inn, was interrupted by demonstrating student radicals from the nearby University of Erlangen, who demanded that the group immediately define its political stance. Suddenly even the pretensions of cohesion were gone; some of the young writers within the meeting rose to support the students outside (who had come with bullhorns but dressed as lovable clowns), while others, including Grass, insisted that the literary readings proceed. There was some talk later about meeting once more in Czechoslovakia, in support of the restive writers there, but Soviet tanks rolled into Prague and all plans had to be canceled (fortunately, I think, in that the West German writers, for all their good intentions, were not sufficiently sensitive to the terrible burdens of the German/Czech past). It would be easy, given the supermeetings abroad and the sudden finale at the Pulvermühle, to speak in melodramatic terms of the hubris and tragic fall of the group. But I would rather say that it died, if medical metaphors are appropriate, of a ripe old age and a number of diseases, some of which (perhaps long hidden by TV cosmetics) had been wasting the collective body for years, and whose fatal force was quickly concentrated by the final crisis.

Nearly twelve years after the last meeting, Günter Grass published his *Das Treffen in Telgte* (1979; *The Meeting at Telgte*, 1981), in which he expressed his gratitude to Hans Werner Richter, who had kept the group going for so long. Times merge, as so often in Grass's writings; what reads, at least at first sight, as a sophisticated story about a Westphalian gathering of the most important German Baroque poets, concerned with the fate of their divided fatherland, actually turns out to be a novella à clef, written as seventeenth-century pastiche, about the later group. The daily procedures of the Telgte meeting clearly correspond to the group rituals: the rough-hewn stool on which poets sit when reading to their colleagues from works in progress, the festive meals, and the exciting discussions of texts and ideas. Hans Werner Richter appears in the mask of the wise Königsberg poet Simon Dach; the rotund Marxist critic Hans Mayer, I suspect, in the figure of the learned Baroque philologist August Bucher, often lecturing but rarely listening to others; and Grass himself, as the young Hans Jakob Christoffel von Grimmelshausen, lively, irresponsible, and much more interested in food, money, and the innkeeper Libuschka than in the finer points of the discussion. (Grimmelshausen also happens to be the most important novelist of the German Baroque.) There are wonderful chiaroscuro scenes in the Dutch manner, with soldiers and servant girls around the blazing fires, and we do not need much historical knowledge to understand the worries of the writers who, then as now, "lack all power except the one of working with exact if totally useless words."

REQUIEM

Group 47 was, paradoxically, always of a double mind about politics. The founders were antifascists close to middle age who painfully remembered how literature had been forced into ideological servitude by the National Socialists and therefore had ambivalent feelings about the social function of writing, which in their opinion should fight fascism, war, nationalism, and all repressive ideologies, but without excessive concrete involvement that might endanger creative spontaneity. Kolbenhoff, Richter, Andersch, and their friends never gave up hoping that their writing would have a *Fernwirkung*, a social impact from a distance. In practice, they excelled as editors, poets, and novelists, and in spite of all political gestures were unwilling—in some contrast to Günter Grass and his later generation—to engage too actively in party politics. With most returning soldiers and many German intellectuals in general, they shared a deep aversion to anything that smacked of organization, structure, and hierarchy. Their assumption, more or less hidden, was that writers were an elite who could eat the political cake and have it, too: writers were not interested in conquering political parties or the parliament, but hoped for indirect influence on the changing mentality of the nation. Richter himself solved the insoluble dilemma of wanting politics without politics by trying to keep the group, as a collective body, out of active politicking while at the same time giving a splendid personal example of continuous moral and social commitment—an example later continued by Grass. Personally close to the Social Democrats, Richter brought Willy Brandt to at least one of the group meetings and, more unwilling than willingly, contributed to the general public's idea that the group, all assertions to the contrary, in substantial matters sided with the Social Democrats. Younger writers voiced increased skepticism about their elders who were in danger of petrifying an antifascism of the past, and who failed to see that the powerful of the present, as one of the younger people remarked, used other means to terrorize people, as for instance affluence and an abundance of commodities. But it was the collaboration of Socialists and Conservatives in the Grand Coalition of 1966, the student movement with its renascent Marxist theory, and the formation of a radical Extraparliamentary Opposition that finally split the group from within. Most writers went on unanimously signing proclamations against the war in Vietnam, but Richter and Grass were inclined to be patient with the Social Democrats and Chancellor Brandt while others, including Peter Weiss, Hans Magnus Enzensberger, Erich Fried, and Reinhold Lettau, sided with the radicals and the Extraparliamentary Opposition, which had ceased to believe in the possibility of efficiently reforming the system from within.

Yet it would be a half-truth to suggest that Group 47 fell victim to a late German refraction of the reformist/radical conflict that in so many different shapes had long defined the vicissitudes of the European intellectual Left. I would suggest that the political conflicts within the group corresponded, in perhaps unsuspected ways, to the changing functions of writer and writing in the economic context of West German society. The group started as a kind of professional workshop and was to end, as Hans Mayer suggested, as a literary "market service" that, from a wide range of productions, preselected a set of texts that received a brand name and were eagerly snapped up by the media and publishers. Such a market service fulfilled an important task as long as fiction, belles lettres of all kinds, and poetry were highly valued, but concepts of literature radically changed, at least for a while, in the late 1960s. Two sets of demands combined against the group: a new generation of readers and writers distrusted fiction and preferred writing as close to social action as possible, while at approximately the same time publishing houses, as they expanded, were forced by industrial necessity to develop their own stable of reliable text-producers rather than go to literary gatherings in which, as Heinrich Böll suggested, legitimate pluralism had given way to mere promiscuity. Perhaps the idea of the group itself, however small or large, had become an anachronism. Whether they knew it or not, the fathers of Group 47 were actually continuing something that had developed during the "Third Reich" among the non-Nazi intellectuals, who met regularly in their apartments to read each other their imitations of Rilke, Heidegger, and rarely, Brecht. If Group 47 was averse to the candlelight and romantic chamber music that were de rigueur in the darkened apartments of World War II and preferred the tough style instead, at least initially it was not so different from the *Kreise* (circles) in the Nazi Reich engaged in protecting introversion and high culture against the brutal political powers. Yet it was impossible to continue the old tradition of the private and protective *Kreis* under the media lights, and as the individual writers had to face the increasing industrialization of publishing, the *Kreis* or *Gruppe*, graced by the presence of a famous publisher, was no longer sufficient. Other forms of organization were needed and, as the fortunes of the group declined, more writers, among them Böll and Martin Walser, were active in establishing a writers' trade union strongly concerned with questions of copyrights, taxation, and pension plans.

Yet Group 47, at its best times, brought together authors of several generations and staged, perhaps in the full sense of the word, some of the central events of contemporary literary history. It provided a sounding board for intrepid beginners, arranged publicity for the advanced, opened the West German reservoir of readers to writers from Austria and Switzerland, and quietly invited many of the isolated authors from the GDR, though not everyone could or would come. The group did not eagerly seek out talented women, and sometimes favored a tepid *Sozialdemokratismus* (trenchantly analyzed by the critic Hans Egon Holthusen) as a kind of conformist ideology that made it easy to be on the side of progress without really trying. And there may have been yet another problem. In 1965 the critic Rolf Schroers suggested in a first-rate essay that it was precisely the flexibility of the group, and its almost unlimited luck in attracting new talent, that prevented other, competing centers of literary originality from forming. His shrewd diagnosis is amply confirmed by the relatively short life-span of all other literary groups, including the Vienna Group or Group 61, established in the Ruhr region to explore the working people's experience. The virtues and problems of Group 47 were bound together inseparably.

2

ON AUSCHWITZ, AND ON WRITING IN GERMAN: A LETTER TO A STUDENT

Dear David,

When you came to my office recently to continue our class discussion of Peter Weiss's Auschwitz oratorio [1965] and to ask why I did not offer a course on Holocaust writing in German, I found myself incapable of giving you a simple answer, and I hope that my present letter will offer to you the beginning of a response—though I fear that I cannot define it with academic impersonality. I always ask who it is who speaks or writes about the Holocaust, and I have not made up my mind really what to think of our new Holocaust industry—whether it is one more abomination engendered by the publish-or-perish demands of American universities, or an essential intellectual undertaking, keeping everybody conscious of what has happened in central European history and of what could happen again, though I would hesitate to say anywhere. Recently, many more Jewish students have attended my seminars on contemporary German literature than in previous years, and I am inclined to believe that they are the children of exiles of German and Austrian background and want to know more about people, events, and books mentioned, perhaps fleetingly, in talks with parents or grandparents. (I remember that my own older daughter, when she was thirteen or fourteen, almost obsessively studied the history of German concentration camps, because she had heard her mother and father utter the names of the places and the dead.)

My own involvement is not easy to describe to anybody who did not live over there in the late 1930s and 1940s, and I have to say that my experiences were constituted by the so-called Nuremberg Laws, which classified me as "*Mischling ersten Grades*" (let's say "bastard first-class"), and the fatal consequences of my parents' decision to divorce in the late 1930s, separating my father of South Tyrolian origin from my Czech-Jewish mother who, when the deportations came, could not claim to be married to an "Aryan" and was shipped off, together with her own mother, brothers, and sisters. (With one exception, all died or were killed in Theresienstadt or Auschwitz.) When my mother received her deportation order, I helped in the packing of her rucksack (which everybody thought eminently practical because there was space for a pair of sturdy shoes), and rode with her in the streetcar to the Prague Hall of Commercial Fairs, the assembly point. I am sorry to say that it was a fellow Czech who struck her in the face because we stood, in his opinion, too close to the front of the streetcar (Jews had to stay in the back). In the meantime my father and his friend Michal Mareš, well-known as mentor to Franz Kafka's beloved Milena Jesenská, walked about the Hall trying to find out whether the transport would leave that evening or later. I could go on telling you a few chapters of the (occasionally) picaresque story of how the Gestapo became interested in the doings of our little student group thinking about the future, and about my stints in various prisons and forced labor camps, but what I would really like to say is that I found myself on the border between Aryans and Jews, living, if you will, since I grew up Catholic, in the narrow space between norms, collectives, and great traditions. There were, of course, thousands like myself all over Nazi-occupied Europe, and to this day, when I go to Germany and Austria, I have an easier time talking to former "bastards" or Jewish survivors than to many other people. From special habits, dress codes, and even furniture in apartments, I have become adept in "reading" what people did in the past. We bastards developed, for it was a matter of life or death, an almost Proustian sense for the semiotics of fascism and antifascism.

We were also—especially if we lived in border regions or in cities like Prague where many languages were spoken—early if instinctively aware of a fundamental issue irrevocably present in our daily experiences: the issue (grievously underrated by many observers here) of the language itself, of German, and whether or not the victims and their friends should go on speaking, writing, and dreaming in the language of the killers. We asked ourselves whether it would not be nobler to be inarticulate in another language rather than articulate in German—whether we should escape into or adopt Czech, Polish, Yiddish, or Hebrew, or go on, against all reason, to cultivate German in a secret act of basic resistance, believing that we were the true speakers, as long as we were able to speak at all, and that the killers were infecting, misusing, raping a pure idiom. The question was answered differently by different people, and there is no right or wrong. There were those who categorically refused to go on speaking their mother tongue; those like Nelly Sachs (Nobel Prize, 1966) who, discovering her Jewish origins in Hitler's Berlin, unhesitatingly wrote her dirges and psalms about the dying of the Jews in German; those who began studying Goethe, Hölderlin, and Rilke so as to explore what German before Hitler was all about; and those like H. G. Adler who rarely wavered in their allegiance to the German classical heritage before or after Auschwitz. There were those who began writing in a new and unknown language, word by word and day by day; those who went into exile in another language and after many years (like Peter Weiss) returned to German; and those, among them Jakov Lind, who after writing many years quite successfully in German, ultimately decided to turn to English after all. I could go on and on, but what I really want to say is that it is dubious, in the age of Auschwitz, to speak about German writing as if these texts were written in Polish, English, French, or Yiddish, or to forget that one cannot speak about the camp guards in their own language without reflections that hurt deeply. If it is difficult to form an English sentence about what happened, it is still more difficult in German.

In our discussions we often tend to forget that Germans and German-speaking Jews were the first victims of the Nazis. Instead of formulating metaphysical generalizations, it would be more useful to turn to the language problem by analyzing, soberly and with philological attention, the German postwar attempts to isolate the Nazi vocabulary infesting the language and to reveal what was really hidden, semantically and ideologically, in the political and administrative language of the Nazi regime. Fortunately, an excellent and intellectually productive beginning was made, in both the Soviet and the American zones of occupation, by Victor Klemperer (a Jewish professor of Romance literature who survived because of his marriage to a non-Jewish wife) and by Dolf Sternberger, an essayist of distinction. Klemperer's *LTI* [*Lingua Tertii Imperii*]*: Notizbuch eines Philologen* (1947; *Notebook of a Philologist*) combines observations about daily experiences in forced labor and in a Dresden "Jewish house" (most of the house's inhabitants were killed in the Allied air raid of February 1944) with expert philological analyses of characteristic terms from Nazi speeches such as *fanatisch* and *arthaft*, the new wave of Nazi names (e.g., Uwe and Ute), and the use of runes in newspaper ads. Dolf Sternberger's *Aus dem Wörterbuch des Unmenschen* (1947; *From the Dictionary of the Nonhumans*), later continued by W. E. Süskind and Gerhard Storz, suggested that "words and sentences" were "gardens and prisons" in which we "lock ourselves while speaking" and proceeded, less metaphorically and entry by entry, to unmask the bestiality inherent in the key vocabulary of Nazi discourse, as for instance in such terms as *Betreuung*, etymologically related to "loyalty" yet often referring to murder. Group 47 had ample reason to believe that postwar German literature should start firmly from a few words that bore no infection.

Recently it has been argued by younger critics close to the student movement that in May 1945, when Germany surrendered to the Allies, not much changed in writing. Those who were there definitely have other views. It is true that not much was published at first, in contrast to the expressionist revolution of 1917–18, but the few books available to the few carried an imprint of absolute authenticity and of a bare and almost innocent honesty in confronting the recent past. Thoughtful Germans returning from concentration camps and the underground, among them Eugen Kogon, Pastor Martin Niemöller, and the philosopher Karl Jaspers, discussed the idea of "collective guilt," which the Allied authorities unfortunately made the centerpiece of reeducation for democracy. It is a great pity that Eugen Kogon's *Der SS-Staat: Das System der deutschen Konzentrationslager* (1946; *The Theory and Practice of Hell: The German Concentration Camps and the System behind Them*, 1973) has been nearly forgotten today. A Catholic intellectual of the Left, Kogon started to write his manuscript only four weeks after he had been liberated from Buchenwald. Nevertheless, combining the philosophical essay with the laconic witness report and sociological/statistical analysis, he wrote a pioneering book, exacting in its details about the internal and external camp administrations, balanced in its judgments about the many groups, including the Jews, in Buchenwald, and, in spite of the dearth of published documentary materials, incisive and almost unerring in its views about the stages of the Nazi race policies and what happened in other and different kinds of camps, including Auschwitz.

In the long run, our discussion of what kind of writing should be appropriate to the age of Auschwitz is totally irrelevant, if it touches on issues of genre alone and does not look for the presence of compassion. I cannot believe that categories of tradition and experimentation, realism and surrealism are more important than the individual text, in whatever mode, as long as it prevents us from believing that Auschwitz was just another event in world history. In German writing, nonrealist narratives long precede the documentary literature of the late 1950s and 1960s; seemingly more distant from history than are documents, these stories and narratives try to approach the core of what happened in the consciousness of people suffering, dying, or surviving. In the novels of Ilse Aichinger and Elisabeth Langgässer—both half-Jewish according to official classification, and who survived in Vienna and Berlin respectively—individual consciousness reflects historical events without false illusions. *Die grössere Hoffnung* (1948; *Herod's Children*, 1963) by Aichinger (b. 1921) does not separate the daydreams and nightmares of a half-Jewish girl from daily life in Vienna under Nazi rule; she and the Jewish children excluded from the city parks play their games of acceptance, escape, and salvation in the Jewish cemetery. The Jewish children are deported, but the girl stays alone with her Jewish grandmother, who kills herself (the girl helps her to take poison); then, in the last days of the battle in the city streets, the girl herself is killed, after she has helped a Soviet soldier cross the Danube bridges. She "jumped over a streetcar track that had been torn out of the ground, and before gravity could pull her back to earth, an exploding grenade blew her to bits."

Elisabeth Langgässer (1899–1950), read only by the happy few today, immediately after the war challenged her audiences by the density of her metaphors and by her ruthless combination of myth, unhidden sexuality, and unsparing language. Her *Märkische Argonautenfahrt* (1950; *The Quest*, 1953), one of the most important novels of the immediate postwar period, does not invite easy reading, for it moves in a strange world of mystical religiosity in which Judaism, ascetic Christianity, and Greek myth paradoxically merge. It is the story of seven Berliners who in August 1945, with the stench of corpses and fires still in the air, set out to find wisdom on a spiritual pilgrimage. During the journey they seek shelter from the rain in a forest hut where their patron "saint" Sichelchen, who died in Auschwitz, looks down on them from the translucent sky and tells them her own story—the life of a Jewish woman of supreme intellectual gifts, a hunchback who, while other girls danced, studied physics and mathematics in Paris and Göttingen, fired by a desire for absolute beauty. She stayed on when the "killers came," serving as the last administrator of the Berlin Jewish welfare center, and voluntarily joined a transport of orphans to the east, moving toward the divine as does "the disintegrating universe itself." There is nothing in German writing of the time that equals the febrile pages in which Sichelchen speaks of her love for the orphan Deborah, a dwarf, and Marcus, "the wobbly hydrocephalic," in whom she finds reflections of a transcendent beauty for which she has longed all her life, and her memories of the welfare center in which the last Berlin Jews assembled daily after their slave labor, before being deported. "Tossing in a heap their coats and jackets with the Jewish star, they would sit together in spectral gaiety, like departed souls that have shed their bodies, and listen to voices from out of cosmic space that thronged into their ghostly ears . . . 'hang on! we're coming . . . !' "

One evening in October 1956 a translation of the U.S. stage version of *The Diary of Anne Frank* was performed in many German theaters, to be followed by the now forgotten play *Korczak und die Kinder* [1957] (*Korczak and the Children*), by Erwin Sylvanus (1917–85), about a teacher who follows his wards to the death camps. Then came the trial of Eichmann (1961) and that of the Auschwitz guards (1963–65), the latter reported in detail by the *Frankfurter Allgemeine Zeitung*, compelling many writers to turn once again to the recent past. The philosophers Theodor W. Adorno and Günther Anders considered the implications of the trials and the need of German education in the future, and a new wave of plays about anti-Semitism and the concentration camps was staged and widely discussed in the mass media, including Max Frisch's allegorical *Andorra* (1961); Rolf Hochhuth's *Der Stellvertreter* (1963; *The Deputy*, 1964); Heinar Kipphardt's *Joel Brand* (1965); and Peter Weiss's *Die Ermittlung* (1965; *The Investigation*, 1966). Witness reports, court proceedings, and historical materials were closely studied, and many young writers—continuing a distinct trend of the mid-1920s and also anticipating the future disavowal of all fictions characteristic of the late 1960s—wrote in the "documentary fashion," working with long quotations, reducing the function of the inventive author at least in theory, and letting history speak for itself to the extent possible in literary texts compiled or written by later authors who were themselves but students of texts. Transferring the device of the movie montage to prose writing, the lawyer and filmmaker Alexander Kluge published *Lebensläufe* (1962; *Attendance List for a Funeral*, 1966), which was "in part fictional, in part not." He asked questions about the German tradition and explored the lives of a dozen German men and women involved in the events of 1933–45, among them the nonfictional army officer charged with interviewing and then decapitating imprisoned "Jewish-Bolshevik commissars" whose skulls were collected, as anthropological specimens, at an institute of the Nazi University of Strasbourg.

On February 20, 1963, Rolf Hochhuth's *The Deputy* was produced in Berlin by Erwin Piscator, the veteran of the radical theater of the 1920s and early 1930s. Immediately it triggered a wide and often violent public discussion concerning the role of the Catholic Church and the Pope during the war, and the possibility or impossibility of showing Auschwitz onstage. I deeply respect Hochhuth's Christian existentialism, which drives him to reveal the terrible gap between history and the institutionalized versions of historical events. However, upon rereading *The Deputy*, which was triumphantly performed in Paris and New York twenty years ago, I have to admit that the play itself, whatever the documentation, comes close to counteracting its own purpose by reducing the conflicts to Schillerian disputes in high places and by constructing, in the fifth act, a stage Auschwitz replete with shootings, melodrama, fires on the horizon, and a blond Nazi secretary putting on her panties adorned with SS runes. We watch the tragedy of a young Jesuit who as a believing Christian has to undergo fearful tests of strength, rather than a play about Jews. In spite of all his doubts about the divine order of the world, the young Jesuit who voluntarily joins a convoy of Jews to Auschwitz and works there removing corpses from the gas chambers (as the Pope should have done) dies a professing Christian, and the Jews are part, if not the objects, of a theological argument, their presence in no way strengthened by the bad poetry they have to utter before arriving at the Auschwitz ramp. The problem is that the "historical" play—acts 2 to 4, consisting of Hochhuth's passionate accusations against Pope Pius XII for having failed to identify with the persecuted—has been put into the framework of a mystery play, acts 1 and 5, in which the author deals with ontological issues of good and evil, history, and people, then ultimately returns to the myth of the Nazi devil, here incarnated in the infamous camp doctor Mengele, complete with a black cape of silk, quotations from Valéry, and implacable hate of life itself. Unfortunately, the historical and political issues of the Nazi regime, and possible resistance against it, are elevated into the remote and immaterial realm of the satanic. In the spiritual battle between the devil and a true son of the Church, simple people suffer and die within a traditional metaphysical scheme. We Gestapo prisoners of 1944 must have been a sadly irreligious bunch; I cannot recall anybody, whether Jew, Communist, Liberal, or Social Democrat, who was much concerned with what the Vatican hierarchy could or should do (Hochhuth's particularly Protestant concern), but I recall many who asked (as does Hochhuth's Jacobson, a Berlin Jew) why the Allies did not bomb German communication lines leading to Auschwitz and other concentration camps with more precision.

It is with some qualms, dear David, that I approach the final part of my annotated reading list, comprising a few suggestions concerning the writings of the Left, old and new. Perhaps I should say, speaking of the late 1940s, the 1950s, and the early 1960s, that public awareness of what had happened to the Jews was strengthened and paradoxically modified by concentration camp reports (some authentic, others a bit fictionalized), because the genre, from its very beginning at a time when the mass deportations of Jews were yet to come, had been bound to experiences and, in many instances, to literary rules defined by the Communist Party. The persecuted were seen in terms of class and party allegiances, and the genre itself was unwilling to perceive them as loyal or assimilated members of a religious and ethnic community. Wolfgang Langhoff's *Die Moorsoldaten: 13 Monate Konzentrationslager* (1935; *Rubber Truncheon*, 1935), the first of these reports, was immediately translated into twenty-eight languages after its initial publication in Switzerland and was promptly republished after the collapse of the Nazi regime. It defined the political perspectives early: 95 percent of the Camp Papenburg prisoners were politically organized Rhenish and Ruhr workers, the few Jews being exceptions, one of whom was an *Ostjude* (astonishingly, the intellectual Langhoff uses a Nazi term to designate a Polish Jew). Anna Seghers's *Das siebte Kreuz* (1942; *The Seventh Cross*, 1942), a renowned and powerful novel that was written in Paris and made into a movie in the United States, fully sustains the characteristics of the genre, bound by class consciousness. In her novel, set in the late 1930s, German camp prisoners are working people; one of them, Georg Heisler, succeeds in escaping to Holland while six of his fellow prisoners fail or wish to fail. A kind Jewish physician who still runs a modest office in town bandages Georg's hand without asking questions and will later be investigated by the Gestapo. The author, the daughter of one of the elders of the Mainz Jewish community, does not say what will happen to him.

My point is that the partisan genre perspective, if not party discipline itself, survived under changed circumstances in the years of the mass deportations. Bruno Apitz's *Nackt unter Wölfen* (1958; *Naked among Wolves*, 1978), a famous and nearly documentary narrative about the last days of Buchenwald, suggests a good deal about how Communists of the Weimar generation looked at their unorganized Jewish fellow prisoners. The novel tells the true story of a Jewish orphan who, smuggled into the camp by a prisoner coming from Auschwitz, survives under the protection of other prisoners until the camp is liberated by the internal International Camp Committee (ICC), consisting of resolute Communists of different nations, and advance units of the U.S. army. It is revealing to note what the narrator feels about Jews and Jewishness, explicitly and by implication: the hapless prisoner who brings the child in a shabby suitcase is called a Polish Jew only once, and the comrades of the committee, including Poles and Germans, delight in speaking about the "Polish child" (hidden, in the most dangerous moment, by a Soviet army POW). I am not surprised that the author has somewhat stylized the name of the Jewish orphan from Warsaw into Stephan Cyliak, a bit on the non-Jewish side. The epic spotlight fully rests throughout the novel on the members of the Internal Camp Committee, consisting of strong, positive heroes, all party members who prepare (as they really did) for the final battle. The thousands of Jewish prisoners are kept in their barracks, subject to decisions made by the German camp commander or the camp committee. When, in the the last days, an evacuation order is given, in the Jewish barracks utter confusion reigns: "They shouted and wept and did not know what to do"—unlike those who partake of the higher party knowledge and resolution. Peter Weiss's Auschwitz oratorio, staged only seven years after Apitz's novel had been published, in its own way powerfully sustains the perspective of the Old Left.

The German New Left of the late 1960s and later had its particular difficulties because it was nothing if not theoretical. While many older Social Democrats or Communists had gone through the prisons and camps, the younger student generation, in the near absence of Jews in German political life, relied on antiquated ideas of class warfare to explain anti-Semitism. While Jean Améry—born in Vienna, a member of the Belgian resistance, and a survivor of Auschwitz—in his passionate autobiographical essays warned against ideological abstractions, attention was concentrated more on the progressive decay of late capitalism (a rather protracted process) than on the events of the 1940s. The high-pitched revolutionary expectations, quickly disappointed, combined increasingly with a radical view of the Third World, ranging the PLO and its Arab allies, in the classical role of the "proletariat," against the Israeli and American "bourgeoisie." (In 1976 at Entebbe, when terrorists hijacked an airplane, young Germans helped separate Jewish from non-Jewish passengers.) The chic new anti-Zionism, replacing the fashionable philosemitism of the 1950s, in practice was difficult to distinguish from the endemic anti-Semitism of the past.

This is especially the case in Gerhard Zwerenz's novel *Die Erde ist unbewohnbar wie der Mond* (1973; *The Earth Is As Uninhabitable As the Moon*), and in Rainer Werner Fassbinder's play *Der Müll, die Stadt und der Tod* (1975; *The Garbage, the City, and Death*), which is based on Zwerenz for plot and on Brecht's *In the Jungle of Cities* for atmosphere and idiom. The novel and the play, widely discussed by liberals and the Left, took their cue from the scandals of contemporary Frankfurt real estate operations. Zwerenz, in his fast-moving but rough narrative, described the career of one Abraham Mauerstamm (a real person), who, in collaboration with the corrupt city government and gangs of dropouts, buys up old houses and, in total disregard for public needs, changes the city into a cement desert. Mauerstamm, a Jew, speaks of Israel as a nation that still has to go through the Age of Enlightenment, yet he is duped, more willingly than not, by the Iranian security services, who want to invest dirty money in European operations (the Iranians pretend to be Israeli secret agents). Fassbinder, however, turned this real estate thriller into an apocalyptic play peopled with prostitutes mostly from the 1920s, pimps, unrepenting fascists, and transvestites. The "rich Jew," who has no name, tells us that he does not care if children and old people suffer, since the city wants change and it is he who is the agent of change. When he kills a prostitute (who desires death), the murder will be pinned on another man by his friends in the police. Fassbinder's play resuscitates the traditional image of the rich Jewish fiend, and it may have been common sense—rather than secret censorship, as Fassbinder's friends claim—that has kept his eclectic play, written by one of the most outstanding contemporary filmmakers, off the German stage. In late October 1985 an attempt to perform the play on the Frankfurt stage was frustrated by twenty-five representatives of the Jewish community who occupied the stage and engaged the actors and audience in a discussion of the text and its implications.

In the late seventies, literary discussions were overshadowed, if not silenced, by the telecast of the American *Holocaust* series (partly filmed on the old concentration camp site at Mauthausen) by the West German Broadcasting Corporation, and the sudden, unexpected, and overwhelming response by millions of viewers.

Aired for four evenings during the last week of January 1979 (in Austria, in March 1979), *Holocaust* was followed each time by a midnight discussion, and within hours it became clear that the telecast (arranged by Peter Märthesheimer) was an event of incisive national importance. The series was viewed by twenty million people; thirty thousand telephone calls were made to the TV station (four times more than on the occasion of the NBC broadcast in the United States); and when the government printed twenty thousand copies of a documentary brochure offering additional historical materials, more than a quarter million people wanted to receive copies by mail. The response of the viewers clearly revealed that an entire new generation did not know much about the events of the late 1930s and 1940s, and that everybody else felt a great need for more historical information—even after so much German writing, all of the best intentions. It is a sobering thought: since 1945, the best and most thoughtful German writers have confronted the recent past, and yet it was a telecast with old-fashioned characterizations in black and white, realism, and totally un-Brechtian empathy that shocked millions of viewers into thinking more about Germany history than any books or plays had been able to do. My astonished respect for the impact of the *Holocaust* series on German public opinion is not entirely free of a certain melancholy about the rather limited power of good writing, revealed once again so blatantly.

There is not a single aspect of German life and letters that remains unaffected by the legacy of Auschwitz. Before sketching portraits of a few important authors of the age, I should like to close my letter with a few general remarks. As a non-Jew and a non-non-Jew of the liberal and agnostic kind, I have my own difficulties in speaking about these issues, one of them being the theological interpretation of recent history implied in the biblical term "holocaust," which I hesitate to use. It is used more legitimately by those who believe in meaningful suffering, in the presence or absence of the God of Abraham, and the possibility that Hitler or Kaduk, the most brutal among the Auschwitz guards, was the instrument of a higher power. But even if I can see myself less alien to religious thought than I assert in my more secular moments, I cannot under any circumstances accept any explicit or implicit glorification of the Nazis for whatever reasons, even mystical. I also have to confess that I sympathize with those European liberals of my generation who, having survived the "Third Reich," have great difficulty in perceiving human beings in closed terms of groups, collectives, classes, national loyalties, or ethnic determinants. I admit my contradictory feelings: I do not want to think of people in abstract terms (as Peter Weiss does), yet I perceive in any Jew, gypsy, or Soviet prisoner of war murdered by the Nazis a *reiner Mensch* (pure human being) in the sense of the eighteenth century; after my experiences with Hitler's nationalism, I am out of sympathy with any other kind. Perhaps I should also say that from most of the postwar German novels, plays, and poems about Auschwitz and its time, a characteristic and inevitable limitation of perspective emerges early. If, to historians in Israel, America, and elsewhere, the Holocaust means above all the destruction of the East European Jewish community and the epic world of religious and intellectual culture in the *shtetl*, postwar German writers, with the exception of Becker and Celan, inevitably tend to think of acculturated middle-class Jews in Germany, Austria, Bohemia, and other regions of central Europe, and look deep into the past but do not have anything to say about the future of the Jews. The agonies of assimilation are closely watched and analyzed, but the world of the *shtetl* has not become more familiar to German intellectuals, least of all, I think, to the youngest generation. But again, these are rash generalizations, and I leave you with H. G. Adler, Jurek Becker, Paul Celan, and Peter Weiss, who will tell you more than I can ever do.

H. G. ADLER

Living in London and writing in German of the classical tradition, author and scholar Hans Günther Adler (who does not wish to use his full first and middle names because they recall the name of a Nazi functionary) prefers his own thoughtful solitude and grim independence to ease of communication. Adler was born in Kafka's Prague in 1910 of middle-class Jewish parents acculturated to Austrian liberalism and the legacy of the Weimar classics. He studied music, philosophy, literature, and psychology at Prague University, wrote a dissertation on the eighteenth-century German poet Klopstock, and was active in adult education before being deported with his wife to Theresienstadt, and later to Auschwitz (where his wife died) and Buchenwald. In 1945 he returned to Prague, where the prospects for a German-speaking intellectual of non-Communist persuasion were rather dim, taught children who had survived the camps, and helped rebuild the Prague Jewish Museum. A few days before the Communist takeover he settled in London, where he married the Prague sculptor Bettina Gross and, a true free-lance writer, began publishing his books, essays, and poems in continuing exile. He had long been writing poetry and stories, as did so many Prague intellectuals of his generation, but first he published his anatomy of camp life, *Theresienstadt, 1941–45: Das Antlitz einer Zwangsgemeinschaft* (1955; *Theresienstadt, 1941–45: The Face of a Forced Settlement*), which was awarded the Leo Baeck Prize, and a documentary sequel, *Die verheimlichte Wahrheit: Theresienstädter Dokumente* (1958; *The Secret Truth: Theresienstadt Documents*). Only in the early 1960s did he begin speaking as an imaginative writer in stories and novels. *Eine Reise* (1962; *A Journey*) and *Panorama* (1968) were warmly welcomed by Heinrich Böll, who was among the first reviewers. In the 1970s and since, Adler has continued his sociological and historical research into the history of the German Jews. He himself considers his massive study *Der verwaltete Mensch* (1974), which can perhaps be translated as "Deported People"—a closely documented analysis of the deportation of Jews by the Nazi organizations—his most important contribution to modern history.

Adler's *A Journey*, dedicated to Elias and Veza Canetti, returns to the experiences of a Prague middle-class family. The narrator does not offer a mere fictionalized account of what Adler himself has described, in minute detail, in his historical account of how Jews lived, worked, and died in the Theresienstadt "forced settlement." Rather, in a literary structure that he himself relates to a traditional ballad, Adler is far more concerned with how people think and remember and, when utterly deprived of their humanity, how they reassert what they have lost in their memories of happier times ("we all were habitués of the Semmering and Cortina d'Ampezzo"), in their dreams of returning home, or in their anticipation of cataclysmic events on the threshold of a new time of peace. The Austrian novelist Heimito von Doderer, one of the early readers, suggested that the exuberance of daydreams in the minds of people threatened by a terrible fate does not alienate us from their situation, but on the contrary opens up one way of really understanding their life. All of us, unfortunate and fortunate, share an inclination ultimately to dream, when we know of no other way of changing what we call real.

Adler's *Panorama*, a memoir rather than a novel, was published in the days of the student revolt by a courageous Swiss publisher. An intimate record of a search for philosophical meaning in the time of terrors, it was not read by many young people committed to collective action and theories of class warfare. In this long and reflective narrative, the autobiographical materials are barely camouflaged by some name changes and ironic indirections. It is not entirely surprising that Adler calls his protagonist Josef K[ramer], relating him to another lonely inhabitant of Prague, the central sensibility in Kafka's *The Trial*, written almost two generations earlier. In twelve separate "pictures" we are told what happened to Josef in an important moment or stage of his life, and only in the last chapter are we able to reestablish the continuity of his experience. We see Josef growing up a spoiled child in a Jewish bourgeois family; spending a year in the Czech countryside; attending a *Gymnasium* in Dresden and having difficulties with a nationalist teacher; sharing happy experiences with other boys of his Youth Movement group while camping in the forests of southern Bohemia; involving himself in the ideological discussions of the late 1920s; attempting to make a living as tutor in a rich family and as secretary in a Prague adult education institute (the renowned Urania); doing forced labor building a railroad after the Nazis seize power in Bohemia; surviving in Auschwitz and Buchenwald; and, long after the liberation, spending a day of reflection in a quiet park near an old castle in England, coming to terms with all of his past, and expressing to himself a philosophy of life in which the ideas of presence as an essential reality, of possible grace, and of disgust with fear (which kills people before they are killed) are of fundamental importance. It is an unusual book, in which an innovative structure combines with a deeply conservative commitment of the mind, and with an intense religiosity stubbornly unwilling to embrace religion in any prescribed and inherited sense, unless it be a religion of "ethical attitudes" and not "metaphysical systems."

Adler defines the structure of his narrative by its title and the first chapter, in which the young Josef and his grandmother visit a panorama—that is, in the central European sense, a dark little precinematic room where visitors watch a rotating series of stereoscopic photographs offering views of a landscape, a famous city, or a work of art. The pictures are not less "magnificent" for being "immobile," as the narrator remarks, and for being "taken out of time." To him, the twelve pictures of his life are as "firm" and "true" as those in the old panorama, and while they cannot constitute a "whole," being but "individual stills without a conclusion," they have luminous immediacy; whatever happens, whether in Prague in 1914 or in Auschwitz in 1944, is told in the present tense throughout, internally organized by a plenitude of semicolons and little else. The optical metaphor of the panorama suggests a narrative distant from actual events, but makes it more difficult to recognize the writer's concentrated attention on what is said and heard, the remarkable absence of descriptive adjectives and adverbs, and the presentation of experience, noble and terrible, as a repertoire of sayings, monologues, and commands not too far removed from Gertrude Stein's idea of an aural world. It is no mere coincidence that, among Adler's initial studies, music ranked very high.

In Adler's *Panorama*, narrative method reflects a universe in which time and being are in utter disjunction, and ultimately, a philosophy hesitating on the threshold of religion. Past and future are disqualified as dimensions of time, and time itself is deprived of its ontological privileges; "presence" alone comes to offer a constancy, potentially enabling people to live in quiet harmony with life itself. The past, Josef believes, exists only in human consciousness and not in the outside world (so that, in the deepest sense, it lacks reality); all attempts to establish it out there are but "meditative attempts" at construing conceptual crutches. The future, or rather human desire to know what is to come, is to be condemned for moral reasons. It is inadmissible, Josef holds, to look ahead eagerly, and the search for the future, abandoning presence, comes close to being dirty, unchaste, even sinful—as, fundamentally, does any involvement in time, "which is in constant conflict with being, and is identical with being only in part and incompletely." Out of time, alien to time, presence rather than the present time emerges as the true affirmation of being, a source of resuscitation "surprising and unpredictable." It is imperative, Adler's Josef asserts, to "show a readiness to accept" presence, but such readiness differs radically from "passivity" or "fatalism," modes of behaving that do not reach the truth but merely reveal "desires of insecure people" who are incapable of "participation" in fate. Those who are ready to accept presence are ultimately predestined (though it is not clear by whom), and are blessed by a "grace" that the narrator has often felt palpably in his own life.

In many ways Adler for the last time incarnates the traditions of the Prague intellectual of Jewish origins. He always belonged to those who, like Kafka, went on writing in pure and classical German. If Kafka's close friend Max Brod took the last train before Prague was occupied by the Nazis, and went to Israel and wrote many of his essays in a new language, Adler later left for the "neutrality" of London, at least in a linguistic and ethnic sense, and, surrounded by English, continued to write his poems and prose in a kind of German that would have pleased Karl Kraus, the stern, conservative guardian of Goethe's German in an age of moral decay. Among the witnesses and the survivors, he is a towering and perhaps forbidding figure of courage and absolute demands. It is one of the great intellectual scandals of our time that his most important books, both the personal ones and those in search of historical truth, have yet to be translated into English.

JUREK BECKER

H. G. Adler came from an acculturated German-Jewish middle-class family, whereas Jurek Becker grew up speaking Yiddish and Polish and, unlike Paul Celan, learned his German only after he was liberated from the concentration camps. Among so many writers of Jewish origin who changed languages in the last generation, he is, as far as I know, the only one who, in the GDR, switched to writing and living in German. Like Jerzy Kosinski, Becker was born (in 1937) in Lodz. After the Germans occupied

Poland, Becker spent four years with his parents in the Lodz ghetto and was later transported to the concentration camps of Ravensbrück and Sachsenhausen. In the summer of 1945 father and son settled in Berlin, in a district then within the Soviet zone of occupation, and Jurek Becker attended the local schools, served in the GDR army for two years, studied philosophy, and in the early 1960s established himself as a writer of film and TV scripts.

Becker belongs to a younger generation of socialist writers increasingly concerned about the gap between the idea of a socialist republic and the petty bourgeois realities of what is called "real socialism." In the changing context of GDR cultural policies, his novels *Jacob der Lügner* (1969; *Jacob the Liar*, 1975) and *Der Boxer* (1976; *The Boxer*, in which he turns to his memories and to the difficulties of the survivors) suggested that it had become possible, at least for a while in the late 1960s, to speak of Jewish experiences and the past without immediately mobilizing the melodramatic clichés of Socialist Realism. Yet in another novel, *Irreführung der Behörden* (1973; *Misguiding the Authorities*), Becker sketches the funny and satirical portrait of a clever student who makes a quick career as a writer by conforming to the Party's demands. The real touble started in 1976, when Becker signed the petition that the Wolf Biermann case be reconsidered by the government and refused to go through the public ritual of recantation, as required by the authorities. He left the Writers Union by his own decision and was expelled by the Party, to which he had belonged since the late 1960s; his novel *Schlaflose Tage* (1978; *Sleepless Days*, 1979), about a steadfast teacher who becomes a worker rather than submit to ideological pressure, was never published in the GDR. When Becker asked for an exit visa to teach for a year at Oberlin College in Ohio, the police gave him a passport of extended validity; to this day, Becker lives in West Berlin with the permission of the GDR. In his particular case of dissent, the authorities and Becker himself, for reasons of their own, do not want to let go of each other. Perhaps Becker really feels at home on the other side of the Wall, and the authorities do not wish to create yet another scandal by expatriating a writer who literally grew up in the concentration camps and belongs to a group publicly classified as ODF (*Opfer des Faschismus*, Victims of Fascism).

After Johannes Bobrowski (1917–65), in his poems and poetic

prose, had recalled to German readers (often in a manner close to Chagall) the world of the *shtetl*, Jurek Becker, in his novel *Jacob the Liar*, an immediate best seller in both East and West, told the story of the poor, honest innkeeper Jacob, who is confined to the Lodz ghetto and there, by accident, discovers a way to impart new courage to his fellow Jews and to strengthen their hopes for the future. Jacob is picked up by a German guard on a ghetto street after curfew and told to report to the German *Revier*, from which no Jew has ever returned alive; but after he spends a terrible time of waiting for the worst, the German commandant waves him away. A new problem now arises: through a half-open door, Jacob has heard a broadcast saying that the Soviet army is close to a little town that he knows well; he does not know how to spread the good news, however, without impairing his credibility by confessing that he was sent to the *Revier* and simply was let off. He tells the good news to his friends, suggesting that he has his own radio (an offense punishable by death), and the news spreads like wildfire, with some unsuspected results: "Old debts are being recalled . . . daughters are changing into brides . . . the suicide rate falls to zero." Another friend consults him about postwar economic problems, and a famous actor, who sports remnants of his former elegance, quickly destroys the real radio that he has hidden in his cellar, lest the Germans trace the source of the news to him. Not wanting to lie, honest Jacob invents difficulties with his "electric wiring." But after he sees how much good his one bit of news has done, especially when whispered to people in a sealed train destined for Auschwitz, he tries at least to piece together another news item from torn newspapers from a German latrine and finally finds himself compelled to invent a major battle closer to Lodz so as to console his friends, increasingly threatened by deportation to Auschwitz. For once, he wants to be honest with his best friend and confesses his inventions, only to be told a short while later that his friend has hanged himself. From now on, Jacob's radio functions magnificently again, but after he has reported a hopeful interview with Churchill himself, he and his friends on the block are shipped to the camps, where they all die except the narrator himself.

Becker's use of one of Jacob's younger friends as narrator has the advantage of avoiding old-fashioned realism, not particularly favored among younger GDR writers in the late 1960s, and provides the possibility of questioning the process of storytelling itself, offering alternate endings and generally indulging in the sport of telling the story of the story—enough to give an experimental air to the text, but without seriously undercutting the reader's easy participation. Becker's storyteller is a survivor who combines a good deal of camp-weary cynicism with sincere compassion; there are rules for everything, he has learned, and if you do not follow the rules, do not be surprised to die. People are being shot every day; and if you admire a man's courage, you rely on respectful understatement (as in the case of a famous Jewish physician who kills himself rather than provide medical help for the SS chief). There is a trace of the picaresque in the tone of the story, which is skillfully combined with other individual stories of how young and old Jews live, suffer, and try to survive in the ghetto. A young lover rescues his unsuspecting girl, at least for the time being, by walking her away from the block that is rounded up for transport; a Prussian Jew makes his stiff appearance ("he would not have had any objections against the ghetto, if he had not been right in the middle of it"); and while the roguish narrator repeatedly tells us that he totally lacks Sholom Aleichem's imagination and inventive skills, he amply confirms that *Jacob the Liar*, a story about the life-sustaining force of fictions, should be read as a text in the Yiddish tradition, except that it is written in modern German.

Becker's *The Boxer* was published simultaneously in both the GDR and the Federal Republic, but it was welcomed much less ardently by readers and critics. Far less folksy and talkative than Becker's first Jewish novel, it is a more sensitive and possibly ambivalent book, mostly because of the unresolved relationship between the narrator and the central character. We are reading a report about a survivor, based on interviews and notes gathered for many years, and a plea for understanding those who have been irreparably hurt by their terrible experiences and cannot easily adjust to a new society of collective efforts (even if, as Victims of Fascism, they do enjoy certain privileges). Aaron Blank, whose pious family came from Riga but who spent most of his working life in German-speaking cities, is liberated from a camp where his wife was shot and two of his children died before his eyes. Thereafter he goes listlessly through the prescribed procedures. He hates the "provocative" faces of the new people around him, and when he applies for an identity card, he changes "Aaron" to the more protective "Arno" and subtracts six camp years from his life. A male child named Mark, possibly his own, is found by the Jewish Joint Distribution Committee in southern Germany. A young woman who works for the Jewish Committee lives with him for a while but then leaves him, and Aaron succeeds in moving Mark, with the help of the Soviet authorities, to a children's home not far from East Berlin, where he himself has settled. He works as a translator for the Soviet administration, not hiding his belief that for political reasons it treats the Germans far too gently. He asks Mark's nurse to move in with him, which she does gladly, but finds himself unable to share his life with others; when the nurse has gone, he recognizes that Mark has become the only human being to keep him aware of the world at large. Aaron has great plans for being a good example to his son, but when Mark begins his studies and the search for his own life, Aaron does not wish to interfere. One day Mark leaves for the West, going first to Hamburg and later to Israel; after the Six Day War in the spring of 1968, his letters abruptly cease. Sick, taciturn, and alone, Aaron does not know what really happened; in his solitude he tells himself that perhaps Mark was not really his son and has now found his true family, or that he has died as an Israeli soldier in the war. There are no definite answers.

Becker's well-tested epic procedure (to have a friend tell the story) does not work as effectively here as it does in *Jacob the Liar*: narrator and central character are separated by an age difference of almost a generation, and Aaron's constant interviewer lacks individuality as a human being and almost functions as an impersonal voice, speaking for a professional writer who, committed to the socialist cause (to judge from Aaron's caustic remarks), patiently gathers materials in five neat green copybooks. When Aaron follows Jacob's example by inventing a story about his training as a boxer in the distant past (in order to teach his son to defend himself in the world), the narrator restricts himself to a sober account and does not show what he thinks of the story himself. Yet it may be precisely the grating lack of fit between the interviewer and Aaron that suggests the radical incompatibility of what Aaron has been through with the practical perspectives advanced by socialist society. The best the interviewer can do is to show the wounds that cannot be healed, not even by the nurses in state-run sanatoriums. Becker certainly knows more than Aaron's interviewer; as the last messenger—sad, ironic, and compassionate—from the lost world of the *shtetl* and the Yiddish traditions of storytelling, he is, in contemporary German writing, simply irreplaceable.

PAUL CELAN

Paul Celan is usually called the "pure poet" of the Holocaust age, but it is less easy to grasp why he remained loyal to the German language, and it is an even more difficult if not desperate undertaking to approach his later poetry. His poetry invites readers, translators, and philosophers who want to know what language can do in a time of sighs, shouts, and silence, yet harshly rejects most of our hermeneutic efforts as an invasion of privacy. The continuing discussion of "Todesfuge" ("Death Fugue"), Celan's most famous and yet very early poem, may be a way of admitting that we prefer less rather than more resistance in our reading.

Paul Celan, or rather Paul Antschel, was born in 1920 in the Romanian town of Czernowitz (once at the old Austrian frontier) of Jewish parents who were still close to religious traditions. He himself has suggested that Hebrew was his "father tongue," while his mother, Fritzi, insisted on cultivating his German, spoken at home, and on reading the German classics to him when he was young. Czernowitz was, perhaps more so than Prague, a town of many literary traditions and languages, among them Yiddish, German, Ukrainian, and Romanian, and Paul Antschel's early training reflects a delicate balance between his parents' wishes and social necessity. He first attended a German kindergarten, switched to a Hebrew elementary school, and studied at the Romanian and later the Ukrainian *Gymnasium*, which was mostly attended by Jewish students who wanted to escape the rampant Romanian anti-Semitism. He was fifteen or sixteen years old when he became active in antifascist groups of the Left rather than in Zionist clubs, as his father would have wished, and showed his first German poems to his friends. In 1938 he went to France to take premed courses at Tours (Vienna had been occupied by the Germans), and returned to his hometown just in time to be caught up in the war and the destruction of the Jewish community. In 1940 the Soviet army occupied Czernowitz and, after the usual orations, began deporting many members of the Jewish intelligentsia. In 1941 the Romanians and a German *Einsatzgruppe* came in and within seven weeks killed three thousand Jews, organized a ghetto, and began deporting Jews to Transnistria, a corner of the occupied Ukraine that the German army handed over to the Romanian regime in return for loyal services. These months were never erased from Paul Antschel's memory; as the weekly roundups continued, he wanted his parents to hide, but they refused to do so, were deported, and died (his mother was shot through the nape of the neck). The son, who hid himself for some time, survived in a Romanian forced-labor detachment until the Soviet army returned.

Under Soviet occupation Antschel studied first French and later English at Czernowitz's university, but the Soviet authorities were happy to see the Jewish survivors leave town. He went to Bucharest, where he found a job in publishing as a translator, wrote a number of poems in Romanian (mostly imitative of French surrealist models), for the first time published these and other poems (translated by a Romanian friend), and changed "Antschel" to the more poetic and perhaps less Jewish "Celan." Two years later he went to Vienna, which was still occupied by the Allies, and there, carrying a letter of recommendation from Alfred Margul-Sperber, a well-known Czernowitz writer, he was warmly welcomed by Otto Basil, the editor of *Plan*. Basil printed a number of Celan's German poems and arranged for the publication of *Sand aus den Urnen* (1948; *Sand from the Urns*), which was almost immediately withdrawn by the author, who was appalled by the many misprints and the ungainly appearance of the volume. The Czernowitz legend of Vienna and the real Vienna of 1948 were different cities: within a year Celan had made up his mind to go to Paris to continue his philological studies (German, of all languages), to marry the French artist Gisèle Lestrange, and to live by the word alone, teaching German at the Ecole Normale Supérieure, writing poetry, and doing a lot of translation.

Celan's collections of poetry, written in Paris and published in the Federal Republic, include *Mohn und Gedächtnis* (1952; *Poppy and Memory*), *Von Schwelle zu Schwelle* (1955; *From Threshold to Threshold*), *Sprachgitter* (1959; *Speech-Grille and Selected Poems*, 1971), *Die Niemandsrose* (1963; *The None Rose*), *Atemwende* (1967; *Reversal of Breath*), *Fadensonnen* (1968; *Thread Suns*), *Lichtzwang* (1970; *Light Force*), and *Schneepart* (1971; *Snow Part*), which appeared posthumously. Celan had many admirers but few personal friends among German and Austrian writers and critics, except for Milo Dor, Hans Mayer, and Peter Szondi. After he had been invited by Group 47 once in 1952 but never again, he did not travel much in Germany, though he occasionally read in the media and at the Berlin Academy of the Arts. He received important awards and prizes, among them the Prize of the City of Bremen (1958) and the Georg Büchner Award of the Darmstadt Academy (1960), but in the late 1960s he complained that he did not have many readers any more. In 1970 he drowned himself in the Seine.

Poppy and Memory (1952), the first collection of poems that Celan himself accepted as an integral part of his achievement, distinctly shows, by returning to a few early poems written in Czernowitz, the romantic and symbolist origins of his art. Anachronistic and provincial, these poems struck many readers of the 1950s as surprisingly poetic and new, and the gifted critic Helmuth de Haas, himself a young poet of note, was not alone in admiring "the noble shape" of Celan's poems, which he saw as revealing a "lyrical Proust, even if potentially for the time being." Decorative long lines, often in lively dactylic rhythm, combine with German Romantic verse of the four-line, three-stanza pattern and echoes of Slavic folk songs; the images are deliberately "beautiful," if not melodramatic, and a good deal of fin-de-siècle vocabulary of flutes, hair, lights, cathedrals, and carpets gently fuses with Georg Trakl's favorite hues of brown, gold, and blue. These are meditations about loving, dreaming, dying, and remembering, but not in the idiom of contemporary poetry; it would be easy to speak of the many trite rather than startling metaphors ("the heartbeat of the hour"), the mellifluous Rilke murmur, or the uttering of the poetic line as a *l'art pour l'art* ceremony. Yet these are the beginnings of a poet close to genius. The dirges for his mother (whether in the form of a Ukrainian song or a Romantic poem in the German tradition) burn with memories of her death and the poet's own burdens. The more sprightly "Erinnerung an Frankreich" ("Memory of France") has the harsh edge of paradoxical authenticity, and other poems, including "Kristall" and "Die Krüge" ("The Pitchers"), anticipate the most cryptic of his later poems, pleasant to listen to and yet absolutely unwilling to yield their meaning, beyond a few puzzling intimations.

In *Poppy and Memory* Celan first printed, or rather reprinted, for German readers his "Todesfuge" ("Death Fugue"), the most famous of his poems and perhaps of all postwar literature in German. John Felstiner, one of Celan's most thoughtful translators, recently suggested that "very few lyric poems in this century have cut so deeply into consciousness . . . probing, dividing, and reshaping opinion." It is essential to know that "Death Fugue" belongs among Celan's early poems and does not represent in any way his later work. Celan may have written "Death Fugue," which clearly reveals his early studies of French surrealism, even before 1944, when he recited it to a friend in liberated Czernowitz. The complete biography of the poem certainly includes a Romanian version (prepared by a friend) called "Death Tango," published in Bucharest in 1947, as well as the earliest publication in German, under the title "Death Fugue," in the rare Vienna volume *Sand from the Urns* (1948).

In "Death Fugue" Celan handles a few motifs in recurrent and changing combinations to confront the agonies of the imprisoned Jews (the collective speaker of the poem) with the daily schedule of the German *Kommandant* of the camp, who writes home to his blond Margarete, and who in his blend of aesthetic inclinations and cold brutality reminds many readers of Reinhard Heydrich, the Nazi chief of security services. Daily foretasting death in the "black milk of daybreak" (a contradictory image anticipated by Rimbaud and the Czernowitz writer Rose Ausländer), the Jews have become slaves; the *Kommandant* (as documented later for one of the camps) orders one group to dig its own grave while another plays a dance: "Jab your spades deeper you there you others play on for the dance." The fateful incompatibility of the two worlds is suggested in the final epigrammatic pairing of motifs: "Dein goldenes Haar Margarete/ Dein aschenes Haar Sulamith" ("Thy golden hair Margarete/ Thy ashen hair Sulamith"). In its pure musicality, sustained by the repetition of entire lines, "Death Fugue" astonishingly succeeds, perhaps against its own intentions. But the aesthetic success, or rather the haunting suggestiveness of the poem (in which the lilting dactylic rhythm complies with the *Kommandant*'s order that his Jews dance), constitutes a highly problematic achievement triggering a radical question as to how aesthetics and brutality may be related to each other in a particular work of art.

The conflict between aesthetic perfection and the demands of ethics was intensified but not solved when the critic and philosopher Theodor W. Adorno, in an essay published in the early 1950s but written in 1949, declared that it was "barbaric" to write a poem "after Auschwitz" and thus unwittingly provided an entire generation of essayists with a one-line incantation. Adorno did not know "Death Fugue" when articulating his assertion, and he later believed that Celan was one of the truly representative writers of the age (though not necessarily as author of "Death Fugue"). In the 1950s the poem was widely anthologized and taught in West German schools, but the legitimate argument that German students should learn what had happened did not entirely convince everybody. A few teachers were afraid that "Death Fugue" was a poem potentially to be enjoyed by readers who (to quote Adorno from another context) were ready "to take away some measure of the terrible," while others insisted that students stick to the text itself lest "student discussion deviate from the work of art to the persecution of the Jews." Celan himself later turned against the musicality of his early poetry "of the time of the much touted 'Death Fugue,' which by now has been thrashed out in many a texbook" (1966), and persuaded some translators and editors to remove the poem from important anthologies widely used in institutions of higher education. I think that Celan was right in reconsidering the achievement of "Todesfuge" and directing attention, whether he was aware of it or not, to some of his more traditional poems, in which he remembered the suffering of his parents and fellow Jews (for instance, the dirge for his mother, entirely free of surrealist sophistication), or to a more radical mode of writing that, to quote Adorno on Schönberg, "supersedes the aesthetic sphere through the recollection of experiences that are inaccessible to art" by seeking refuge in broken language and a "shriveled diction."

In the middle and late 1950s Celan's poetry changed rapidly.

From Threshold to Threshold announces, by the programmatic title itself, the radical move to another way of articulating, while the collection *Speech-Grille* suggests the new and irrevocable intensity of the transformation. As one of Celan's interpreters suggests, the image inherent in the title may imply the barred windows through which prisoners or monks speak to their visitors, or the idea that language itself imposes an iron pattern on reality. Celan turns against the tender surfeit of his early poetry, as well as against language as a dubious means of communication: to continue writing is to record individual encounters with scattered words. Musicality has given way to razor-edged stanzas fascinating to the reader's eye; long and ornate verse yields to irregular three- or four-beat lines in disjointed syntactical patterns; genitive metaphors are replaced by strange compounds. Celan dehydrates his poetic landscape: stones and rocks circumscribe the horizon, and a sterile plain threatens with mud, flint, sand, pebbles, lava, and basalt. Life, or what is left of it, resides in the eye, which, enhanced (if not inflated) to inhuman proportions, hovers over infertile wastes, its anatomical parts almost obscenely revealed: retina, lid, lashes, and eyeball, a hungry vortex waiting to swallow up everything. The world, once rich with roses, melancholy willows, and courtly words, has been reduced to a terrifying encounter between bloodstained eyes and merciless rocks.

I read the poem "Engführung" ("Stretto") as Celan's own reconsideration of "Death Fugue" almost fourteen years later and from a full awareness of what was disturbing in a poetic attempt to speak about mass murder in a composition of seductive orchestrations. As a musical term (*stretto*), "Engführung" still relates, perhaps demonstratively so, to the structure of the "Fugue," but it refers to the particularly dense filiation of the compositional texture in the third part of that poem, as Peter Szondi suggests in his interpretation of the poem; instead of being offered the melodramatic fragments of a story, we are compelled to enter a forbidding landscape of agony, "the place where they lay,/ it had a name—it had/ none—." As we listen to many voices emerging from nine shreds of texts, to broken syntactical constructions often close to stuttering, to contradictory images of ashes, night, and poison, and to difficult allusions to Democritus and Dante, we witness that unspeakable moment in which the Jewish prisoners are shot while praying: "choirs, at that time, the/ psalms. Ho, ho—/sannah." In the Hebrew words, a voice assures us, "are temples yet/ a/ star/ probably still has light." It is a poem openly sharing its paralyzed incapacity to tell what happened, without choking, and offers one of the possible responses to Adorno: after Auschwitz, poems could not be written any more, except those created on the grounds of that place.

In *Reversal of Breath* Celan pushes his search for the absolute essence of poetry further than ever. Here he finds himself caught between the extreme demands he makes on his idiom, and his diminishing hope of still communicating his search. The more he advances in his relentless quest, the more exclusively he relies (as in *Thread Suns*, clearly indicating the danger of total exhaustion) on a butchered language all his own, fiercely disregarding the contemporary readers. Individual poems consist of broken stanzas of a few words, and an increasingly obsessive concern for compounds sustains the line with a chain of kenninglike riddles ("cheektower," "ashneedle," "clipperbliss," "nipplestone"). Celan sees himself going to the verge of utterance: "In the rivers north of the future/ I cast my net," he says of his pursuit of something "northerntrue" and "southernclear" that represents only his own poetic intent, "even devoid of language," if need be. The poem "Accumulation of words, volcanic" moves cautiously, as if for the last time, within the confines of human communication; in a planetary landscape of geological sedimentations, the poet sees himself cast against "a floating mob of antipeople" who concentrate intently on the mere copies and imitations that constitute their lives. Yet these efforts come to an end when the poet creates his "wordmoon," causing an ebb tide and revealing hitherto hidden "heartshaped craters" testifying to forgotten primeval events, "the birth of the kings." The cosmic images cannot entirely obliterate the vision of a luminous and enduring counterworld rising from the poet's words.

Celan rarely defines his poetics, and his speech upon receiving the Georg Büchner Prize (1960) and his Tel Aviv address (1969) are superseded by his far more radical practice of writing. Essentials are suggested: his resolve to continue Mallarmé's thought to the bitter end; his belief that modern poetry is moving toward silence (suggested a decade before Susan Sontag); and his insistence that the successful poem must balance on the borders of its own existence—that the poem, in order to be, must constantly pull itself back from the realm of the "never again" into the sphere of the "as yet." Restlessly hovering on the borders of potential communication, Celan's poems (which he hoped would be carried to the shores of a "heartland," like messages in a bottle) encompass a good many explicit concerns, literary, political, and religious. Celan has no qualms about openly criticizing fellow poets for becoming excessively involved in conveying social messages before they have tested their language; in "Huhediblu" he rages against "the empty skins of the vigilante poets" who produce toadlike sounds (*Geunke*) from their facile "fingerguts" (*Fingergekröse*) or mere "holiday desert." In Celan's earliest poems, filtered memories of his own political commitments appear. In "Shibboleth" thoughts of past defeats that destroyed the hopes of his particular generation are articulated in poetic allusions to the Austrian civil war between the Socialists and the Conservatives (February 1934), and to the defense of the Spanish republic against Franco: "February. No pasarán." He shows his generation's distrust of dogmatic metaphysical commitment: in a poem dedicated to Nelly Sachs he recalls an argument about her "Jewish God," yet admits that she may have been right to say that theological questions do not require definite answers. Heaven and earth are reversed in their hierarchies; the sky is covered with "pocks" and "pustules," like the skin of a sick man. In a moving poem about the Umbrian landscape of Francis of Assisi, Celan expresses doubts about the blessings of traditional Christianity. Elsewhere glimpses of transcendence appear, and in one of his late poems Celan suggests in almost mystical terms the presence of a more than human force of "light" and "salvation."

Being the last European symbolist, and heir to Hölderlin, in the age of the concentration camps, Celan pressed his search for an ultimate and permanent language (the only one that can legitimately keep alive the memory of so much agony), and found himself a prisoner of the inevitable dilemma confronting the poet intent on unremitting advance. He wanted to say something absolutely pure and uttered his words far ahead of those whom he wished to address; discovering "Songs Sung beyond Humanity," he could not avoid the danger of speaking only to himself and a few loyal friends. He did not shrink from the monologue uttered in a harsh landscape of rocks and stones and, refusing to say something that had been used before, he accepted the role of the nay-sayer and set his sights on the final "noem" (*Genicht*) in which language is stripped to its bare bones: "deep-insnow/ eepino/ ee i o" (in Hebrew, the consonants would survive).

Sometimes I feel that it would be easier to understand Celan's life, writing, and death by grasping more closely the meaning of his poetic existence among the many languages. German was, in the deepest sense of the word, his *Muttersprache*, but it was also the idiom of those who had ordered his mother killed. For a long time, however, he did not sympathize with his father's world, incarnated in the Hebrew of religious tradition. Perhaps his surrealist poetry in Romanian, written in postwar Bucharest, was not merely an act of assimilating to changing conditions but also an existential gesture to avoid conflict, and his many first-rate translations into German, including those of Mandelstam's poetry, may be ways of trying to cleanse what history had left unclean. His astonishing decision to go to Paris to study and teach German implies that he ultimately accepted a fundamental challenge. While he continued to say that German passed "through the thousand darknesses of death-dealing utterance," in his later poems he came more and more to speak in moments of overwhelming tension, in his father's Hebrew: "kumi/ori, rise, and be full of the light." For a poet who had his home in his writing and nowhere else, it was a conflict difficult to endure.

PETER WEISS

It may seem unfair, after Becker and Celan, to speak about Peter Weiss, who by his own choice belonged among the writers of the Left rather than among those haunted by their fate of being Jewish among Germans. His writings and his life, I believe, were attempts to escape from the solitude of the Jewish exile and its introversions—first into the exhilaration of the avant-garde arts, and later into an activist commitment promising meaningful self-effacement in the ranks of the revolutionaries who, if not in Germany any more, could be found at least in the Third World at large. To Peter Weiss (1916–82), born in Nowawes near Berlin, isolation came slowly, inevitably, and mercilessly: while the Nazis marched in the Berlin streets, the boy was told that his father was Jewish, and the subsequent years of exile in London, Prague, and Stockholm were a period of more than geographical separation from his past. Obsessed with adolescent thirst for romantic self-expression, he painted, made experimental movies, wrote poetic prose (for many years in Swedish), and withdrew from a world in which the Allied armies were fighting the Germans and the fires burned in the concentration camps. Analyzing and judging his experiences in piercingly sincere autobiographical narratives, including *Abschied von den Eltern* (1961; *Leavetaking*, 1962) and *Fluchtpunkt* (1962; *Vanishing Point*, 1966), Weiss hesitatingly returned to his native tongue and pondered whether or not he was guilty of inhumanity, having indulged in the vagaries of the private self while others suffered and died.

In *Marat/Sade* [1964; 1965], the conflicting voices of Weiss the existentialist and Weiss the political activist were heard, each asserting his own point of view, but in the mid-1960s Weiss formulated a firmer response to the challenge of his past. In his "Ten Working Points of a Writer in a Divided World," first published on September 1, 1965, in a Swedish newspaper (and later translated into many languages), Weiss committed himself to the Leninist forces of historical change, above all those exemplified by events in the Third World, and combined his investigation of the Auschwitz concentration camp with a simplified interpretation of National Socialism. In the late 1960s he developed his own kind of documentary theater in the tradition of agitprop and early Piscator, insisting, however, that the documents had to be selected and presented from a partisan point of view. In his revolutionary masques *Gesang vom lusitanischen Popanz* [1967] (*Song of the Lusitanian Bogey*) [1968] and *Viet Nam Diskurs* [1968] (*Discourse on Vietnam*) [1970], monolithic arguments, more likely to strengthen the believer than to convince the skeptic, are charged with the theatrical force of chorus recitations, group movements, and ingenious pantomime. In his play *Trotzki im Exil* [1970] (*Trotsky in Exile*) [1971], written to counteract Stalinist falsifications, he explores his own point of view as an independent radical of the Left. In *Hölderlin* [1971] he asks once again what the writer should do in an evil world and suggests an answer in the final theatrical encounter of the poet

Hölderlin and young Karl Marx, who tells us that, fortunately, thinker and poet both go their legitimate ways, the one "politically analyzing historical situations" and the other "giving shape to his deepest personal experience." *Trotsky* and *Hölderlin* may be clumsy and occasionally sentimental plays, but there is nothing haphazard or unreflected in the three volumes of *Die Ästhetik des Widerstands* (1975–81; *The Aesthetics of Resistance*), an intellectual autobiography of Weiss as he would have liked to be (and was not)—that is, a thoughtful proletarian *goy* who experiences all the secret victories and defeats of the German Left. Dense, probing, and difficult to read, it is a novel of essential importance that should have been translated long ago.

In the chronicle of his exile Weiss says that many critics characterized his early paintings as imitative. I would add that his early German plays, published in 1968 in the two-volume collection of his theatrical writings, are those of an epigone trying in isolation to combine what has been developed in many arts by others. In *Marat/Sade* Weiss reached an essential turning point as playwright and critic of society: while observing the rehearsals of the play on the stage of the Rostock Theater (GDR), he moved closer to identifying himself with the radical figures of his imagination. *Marat/Sade* basically consists of a play within a play: an aging and obese Marquis de Sade produces his own script about Charlotte Corday's murder of Jean Paul Marat for the edification of both patients and authorities at the Charenton insane asylum. In a complex time pattern involving the day of the actual murder (July 13, 1793), the moment of the commemorative performance (July 13, 1808), and the hour of the present-day theatrical experience, history itself emerges as a counterforce to mere theatrical concerns. Sade, who has been committed to Charenton for political reasons, does not have an easy task: discussing life, death, and revolution, he steps into his own play in order to answer Marat (played by a paranoid), while as producer he must continually defend his text to Coulmier, the director of the institution, who is disinclined to tolerate radical formulations because they unmask the discrepancies between the revolutionary rhetoric and the bourgeois practices of the triumphant liberal regime he represents. In Weiss's revised 1965 text Sade mockingly laughs at his inability to discipline the fury of the patients whom he has paradoxically provoked by his therapeutic play:

stamping and shouting "Revolution Revolution/ Copulation Copulation," they rush forward and are beaten by the nurses at Coulmier's command; only the falling curtain of the real, not the fictional, theater rescues the modern audiences from raging chaos. We, the new accomplices of Coulmier, are to be attacked by the final thrust as well.

The antagonists rarely speak to each other, but they do articulate two cohesive views of humanity: Sade is sustained by romantic self-pity, "existentialist" solipsism, and a circular view of history, whereas Marat incarnates the abstract rhetoric of the revolution, a scientific view of mankind, and an unhesitating belief in productive action. Sade rages against the indifference of a nature that does not impart a sense of meaning, blindly killing in bleak monotony (an "individual" death is therefore a great achievement); Marat believes it is Sade's personal apathy that prevents Sade from intervening to halt the social evil of the world. But Sade rejects the idea of man's acting beyond himself; since man is largely unknown to himself, he should concentrate on exploring his own ego and consider the impersonal issues of the moment (be they patriotism, nationalism, or the turmoil of the masses) as inconsequential specters. Marat asserts that it is imperative to live by acting in the historical moment, and that the particular moment demands that the revolution be defended against the middle class, which lives by exploiting the fourth estate; hence a second stage of the revolution is necessary. Alternating monologues formulate Sade's narcissism and Marat's commitment, but the question is whether these alternatives are not superseded by the views of the radical socialist Jacques Roux, who, a premature Leninist, interprets the revolution strictly in economic terms, demands concrete measures for distributing the means of production, and insists, in an idiom devoid of enlightened rhetoric, on well-aimed and violent action *now*.

In the early summer of 1964 Weiss attended the Frankfurt trial of the administrators and guards of the Auschwitz concentration camp. Drawing on actual source materials, he then transcribed what he had heard in *Die Ermittlung* [1965] (*The Investigation*) [1966]. Unspeakable suffering and mindless henchmen are once more confronted, and the dramatic event, freed of theatrical dross, turns into a fierce and sober ritual that keeps alive the memory of those murdered in camps, ditches, cellars, and prisons. Rather than "imitating" facts, the playwright compresses the monstrous realities of the courtroom with unobtrusive energy, successfully transforming the legal procedures into a dirge in which the killers judge themselves. The eighteen accused retain their individuality (because they retained their names in the camp), while the nine witnesses, or former "nonpersons," are assigned mere numbers and articulate what many others actually said before the judges. Weiss asserts that he is simply offering a "concentrate" of the court proceedings, but he actually does much more. He has changed the prose statements of the court session, as preserved in the stenographic record, into a consistent free-verse line of three or four beats that seems equally to shun everyday idiom and heroic five-beat blank verse. He conducts his investigation in an effectively structured way, first leading his listeners into the camp (cantos 1–2), then exploring the daily hell of the prisoners (3–4), and symbolically confronting one of the victims with one of the killers (5–6). Then, in the second part, he builds up a terrible sequence of annihilations: death by shooting at the black wall (7), death by injected poison (8), death by hunger (9), death in the gas chambers (10), and death in the fiery ovens (11). If this is theater, it is one of "total drainage of emotion" (Adolf Klarmann's words) rather than of alienation or empathy.

In his thoughtful and highly personal essay *Gespräch über Dante* (1965; *Conversation about Dante*), Weiss reveals the fundamental source of his formal intents: the thirty-three parts of his investigation relate to the structure of Dante's *Inferno*, and the mystical number itself emerges as a sign of involvement and despair. Dante created his universe thinking of a Beatrice, and his modern heir thinks of the fate of a Jewish girl whom he might have saved from the camps by acting more resolutely on her behalf. His structure of thirty-three parts, giving form to the most infernal matter in human history, implies a cry for forgiveness, and the most impersonal cipher (as so often in his work) hides his most personal plea.

But Weiss pushes his artistically sharpened investigation beyond reestablishing the facts and in his own way suggests a definite interpretation of the concentration camp system. He places the statements of Witness 3 in such a structural context that they inevitably dominate ideologically. Witness 3 has more of a personal past than the others, describing himself as a physician who was politically active long before being sent to the camps. Precisely because he had been concerned with political theory, he was able to see the continuities linking the camp society with the society outside the barbed-wire fences. What he discovered was a world ontologically no different from that outside: the attitudes within the camp were potentially present in the competitive society outside and only more fully "realized" in the death mills; many captives (he is evidently thinking of the German Jews) once shared national and acquisitive aspirations with those who later became guards. Their functions are, within the acquisitive system, interchangeable: "if they had not been designated/ prisoners/ they could equally well have been guards." Weiss takes great care to let these analyses go practically unopposed. Witness 5, who suggests a kind of "existentialist" interpretation of the camps by saying that they radically differed from the society outside, unwittingly supports Witness 3 when she describes the "radically different" laws as those of theft, brutality, and expropriation; the only people who directly oppose Witness 3 are the murderers themselves or their defense attorney.

Yet I cannot entirely agree with Witness 3, for my mother, who died in a camp, was not a potential Nazi guard. While I am certain that Witness 3 rightly stresses the later collaboration of important German industries with the camp administrations (established beyond a doubt by the Nuremberg tribunal), I suspect that he is totally unaware of concerted economic efforts by the SS that resulted, after 1939, in its establishing an economic empire of its own. Planning to monopolize power, the SS tried to build a production system that would undermine private industry—called "liberal" by the SS newspaper hacks—and the competing strength of Hitler's party organization. In economic practice and intent (though often counteracted by other orders), the policies of the SS Reichswirtschaftshauptamt (Central Economic Office) in the later years of the war closely resembled the economic operations of the Stalinist Secret Police Ministry, which staffed vast construction and gold-mining industries with slaves guilty of being Polish or Estonian. Old-fashioned concepts of capitalist exploitation certainly do not suffice to explain the origin of the German or any other camp system, nor the shabby sadism of the guards. It is an inalienable element of the reductive view that Weiss, throughout *The Investigation*, never uses the terms "Jew" or "Jewish" (at most, he speaks of those "killed for racial reasons") and deliberately counteracts any possibility of arguing against Witness 3, who, taking away the invisible dignity of dying from the dead, asserts that the victims were but potential camp guards. Witness 3 is as blind to history as Weiss's Trotsky, who pontificates to an enquiring German student (act 2, scene 12) that, in the confrontation between exploited and exploiters, "the Jews' fight for survival is of minor significance" because they are *merely* "the victims of an internal capitalist quarrel."

Weiss himself has called the three volumes of his *Aesthetics of Resistance*, written between 1972 and 1980, his most essential undertaking. Even a first reading of the difficult text (presented on the printed page without paragraphs and in monumental density) should not entirely disregard his additional *Notizbücher: 1971–1980* (1981; *Notebooks: 1971–1980*), a literary diary in which the author comments on gathering his materials, describes his travels to interview witnesses and old friends, and, in bitter irritation, defines his difficulties with the radical students (so young) and with the officious functionaries of the establishments of West and East. *The Aesthetics of Resistance*, a novel of striking intellectual power that explores Weiss's "search for himself," combines the wishful thinking of a fictional autobiography of his life as it should have been with a history of how fascism was resisted in Spain, in the cities of exile, and most important, in the Berlin underground. We hear the voice of a more or less authentic proletarian whose father (rather than being a capitalist factory owner like Weiss senior) had his active part in the Spartacus rising of 1919 and, by his stories about the continued fighting in the early 1920s, contributes to the political training of a young man who is eager to understand history as class warfare and the function of art and literature in these conflicts that are determined by the power of economy. In Spain the young man experiences the gory realities of the civil war and the inner conflicts among the defenders of the republic (i.e., the way in which the Communists get rid of dissenters whom they call Trotskyites or foreign agents). After the Spanish republic is overrun by the fascist armies, he finds himself first in Paris and then, with the help of friends in the trade unions, in exile in Stockholm, where he long debates whether or not to join the Communist Party (he does, in spite of all the Spanish experiences and the Moscow trials). Working in a factory, he serves the party apparatus at least in a small way by carrying manuscripts to underground printing presses, and tries to learn from his friends and from those who, through couriers, are directing resistance in Germany itself. In the last part of the novel much of the story shifts to Berlin, showing the last days of the "Red Orchestra" resistance group in the Nazi Air Ministry (which provided information by secret broadcast to the Soviet army) and the terrible way in which the members of the group, men and women, were executed by the Nazis. A striking contrast emerges between the active and hunted men and women of the Berlin resistance group (of different ideological orientations) and the exiles in Sweden and elsewhere, who cannot agree on a shared minimal program that would unite Socialists, Communists, and independents in their ideas about the political and intellectual future of Germany.

The playwright Weiss felt attracted to the fate of entire societies or characters of historical distinction, but the prose writer never tired of indulging in his own kind of narcissism, illuminated by the thunderbolts of recent history. If, in some of his early writings, he came close to accusing himself of not being Jewish enough to be persecuted with the others, the author of *The Aesthetics of Resistance* whips himself for not being a dyed-in-the-wool proletarian. While others (Max Frisch, perhaps) may play games with substitute biographies, Weiss in his high seriousness and total lack of self-irony systematically constructs himself a counterlife, with the result (revealed in the *Notizbücher*) that he often confuses facts and fictions in his own experience. Readers have a difficult time for other reasons, too: the storyteller has a sensitive ear and a hungry eye, but he does not really do much and speaks even less, while the corporeality of his comrades and friends, who never drink a glass of beer or make love, vanishes in a fog of opinions—we hear voices about voices, arguments about arguments, discussions about great works of art and the political alternatives of the divided Left.

Weiss, I suspect, writes much more suggestively about Spanish landscape or works of art by Kafka, Picasso, or Géricault (not to mention the unifying interpretation of the Heracles relief on the Berlin Pergamon altar) than about the ramifications of the changing party line. Coming to Marxism with a delay of thirty years and reliving the late 1930s, Weiss has never forgiven the great organizations of the Left for having been unable, or unwilling, to sustain the Popular Front against the fascists. Though his views of political life in the West often seem as sophisticated as a Hanoi propaganda broadcast, he studied the history of socialism and Soviet communism exhaustively and in scholarly detail, and his portraits of some of the political and intellectual figures in exile, among them Brecht (an unwashed genius surrounded by submissive women), are of uncanny precision. Some of the important figures in the novel are high functionaries of the Communist International, but Weiss never abandons his real aim of showing politics "from below." Thus he describes what political change meant for a working man, a volunteer of the International Brigade, a girl in a youth organization, and a lonely courier hiding in Germany (as did the real Lotte Bischoff, who was brought ashore by Swedish sailors to take information to the Resistance in Berlin, and who survived miraculously).

Weiss, who actually belongs to the generation of Günter Grass and Heinrich Böll, first published a German prose piece in 1960, and his difficulties with writing and living are more intimately related to his deliberately discarding and then reclaiming his native German than many of his Marxist interpreters are willing to admit. His turn to painting, the graphic arts, and experimental movie-making may have been one way to escape the necessity of deciding in which language he meant to live. He clearly preferred Swedish for a number of years before writing in German again and ultimately defining himself as a German writer residing in Stockholm. His conversion to Leninist theory (later characterized by himself as going in the direction of Rosa Luxemburg and Antonio Gramsci) offered him another possibility of solving many of his problems at once: proletarian internationalism made writing in German less painful, and the explications of what happens in history in economic terms, including the Marxist reduction of Auschwitz to a place without Jews, made it easier for him to identify universally with all the persecuted of the world, without complicating matters with particular questions of religious heritage and the Jewish tradition, dimly remembered and perhaps repressed anyway. He arrived late, but he has often compensated for his lack of a personal idiom by displaying a forceful scenic imagination that challenges the most intelligent directors of our time. Repelled and attracted by images of sickness, flagellation, torture, and death, and darkly obsessed by the awareness of his own past failure to combat inhumanity, Weiss has tried harder than any of his contemporaries to fight the introspective middle-class bohemian in himself by concentrating his energies on social aims independent of his vulnerable sensibility; nobody else has gone so far as to write himself a scenario for a new life, down to the last rented room in the Stockholm suburbs. In his Charenton play Sade compares Marat in his bathtub to an embryo swimming in the amniotic fluids that protect it from the confusing world outside, and regrets that the people's tribune, transfixed in rigid thought, can no longer be affected by unpredictable experience. To both lonely Marat and self-tortured Peter Weiss, revolutionary ideology had become another womb that marvelously protects a sensitive skin.

3

WEST GERMANY: SOCIETY AND LITERATURE

THE STUDENT REVOLT AND THE QUESTION OF REVOLUTIONARY VIOLENCE

In the 1960s and 1970s it became clear that the structure of the West German population had changed visibly. The number of people dependent on "natural conditions" in their working life, above all in the primary sector of the economy, fell by half between 1950 and 1971, while in the same period the number involved in a working process "outside nature" rose to 83 percent. The traditional parties competed for the support of the new middle class of multiplying civil servants and white-collar employees in the service industries, underplaying their ideological commitments, which ultimately derived from nineteenth-century assumptions. The Conservatives, largely dominant among the middle classes and in the Catholic regions, attracted new votes of Protestants, housewives, and working-class people, while the Social Democrats, historically a party of the Protestant proletariat, revised their old Marxist program at their Godesberg Conference in 1959 and acquired new loyalties among Catholics, civil servants, and even farmers. The federal elections of 1965 irrevocably transformed the West German political scene, less perhaps by the immediate statistical results (CDU/CSU 47.6%;

SPD 39.3%) than by making it possible to conceive of a grand coalition of Conservatives and Socialists. In 1966 growing unemployment and a large budget deficit combined to create the first economic recession after the long years of the economic miracle; Ludwig Erhard, who had engineered that miracle, was forced to resign as chancellor, and the coalition of Conservatives and Social Democrats headed by Kurt Georg Kiesinger, a former member of the Nazi Party, and by Willy Brandt, who had returned after the war from his Scandinavian exile, was formed in 1966, ending the long period of Socialist opposition to the government. The coalition was eminently successful in combating recession, but the concentration of massive party power in the Bonn parliament and elsewhere made it more difficult for any opposition to be heard (as had happened in Austria ten years earlier). In the big cities and university towns student unrest increased, pitting students and police against each other in a spiraling violence of street battles constantly renewed.

It is characteristic of the late 1960s and 1970s that it was no longer a group of writers and critics that dominated the intellectual scene, but the events and ideas of the student revolt. A few critics maintain that the student revolt destroyed literature, but I would rather say that it radically revised the expectations of a whole generation about what literature could and should be. Many of the activists of 1966–69 are today in positions of influence in the cultural establishment, including TV; essential ideas of the student movement have been preserved if not *aufgehoben* (in the Hegelian sense) in the media and have combined, rather easily, with the emerging ideology of the Greens and the new peace movement. The short chronology of the student revolt does not reveal much about the long-range impact of the events and the subsequent diffusion of its idioms into the experience of nearly everybody. Some of the speech habits of the student movement, originally derived from the difficult scholarly writings of the philosophers and sociologists of the Frankfurt School, have long since turned into public clichés. After a few local rumblings in 1965 and 1966, mostly in West Berlin, students took to the streets everywhere for two years, challenging the political and academic establishment across the nation (1967–68). In the spring and fall of 1969, however, it became increasingly clear that the students, most of them from the humanities and political sciences, were isolated from the white-collar and blue-collar working people. The national movement, mainly represented by the Sozialistischer Deutscher Studentenbund (SDS), or Socialist Federation of German Students, rapidly disintegrated into opposing factions, lost many of its activists to newly established splinter parties of the radical Left, or yielded its emancipatory impulse to new groups such as the feminists. In spite of all the alleged frustrations of being a student in a capitalist society, the number of students in the field of German alone rose, in the Federal Republic and West Berlin, by 40 percent between 1966 and 1971.

Kenneth Kenniston wrote in the late 1960s that the international student movement showed the "failure but also the extraordinary success of the liberal-industrial revolution," since the students rose "where conditions were best." He was right to say that "those who complained most loudly about being suffocated by the subtle tyranny of the establishment, usually attended the institutions where student freedom was greatest." It is true that the West German student revolt originated at the Free University of Berlin and quickly affected the historically younger institutions like Frankfurt University, while institutions of older traditions such as Munich, Würzburg, and Freiburg sustained rather than pioneered the revolt. The Free University, at least initially, was the freest of them all, having grown from the secession of a group of students and professors reacting against the ideological and political restraints imposed by the Soviet zone authorities on the old Berlin University located in the Soviet sector. It was established on December 4, 1948, at a convocation at the Titania Palace Cinema in the Western sector of the city, and lectures and seminars were at first improvised. The Ford Foundation provided an operating capital of $1.3 million and guaranteed the survival of the intellectual secessionists, who ultimately settled in the quiet Berlin suburb of Dahlem. Alone among German universities, the FU was established programmatically as a "community of teachers and students" opposing the traditional oligarchies—in the East, the functionaries, and in the West, the faculties. The charter deliberately created a counterbalance to the traditional power of the academic elders by establishing a student assembly in which university affairs were discussed and voted on according to strict parliamentary procedure. Many of the students joining the FU at its inception came from the GDR universities, where it had rapidly become impossible to continue academic studies without joining a party-organized group or submitting to the crudest indoctrination by party activists. These refugee students contributed their political awareness, actively helped organize secret student dissent in the GDR, and even tried to storm the Wall when it was erected overnight by the East German authorities in the late summer of 1961.

The early history of the FU (so different from later developments) was recorded in Dieter Meichsner's novel *Die Studenten von Berlin* (1954; *The Students of Berlin*), which can be read as an atmospheric document of changing expectations. The hefty narrative employs Dos Passos's methods of synchrony to show what happened to a group of young people of different backgrounds and beliefs who, after the traumatic experiences of the war, all came together at the FU to pursue their studies. One of them had barely survived the bombing of Dresden; another had been a lieutenant in the army; a third belonged to the Communist underground; a fourth came from a well-to-do family; and so on. The historical events are given ample scope. There are long and fascinating discussions between students and professors as to whether it would be better to submit to political necessity or to leave the Soviet zone. (I remember similar discussions at Charles University in Prague in the spring of 1948.) There are also instructive portraits of East German youth functionaries and how, once in power, they manipulated the antifascist and socialist idealism of young people returning from the war. Meichsner makes no bones about his political sympathies: he likes Harald, the disenchanted Communist who goes on a secret mission to help his fellow students in the Soviet zone and is promptly arrested there. And he certainly does not like Monika, who turns into an early example of the *Wirtschaftswunderkind* and, regretting that most of her colleagues are "so terribly political," marries a conservative young lawyer. A large part of the narrative is devoted to the workings of the student parliament and to the intrigues of older professors attempting to undermine, if not sabotage, the participatory role of the students in university life. It is a book to be read alongside the theoretical texts of the student revolt in today's perspective.

The construction of the Wall, cutting through the city of Berlin, changed (among other social relationships) the FU student population: students from the East could no longer cross over without risking their lives. The FU then attracted restive and politically aware young people from all over the Federal Republic who were eager to leave their stuffy hometowns, parental tutelage, and a republic governed by the conservative establishment. If the first generation of students was radically liberal almost by instinct and was philosophically inclined to existential moods, the members of the following generation, trying to escape from the traditionalism of their families and the increasing consumerism of West German society, demanded a higher quality of emancipated life right then and there and studied the early writings of Karl Marx, the critical theories of Theodor W. Adorno and Walter Benjamin, the works of Herbert Marcuse and Wilhelm Reich and, somewhat later, Marx's *Das Kapital* and *Quotations from Chairman Mao*. The earlier opposition to the regime beyond the Wall was less relevant than fighting authoritarian structures on the western side of the Wall, and by the mid-1960s a utopian disappointment with the shortcomings of democracy (represented for many by the capitalist system) triggered growing conflicts with the university authorities. The students demanded free speech for guest lecturers whom the administrators thought inopportune, opposed U.S. military intervention in Vietnam, and in December 1966 clashed with the police in the first street battles in the center of West Berlin.

Later observers of the West German student movement suggested that its politics were intertwined with larger strains of wanting to change life itself immediately and fundamentally. Kommune I, emerging from the Viva Maria Group (inspired in turn by the technicolor revolution enacted by Brigitte Bardot and Jeanne Moreau in the movie *Viva Maria*), demonstrated that many younger people, as in other countries, wanted an alternative to old-style politics. The Kommune mixture of Dada, anarchist nostalgia, and amateur psychotherapy was more useful to the media than to the cause. Kommune member Dieter Kunzelmann (who later turned up in a Near East terrorist training camp) publicly declared that his orgasm was more important to him than Vietnam, while Fritz Teufel (conveniently meaning "the devil") was in and out of prison for preparing "bombs" to be used against Vice-President Humphrey (they were made of pudding) and writing leaflets inciting to arson (found by the court to be works of art), before he finally did go to prison for attempted arson and trying to plant a bomb at a gathering of Berlin lawyers for their yearly dinner dance. From the beginning of the student movement, private desires and public concerns were jointly present. I wonder whether the later characteristics of a "New Subjectivity" and the renewed attention to the psychological problems of the individual, so obvious during the disintegration of the student revolt and later, were not inherent in the nascent rebellion from the outset, perhaps in political camouflage.

In the late spring of 1967 the students and Berlin police began confronting each other in increasingly brutal tests of strength, until the events of June 2, 1967 turned the FU student revolt into a movement of national importance, starting riots against the authorities all over West Germany. On that day the Shah of Iran and an official entourage including Willy Brandt visited West Berlin under heavy protection by police and groups of pro-Shah Iranians. After the guests had entered the Opera House to listen to Mozart's *The Magic Flute*, the police began chasing the student demonstrators gathered in front of the building. Benno Ohnesorg, a nonpolitical Protestant student new to demonstrations, was shot and killed while trying to escape the police. (Detective Sergeant Karl-Heinz Kurras was later not even sentenced for manslaughter.) Ohnesorg's body was carried home to Hannover through the GDR, and students marched in West Berlin and all other West German university towns, demanding the formation of an encompassing Extraparliamentary Opposition (APO) that, for many, was to embody opposition to parliament and all it represented.

The year 1968 proved restless and bloody, witnessing the rise and fall of the student movement within six months. Seminars and university buildings were occupied throughout the Federal Republic; in early February one thousand Freiburg students stormed the local jail to free their arrested colleagues; in late February, an "International Vietnam Congress" in West Berlin mobilized twelve thousand demonstrators to demand the dissolution of NATO (chief slogan: "U.S. equals SS"), while eighty thousand citizens assembled in front of the city hall in a counterdemonstration sponsored by the trade unions and the city government. On April 3, 1968, two department stores in Frankfurt burned (the arsonists were later among the most prominent terrorists), and on April 11 Rudi Dutschke, the most prominent Berlin SDS theoretician, was shot and grievously wounded by the psychopath Josef Bachmann, who later hanged himself in his prison cell. The leadership of the SDS was rather quick in "positively" asserting that the crime was "plainly" the consequence of a political conspiracy "mounted by the Springer [newspaper and publishing] Corporation and the [West Berlin City] Senate." The shooting was followed by five days of bloody Easter holiday rioting in Berlin and West Germany, leaving two dead and over four hundred wounded in the worst street battles since the Weimar Republic and the nascent Nazi movement. Student groups organized a "Springer Blockade," tried to storm the corporation's high-rise headquarters near the Berlin Wall, and often prevented the distribution of the conservative Springer papers by blocking garage exits or burning delivery trucks.

In May, however, the student movement suffered an incisive defeat in national politics that shattered its febrile energies and confirmed its ultimate isolation from the working people, whether readers of Springer newspapers or not. The students and the Extraparliamentary Opposition had concentrated on opposing the Emergency Laws, long under discussion in the federal parliament in Bonn, which authorized the government to establish emergency procedures in time of war and natural catastrophe. But the trade unions and the Social Democrats separated themselves from the students on this issue: holding their own protest demonstrations, eventually they agreed, at least on the national level, to a revised version of the laws. Thus the students were left in the cold, without specific aims or effective allies. The SDS disbanded two years later, and the continuing disintegration of the movement in sporadic and helpless violence at the universities created a new situation with changing group interests and shifting alliances. The terrorist groups, unwilling to give up the struggle against the system, now took their cues from the urban guerrilla movement elsewhere. The poet Hans Magnus Enzensberger called for the "creation of French conditions" (in which the students and workers had briefly united), but Berlin was not Paris. Ninety-two percent of all Berlin citizens (as *Der Spiegel* reported in June 1968) expressed their opposition to "the use of violence by protesting students"; the antistudent group included 78 percent of all Berlin blue-collar citizens under thirty years of age.

Uwe Timm's *Heisser Sommer* (1974; *Hot Summer*) is one of many novels looking back on the student movement. It is so entertainingly written that the reader only belatedly realizes its Communist Party bias: the message to the students is that they would have been more effective had they joined organized power. Timm's protagonist Ulrich, a sort of student Everyman at the University of Munich, cannot hold our attention as an individual: we are asked to accept him as a "type" who finds himself involved with fellow students representing a spectrum of orientations and attitudes, including defeated SDS radicals, Trotskyists, terrorists, and dropouts smoking hash and cultivating cabbage patches. Timm knows a good deal about the speech habits of his generation and the private worlds of restive students. His Ulrich starts out as totally unpolitical (he has a difficult time making love to his girl in a dingy rented room), but fortunately, after many confusions, false commitments, and disastrous term papers, he meets Roland, a positive hero appropriately committed to the Communist Party. Ulrich then begins to learn about the political struggles of the underprivileged and finally returns to Munich to become a schoolteacher and work for the People, like a character in an early Soviet novel. Timm's novel is itself a product of the disintegration of the student movement, in that it looks back half longingly, half critically, and wishes to tell the aging students how to act effectively in a changed world. In its own way, it clearly reveals why the student revolt never had the chance of turning into a revolution, and why the students, enclosed in their elite world of philosophy seminars and monthly subsidies from their parents or the government, were unable to form an effective alliance with what they called the "revolutionary Proletariat" (largely absent from the scene) or the "fringe groups" (*Randgruppen*) that were suggested, at least by theory, as a proper substitute for the missing plebeians. But it was precisely at this time of lost illusions that a new period of German writing began, and whether or not we wish to call these later years the age of the "Turn of Tendencies" (*Tendenzwende*) or the "New Subjectivity," we cannot ignore the fact that by the mid-1970s people began speaking of the student movement as belonging to the more or less distant past.

Considering the intellectual importance of the student movement, it is surprising that younger intellectuals and writers have failed to explore their recent past rationally; true confessions and sentimental memories are not missing, but good analyses are. Most observers perceive the student movement legitimately as continuing the "Ban the Bomb" Easter marches and the opposition to the remilitarization of the Federal Republic in the 1950s. It is possible to argue that the student revolt largely coincided with the effects of the first economic recession in the Federal Republic, though it would be difficult to show how. I would rather agree with those who say that the student movement was sustained by young people of an affluent society, born in the World War II baby boom, who in the mid-1960s found themselves confronted by professorial father figures, depressed by impersonal regulations, and frustrated by a terrible feeling of loneliness in a sham society of material values. If many of these young people wanted to study in West Berlin, it was not only to avoid serving in the Bundeswehr (an exemption made possible by Allied statutes), but also to live in a city still deeply wounded, hidden in its agonies, shabby in a heroic sense, and far from dominated by the *Wirtschaftswunder* chic prevailing in Munich and Düsseldorf.

The student movement was strengthened by the government's Grand Coalition of 1966, which immobilized an effective opposition within the parliamentary system. Students certainly showed intense energy in defining their "home" demands concerning the administrative and pedagogical reorganization of the universities, and in expressing their passionate commitment to liberating Iran, Vietnam, and life itself, yet they were incapable of translating these desires into the middling terms of national policies. In some essential aspects, the student revolt was but another stage in the long history of German expressionism in which the rebellious children of the restored middle classes rose once again against the world of the parents, who were committed solely to material values, money, and immobility. But instead of creating plays and miraculous poetry, as their grandfathers and grandmothers had done, the new generation articulated its restlessness by embracing the poetic rites of communal living (in Germany, if five students rent an apartment together, they do so on purely philosophical grounds), by instituting educational counterinstitutions of their own, and, all the more so as national conditions proved intractable, by expressing their wishes and expectations in sublime social and literary theories almost free of inimical earthly matter. Most students of 1968 liked to occupy seminar rooms and libraries, and not post offices or railway stations as did the Spartacists of January 1919.

Ultimately and inevitably, it was the question of violence that revealed the fundamental problems of a movement that wanted to be political but was incapable of overcoming its fatal and often self-willed isolation as an academic elite. In the earliest stages, young people were willing to discuss and convince (though many professors were physically prevented from talking back); only later did some theoreticians begin defining violence against objects rather than against persons as useful and necessary. Street battles, throwing rocks at U.S. Information Libraries, and the destruction of Springer trucks were considered initiation rites of a revolutionary courage intent upon provoking counteraction. As early as June 1967 Jürgen Habermas, a philosopher in the tradition of the Frankfurt School, warned the students against their "fascism of the Left," but to no avail; the speaker following him alluded condescendingly to "well-meaning professors" who believed that it was time to rethink the strategies of revolt.

The New Left is not particularly eager to look closely at the link between the beginnings of West German urban terrorism and the failures of the student revolt. Few intellectuals (perhaps with the notable exception of Klaus Mehnert, Iring Fetscher, and Hans Egon Holthusen) have substantially contributed to analyzing the series of crimes planned to change society in the late 1960s and early 1970s, which included fires set in Frankfurt department stores; bombings of U.S. army headquarters and other installations; attacks on the Hamburg offices of the Springer Publishing House and on the German embassy in Stockholm; the spectacular murders of the federal prosecutor, a bank president, and an industrialist; and the actions of young West German terrorists on the international scene (at the Vienna OPEC conference, Entebbe, and Mogadishu). The great majority of terrorists, whether students or not, came from academic and professional families: Andreas Baader's father was a Bavarian state archivist; Gudrun Ensslin was a minister's daughter; and Ulrike Meinhof came from a renowned clan of Württemberg theologians and scholars. Among the active sympathizers young lawyers, journalists, and teachers far outnumbered any members of the working classes (one of the latter, a lonely and hapless mechanic, indulged in tinkering with the elegant getaway cars). The four major groups operating in West Germany and elsewhere—the Baader-Meinhof "Red Army Faction" (she was the brain, he the stud); Doctor Huber's "Socialist Patients' Collective," organized at a Heidelberg University clinic; the Berlin and Munich Tupamaros; and the later "June 2 Movement"—excelled in constructing highly complex theories reeking of university seminars. Concerned far more with media access than with the opinion of their fellow citizens, they stubbornly proclaimed that their revolutionary actions would turn the latent fascism inherent in dying capitalism into its "manifest stage," thereby arousing the fighting spirit in all citizens. Commando-trained in the Near East and misusing Marxist vocabulary, these middle-class dropouts emotionally blackmailed the left-of-center intellectuals rightly disgusted by memories of the Nazi terrorists. I remember only rare words of true compassion from intellectuals for those who had been hurt, maimed, or killed, intentionally or haphazardly, by the urban terrorists: members of the U.S. forces serving in Germany; a judge's wife nearly paralyzed when a bomb meant to kill her husband went off in her Volkswagen; the twenty-three workers injured in the bombing attack on the Springer concern; or the driver of the prominent industrialist, mercilessly killed with him and left lying in the street. Tears do not come easily to the younger heirs of Hegel.

In public and literary life the *Radikalenerlass* ("decree concerning radicals") agreed on by the Socialist chancellor and all the governments of the *Länder*, whether run by Socialist/Liberals or Conservatives, caused far-reaching discussions inside the country and abroad. Semantics are important: the partisan habit of speaking about *Berufsverbote* (decrees prohibiting the citizen to work in a chosen profession) tends to obfuscate the fact that the "decree concerning radicals" of January 28, 1972, sought to define general norms for judging whether or not an applicant for a federal job in the civil service or elsewhere was loyal to the constitution.

The problem is, of course, that in German tradition most academic and many other jobs commanding prestige and extraordinary benefits are those in federal/public service; many former students who had been active in radical organizations in the mid-1960s were suddenly confronted seven years later with the possibility of an investigation of their political past. There were many public protests, legitimate and illegitimate (the latter in the case of Communist functionaries who kept silent about the close supervision of each citizen in the GDR, where jobs and promotions are allotted strictly according to political behavior recorded in the cadre documents). Then the Social Democrats called for a revision of procedures: in a new "Basic Statement" (1976) the *Länder* were given leeway to either interpret the decree more liberally or stick to the letter of the original wording, and litigation shifted to the courts. (In 1973–75, of 454,585 applications for federal employment, 323 were rejected.) At the height of public discussion Peter Schneider, one of the most thoughtful writers to emerge from the student generation, published his short narrative . . . *Schon bist Du ein Verfassungfeind* (1975; . . . *Before you know it, you're an enemy of the Constitution*). In the form of a young teacher's diary, it reveals the indignant reaction of young intellectuals confronted with the decree while the school system continued to be administered by aging ex-Nazis. However, we also encounter the curious assumption that academically trained people should not be sidetracked into employment by private industry or institutions, which are judged to be incompatible with personal dignity and the development of intellectual potential. It is not easy to reconcile being a radical with the desire for a good federal job with tenure.

FACTS, NOT FICTIONS

Hans Magnus Enzensberger's famous essay "Gemeinplätze, die neueste Literatur betreffend" (1968; "Commonplaces on the Newest Literature," 1974) has often been quoted as a literary manifesto of the student revolt. His essay actually reveals the self-accusations of those who had produced politically committed literature for more than a decade and suddenly felt the need to identify with a younger generation ready (or so it seemed) to prefer the immediacy of social action to literature as such. Enzensberger, who in the 1950s had published an excellent dissertation on Brentano's Romantic lyric, in his essay combines abrasive irony with many striking insights; he cannot but join the elite literati celebrating the "death of literature," but he reminds them and himself that the "death of literature" is itself a literary metaphor in use since Lautréamont and the mid-nineteenth century. He testily argues that German postwar writing merely provided a new alibi for a defeated nation, satisfied the hunger of the state for prestige among other nations, and asserted an antifascism constituted (alas) of "just having better taste than the Nazis." His basic point is that one no longer expects any social effects from elite writing; even the most daring formal experiments, earlier thought to contribute to or imitate social transformations, have been totally absorbed in the verbal and graphic codes of commercial advertising. All writers can do is make Germany politically literate; the present need calls for social documents, reportages, or Ulrike Meinhof's exemplary columns in her periodical *konkret*. Fortunately for German writing, Enzensberger did not apply his own advice to himself, but continued to write intelligent poetry as his secret vice and, before the 1970s were out, had come to admire the poet Gottfried Benn, a melancholy enemy of history once utterly disdained by the Left.

The new distrust of mere fictional writing immediately strengthened the documentary commitment of the media, and newly encouraged those writers who for some time had insistently clamored for greater attention to the working environment in the mines, workshops, and factories of the nation. In 1961 the librarian Fritz Hüser and the writer Walter Koepping (both close to the archives of the German trade unions in Dortmund) had organized a series of conferences on modern forms of industrial literature, and some of the active participants in these discussions, among them Max von der Grün, established a "Group 61" with a program in pronounced opposition to Group 47, which they considered too remote from everyday life. Group 61 called for a literary and aesthetic discussion of the industrial world and its technological pressures, a new scrutiny of the socially committed literature of other nations, and a sustained effort to revive an interest in earlier German writing by and about working people in the industrial Ruhr and elsewhere. The student revolt promptly radicalized many members of Group 61; in the general meetings of the late 1960s, insistent younger voices protested against the deplorable "literarization" of the group's activities, and in 1969 the radicals, including Günter Wallraff, seceded to establish their *Werkkreise "Literatur der Arbeitswelt"* ("Literature of the Industrial World" Workshops) in order to raise the social consciousness of all wage-dependent white-collar and blue-collar people. The difference between Group 61 and the workshops was basically generational: if Group 61 held on to traditional concepts of culture, creativity, poetry, and the "working man" (and stayed close to the trade unions), the workshops combined the seminar terminology of the Frankfurt School with Brecht's demand to "change the world," looked somewhat askance at the unions, and sported ideas derived from the Factory Correspondents' Movement (*Rabkor*) of the Soviet 1920s and the Bitterfeld movement of writing activists in the GDR. Actually, workers were only sparsely represented among the members of Group 61 and the workshops. Nor is it really a surprising paradox that the middle-aged writers of Group 61 were reluctant to give up fiction entirely, while the younger radicals (most of whom had an elite education) opted for reportage, the documentary tape, and "found" rather than "created" literature. In the mid-1970s these trends were swept away by a new wave of me-writing that renewed interest in the sensibilities of the private self.

Max von der Grün's father was a shoemaker and a Jehovah's Witness (he had survived a Nazi concentration camp), but the son, born in 1926, fought as a paratrooper in World War II and, after his release from an American POW camp, worked as a mason and miner and was fired from his job when he described a work accident in one of his early narratives. After publishing *Männer in zweifacher Nacht* (1962; *Men in Double Night*), about his experiences in the mining region, and *Irrlicht und Feuer* (1963; *The Will-o'-the-Wisp and the Fire*), a novel about the consequences of automation that was translated into many languages, he settled as a free-lance writer in the industrial area of the Ruhr and was among the founding members of Group 61, which he later defended loyally against the "leftist pretensions" of the younger radicals. His novel *Stellenweise Glatteis* (1973; *Slippery Road Ahead*) tells the story of a minor industrial Watergate. In a chemical plant a new communication system enables managers to eavesdrop on workers in the shops, and the middle-aged truck driver who accidentally discovers the true function of the system and reveals it to his fellow workers is promptly dismissed. After a wildcat strike and legal proceedings the driver is rehired, but while his rights are now guaranteed, he feels insecure. From personal experience he has now learned what it means for an individual to face the organized power of institutions of corporate management, the trade unions, and the particular interests of political parties. He is caught in the wheels of the social mechanism: management wants to buy him off; the trade unions have no stake in his fight (they have bought the chemical corporation through their own powerful bank); and his daughter, a young Socialist, blames him for his lack of theoretical awareness (he does drink a lot of beer). In the end, his main supporter is an old Communist (Weimar Republic vintage) who has to hide his sympathies for the Ruhr Parsifal from his own comrades. Von der Grün does not avoid melodramatic episodes (arson, a car accident, and a sex murder), but keeps his chapters brief and his idiom uncomplicated, aiming at readers apt to switch from a book to TV. Most of his stories and novels have been popular fare on West German television for years.

Günter Wallraff (b. 1942), who is related to one of the richest clans in the Rhineland, worked as a bookseller and wrote derivative poetry before he found himself in conflict with the West German army, in which he was reluctant to serve. His experiences prompted him to write in the muckraking tradition of Upton Sinclair, though without Sinclair's epic breadth. Though originally one of the more prominent members of Group 61, he decided to join the seceding founders of the workshops, and by "infiltrating" plants, docks, and media offices he obtained documentary evidence that he used with impressive theatricality. Like a Russian middle-class Narodnik of the nineteenth century, he captures for himself and his readers the *frisson* of sharing in the alien life of people laboring in the plants of Ford (Cologne), Siemens, and Thyssen. In his prose collections such as *Wir brauchen Dich. Als Arbeiter in deutschen Grossbetrieben* (1966; *We Need You. As a Worker in German Corporate Plants*) and *13 Unerwünschte Reportagen* (1969; *13 Unwanted Reports*), he reveals an excellent ear for the give-and-take between foreman and workers, but when he tackles modern technology in terms last found in Charles

Dickens, he is far less impressive. *Ganz Unten* (1985; *Far Down*), his report on the experiences of Turkish workers in West German industry (in preparation for which he transformed himself into the immigrant "Ali"), sold nearly two million copies within a short time, but he somewhat weakened his cause by occasionally relying, against his usual practice, on secondhand testimonies.

Erika Runge (b. 1939 in Halle, now in the GDR), who produces documentary films for TV, has a sharper and more critical mind than the romantic Luddite Wallraff. Following the example of Oscar Lewis and Studs Terkel, she taped conversations with underprivileged people who would have been without a voice otherwise. Her *Bottroper Protokolle* (1968; *Bottrop Protocols*) gathers conversations with people in a coal-mining region particularly affected by the closing of the pits and by structural unemployment. By juxtaposing her taped transcriptions (offering us what was said by a venerable prewar Communist, the village priest, a housewife, a salesman, and others), she creates a rich if partisan document of oral history reaching far back into the Nazi dictatorship and the economic crisis of the late 1920s. She admits to a certain amount of editing, rearranging tapes into effective sequences. It must have been a disappointment to her that most people revealed their "false consciousness" (at least from a Marxist perspective) by giving priority to football games, family problems, or how to make money in a rock band, rather than supporting the demand for the immediate nationalization of the mines, which the old comrade suggested as the quickest way to decrease unemployment. By the mid-1970s Erika Runge too felt frustrated by the documentary mode and turned to other forms of writing.

THE NEW WOMEN'S MOVEMENT: FIRST VOICES

The new German women's movement has its organizational origins in the Socialist Federation of German Students (SDS) and was burdened for a considerable time by the theoretical preconceptions of the student revolt. In the United States, liberal women's groups willing to work within the system, and the radicals of the Vietnam period, often took a more or less pragmatic view of effective alliances, but the women of the new German movement, all middle-class, all students, and most of them Marxists, were slow in recognizing the long traditions of the older German women's organizations, ranging from liberal groups to the disciples of Aleksandra Kollontai; initially at least, therefore, they spent a good deal of energy in scholastic self-definitions, isolating themselves from potential allies. Within the German SDS, organizational habits did not seem to differ from those in similar organizations in the United States: the men talked and did the deeds while the women, so they strongely felt, kept the coffee pots simmering, handled the stencils, and provided consolations of the flesh to the tired heroes. At a Frankfurt conference of the Studentenbund in the spring of 1968, Helke Sander (an important feminist filmmaker today) demanded full equality for comrades of both sexes and told the meeting that "the expectations of women" should be included "in future plans." When the conference was unwilling to discuss her speech at length, one of the enraged women delegates pelted her male comrades with tomatoes—an allusion to the tomatoes thrown by men at the women delegates during a 1966 meeting of Students for a Democratic Society (SDS) in the United States. After a Women's Liberation Action Council had been founded in Berlin in January 1968, similar councils were established among women students in many other university cities; within the year, eight groups were represented at the Hannover SDS conference of delegates. Many women and men among the students shared the orthodox belief that the primary conflict was that between capitalism and the exploited classes, patriarchy being a capitalist structure; but whatever the dominant theory, women were no longer willing to ignore exploitation and the private, or intimate, forms of social oppression. As a first concrete step, *Kinderläden* (children's centers) were organized as collective and revolutionary cribs, training toddlers and children in antiauthoritarian principles, and giving young mothers more time to pursue public activities.

Marxist women in Germany were able to strengthen their arguments by referring to August Bebel's *Die Frau in der Vergangenheit, Gegenwart und Zukunft* (1883; *Women in the Past, Present, and Future,* 1886)—reductive in its view of overall economic causation and nearly puritan in sexual matters—and to Clara Zetkin, an eloquent spokeswoman for women's rights as a Communist member of parliament in the Weimar Republic. It was more difficult to recover the past of the well-organized non-

Marxist older women's movement, which included Louise Peters, who edited a women's newspaper in the revolutionary period of 1848; Helene Lange, who demanded equal educational privileges for women students; and Helene Stöcker, who had written about a new sexual ethic before she had to escape from Nazi persecution to New York. Nor was it easy to remember the dominating role of resilient women in German families shattered by Hitler's dictatorship, the war, the fire raids, and hunger.

It was the independent journalist Alice Schwarzer, author of *Der kleine Unterschied und seine grossen Folgen* (1974; *The Little Difference and Its Great Consequences*), who, taking her cue from events in Paris, concentrated public attention on the infamous paragraph 218, which made abortion illegal. By encouraging public confessions of women who had had abortions, in the early 1970s she created a new mass basis for social action in the middle classes that went far beyond the ghetto of the students' groups, which by that time were indulging in mutual sectarian warfare. A federal congress at Frankfurt in 1971 brought together women from twenty cities of the republic. Increasingly, Marxists were confronted with radical feminists and lesbian groups that were inimical to any economic reduction of the situation. Believing that capitalism was but one of the despicable shapes of patriarchy, these groups were ready to explore the predominance of male codes of repression in language, everyday behavior (night and day), and all forms of culture. American and British feminist writings, from Kate Millett and Shulamith Firestone to Juliet Mitchell, were studied assiduously. By the mid-1970s, networks of new women's institutions were created all over West Germany, including women's bookshops, publishing firms, university courses, residences, and health centers that continue to flourish today. The revised version of paragraph 218, submitted to parliament by the Socialist/Liberal coalition, was declared unconstitutional by the Supreme Court. While another watered-down version was being discussed, the surge of public enthusiasm subsided, and local women's groups of different orientations turned from a concentrated and national political effort to cultivate a new sensibility often implying a new pride in motherhood, or to support the peace movement or the Greens, who were not at all unified in their stand on abortion. It was a time when women's writing rapidly demanded attention from a new generation of readers in all German-speaking countries, including the GDR, in which the economic equality of the sexes, guaranteed by law, did not inevitably affect the habits of patriarchy in daily life.

Social historians have quickly developed a view of the new women's movement in successive stages of development. It may be possible to separate an early, or student, phase from the mass actions against the old paragraph 218 and from the subsequent phase of feminism as counterculture (tense with conflicts among the Marxist/Leninists and the radicals). It would be more difficult, however, to trace similar stages in imaginative writing. I would say that the privileged kinds of women's writing emerged almost simultaneously in the early 1970s: confessional or autobiographical prose; the historical panorama of women in German history; and, most attractive of all, a kind of irrepressibly fantastic fiction subverting traditional realism as an expression of ancient patriarchy. The autobiographical texts include reports and novels. (Whatever term is used, it should not hide the most intimate closeness of the text to actual experience.) Among these, Karin Struck's *Klassenliebe* (1973; *Class Love*) and Verena Stefan's *Häutungen* (1975; *Shedding*, 1978) were widely read as pioneering best sellers.

Class Love is a collection of letters and diary notes in which Struck relentlessly explores her personal experiences in the spring and summer of 1972. She travels and lectures in the service of the German Communist Party (which she has left long since), and feels caught between her nuclear family and her tortured loyalty to another man, described in sufficient detail to be known to the *cognoscenti* as an important writer of the radical scene. It would be easy to say that the text is uneven, self-indulgent, and sentimental, yet this is the only way in which the young woman feels able to cope with her aversions and longings. A refugee from the GDR and the daughter of a workingman among intellectuals, she is unable to articulate abstractions as easily as her husband or her lover. She feels "without language, without a country, and without a class" and incessantly urges herself to hope for a more serene and fulfilled existence, "love, love, tenderness, to be a mother, a woman" (without really giving up her male role models). Feminist readers of the Left were often irritated by Struck, not so much because of her attacks on Brecht for exploiting his companions in bed and on the stage, but because she almost proudly announced her biological closeness to nature and the procreative flesh, an attitude more clearly confirmed by her later novel *Die Mutter* (1975; *The Mother*). In the German context in which many remember the Nazi glorification of biology, mystical ideas about nature-mothers are more difficult to advance than in other countries, quite apart from the realities of paragraph 218.

Verena Stefan's *Shedding*, a loose collection of notes, poems, and confessions, gently expresses a young woman's quest for self-realization on the Berlin counterculture scene of the early seventies. The public questions of the late sixties have now been totally superseded by the assumption that sexuality itself sustains and reflects old and new relationships of power. The young woman, who works in a hospital as a trained physical therapist and studies sociology at the university, goes through her own intense novel of development, learning, doubting, rejecting, and finding. (Questions of profession and money are excluded from any consideration, and trips to America and Mexico are undertaken as easily as a subway ride to Dahlem.) Her first partner, Dave, an American black, fights "against the tyranny of whites over blacks and yet constantly re-creates the tyranny of men over women." Another relationship with a leftist intellectual in the ghetto of "loquacious Marxists" (who religiously attend late performances of old Westerns) promises liberation but also ends in disappointment, because the man cannot see her as a person in her own right; in spite of all the theories about the economic causes of all ills, he demonstrates, in bed and elsewhere, that "the terrors of sexuality have been operating autonomously, and will persist, in spite of economic upheavals." She moves in with women friends and meets the painter Fenna, who is as willing as she is to explore new ways of living together. The two women, perhaps Fenna more than the writer, are happy in their untroubled togetherness, without forcing a feverish affair. In a conclusion in which the writer shifts to speaking about herself in the third person, the young woman now called Claudia longs for Fenna, who concentrates on her paintings, and a newly found pride merges with the awareness that "der Mensch in meinem Leben bin ich" ("I am my own woman"). Stefan legitimately complains, in an introduction unfortunately missing from the

American translation, about the impossibility of using appropriate German terms in writing about sexuality (all terms being male by implication), but I would also ask whether she pursued her search for a new language and a new narrative mode far enough. This may be why *Shedding*, which in West Germany sold nearly two hundred thousand copies initially and triggered a wave of similar texts, left far less of an impression on the American scene, and why the poetry of Karin Kiwus and Ursula Krechel (in which feminist issues are often implied rather than directly expressed) and the writings of Brigitte Schwaiger and Elfriede Gelinek, two Austrian women of the stiff upper lip, have shown far more staying power for a widening circle of readers.

It was not among the most pressing priorities of the new women's movement to look back into the past. But Ingeborg Drewitz (b. 1923, Berlin), who published her first stories and plays in the late 1940s and early 1950s, has chosen the burden of illuminating the present moment against the horizon of recent German history, from the early Weimar Republic down to the student revolt. Four generations of women in a Berlin family, reminiscent of the Drewitz clan but conveniently more plebeian in fiction, struggle for survival and awareness of their selves. The story of Gabriele, born in 1923, and later that of her daughter among the revolutionary students, offers an instructive and almost autobiographical opportunity of showing what happened in German history as seen through the eyes of a woman who refuses to submit. Rather than gathering masses of descriptive detail in a family saga, Drewitz concentrates on important if not emblematic moments from Gabriele's experience: when Hitler triumphantly returns to Berlin after the fall of France, she holds hands in a streetcar with a young man eager to escape from the blaring radios and crowded streets to the suburban forests and rivers. Only gradually does Gabriele come to know what kind of life she really wants to have. She defends her intellectual interests against her traditionalist husband, whom she leaves for a time to conclude her studies and to commence her career as a broadcasting editor. And yet, thinking about the persecuted, the Jews deported to the death camps, and the burning city, she ultimately believes that thinking women experience themselves as *caring* (even if rejecting the automatic roles of mothers and wives), and that emancipation would be reckless if it did not remain aware of the fragility of all human beings, and of death. The radical liberal Drewitz (long committed to public functions in the P.E.N. Club and the Writers' Union) explores alternatives and contradictions, free of all impatient dogma. While elements of didacticism are not entirely absent, as in some of her other books, there are also moments of intense feeling reminiscent of her other autobiographical novel *Oktoberlicht* (1969; *October Light*). The city of Berlin itself begins to emerge with its own life, from Moabit to Oberschöneweide, and from Gotzkowsky Bridge to the back rooms of the Café Möhring on the Kurfürstendamm.

French feminist theories about the continuing power of patriarchy in language and established kinds of literature were slower in reaching Germany than the United States, but writing women, committed to the idea of self-realization, immediately went beyond the autobiographical narration and the historical panorama to challenge the legacy of realism (however useful ideologically). It is not surprising that the most provocative texts in the mode of a new and liberating fantasy were written by women trained, or still living, in the GDR, where the theory and practice of literary realism strongly survives as something either to do or to argue against. The poet Christa Reinig (b. 1926), who left the GDR in the mid-1960s, defended her narrative *Entmannung* (1976; *Emasculation*) against disapproving feminists by arguing that it documented, however obliquely, her way to the women's movement. It is a sad, grotesque, happy, and intentionally disordered book that, by virtue of its formal chaos, protests against law-and-order patriarchy, whether alive among the Marxists in the West, or masked in the "alleged equality of women" on the other side. There is a fragmentary story about four women (a physician, a housewife, a reflective kleptomaniac, and a factory worker) who, together with a playboy and a surgeon, try to discover and practice alternative forms of daily living. Ultimately, the living and the dead happily meet in a magic theater to attend a performance of Mozart's *Magic Flute*, a witty persiflage of Gustaf Gründgens, the famous German actor and theater manager. *Emasculation* is not a book to please ideologists of any stripe, except those who firmly believe in the productive force of literary dislocations, wit, and parody.

Irmtraud Morgner's *Leben und Abenteuer der Trobadora Beatriz nach Zeugnissen ihrer Spielfrau Laura* (1974; *Life and Adventures of the Trobadora Beatrice as Chronicled by Her Minstrel Laura*) has rightly been called the most important novel to reflect on issues of women's emancipation in the GDR. Its fantasy ploys and collage elements are part of the message, skillfully balancing a fundamental affirmation of socialist principles, as proclaimed by the GDR state, with frank irritations caused by the male chauvinist praxis of everyday life in the republic of workers and peasants. Instead of telling a linear story of how Beatrice, the most famous Provençal "trobadora" of the early Middle Ages, returns to life to search for a truly humane society in the GDR, she alternates the adventures of a wide-eyed and yet wonderfully earthy Beatrice with those of her friend and ally Laura Salman, engineer, mother, and author. The novel introduces excerpts from contemporary literary texts and political documents (including the new GDR law on abortion, which is left to the decision of the individual woman); dwells on instructive episodes of memory swapping between women and men; and concludes with a novella of miraculous androgyny set in the most modern research institutes of East Berlin and Moscow. If the novel were not so long, it would be doubly effective, as indeed it should be in a country where, in spite of all slogans of socialist solidarity, in the early 1970s more than 50 percent of all employed were women, who also did 78.7 percent of the housework before and after their working hours in offices and factories.

Characterizing the present situation, an American woman observer recently remarked that "creative female incursions through film and literature into the public sphere have given the German women's movement its most sustained momentum since the mobilization of the abortion struggle" (of the early 1970s). Such a statement can be read in two ways. It attests to the new wave of creative impulses liberated by women's groups, but it may also suggest that women are again most effective in the aesthetic realm, however closely it may or may not relate to social experience.

FROM THE SEVENTIES TO THE EIGHTIES: THE "RED BLUES," THE PSYCHOBOOM, AND THE GREENS

The seventies were years of changing feelings about the quality of life in the Federal Republic. Within a decade, what began as a grand honeymoon of sweet hopes and almost limitless expectations turned into a time of sour irritations, creeping disillusions, and a disquieting new belief that the good future was perhaps an affair of the past. In the elections of 1969 the Socialists (42.7 percent) gathered sufficient middle-class support to constitute, together with the rejuvenated Liberals (5.8 percent), a left-of-center coalition that, for the first time in the history of the Federal Republic, relegated the strong CDU/CSU (46.1 percent) to the benches of the opposition. The new cabinet, headed by Willy Brandt and the urbane Liberal Walter Scheel, well liked by people in business and middle management, immediately launched a wide range of social, economic, and legal reforms that were to touch the lives of every citizen, and pursued the new *Ostpolitik* designed to reduce tensions between West Germany and its neighbors in the Slavic east, who were burdened by lacerating memories of the war. The elections of 1972 confirmed that a majority of citizens, and not only those from working-class backgrounds, were happy in support of the Socialist/Liberal coalition: the Social Democrats received more votes than ever in their history (45.8 percent) and the Liberals made strong gains (8.4 percent), while the Conservatives (44.9 percent), unsure of future politics, lost out to the left-of-center competition.

The year of the Socialist victory, however, was also the time of the first reversals, as mounting economic problems began to endanger costly social reforms. Then the oil crisis hit West Germany with its full force, raising the cost of living and emptying the roads of cars (on Sunday, driving was forbidden by government decree). After many years of expanding social privileges offered by the welfare state, and of widening participation in the democratic process, citizens were confused and shocked when these economic problems combined with unexpected political issues. A member of Willy Brandt's personal staff was discovered to be a mole who had systematically transmitted information from the chancellor's office to the intelligence apparatus in East

Berlin. Brandt resigned from office in 1974, and with the appointment of Helmut Schmidt as chancellor in his stead, a public attitude of prudently managing pressing economic problems (the presence of millions of foreign workers, and the continued loss of exports) prevailed. Many German intellectuals, untrained in the fair exchange of arguments and unschooled in the art of political compromise, yielded to eschatological moods and were unwilling to think of the future in the light of recent achievements that included the new *Ostpolitik* détente and a much-discussed reform of the educational system that had increased the number of university students of working-class background from 8 percent in 1967 to 14.6 percent in 1975.

There was also the matter of personalities: to many, Willy Brandt, the antifascist exile and defender of West Berlin in a time of grave danger, possessed a historical if not romantic aura that his successor in office definitely lacked. While many intellectuals had greatly admired Willy and his friend Grass, they had a more difficult time being fair to the cool and sober economist Schmidt, whose grim task it was to face one crisis after another, urban terrorism being just one of them. The media and the critics watching the intellectual scene were busy diagnosing a turn from utopian expectations to more pragmatic dealings, within narrower confines, with the possible, and from great collective commitments to the surprising rediscovery of what it meant to have a private self. Some observers talked about the *Neue Subjektivität* (New Subjectivity) emerging into full view, while others, more ironic, discussed the "Psychoboom," and everybody who wanted to be "in" switched from quoting Marx and Adorno to adoring Freud, Jung, and Reich.

The literary discussions of *Neue Subjektivität* were useful, because they revealed the ideological orientation of those who operated with these concepts in one way or another. In the magazines of the New Left, contributors constantly asked the embarrassing question how it was possible that so many comrades (now turning into German yuppies) were reading fiction again. Preferring honesty to self-delusion, the questioners suggested that all past efforts to develop "proletarian ersatz identities" had failed: young people once more were on the move to ascend the magic mountain of subjectivity, which perhaps constituted a gesture of political relevance in a capitalist society adverse to tolerating the independent self. Other critics valiantly tried to separate the new young writers of the Left, who were hesitantly exploring their subjectivity, from Peter Handke's retrogressive introspections or Botho Strauss's psychological games, but it was difficult to ignore the shift of interest to many kinds of writing proscribed by the student movement of 1968. In her symptomatic poem "Jetzt ist es nicht mehr so" (1977; "It isn't that way any more"), Ursula Krechel speaks for the changing emotions of her generation when she recalls the collective rituals of the late sixties, the happy demonstrations and the movies afterward, the easy way of recognizing comrades by their haircut and their laughter, the foolish certainty of telling every workingman in the subway what he really needed. It is not that way any more: now there is ample time for long discussions in bed when two people are alone with each other, "perspiring but cold down to our toes/ we see for the first time the white/ in our eyes and we are terrified."

In his story "Lenz" (1973), Peter Schneider asks essential questions about the future of student radicalism and the incipient change of feelings among the doctrinaire Marxists. Alluding to Georg Büchner's narrative, he suggests that political energies would be far more effective if they were intimately related to the sensuality of experience and the individual's wish for personal happiness, engendering a willingness to defend the happiness of others. The brief narrative, which within a short time sold one hundred thousand copies, works with the romantic motif of the voyage to Italy in quest of deeper fulfillment. Schneider's protagonist is a sensitive Berlin student who, as is de rigueur, does not really study, but works in a factory to enlighten the masses and attends a study group interpreting Mao. He hocks his guitar and buys a ticket to Rome, trying to escape from German "neurotics and theoreticians" incapable of offering passion or salvation, as well as from oppressive memories of an affair with a working-class girl rightly unwilling to open his way to the proletariat through the orifices of her body. Italy, as he expects, turns out to be a country of strong colors, sounds, and humane encounters, but happiness eludes him. At a fashionable cocktail party in Rome, he watches left-wing film producers "in stylized sailor suits" and Communist authors in "some uniform of the Red Army or expensive blue jeans," and discovers that the discussion is as sterile as at home: in Berlin his friends derived their intimate frustrations from the conflicts between labor and capital, while here everybody believes that class conflicts are caused by unresolved family relationships. He goes north to Trento and finds true paradise among real working people who are involved in revolutionary action, to the left of the Communist Party, against the industrialists of the region. Living in the proletarian family of the people's leader, he even accepts a clean and orderly way of living that would have repelled him as typically bourgeois in West Germany. When the Italian police expel him from the country, he returns to Berlin gladly, believing that he has learned an important lesson about thought and feeling, a new patience with the small things in life, and the essential ability to relate sensuous experience to abstract concepts. Dialectical materialism, the tale tells us, can productively absorb fundamental elements of the New Subjectivity, and exploring their own feelings will do the revolutionaries no harm.

Among the many autobiographical sketches and authentic memoirs of the retrospective 1970s, Bernward Vesper's *Die Reise* (1977; *The Trip*) was widely read, especially by younger people, as a document articulating the confusions of the time. The young author, who began writing immediately after the student revolt withered away, himself suggests, in his fragmentary correspondence with his publisher, that his manuscript should be published (in his own American idiom) "as far-out notes of the inner space." Vesper (1938–71), the son of a well-known nationalist author who collaborated with the Nazis, grew up on his parents' country estate on the southern fringe of Lüneburg heath (a way of life that did not really change much after 1945). Falling victim to his father's ideas, as a boy he distributed leaflets for a neo-Nazi party that failed to attract voters at large. He studied in Tübingen and West Berlin, turned radical, became a friend of Gudrun Ensslin and Ulrike Meinhof and, "after they had gone their terrorist way," experimented with LSD, mescaline, and other drugs. He showed symptoms of mental disturbances, was put in a Hamburg clinic, and committed suicide, as did Gudrun Ensslin, the mother of his son. His unfinished manuscript was posthumously edited by a friend, and the outlines of its organization emerged clearly: the report of his wanderings (à la Jack Kerouac) with a young New York painter from Dubrovnik to Munich; recurrent attempts to articulate an LSD trip in prose and illustrations; and, most substantive, a "Simple Report," in which Vesper tells the story of his boyhood and youth at home in translucent and nearly classical prose, his own negative comments appearing in the defensive confines of parentheses. He proudly proclaims his new narcissism and feels equally distant from the *Schickeria*, or radical chic set, and the "vegetables," as he terms his middle-class fellow citizens, whose affections are absorbed by their families and cars. He could not have lived among either group.

From the mid-1970s on, the issue confronting the Socialist/Liberal coalition was to balance the competing demands of the social programs and the economy, which was stagnating or hovering on the brink of recession. Chancellor Helmut Schmidt was given far less recognition, especially among intellectuals, than he deserved for his clear-eyed attempts to work out practical solutions acceptable to the coalition partners, asking for more and more cuts in welfare programs, lower taxes, and greater support for private investment. In the elections of 1976 the coalition barely made it; many voters felt disenchanted again with the traditional party system (not necessarily a hopeful signal in the German context), and the new *Bürgerinitiativen* (citizens' initiatives), or environmental self-help groups of concerned citizens, consolidated their regional and federal organization. In the late 1970s the coalition faced, in addition to its economic worries, an increase in terrorism on the left and the right. Public discussion continued about security measures, antiterrorist laws, and the legal rights of individual citizens, and the NATO "double-track" decision of 1979 to initiate arms limitation talks with Moscow but also deploy medium-range missiles in Europe (and Pershing IIs in West Germany), triggered a new peace movement continuing the traditions of the 1950s on a popular basis and strengthening the nascent Greens. In 1980 Schmidt once more defeated the Conservative opposition, but the coalition did not hold together for long. In 1982 a new coalition of Conservatives and Liberals was formed by Helmut Kohl, who developed an action program to fight unemployment and inflation (high to German perceptions, though relatively low as seen from outside) by means usually favored by Republican administrations in the United States. The 1983 elections confirmed that the citizens, at least those trusting the established system, were in search of conservative solutions again: two million Socialist voters deserted the party, throwing it back twenty years; the Liberals lost more than one third of their support; and the Greens, supported by pacifists, feminists, and environmentalists, showed a gain of 5.6 percent and for the first time sent twenty-eight delegates to the federal parliament.

The citizens' initiatives that emerged in the early 1970s, and went through a number of transformations later, conformed to the German urge to be in politics without indulging in party affairs, traditionally considered by many members of the middle classes as apt to dirty a pristine mind. Initially, citizens' initiatives developed spontaneously when white-collar people in a particular neighborhood wanted a new playground for their children that was not foreseen in the city budget, or fought pollution or the building of a new road brutally disfiguring an ancient cityscape. But the occupation of the building site for a nuclear plant at Wyhl (Upper Rhine, 1975) signaled a decisive turn toward fighting nuclear and other technologies, a trend that was continued in massive and occasionally violent demonstrations at nuclear plant sites at Brokdorf, Kalkar, Gorleben, and elsewhere. Sociologists say that in the late 1970s the citizens' initiatives changed into a broadly based ecological movement from which the Greens in turn emerged in 1977–78, at a time when a new xenophobia was also making itself felt.

The Greens, who had chosen the open sunflower as their emblem, gathered the dispersed energies of the citizens' initiatives and the peace movement. Against all predictions, they initially attracted sufficient electoral support to be represented in many city governments, in individual states, and in the federal parliament. Much political speculation now centers on whether or not the Greens, usually unpredictable, will one day collaborate closely enough with the Socialists to build a new majority and defeat the Conservatives and the Liberals, who have been weakened in recent years.

The Greens are a conglomerate of movements and a political party that does not want to be one. They are largely people between eighteen and forty-five years of age, solidly white-collar and professional, male rather than female, and of far better education than the average voter. Their fundamentalists, never absent in German political life, do not wish to see the organization involved in impure everyday affairs, while their pragmatists argue that you cannot be effective outside the social institutions. The Greens have not hesitated to accept the $1.40 per voter of taxpayers' money that the government provides to competing political parties, so as to make electoral campaigns independent of private funding; however, the question of salaries for delegates in the parliaments has created doctrinal difficulties, and all Green officials, including delegates in the federal parliament, serve according to a rule of rotation in office, making it impossible to accumulate power (or expertise). The Green slogan of *Ökopax* ("Eco-Peace") stresses the essential commitment to a humane environment (as opposed to more industrial growth, roads, and airport expansions) and to rescuing Germany from becoming the charred theater of an atomic war (they urge an immediate withdrawal from NATO and instant removal of U.S. missiles from German soil).

Yet the Green *Weltanschauung* goes much further, demanding universal changes in thought, society, and life, which all "hang together" organically. The brown Greens of the older generation hanker after a strong Germany asserting its ancient *Geist* against what is called the "vodka-cola culture," while the red Greens, ranging from former Maoists to disenchanted Social Democrats, favor revolutionary action against the Establishment and dispute the principle of nonviolence inspired by Martin Luther King. Feminist Greens have trouble with conservative women Greens who argue that abortions kill as brutally as do toxic chemicals. Green flower children of many age groups argue about possessive and nonpossessive love, and a few gurus quote a hodgepodge of the medieval mystic Meister Eckhart, Marx, and Christ. Green ideology is a strong brew of many intoxicating ingredients, particularly attractive to young writers, jaded intellectuals, and true innocents like Heinrich Böll. At a conference at the Munich Max Planck Institute in 1980, scheduled to take an analytical look at the social scene of the seventies and eighties, a critical observer noted that the new movements were in danger of importing, in colorful new costumes, conservative impulses and reactionary ideas "from below," preparing the ground for an "unholy alliance" of contradictions, "new motherhood and sociobiology, an alternative critique of science, and a theory of ecosystems, neonationalism, and a spontaneous sensuality." Personally, however, I am much more disturbed by the Green insistence on the *total* transformations that *must* occur, if the world is to be saved at the last minute, because I still remember what can result from a volatile mixture of cataclysmic emotions, cries for closer "ties with the earth," and the inevitability of absolute change.

4

HEINRICH BÖLL (1917–1985): CITIZEN AND NOVELIST

EARLY WRITINGS

American readers tend to know more about Grass than Böll, but people in his native country and in the republics of Eastern Europe consider Böll the ranking representative of postwar German literature. As a writer, Böll has had a difficult time in the United States: his sentimental writings about defeated and hungry Germans did not particularly speak to American audiences of the self-satisfied 1950s, while the new generation of the 1960s, potentially closer to his ideas, preferred Hermann Hesse and Herbert Marcuse. Böll probably knew more about American writing than anybody else in Germany, with the possible exception of the literary critic Günter Blöcker and the writer Gabriele Wohmann, but he felt more at home among the Soviet and Czech dissidents whose closely knit, ascetic, and friendly communities exemplified, to his mind, the ideals of humane society at large. He would have been happy in a New York ethnic neighborhood of, say, 1910 or 1920, but he never encountered such womblike communities when traveling in the United States, visited rarely, and kept a wary distance from American critics and intellectuals. When he received the Nobel prize, only two of his many novels were in print here (I checked that very day).

Heinrich Böll was born in Cologne in 1917 to a family of craftsmen whose Catholic forefathers had left England under Henry VIII. His childhood in the Cologne tenements, the legacy of his native Catholicism, and his experiences in Hitler's war marked him for life. His father was a carpenter and woodcarver who worked for local churches and monasteries. The family enjoyed a few years of petit bourgeois well-being in the mid-1920s, but the economic crisis of 1929 destroyed all hopes for continued prosperity. The Bölls (Heinrich was the eighth child) settled in a flat in the old quarter, where, increasingly hard pressed economically from month to month, they were often caught between pawnshop and bailiff. But parents and children were close to each other, and the door was always open to relatives and friends, including many members of the Catholic Youth Movement (averse to the Nazis); young Heinrich must have been among the three or four students in his school to avoid enlisting in the Hitler Youth organization without major difficulties. After finishing school he worked in a bookshop in nearby Bonn, hung around at home reading Balzac and Flaubert, and after six months in the Labor Service, listlessly enrolled at the University of Cologne but rarely attended any lectures. He and his friends, he later said, were paralyzed by a sense of imminent and inescapable war. Böll was among those who served, as soldier and corporal of the infantry, from the first day of the war to the last, first in Poland and later in France, Russia, and Romania. He was wounded in action four times but by 1944–45 had developed an ingenious technique of survival, operating with false travel orders, injections to induce high fever, and half-legal home leaves that brought him close to being AWOL. In April 1945, however, when the front moved close to the West German village where he was hiding with his wife, he decided that he would have a better chance for survival in a regular army unit than as a deserter who might be caught by the German MPs. Joining a front-line fighting unit, he was promptly taken prisoner by the U.S. army. Moved to a French camp, he was released in November 1945 as unfit for work and went home to a Cologne totally destroyed by Allied bombs.

Thereafter Böll never left Cologne or the adjacent region for any length of time, though in his fits of creative irritation he often got restless, tried to live in small villages, or rented a room for writing as Kafka had once done. In the 1950s he bought a modest farm in Ireland for himself and his growing family, but his real Dublin was Cologne, where he had spent the happiest years of his youth. Immediately after the war Böll produced many short stories that were widely published in little magazines but failed to impress readers busily catching up with Hemingway, Thomas Mann, and Kafka. The change came in the early 1950s. In 1951 he was awarded the Group 47 prize (approximately $250.00, then provided by the McCann Company, a U.S. public relations firm). Two years later his novel *Und sagte kein einziges Wort* (1953; *And Never Said a Word*, 1978), about a returning soldier and his difficulties in adjusting to marriage and a life of poverty and isolation, was a success nationally and internationally, which made it possible for him to concentrate on his writing while his wife Annemarie continued to teach for a while in a local high school. Together they translated many books from Irish, English, and American literature (including Synge, Behan, and Salinger), while his wife served as his first editor and literary adviser.

As a writer, Böll developed slowly but steadily. His first problem was to cool his sentimental feelings for the troubled characters he created and to bring together the individual splinters of life, shown in his sketches and short stories, in the structures of more encompassing novels. His earliest protagonists were soldiers at the front or maimed in hospitals, ordered to do absurd jobs in the barracks, dying in the fields, retreating home to women who had changed, or going hungry in the rubble of destroyed cities. History appeared as an absurd force crushing individuals; only when sensitive men and fragile women encountered each other in love and compassion (whether a German corporal and a Hungarian girl, or an infantry soldier and a Jewish schoolteacher) was time suspended for a moment of bliss, innocence, and meaning. Initially Böll wrote on a level far below the war writings of the 1920s or 1940s, from Henri Barbusse to Erich Maria Remarque; his encounters between soldiers and girls were occasionally close to unabashed B-movie kitsch, like the *Liebestod*-and-fate story of the soldier Adam and the noble Polish prostitute Olina in *Der Zug war pünktlich* (1949; *The Train Was on Time*, 1956). By the mid-1950s Böll was close to overcoming his amateur handicaps. In his novel *Haus ohne Hüter* (1954; *To-*

morrow and Yesterday, 1957) he distinctly widened his epic interests and tested new methods of handling more complex patterns of internal monologue that separated the fictional characters, in their full individuality, from the diminishing narration by an authorial voice. Instead of watching romantic lovers, we are faced with fearful down-to-earth family problems at a time when fathers are wounded, killed, or missing in action; what we hear are authentic voices of troubled people, old and young, trying to build a new life in a newly acquisitive society. Upper-middle-class women like Nella, in *Tomorrow and Yesterday*, may spend their time dreaming of a happier past, but plebeian Ms. B. has to take a rich baker as "uncle" because she needs money for her dentist bills.

Böll's important novels of the late 1950s and early 1960s—*Billard um halbzehn* (1959; *Billiards at Half-Past Nine*, 1961) and *Ansichten eines Clowns* (1963; *The Clown*, 1965)—move on a higher level of achievement than his earlier narratives. These novels do not break new ground structurally, but work firmly and inventively with narrative strategies tested in earlier books, as for instance leitmotiv or recurrent tag techniques, and an almost symphonic score of "voices" speaking for the historical experiences of three generations and reaching far back into the German past. Böll uses his skills to suggest that we must resist those who viciously harm other people. In *Billiards at Half-Past Nine*, about a prominent family of architects, the offended, persecuted, and exiled "lambs" strike back, resolutely if not always successfully, at those who have "partaken of the host of the beasts"—the Nazis, the powerful, the rich, and the vicious. If no other choice is left to the new underground man, as he appears in *The Clown*, he can at least totally reject state and society, express his intentionally inarticulate opposition to the Establishment by painting his face white, and play a guitar on the steps of the Bonn railway station. In Böll's early stories people suffered because they were overwhelmed by meaningless fate, but in the novels of the 1950s Böll writes as a political author exploring the concrete vicissitudes of German history. Instead of projecting his humble people against a diffuse background of rubble, dirt, and dust, he clearly defines their political attitudes and those of their enemies in terms of the "Third Reich" and the new republic, and chooses his friends and adversaries with passionate precision.

Obsessively returning to May 1945, the time of liberation, Böll tells us directly or by symbolic implication that it was a marvelous chance irretrievably lost, and thereafter, as narrator, satirist, and public figure, tackles the question whether or not the new Federal Republic of Germany really differs from the Wilhelmine empire or the "Third Reich." His answer is not always in the affirmative.

POLITICAL VIEWS AND LITERARY IDEAS

In the 1960s and after, Böll's fiction related more than ever before to his political ideas and intensifying irritations, and it is almost impossible neatly to separate (as can sometimes be done with Grass) his narratives from his many essays, statements, and interviews. Böll the returning soldier wanted to write and do nothing else. After the currency reform and the establishment of the Federal Republic, keen disappointment prompted him to express his opposition to new, or not so new, institutions, and to move slowly from more or less Rhenish concerns about Cologne Catholicism unchanged by changing history to the national issue of the Church and West German rearmament and, in the late 1960s and 1970s, to defend publicly his challenging ideas about party politics, the student movement, hapless terrorists, and the exemplary virtues of the dissidents in Soviet Russia, Czechoslovakia, and elsewhere. In the late 1960s and early 1970s Böll was widely visible in several roles: as one of the founding members of the Verband deutscher Schriftsteller, or Union of German Authors, calling, in a famous speech in 1969, for the end of the writer's "modesty"; as president of the West German and the International P.E.N. clubs (1970–72 and 1971–74 respectively); and as the 1973 recipient of the Nobel prize (after Hermann Hesse in 1946 and Thomas Mann in 1929). In a famous 1972 *Spiegel* article, Böll protested against the despicable manner in which the tabloid press immediately ascribed a local bank holdup to the Baader-Meinhof group. He warned against a new wave of political hysteria sweeping West Germany but, while wishing to clarify the situation of the terrorists gone underground, actually contributed to the continuing polarization of public opinion about legality and due course of law under less than ordinary circumstances. Courageously, he demanded that terrorists be given due legal process and be tried according to the laws of the republic in open and fair procedure, and condemned in no uncertain terms the sensation-mongering tabloids that triggered lynch-mob instincts among their readers. He was, I believe, on more dubious grounds when telling an audience deeply shocked by violence that the theory of the terrorists was more violent than their practice, and furthermore that all the terrorists had done social work and thus, perhaps, had reasons to declare war against society at large; or when he asked those members of the legal establishment who had once been persecuted by the Nazis not to forget what it meant to be persecuted by the police (forgetting himself that these people were once hunted down because of their ideas, not for blowing up cars or robbing banks). Tempers ran high; responding to his more liberal critics a short time later, Böll (suddenly revealing his metaphysical or rather Dostoyevskian assumptions) publicly suggested that for him, as author, terms like "persecution," "mercy," and "criminality" had different dimensions than they did for civil servants, lawyers, and police officials. At that time, 149 well-known German writers expressed their solidarity with him. In Paris, a little later, Solzhenitsyn indicated that Böll had shown the greatest personal courage in taking out important samizdat manuscripts from Soviet Russia, including some of Solzhenitsyn's own.

Böll's political sympathies and feelings were formed early in life when his parents, impoverished in the 1929 crash, lived outside all restrictive rules of middle-class economy, and then again when he returned, in the rubble of Cologne, to an egalitarian community of people barely surviving by bartering and by sustaining each other in mutual love and charity. In 1929 and immediately after 1945 there existed, at least in Böll's memories, openness, warmth, and a total absence of bourgeois urges, a kind of prelapsarian community open to everybody; if there was hunger and the ever present dust of the ruins, people were also willing to share, talk, and feel with each other. The beginning of the end, Böll often implies, came with the currency reform and the subsequent restoration of a "capitalist model" of economy; equality was destroyed, and a real chance to develop a new kind of thinking about property, economics, and religion was lost to acquisitive urges strengthened and manipulated by the Establishment.

Böll's City of God, or the alternative society, can be found on the fringes of organized economy. His bitter aversion for Church authorities derives much of its intensity from his belief that the Catholic hierarchy, after concluding the Concordat with Hitler, did not show active compassion for the hungry after the war. Many priests died in concentration camps, but the parishes did not accept many refugees under their roofs (if they had any), and by 1948 the Church as an institution fully sympathized, Böll insists, with the politics of restoration, and by relying on the church tax (10 percent of the income tax of each Church member), turned into an accomplice, if not a pimp, of capitalist economy. In his bitterest moments Böll speaks of the "criminal and untenable" involvement of the West German Church in the evil ways of the acquisitive world, and praises the Franciscan virtues of South American and Czechoslovak priests. It is not really paradoxical that Böll, in comparing the Soviet army and the Wehrmacht, suggested that the Red Army, at least after 1942, had restored the feudal gap between officers and soldiers, while in the Wehrmacht the same food rations were distributed to everybody and there was at least "a suggestion of socialism" (1976). In the early 1960s Böll insisted that communism still offered a hope and a chance for people, but his communism, I suspect, is one for angels, free of imperialist drives, innocent of Hegelian theories, and eager to sustain sponaneity. Böll is closest to describing his attitudes when he speaks of himself as a non-Marxist liberal of the Left with strong anarchist desires. What he had in mind was an almost mystical way of life, sustained by tenderness and a spontaneous unwillingness to exercise power, a marvelous condition of *Herrschaftslosigkeit* in which there is no dominance, only luminous togetherness.

It is revealing that, in his polemics against the new Establishment of the republic, Böll for at least ten years had great difficulties in allying himself with an institutionalized political party. In 1963 he insisted that he did not belong to any group whatsoever and expressed reservations about the growing involvement of Group 47 with the Social Democrats. Then, in a speech about the "Freedom of Art" (1966), he said that where the state should be, he merely "perceived a few rotting dregs of power . . . defended with ratlike fury." In supporting the restive students (he did deplore their intellectual arrogance and the absence of worker support), as well as in speaking against the Emergency Laws, he came close to wishing a plague on the houses of both the Conservatives and the Socialist/Liberals and declared that, as a writer, he belonged "by nature" to the Extraparliamentary Opposition (APO).

In 1971–72, overcoming some of his hesitations to commit himself to candidates in party politics, he joined Grass and other writers in support of Willy Brandt, stressing his loyalty to the man rather than the party. He continued to distrust the Socialist/Liberal government after expressing his views on how to deal with the Baader-Meinhof terrorist group. The federal police checked on some of his visitors and searched his son's home, and official explanations of these procedures were less than satisfactory. Böll was among those writers who early supported the massive demonstrations against the Brokdorf atomic reactor in 1976. Among the intellectuals of the older generation, he was closer than many to the thoughts of the Greens, and it was not suprising to most of his readers that, in the electoral campaign of 1982, he signed a writers' manifesto urging the citizens to vote for Petra Kelly and her Green candidates.

The problem was that Böll was not only blessed by memories of a happy family togetherness that sustain his images of an alternative society, but also burned by early fears and anxieties of which he spoke less often. He once admitted that he was seized by recurrent fears that everything would change politically from one day to the next, as happened once before. On another occasion he discussed a "primal German fear of living" resulting from the two inflations that are an ineradicable part of the historical experience of his generation. In the deeply probing interviews conducted by the writer Christian Linder (March 11–13, 1975), Böll alluded to that "deepest anxiety" that he first felt when, as a boy happily playing in the Cologne streets, he was suddenly forced to hide in a doorway because the Nazis were marching through the city to demonstrate their power; deprived of his "home" in the streets, he suffered an emotional wound that never healed. Speaking about his "street anxiety," Böll told his interviewer that it may account for the sudden and unexpected ways in which he sometimes reacts to political challenges or provocations, responding less to the gist of the arguments than to a crude tone of voice immediately reminding him of what was most evil in German history. I am not suggesting that there is a hidden strain of violence in Böll's sensibilities, but rather that a latent political claustrophobia prompts him to strike back when he feels pushed against the wall. While Grass, as a political speaker, usually keeps his cool, Böll, when provoked by that tone of voice that triggers unforgettable fears, had responded with sudden fits of rage, had difficulties in articulating a sustained and rational argument, and used strong terms for which he apologized a short time later. As some of his narratives show, Böll knows a good deal about peaceful people who burst out in sudden violence when they feel totally helpless. It is not impossible that his fragile anarchism was but another version of the traditional German attitude that views the pure self "inside" and the evil powers of the world "outside" as irreconcilable enemies.

Increasing social commitment did not prevent Böll from continuing to write many literary reviews and illuminating essays on his favorite authors in German, Russian, and American literature. While no theorist of literature (as are so many of his colleagues in contemporary Germany and France), he contributed often to what I would call a latter-day apologia for literary realism, equidistant from self-sufficient language experiments and mere documentary writing, and he substantially enriched our readings of Dostoyevski and Solzhenitsyn. In his earliest literary essays, above all his defense of "Rubble Literature" (1952) and "Washhouse Writing" (1959), he defended the gray world of his little, indeed "superfluous," people against the critics who argued that his narratives were joyless and boring. He suggested, as did some of the great German and Austrian realists of the nineteenth century, that "greatness" and "smallness" were not dependent on social location, and that human sufferings and happiness were not determined by social forces alone. In a series of lectures at Frankfurt University in 1964, he said that he wanted to constitute "an aesthetic of the humane" and offered a wide range of scattered views concerning his critics, who always talk politics when approaching literature; the undiminished presence of the Austrian realist Adalbert Stifter; and the importance of H. G. Adler (whose writings I have discussed in chapter 2). He defined his own work as one concerned with humane fundamentals, "dwelling somewhere, the neighborhood, our households, money, love, religion, and eating together." These Frankfurt lectures and his 1973 Nobel prize acceptance speech in Stockholm suggest that Böll distrusted words without reference to experience, or words offering nothing but information. Böll disliked purely experimental texts consumed by themselves, communications that do not "trigger any communication," words "which do not cause alarm." Yet he did not believe that contemporary writers should pretend there is no gap between texts and social experience, even in documentary literature; instead of dealing with what they think is mere information, they should explore these gaps, whether they be "irony" or "poetry, God, resistance, and fiction." Writing, Böll said, was "the conquest of a body which is still unknown," a "movement from somewhere to something" that the writer has to discover for himself. In his Nobel prize acceptance speech, Böll uttered a strong warning against the documentary writing of the late 1960s and early 1970s, which reduced literature to convenient reports for radical activists.

Böll felt particularly close to the Russian traditions of the nineteenth-century narrative. In his extensive responses to Manès Sperber, who asked specific questions about his development as a writer, he suggested that Dostoyevski was responsible for turning his early energies to writing, perhaps together with some authors of the modern French "Catholic Renaissance," above all Georges Bernanos. Böll said that he heard some lectures about Russian religious writing in 1934–35, watched the movie of *The Brothers Karamazov* with Anna Sten, and soon thereafter acquired a secondhand copy of Dostoyevski's *Crime and Punishment*, beside which all German literature that he had read so far, including Goethe, appeared "rather pale" (only Kleist and Hölderlin would compete somewhat later). Yet it was not Raskolnikov, too abstract, who overpowered him: he was deeply impressed by Dostoyevski's knowledge of a petit bourgeois milieu that reminded him of his own life, and he was fascinated by Dostoyevski's exact feeling for the economic decline of the lower middle class and for their "specific hysteria," which was simply an attempt to protect themselves against annihilation.

Böll visited the Soviet Union many times from 1962 on and had many loyal friends among the dissidents there and in the West. In the late 1960s he described Solzhenitsyn's novels as miraculously combining the essence of Russian tradition and the best of Socialist Realism. He attentively followed, in many later essays and articles, the successive publication of Solzhenitsyn's novels in the West, and welcomed him in his own house when the Russian writer arrived in West Germany on the first day of his forced exile. Böll always warned against manipulating the achievements of Soviet and Russian writers for political purposes, but he had, I believe, his own difficulties with Dostoyevski's and Solzhenitsyn's ideological attitudes. Deeply rooted in the spirituality of the Orthodox Church, they constitute a Slavophile response to the libertarian West, a rage for law and order that often totally diverges from Böll's own social desires. Böll was convincing in showing that Dostoyevski wanted order because of the chaos in his own sensibility, but he was far less prepared to confront the ideological gist of Solzhenitsyn's speeches to American audiences, preferring to direct his arguments against the U.S. trade unions, Solzhenitsyn's onetime hosts, rather than to argue against his friend's anticommunist pronouncements.

LATER NOVELS: THE SIXTIES AND SEVENTIES

There was, in spite of his widening concerns, a distinct element of moral and formal continuity in Böll's narratives of the late 1940s and 1950s, but in the 1960s he turned restive and impatient. A more intense social commitment combined with striking experimentation in viewpoint and style, and humor changed into bitter irony and belligerent satire. It became clear only later that in the major prose pieces of the 1960s, *Entfernung von der Truppe* (1964; *Absent without Leave*, 1966) and *Ende einer Dienstfahrt* (1966; *The End of a Mission*, 1967), Böll had tested his narrative procedures and gathered his energies for *Gruppenbild mit Dame* (1971; *Group Portrait with Lady*, 1973), a novel of the first rank, and for his more recent *Fürsorgliche Belagerung* (1979; *The Safety Net*, 1982), which signaled a new attitude of sweeping tenderness for all people, old or young, caught in the backlash of contemporary political conflicts. *Absent without Leave* and *The End of a Mission* clearly relate to each other thematically, because in these novellas Böll warns his readers against the moral and political dangers of rearmament. Demonstrating his frank sympathies with deserters, instinctive pacifists, and all those who balk at military orders, he again defines his fundamental opposition to German nationalism past and present and to the West German Bundeswehr. Yet the two stories are so surprisingly different in tone, texture, and narrative procedure that the reader is often distracted from the message by Böll's new experimental skills.

In *Absent without Leave* a well-to-do citizen of Cologne, now nearly fifty years old, haltingly talks about an afternoon in late September 1938 when he was a young soldier. He cannot and does not want to develop an orderly story with a beginning, middle, and end; as a late and possibly unwilling disciple of Laurence Sterne, he finds himself (for the alleged benefit of the reader) involved in constant digressions, grotesque and sad, with ironic discussions of his narrative incapabilities. He uses, to extend one of his movie metaphors, a camera that refuses to concentrate on shooting a sequence of simple takes to constitute a plot, and yet in panning finally presents us with the realities of German life about one week before the 1938 Munich conference. The actual story that (at least by implication) unfolds is the oldest in Böll's repertory: a young soldier encounters a girl whom he has loved from afar, marries her more or less on the spot, and spends a few blissful days with her while absent without leave from his unit. We discover how fateful these days were for him when, in the middle of the text, we learn that the girl, the mother of his child, was killed in an Allied air raid. Later one of her brothers was shot by a French soldier while trying to cross the lines, and another was executed by the German military police for organizing a band of deserters in the cellars of burning Cologne. The narrator himself confesses that his war experiences have left him with a slight speech defect: he stammers when telling the reader the bare outline of the story, which includes documentary materials from the 1938 newspapers and ironic suggestions about how to interpret these materials.

Böll plays a totally different game in *End of a Mission.* Here he uses an omniscient narrator who delights in finicky detail and communicates a story of explosive disorder in the well-tempered prose of the classical tradition that extends from Goethe to Thomas Mann. The structure and tone of the narrative themselves imply order, law, and neatness: we are invited to attend a trial in a local court right through the sentencing, and the story, as trial report, faithfully adheres to the niceties of legal proceedings and, since the narrator is much concerned with unity of time, follows the officers of the court, the accused, and the audience to lunch and dinner in their respective homes, inns, and restaurants, reporting on their menus in circumstantial detail. The defendants are two honest carpenters, father and son, who on a hot day in July 1965 set fire to a jeep of the West German Bundeswehr, then clanged their pipes together in the rhythm of *Ora pro nobis* and performed a little celebratory dance around the burning wreck. They assert that they were merely arranging a "happening," and a professor from the Academy of Arts confirms in a lengthy Dada disquisition that the destruction of the army jeep was merely a "quinquimusal event" involving the muses of architecture, sculpture, dance, music, and literature. The tolerant judge, knowing that the authorities do not want any national publicity, sentences the accused to six weeks in prison, while the army has to return the wreck of the jeep to the carpenters because it is the material of their art. As readers, we are asked to reflect on the contrast between the narrated events and the leisurely tone of the story; although Böll wants us to see that the Olympian narrator whose prose exudes so much calm is really an accomplice of the law-and-order authorities, many a reader may succumb to the seductive power of the prose or, at the most, perceive a strain of mild irony in sympathy with Rhenish tribal ways, rather than feel the undercurrent of fierce restlessness urging us on to active political engagement.

In the 1960s Böll engaged in intense discussions of national politics and for nearly five years worked on *Group Portrait with Lady* (1971; 1973), his most important novel, which was immediately translated into sixteen languages. He had long been tempted, Böll told his editor, to tell the story of a middle-aged woman who carried the heavy burdens of German history between 1922 and 1970; in doing so, Böll combined some of his oldest thematic interests (for instance, that of charitable women, or the fate of star-crossed lovers in war) with narrative innovations untested in his writings before, and, contrary to all past habits, with a new and surprising sympathy with characters less than morally perfect. The central figure is forty-nine-year-old Leni, née Gruyten, a kind of saintly slob, but there is also a cast of hundreds who belong to her Cologne clan and the clans of her friends, lovers, acquaintances, adversaries, and fellow citizens—people who are good, evil, and of mixed morals. Cologne and German society at large unfold in a historical panorama of teeming mass and illuminating force. With the exception of Uwe Johnson's tetralogy *Anniversaries* (1970–83), I know of no other fiction in German writing of our time that is closer to the contradictory realities of how simple people survived Hitler's Reich and how they tried to build new careers in a changing society. We are invited to listen to the story of Leni's life from her earliest days in the house of her father, who makes and willfully loses a fortune in building fortifications for the army. We hear much about her friends and teachers, including a nun of Jewish origin who is of lasting influence on Leni's sensibilities, and meet her cousin Heinrich, whom she secretly adores (he is executed as a deserter and traitor). We encounter the young soldier Alois Pfeiffer, whom she marries in a moment of youthful confusion (her family is not unhappy that he dies in action near Grodno in 1941); her great love Boris, a young Soviet POW whom she meets, by an almost miraculous concatenation of circumstances, in a flower shop where they both work in the last years of the war; and, nearly twenty years later, the Turkish *Gastarbeiter* (guest worker) Mehmet, to whose adoration she tenderly responds. But there are others who pine for her: a music critic charmed by her artless ways, and her boss Walter Pelzer, who always knows how to make a fast *Deutsche Mark* or *Reichsmark*, whatever the regime. When, pregnant by Mehmet and refusing, as always, to be as rapacious as others in the new consumer society, she is threatened with eviction from her old apartment, her friends (including the narrator, who is moved to tears by her innocence), constitute a Leni Rescue Committee to protect her from her creditors and the authorities. The great finale is one of romance: happy endings abound; old friendships are confirmed, new ones formed; and, anticipating a better society, everybody holds hands with everybody, or nearly so.

In many of his novels, Böll liked to speak in internal monologues from inside his characters. However, seemingly affected by the increasing distrust of mere fiction that characterized the late sixties, in *Group Portrait with Lady* he follows, tongue in cheek, the experimental way of his fellow writers who explore documentary evidence. We are prompted to participate in his actual process of reconstituting a biography by questioning witnesses, sifting through documentary materials, and taping interviews with friends or friends of friends. The well-documented story of Leni may have the ontological disadvantage of being totally fictitious, but it also has the virtue, Böll ironically implies, of being more alive poetically than factual reports and of offering incisive insights far more essential than those suggested by mere information.

Böll's Leni Gruyten, in whom all the good women of Cologne return in statuary splendor, certainly embodies his most ardent beliefs about our possible salvation in a venal society. In spite of or rather because of her sensuous nature, Leni is the Holy Virgin of a Christianity without theology, transcendence, or Christ, and in her own way radiates innocence of a kind, willingness to love, and unquestioning charity. Those who have known her for a long time describe her as "enormously sensual," meaning that Leni is not at all afraid of the earthy and excremental element of life; she has a marvelous sensibility that allows her to experience what reductive physiology would call an orgasm by resting in the heath, or by simply feeling with her toes a little crack in the pavement that lustfully recalls the days when she played there as a child. Most of the time as virtuous as a Dickens heroine, she becomes direct, strong, and tender when the right man comes along, being so much endowed with the grace of the flesh that she has only to lay her hand on her lover's arm to give him a moment of blissful release, emotionally and physiologically. Leni has ceased to receive communion because she feels that the thin wafer lacks full corporeality, but she has no difficulty in understanding the meaning of bread and wine. When, in a moment of true revelation, she offers a cup of coffee to Boris, her Russian lover, while being watched by the glowering Nazis, her tender and courageous gesture has the full force of a sacrament that transforms the humiliated Soviet POW back into a human being.

Nearly a generation later, when the consumers and corporations have taken firm hold on German society, a friendly capitalist who has long known her will say that Leni spreads the dangerous ideas of "communalism" and "paradisism," which, if allowed to prevail, would "like some infectious disease undermine, erode, disintegrate . . . the basic principle of our achievement-oriented society." In Marx's terms, Leni has appeared on earth to spread the joyful gospel of "being," not "having." Yet saintliness, whether old or new, is not easy to demonstrate to modern readers. Leni herself is far from being articulate, to say the least, and we have to learn about her by indirection from Sister Rahel (originally Jewish), her spiritual mother (if "spiritual" is the right word) and from Margret Schlömer, her best friend. Margret is the Mary Magdalene of the story: less sensual than Leni, she gives herself continually (and sometimes for money) because she does not want to deny pleasure to boys and men. "Her undoing," the author suggests, "was not her desire for the pleasure of love, it was the fact that so many pleasures were desired of her which she was endowed by Nature to bestow."

Böll's art is decisively changing: the novelist and the moralist cease to see eye to eye; the binary patterns of good and evil, of "lambs" and "beasts" that dominate his early fiction, are at least occasionally suspended; and for the first time Böll begins to look at some of his dubious characters with understanding and even outright sympathy. The older, largely Manichaean, value structure is still there: nationalists and most capitalists operate on the evil side, while most of Leni's lovers, pre-Stalinist members of the Communist Party like Ilse Kremer, and all true plebeians who like to give, weep, drink schnapps, and smoke cheap cigarettes retain their little halo. Yet the author cannot hide his admiration for that particular mixture of rapaciousness and being human that is so typically Rhenish and defies all labels. Leni's longtime boss Pelzer, "cunning little Walter," grew up in a petit bourgeois family constantly threatened by economic collapse (as did the Bölls) and learned early to seek out material advantage in any situation. Totally unconcerned with who was in power but very much interested in getting his cut of the pie, he sheltered Leni and Boris in his flower shop during the Allied advance and, three days before the collapse of the Nazi administration in Cologne, mailed a registered letter to party headquarters resigning from all Nazi organizations. When the Allies finally arrived, he could say he was not a Nazi, received permission to run his flower shop again (since people kept on dying), and retired as a successful businessman now looking somewhat ruefully on his colorful past and complaining that his daughter, an archaeologist, was constantly bothering him about the Third World without really knowing the First. We come closer here to the realities of recent German history than by looking at the devilish (though somewhat allegorical) Nazis in Böll's earlier prose.

Yet Böll does not want to cope with the past without turning to the future of German society. He celebrates Leni as a Madonna of his homespun religiosity, which is difficult to separate from his social concerns. Fulfilling the desires of the eighteenth-century German rationalists in his own emotional way, he radically separates the possibility of living a Christian life from Christ and the Christian institutions here on earth. Yet his sensibilities are Catholic: not wanting to miss the traditional rituals and sacraments, he boldly presents us with revelations about Leni, and earthy sacraments in which a cup of hot coffee functions as Holy Communion. It is essential to his vision that Leni does not stand alone in the world of the Nazis or, later in the Federal Republic, in that of the capitalist profiteers; she always gathers around her an extended family of lovers, admirers, relatives, and friends that anticipate a glimpse of heaven on earth. By simply *being*, Leni attracts those ready to form the nucleus of an alternative society, but it is not a Cologne version of Haight-Ashbury that emerges. Leni and Böll are good conservatives who, refusing to collaborate with power and money, instinctively return to a preindustrial realm of large families, tender love between men and women, the simple joys of a good breakfast, and old German folk songs (intermingled with Schubert and Brecht) rather than rock or punk. There is a good deal of regression in such a future, and Leni is such an alien in the historical world that she has to be told—in 1943–44!—that the Nazis have long been persecuting Jews and that it is dangerous to ask for a copy of Franz Kafka. This is innocence at its best, or at its worst.

In the early 1970s Böll found himself more deeply involved than any other German writer in the corrosive exchange of arguments about the terrorists, the strident illiberal newspapers (eager to denounce him as a terrorist sympathizer), and the presence of the security services nearly everywhere. His rage showed in many political statements and in short narratives, but it was not of the analytical kind that triggers energies of innovative art. Rather it prompted him in *Die verlorene Ehre der Katharina Blum* (1974; *The Lost Honor of Katharina Blum*, 1975), which was made into a successful movie, and *Berichte zur Gesinnungslage der Nation*

(1975; *Reports on the Ideological Situation of the Nation*), a parody of contemporary security reports, to rely on his well-tested repertory of characters, situations, and narrative ploys. Only in his more recent novel *Fürsorgliche Belagerung* (1979; *The Safety Net*, 1982) did he, from renewed distance, powerfully reassert himself as a novelist and move ahead to explore new ground.

In *The Lost Honor of Katharina Blum*, which he himself called a "pamphlet novella," he wants to defend, in a parable as it were, the dignity of the individual citizen against the unthinking harshness of the police and against the defamations of a sensation-mongering right-wing press that ultimately destroys the individual's integrity, privacy, and honor. His Katharina Blum is a kind of Leni without Leni's past, who at a Cologne carnival party meets a young man, invites him to stay overnight in her apartment, and in the morning has to face the police and the media because the young man, with whom she has fallen deeply in love, happens to be a deserter who has also helped himself to some Bundeswehr funds. Although Katharina did not know what the young man had done, the aggressive press mercilessly denounces her as an accomplice of dubious morals, and her hospitalized mother is squeezed for information and dies of shock. When, encountering an unscrupulous reporter in her own apartment, Katharina suddenly recognizes that she has become a mere object on the news market (and the reporter wants to sleep with her before proceeding with the interview), she shoots him in a fit of rage. She then gives herself up to the police without regretting anything, hoping that she and her lover, who will be given a ten-year sentence, will meet again after they have both been released from prison. I am not surprised that Böll had a difficult time defending himself against critics who said that Katharina Blum was yet another of his Rhenish saints. It was even harder to answer the question why it would be politically effective to respond to melodramatic newspaper reporting on the right with a little sentimental melodrama on the left.

Böll's novel *The Safety Net* was a near flop in his native country, but it strikes me as an important book signaling an attitude of paradoxical calm, controlled melancholy, and a sweeping compassion for everyone threatened by the political backlash of the terrorist wave. We experience three days in the life of a West German family prominent in politics and the media, and in that of an ever present group of security agents guarding their residences, gardens, and cars. There is no dearth of dramatic events, yet we are prompted to learn slowly and in significant detail how the guarded and the guardians uneasily come to coexist, how all privacy is in danger of being destroyed, and how difficult it has become for the younger generation, intensely committed just a few years before to utopia, to live in an age of growing disillusion. Given Böll's predilections, the central characters are surprisingly upper-middle-class: old Herr Tolm, the owner of a provincial newspaper after the war, who has now been elected president of the West German Newspaper Federation; his daughter Sabine, who is leaving her husband (a textile industrialist) and a comfortable home because she loves a pensive police officer who has been among her guardians; Tolm's son Rolf and his group (including his Marxist girlfriend), all melancholy activists of yesteryear now living together in an old parish house without jobs and without expectations; and Rolf's former wife Veronica, who, having chosen the other path, is being trained in a North African country as a member of a terrorist commando group but who, after her lover dies in a trap set by German security agents, surrenders to the police. Veronica's young son sets fire to the Tolms' residence, but he does not know that the authorities have also been waiting to raze the stately building and to shift the entire village elsewhere, because there are rich deposits of coal underground.

German critics had their difficulties with *The Safety Net*: having been trained by Böll himself to expect that, as an aggressive moralist, he always shares his values with the narrator of his novels, they now found themselves confronted with a book that wants to show people rather than to judge them. Here Böll does not automatically disqualify a German family of means and considerable power from probing and largely sympathetic scrutiny. We are close to a particular kind of irony (which some years ago Böll himself despised as "bourgeois") that is unwilling to take sides right away. The internal monologues, allowing people to think and speak about their particular worries, constitute an epic world of rich detail and body. Böll, who dedicated his novel to his own adult sons, has come to feel compassion rather than rage. Whatever its structural and economic terms, the system has overwhelmed even those who believe themselves capable of directing and determining its functions: President Tolm rightly suspects that he himself is being manipulated by younger power interests in his corporations. As for the younger intellectuals, if they do not wish to conform without reflection or destroy themselves in senseless acts of terrorism, they have only the choice, it seems, to withdraw into dubious idylls like the one in Rolf's garden, where former activists coolly analyze the power situation but despair of deeds, or those meetings in a large apartment where Rolf's brother Herbert gathers a few friends to cultivate a "natural way" of living in a high-rise building in the center of town. At times, the attitudes of the generations seem curiously reversed: somewhat surprisingly, old Tolm speaks of his youthful hope that, in spite of everything, socialism will emerge from the confusion, whereas Rolf and his friends, after the Establishment has refused to take their ideas seriously, remain transfixed in distance, stoned solitude, and cold pride—a new ice age of ossified feelings. "In a world marked by alienation," Julie V. Iovine suggests in her review of *The Safety Net* in *Grolier's Literary Annual* (1982), ". . . it is a significant achievement to see the human face, however grim, and recognize its claims for our sympathies."

From the discontinuities of recent German writing and the shifts and turns of the generations, Heinrich Böll emerged as a resilient and, in more than one way, reliable writer who at times disappointed his critics but rarely his loyal readership among the middle and lower middle classes. Unlike Grass, Böll developed slowly in his political stance and way of writing: he needed more than fifteen years to emancipate himself from his local concerns with Rhenish Catholicism, and nearly as many years to show that he was ready to handle a narrative of complexity and sweep. He often felt restive and enraged but, in his writing techniques, did not wish to disaffect his readers. Once he had explored and skillfully used a narrative method, he was not easily disloyal to its virtues. His Swiftian satires did not change for more than a generation, nor his versions of the internal monologue for decades, yet the clarity of his communications remained unimpaired; even when experimenting, he wanted to be as pellucid as Anthony Trollope. As citizen and political writer, Böll had fundamental loyalties that did not change over the years; he widened his concerns from a fixation on Rhenish Catholicism to being Konrad Adenauer's gadfly, and later from the issue of West German rearmament to those of East European dissidents, the terrorists, and the West German security forces. Still, he remained a largely conservative anarchist who wanted to reestablish the order of families sticking together, of small groups of people who love each other, and the laws of hospitality, charity, purity of heart, compassion, and community (not society).

It may be another question entirely whether Böll's commitments did not really reconstitute a traditional attitude that conceived of the happy and righteous, on the inside, and the organized powers of the world, on the wicked outside, as basically inimical. Böll once complained that critics always talk about politics when discussing German writing, but he himself for a long time invited them to do so by dividing his narrative universe all too neatly into the Good and the Bad. Only later in life did he offer views of a disordered world in which it was difficult to rely on sentimental clichés. In Böll's early writings we found ourselves rather easily on the right side, but this is not the case in his more recent works, above all in *Group Portrait with Lady*, *The Safety Net*, and his posthumously published sequence of interior monologues and conversations, *Frauen vor Flusslandschaft* (1985; *Women Facing a River Landscape*), in which he returns to his portraits of strong women resisting the dehumanizing power play of Bonn politics. In these works we have to make subtle choices and consider in what ways the fine art of the novelist coincides with or perhaps contradicts his ideas about the world. After many years of being the "good German" and an author of popular moral tales, Böll finally came to be, before he died in the summer of 1985, a first-rate novelist of stature and authority.

5

THE GERMAN DEMOCRATIC REPUBLIC: AN INTRODUCTION

THE ANTIFASCIST DEMOCRATIC ORDER: 1945–1949

Writers returning from exile, political prisoners freed by the advancing Allied armies, and hungry soldiers had great hopes for the future when the first Berlin papers began to appear in the early summer of 1945 on newsprint provided by the Soviet army, and the first cinemas and theaters opened again. (Lessing's *Nathan the Wise* was among the first stage performances in the liberated city.) A contingent of German Communists led by Walter Ulbricht, charged with organizing political life according to blueprints prepared long before, had been flown in by the Soviets in a special plane in April 1945, while the fires in Berlin still smoldered. On June 10 the Soviet authorities gave the order that antifascist political parties be organized again, long before the U.S. or British occupation armies resolved to do the same. The basic strategy was to establish an "antifascist democratic order," or rather the old Popular Front conceived in the mid-1930s as a belated attempt to organize broad resistance against Hitler. Soviet authorities, including Colonel Sergei Tulpanov and Major Alexander Dymshitz, responsible for cultural activities, were eager to invite Christian Liberals or even Social Democrats to participate in creating forms of political and cultural life closely reminiscent of the best years of the Weimar Republic. The Communist Party of Germany (KPD), reestablished in June 1945, demanded that a "parliamentary and democratic republic" be created and blithely declared itself on the side of free commerce and "private economic enterprise." In quick succession, other parties were established: the Social Democratic Party, the Christian Democratic Union (CDU), the Liberal Democratic Party, and, somewhat later, the National Democratic Party for former officers and repentant Nazis, and the German Peasant Union for conservative farmers in the countryside. Among the ruins, the first measures expropriating Nazi estates and distributing the lands to refugee peasants and landless rural workers were approved more or less in unison. After 1948, when Tito broke with Stalin and, on the German scene, the Western Allies and the Soviets watched each other with growing suspicions, the realities of the antifascist democratic order emerged more clearly. In the spring of 1948 the Communists and Socialists had fused their organizations into a new German Socialist Unity Party (Sozialistische Einheitspartei Deutschlands, or SED) in which, however, illusions of parity were soon destroyed. To overcome potential opposition from the other parties, new mass organizations like the Free German Youth were established and thereafter applied their SED pressure whenever and wherever needed.

In striking contrast to what happened in the U.S. zone of occupation, where a group of returning soldiers (not particularly known as writers yet) emerged as new representatives of their generation, literary life in the East Zone was re-created by famous writers and artists of the Weimar Left who resolved to return to Berlin. After twelve difficult years in California, Palestine, Mexico, or the Soviet Union (where many German refugees disappeared during the Stalinist purges), these writers made a conscious decision to go to Soviet-occupied territory, because they felt they would be welcome and needed. Most of these writers had been members of the Association of German Proletarian Revolutionary Writers, which had been established in October 1928 in imitation of the Russian Association of Proletarian Writers, to support Communist policies. They all shared memories of intense ideological conflicts between the orthodox partisans of Socialist Realism, who favored tradition, and the advocates of literary innovation (condemned by the Hungarian Marxist writer Georg Lukács, who was to have a profound influence on early literary discourse in the GDR). Some of these authors, for instance Eduard Claudius, Willi Bredel, and Hans Marchwitza, were genuine working-class people who wrote from harsh experience. Others, among them Anna Seghers (1900–83) and Johannes R. Becher (1891–1958), came from middle-class and upper-middle-class families but had discarded their challenging lyric or narrative experiments in order to serve the party cause more loyally. On July 3, 1945, the Kulturbund zur demokratischen Erneuerung Deutschlands (Cultural Union for the Democratic Renewal of Germany) was founded in Berlin to bring together intellectuals of good will in all military zones of occupation. Traditionalists and innovators, Communists and non-Communists eagerly joined, among them Ricarda Huch, the aging Gerhart Hauptmann, and the expressionist painter Carl Hofer. Writers close to the Communist Party were publicly admonished by their fellow exile Ulbricht himself not to make the Kulturbund a branch of the party organization. In the name of the Kulturbund, the new monthly *Aufbau* (*Construction*) was published by an editorial board representing a wide range of interests; in its pages German readers were privileged to read prose by Heinrich and Thomas Mann, Hermann Broch, James Joyce, and Virginia Woolf. New novels were slow to appear, but Anna Seghers republished *Das siebte Kreuz* (1942; *The Seventh Cross*, 1942), once a best seller in the United States, and published a novel written in exile, *Die Toten bleiben jung* (1949; *The Dead Stay Young*, 1950). Theodor Plievier published *Stalingrad* (1946; 1948), the most important novel about World War II in German. Stephan Hermlin, who had fought in the French Resistance, and Franz Fühmann, who had been a loyal German soldier before his experiences in the Soviet Union, published poems that were subtly organized and intense with burning memories.

Film production and the theaters revived early: in the old Berlin studios of the UFA (Universum Film Aktiengesellschaft), challenging movies were made by Wolfgang Staudte, Erich Engel, and Kurt Maetzig, and within a short time seventy-five theaters were again open in Berlin and the Soviet zone, presenting the classical repertory and, at least in the beginning, more Noel Coward and T. S. Eliot than was ever to be seen in later years.

Brecht returned in a troubled moment. He had left the United States a day after being praised by the House Un-American Activities Committee (innocent in matters literary) for being a good witness, but he had stayed on in Zürich for some time while carefully preparing the ultimate step. When he returned to the Berlin Volkstheater and later to his Theater am Schiffbauerdamm, the Popular Front was gone and his epic theater, antitraditionalist and not realist either, was out of favor with the new SED functionaries.

1949–1961: THE TRANSFER OF THE SOVIET MODEL; INTERNAL RESISTANCE

Official histories of the GDR, having strict terminologies for describing the stages of political and social development, speak of the "construction of the fundaments of socialism" in 1950–61. Others, however, prefer to speak of the period when the Soviet model of dealing with industrial and cultural problems was transferred to the GDR, and the working people resisted it. On October 7, 1949, twenty-four hours after the Federal Republic had been established in Bonn, the GDR was proclaimed in East Berlin. In the new State of Workers and Peasants, the Socialist Unity Party (SED) assumed undisputed leadership and relegated the other parties, as "transmission belts," to conveying its initiatives to the masses. The industrial base was built up ruthlessly, with little regard for the wishes of citizens eager to buy food without ration cards or a new pair of quality shoes. After some anticipatory rumblings in the controlled media in March 1951, the Plenum of the SED Central Committee passed a belligerent resolution against "formalism," which allegedly endangered the humanist and democratic character of socialist culture. The Plenum mobilized the intellectuals to defend Socialist Realism, that reflection of changing reality in its historical movement toward socialism, as the only productive and permissible way of dealing with past, present, and future in any work of art. After four years of tactical tolerance, artists in the GDR found themselves confronted with the Communist Party norms of 1934, long enforced in Soviet Russia and more recently in Czechoslovakia and other people's democracies. Stalin's death and the brief ascent of Beria left the SED in some confusion, and a post-Stalinist "New Course" of many promises was proclaimed on June 9, 1953—too late to assuage the weary people, who had been pressed too hard for too long, without being able to articulate their desires. On June 17, 1953, a spontaneous strike of construction workers building the Berlin Stalinallee triggered demonstrations in the center of East Berlin and in the major industrial centers in the provinces, among them Magdeburg, Gera, and Jena, and economic demands escalated into a cry for free elections. A few Party offices were burned down, and political prisoners were freed by the striking workers, but Soviet tanks and the People's Police intervened. The rising collapsed, and the shattered SED reorganized itself through purges, trials, mass exclusions of functionaries and members, and ritual declarations of loyalty (Brecht wrote an ambivalent text of which the authorities published only the affirmative half). It was, for the time being, the last protest in the streets. Having learned its lesson, the SED was admirably successful thereafter in perverting the history of the rising (which it ascribed to foreign agents), in gradually appeasing the demands of the working people for consumers goods, and in separating the restive intellectuals from the working population.

The writers felt that their time had come at the Fourth Writers' Congress in January 1956, when some of the pre-Stalinist intellectuals briefly united with a few members of the post-Stalinist generation in more or less camouflaged language, perfectly understandable to SED ears, criticizing the oppressive ways in which Party authorities had made it difficult for even the loyal to be loyal. Each speaking in his own way, Anna Seghers, Arnold Zweig, and Willi Bredel did not hide their dissatisfaction with the cultural bureaucracy. The authorities immediately retreated and promised not to enforce "dogmatic and ossified formulas" any more. Within a short time, demands were heard that the import of Western literature be increased and that the publishing houses be made independent of the state organizations. But abrupt changes in the Polish government next door and the Hungarian revolution of 1956—both closely watched by GDR intellectuals—brought to a quick halt what could have been a first GDR thaw.

Georg Lukács, the patriarch of GDR literary criticism, had

been compromised by his participation in the Hungarian Nagy government, and the SED ominously talked about eradicating the "revisionism" threatening the republic. The young philosopher Wolfgang Harich was sentenced to ten years for organizing a group of scholars to undermine the state, and the philosopher Ernst Bloch, who had returned to the GDR in 1948 from Cambridge, Massachussetts, was deprived of his professorship; his ideas, widely influential among the younger intelligentsia, were condemned by servile colleagues at the universities of Leipzig and East Berlin. To control the restive intellectuals more easily, party authorities initiated what was later called a "cultural revolution": the publishing house at Halle was urged by the Party to arrange a literary conference at Bitterfeld, the center of the new petrochemical industry. On April 24, 1959, a new movement was launched there to discuss and mobilize writing talent among working people and to send established writers to factories, mines, and fields, where they could learn what real work was all about; Party and state declared that they would give priority support to writers willing to go the "Bitterfeld way" (*Bitterfelder Weg*). Revealing a great admiration for Mao Tsetung's cultural policies, party officials like Alfred Kurella insisted that the Bitterfeld way would bring literature and working people close together again, but other readers of the official announcements had little difficulty understanding that the Party again had doubts about its own intellectuals, and preferred to create an anti-intellectual counterforce of factory writers and people's correspondents to keep imagination on a close leash. The new slogan was "Start writing, buddy! We need you!" (*"Greif zur Feder, Kumpel! Wir brauchen dich!"*).

ADVANCES AND TRANSFORMATION IN THE SIXTIES

The alternate tightening and loosening of the political and cultural screws recurred in the 1960s, though the terminology changed. This was the decade of marching forward on the "road to a developed socialist community," as the official historians asserted, or as others have suggested, a period in which the GDR, in spite of intermittent crises, went on to develop the highest standard of living in the Eastern bloc and to become tenth among the industrial nations of the world. The late 1950s had been less than propitious: in 1958 the five-year plan had to be scratched and a new seven-year plan, closer to Soviet models, substituted for it; industrial output lagged seriously, and the increased tempo of collectivization changed the peasants, by good words or brute force, into members of "agricultural production communities" that did not necessarily increase productivity. The mounting number of people escaping to the West (in 1959, 143,000; in 1960, 194,000; in April 1961 alone, 30,000) was bleeding the already overaged work force of highly qualified younger people. Therefore on August 13, 1961, the authorities erected the Wall (officially called the "antifascist protective ramparts"), which was first improvised by wire and brick but later became a deadly system of cement, barricades, watchtowers, death traps, and mine fields. Only the truly resilient and ingenious, among them a number of soldiers from the People's Army and the border police, were successful now in reaching the other side unharmed. For better or worse, ordinary citizens had to adjust to the regime, which, displaying considerable psychological skill, appealed to the growing patriotism of the non-Communist citizens (often offended by the condescending snobbery of visiting West Germans, puffed up by their economic miracle) and rapidly increased the construction of new apartments and the production of consumer goods.

In 1963, GDR economic life was reorganized according to the principles of a "new economic system of planning and achievement," based on cybernetic assumptions that were suddenly more popular among the new set of young engineers than the heroic slogans of yesteryear. The Spartan community of the 1950s, sustained by battles of production and heroic shop workers, was being transformed into a consumers' society without unemployment, where members of the technical and scientific intelligentsia, whose emergence was of symbolic importance, could now buy a new Wartburg car and go on long-deserved vacation trips to Hungary or Bulgaria. In 1966 there had been only 9 cars per 100 people, but by 1970 the number had increased to 15; the number of television sets rose from 54 to 59, and that of refrigerators from 31 to 56. These were years when ideological hardliners and young poets asked whether the meaning of socialism was really exhausted by acquiring a new washing machine.

The building of the Wall immediately affected the intellectuals, who had hoped for more internal latitude. The guiding idea of how GDR culture functioned in a wider context had to be revised. If, in earlier years, the SED functionaries had stressed the unity of all German culture, they now discussed a "socialist German national culture" inside the Wall, and in later definitions of the GDR constitution, wavered between asserting the existence of "one nation in two states," and a "socialist state of workers and peasants" distinct from the capitalist Federal Republic. After the stream of people escaping to the West had been successfully halted, the authorities made some concessions to the subterranean concerns of the intellectuals. Ernst Fischer's defense of Kafka was published in the periodical *Sinn und Form (Meaning and Form)*, which continued to open its pages to innovative criticism and important writers from abroad (though the GDR delegation at the 1963 conference at Liblice, near Prague, declared that Kafka was of merely historical importance). At the Academy of Arts Stephan Hermlin presented a new group of younger poets (among them Wolf Biermann) who read challenging texts, while important novels written from loyalist positions articulated ideas that had not been discussed publicly before. Thus Dieter Noll's *Abenteuer des Werner Holt* (1960–63; *Werner Holt's Adventures*) offered a differentiated image of the recent German past; Erwin Strittmatter's popular *Ole Bienkopp* (1963) showed a stubborn peasant in conflict with unimaginative functionaries (he anticipates the collectivization of peasants, while for tactical reasons the functionaries still resist); and Hermann Kant's entertaining *Die Aula* (1965; *The Lecture Hall*) presented a functionary of the new generation who admits that he has often been an egotist in the past.

The second Bitterfeld conference, arranged in 1964 by the newly organized Ideological Commission appointed by the SED Central Committee, clearly reflected popular demands for a new efficiency in production, to be guided by cybernetics. While the Bitterfeld way was extolled as the only one leading to the new "socialist national culture," it was now defined in terms of a "new economic planning" that moved away from the romantic heroism of shop workers on the production lines toward the higher achievements of "planners and managers" responsible for new scientific forms of economic organization (in the new critical discourse, the "plane of the kings"). Bitterfeld slogans were invoked for a few more years, but now were emptied of the original impulse; paradoxically, they survived in the radical West German Werkkreise, which tried to organize a spontaneous literature by working people in factories and workshops. In nearby Czechoslovakia at the same time, Marxist and non-Marxist intellectuals and working people were discussing the principles of a "socialism with a human face," actively supported by many Communists in Austria, France, and Italy. A few GDR scholars and writers happily managed to move to Prague in order to live there in more clement air, and the Party had to defend itself against both capitalist temptations (75 percent of all GDR citizens are able to watch West German television) and Marxist innovation, never tolerated in the GDR itself.

The eleventh Plenum of the SED Central Committee, convening on April 15–18, 1965, defined the new sins of "liberalism and skepticism," throwing in "American immorality" for good measure; Erich Honecker, the rising party star, told the intellectuals sternly that the GDR was a "clean state," of "unchangeable norms of ethics and morals, decency and good behavior," and totally averse to a literature that "reduces life to sexual instincts." The list of sinners was as varied as it was inclusive, comprising among others the famous physicist Robert Havemann (potentially a theorist of a GDR socialism with a human face); Stefan Heym (who was writing a novel about the events of June 1953); the playwright Heiner Müller; and above all the poet Wolf Biermann, who had betrayed the basic ideas of socialism and did not hesitate to incorporate "pornographic elements into his verse." The state organization of writers took Honecker's cue and on its own part censored "the liberals and skeptics." Soviet intervention in Prague in the summer of 1968 did not make life easier for those who had watched the Czechoslovak developments with attention and sympathy.

The way in which the authorities, almost with the fervor of recent converts, preached the importance of science, cybernetics, and information theory challenged many writers to rethink the role of the individual in society. The official discussion tried to absorb the articulation of the conflict between the demands of the technological system and those of the individual hungry for socialist self-realization, by speaking about "contradictions of a nonantagonistic kind" (writers are allowed to criticize the absence of onions in the state shops, but not the central party principles). The situation was complicated by the emergence of a distinctive young generation of poets rich in talent and a powerful rhetoric of self-assertion. If many of the republic's older poets had been burdened by awareness of their bourgeois origins and past errors, these younger men and women, trained in the factories and in the army of the people's republic, combined a certain distaste for the past, including traditionalist poetry, with a cocky attitude about being the people of the future, who could claim particular privileges since they had a clear view of what in "the real socialism" was still waiting for fruition. These younger poets first gathered their texts in the anthologies *Sonnenpferde und Astronauten* (1964; *Sun Horses and Astronauts*) and *In diesem besseren Lande* (1966; *In This Better Country*) and proceeded to publish a surfeit of individual volumes radically different from the poetry of the fifties. These young people made the ironic and sober Brecht their classic, and also showed that they had read a good deal of Klopstock and Hölderlin (following the example of the GDR Christian poet Johannes Bobrowski) and much contemporary Latin American poetry as marvelously translated by Erich Arendt. To Volker Braun, Karl Mickel, Sarah Kirsch, and Wolf Biermann poetry was again, as it had been perhaps in the first postwar years, a challenging genre of many forms, allusions, and intonations. Generational feelings were expressed freely (which was anathema to the older functionaries), and the new penchant of the young for extolling the romantic forms of nature and of tenderly speaking of an occasional one-night stand (offensive to the puritans) triggered a discussion of the new "poetry wave" that went on from 1966 almost to the mid-1970s.

Among the many gifted writers of the early sixties generation, Volker Braun (b. 1939) emerged as a poet and later a playwright of extraordinary intensity and force. He worked for some time in the new socialist superprojects, including the Black Pump Kombinat, studied philosophy at Leipzig University, and later worked as dramaturge at the Deutsches Theater and the Berliner Ensemble, though he was too young to have met Brecht personally. Braun's *Provokation für mich* (1965; *Provocation for Myself*), his first collection of poems, some of which were written in the late 1950s, used Walt Whitman's exuberant long lines and an expressionist accumulation of exclamation marks to articulate the wishes of young people who have been trained on the construction sites of the new republic, a rough frontier of sorts, and want happiness, lust, and a full life now, and not in a nebulous future discussed in official speeches. Braun's impatient poem "Demand" has often been quoted in East and West, and for good reasons: "Don't give us what's finished! We want half-finished products/ . . . Let's have the forest and the knife/ Here experiments prevail and not routine!" In his robust love poetry he proudly celebrates the black-jacketed "Adonis of the atomic age" and his Betsy, that "three-stage rocket, legs, breasts, and eyes" (a view of love perhaps equally unpopular among older functionaries and younger feminists). In his communication to "older youth" he clearly addresses the aging officials, revealing what the young feel about their own joys, "far too inclusive" to be produced serially and according to plan. His much-discussed poem "Jazz" probes the relationship of self and collective, the central issue of all his writing. In the image of a group of individual musicians, he finds the "secret" in the way in which each musician offers the best of his art to the performance of the group: "Here is the music of the future: Everybody's creative!/ You have the right to be yourself, and I am I." In his verse collections of the 1970s, including *Gegen die symmetrische Welt* (1974; *Against the Symmetrical World*), in which he turned to the lean language of the later Brecht, and in a spate of plays about problems of industrial production, among them his much revised *Die Kipper* (1972; *Unloading*), Braun continued to ponder the future of the self and the work collective, gradually allowing more substance to the collective than to the individual. In the mid-1970s he wrote *Unvollendete Geschichte* (1975; *Unfinished Story*), a GDR variation on Romeo and Juliet showing, without illusions and close to daily experience in the provinces, what happens to the daughter of a party functionary who falls in love with a young man who, not a particularly good "cadre," is suspected of wanting to leave the republic. In his *Hinze-Kunze-Roman* (1985; *A Hinze-Kunze-Novel*), often reminiscent of Diderot's inventive narrative techniques, Braun listens to the ongoing conversations of a prominent SED official and his driver who compete for the favors of a woman of strong character who prefers local Berlin dialect and a professional life of her own. Braun wittily contrasts the official clichés, used even by the functionary with some hesitation, with the sturdier views of his driver, who happens to be a former student of literature. Both the tragic novella and the comic novel should be required reading for anyone talking about the Republic of Workers and Peasants.

Karl Mickel, Braun's friend and Saxon colleague from Dresden (b. 1935), was trained as an economist and read a good deal of older literature. Braun started by writing combative and exhortative poems in the tradition of German expressionism and its forerunners, whereas Mickel explores contradictory combinations of the stridently contemporary and the grand legacy from Homer to Dante and the German eighteenth-century classics, and provokes by deliberate contrasts, parodies, and allusions. His poems in *Vita nuova mea* (1966) and *Eisenzeit* (1975; *Iron Time*) show an Augustan consciousness of the copresence of the ancients and the GDR moderns. Turning his attention to genre scenes in East Berlin backyards, the smoke-filled apartments of his hard-drinking friends, and his many nights of honest but fleeting love in rented rooms, he brilliantly handles genuine and invented quotations from Dante, Donne, and Brecht and inevitably irritates the official culture watchers in that, in contrast to Volker Braun, he seems to reveal far more interest in the erudite games of literature than in the results of economic and ideological planning. As a lyrical poet who often hides his true sensibility under the guise of the smart aleck, he has done much to resuscitate the traditions of the ode and the hymn in his theoretical studies as well as in his poetry, which usually requires as many learned annotations as do T. S. Eliot's *Four Quartets*. "Der See" ("The Lake"), an early poem that has particularly provoked literary orthodoxy, demonstrates all the virtues of his lyric vitality: the hymnic gesture of an ironic beginning ("lake, you jagged bowl, full of bodies of fish, you countersky under my keel"); the rough verse in praise of the surfeit of existence in the dark depths ("the inexhaustible cycle of corpses and spawn"); and ultimately, the resolve of the poet to turn into a mighty lake himself by imbibing all its waters ("through me through now a river in the middle of their dwellings/ I rest digesting fish"). Far from being an insult to the socialist image of people, as official criticism claimed, "The Lake" reminds us of early Brecht's insatiable *Baal*; it is an incarnation of everything vital that is sadly missing in GDR experience.

BETWEEN LOYALTY AND DISSENT: GÜNTER DE BRUYN, FRANZ FÜHMANN, AND STEFAN HEYM

THE LESSONS OF GÜNTER DE BRUYN

In the late 1960s the novelist Günter de Bruyn (b. 1926, Berlin) made headlines in both East and West as the first to write about the everyday problems of love and marriage in socialist society in an ironic and probing way. De Bruyn relinquished the pretension that the new GDR of the 1960s consisted of red-cheeked peasant girls and muscular metal workers quoting Lenin. His lovers and married couples, loyal or disloyal to each other, are all more or less privileged members of the party intelligentsia; the rare proletarian usually appears as the cleaning lady who comes on Tuesday and Friday. De Bruyn does not limit his narrative interests to socialist marital comedy alone; what he really wants to do is to probe personal integrity in a society intoxicated by mere success. He does not hesitate to shift his attention from honest or cowardly lovers to honest writers and intellectuals who resist material temptation or to those who sell their talents or the truth for a fee, a promotion, or a state award.

By 1968, East German literature had its share of love stories, regular and irregular, but de Bruyn's novel *Buridans Esel* (1968; *Buridan's Ass*, 1973) uses the traditional tale of the milquetoast husband caught between docile wife and attractive young girlfriend to explore the contrast between public aspirations, once so revolutionary, and a private behavior still dominated by petit bourgeois puritan norms, with no change in sight. Karl Erp, a middle-aged party member, is a husband and father of two, an efficient director of an East Berlin district library, and the proud owner of a little Trabant car. He feels attracted to Fräulein Broder, a young woman who has not even passed the librarians' examination but inexplicably charms him with her intellectual intensity and her precision of speech. Erp tells himself that she really incarnates all the ideas that once inspired him when he was an enthusiastic member of the State Youth Organization, ready, in his blue regulation shirt, to change the world. Having deliberately provoked a quarrel with his wife, he moves in with Broder, who admires him as an exemplary comrade. They are happy together for a few days but not much longer, because in Broder's rented room everyday irritations interfere with their newfound bliss. She does not like to talk before going to work and tries in vain to get him to shut up during breakfast. He in turn is appalled by the constant noises from the apartments of the neighbors, the water dripping from the ceiling, the communal W.C., the impossibility of taking a shower and, most disturbing of all, her unwillingness to make love before nicely setting her hair. In the office most of Karl's comrades are shocked by his behavior, but an influential old comrade, deeply impressed by Karl's seeming courage of decision and rejuvenated seriousness of purpose, offers him a better and far more important position in the Ministry of Education. In the meantime Karl, the petit bourgeois, has changed his mind about Fräulein Broder, her shabby one-room abode, and her dreams of working for the people in distant villages. To the surprise of everybody (perhaps with the exception of the reader), he returns to his comfortable apartment, the little car that he missed so much, and his wife Elisabeth, who, however, has completely changed in his absence. Elisabeth has returned to her studies of art history and merely tolerates his presence now for the sake of the children. The narrator clearly suggests that everybody would have been happier ultimately, if Karl had not returned to a life of easy routine. Elisabeth, who will expand her experience by being a productive art historian, and Fräulein Broder, who does go on to a job in a village, are the true heroines of the novel. The successful Karl, now directing library affairs from a position high up in the hierarchy, is to be pitied as a coward and a mere inventor of empty self-justifications.

Yet *Buridan's Ass*, so intense in its aversion to compromise, is itself, at least within the GDR context, a narrative compromise between the required traditions of realism and spritely innovation. Even the "positive hero," that first requirement of Socialist Realism, is not absent entirely, since de Bruyn introduces the wise and sturdy comrade in one of Karl's office colleagues. The residual realism actually works to good purpose, giving us the irritating but highly informative daily detail of how the first generation of successful party officials lives, loves, and attends "parties" (the American term is always used). But I am not certain that de Bruyn's desire to counteract the realist tradition by contrary narrative ploys really functions in this particular case. Imitating Laurence Sterne and his German disciple Jean Paul, de Bruyn willfully builds and deconstructs the narrative, telling us in chapter 8 what has to be postponed until chapter 17, making irreverent remarks about his characters whenever they are too sentimental or insincere, and suggesting alternate plots that he pushes to absurd and entertaining conclusions. Yet he deprives us of any real suspense, because early in the game he turns his characters into puppets so as to demonstrate a problem, rather than creating figures who retain some capacity to surprise. For better or worse, the narrative voice dominates almost exclusively; we have to take the witty with the occasionally glib.

De Bruyn's *Preisverleihung* (1972; *The Award Ceremony*), his second novel of symptomatic importance, also takes place in the privileged society of journalists, translators, writers, and university teachers and asks disturbing questions about intellectual integrity. Paul Schuster, an East German writer and journalist, has been awarded a state prize, and Theo Overbeck, a struggling assistant professor at the university, has agreed to give a little *laudatio* at the award ceremony. Behind this situation lurk many complications. Theo was once Schuster's editor, struggling to bring out his indubitable talent, and later married Schuster's girlfriend Irene. Yet when Theo reads the prize-winning book (the old manuscript, revised to please the Establishment), he realizes that it no longer deserves any praise and tries to get out of making a speech. He speaks to the head of his department, who tells him that certain compromises are necessary in the interests of progressive society. When the time of the ceremony approaches, and the representatives of the government, Party, and the working intelligentsia gather at the Academy, Theo is torn between the demands of honesty and the necessity to conform. In utter confusion he offers a speech made up of a jumble of clichés, sudden insights, and almost meaningless babble. Anticipating an unpleasant confrontation with his department head, Theo takes pills to calm his nervous stomach. His wife, Irene, cannot easily overcome the sudden shock of recognizing Theo's potential resolve to tell the truth about Schuster's book and so jeopardize his own promotion, the comfortable three-room apartment in a modern downtown building that goes with it, and perhaps even a small car in their tenured future.

De Bruyn clearly wishes to operate within distinct confines, for he accepts the basic premises of the social order and its literature, including the assumption that the writer should not risk alienating the sympathies of the untrained reader by experimenting too ruthlessly. De Bruyn was instrumental in bringing to public attention the bedroom problems of a society that has totally changed its economic structure and yet retains, in matters of sex, love, and marriage, the code of the nineteenth-century Protestant petit bourgeois. He has challenged his own colleagues, if not the Establishment, by his characterization of Paul Schuster, who stands for all writers who sell out by satisfying the pragmatic demands of institutions (an East German version of the talented kid from Ohio who becomes a reporter for *People* magazine). The problem, de Bruyn argues, is that Paul Schuster succeeded in placing a sieve or filter between his observing self and his writing self, but that the filter later proved superfluous because the self "became blind to certain aspects of reality." Yet de Bruyn carries some filters in his own mind. There is a curious, disturbing, and politically revealing passage in *Buridan's Ass* that distinctly shows the problems involved: as the lovers drive through the flat countryside close to the border between the GDR and West Germany, we hear that the "little watchtowers (*Wachttürmchen*) were standing at attention" while the "barbed wire peacefully rusted away." It is unclear who creates these images. Is it the sentimental lovers or the narrator, who is usually so sober and appalled by any cliché? For de Bruyn's sake, I hope that he is telling us what the silly lovers see, rather than what he himself as narrator wants us to perceive.

FRANZ FÜHMANN: A CHANGE OF HEART

Franz Fühmann (1922–84) long believed that he could substantially contribute to the literature of the GDR by writing about his experiences as a young Nazi soldier who underwent a conversion to socialism, but ultimately the functionaries wanted more. Fühmann was born in Rokytnice, a small town in the north of Bohemia split by the conflict of nationalists and socialists. His father, the town apothecary, established the local branch of the Nazi Party. When war came, the son immediately volunteered for the Wehrmacht and fought in Russia and Greece, fanatically believing in the transformation of Europe by the new German *Geist.* His extraordinary poetry was published first by a little firm in Hamburg well-known for its resistance to Nazi writing, and later by the weekly *Das Reich*, effectively organized by Goebbels himself to show that there were intellectuals inside and outside Germany who were willing to collaborate. On the last day of the war Fühmann, returning from home leave, was taken prisoner and shipped off to a Soviet camp where, reluctantly at first and with dedication later, he attended training courses in dialectical materialism. Embracing the new creed, he returned to East Germany eager to write for the new republic and to reeducate his fellow citizens by telling what he had gone through. His *Die Fahrt nach Stalingrad* (1953; *The Journey to Stalingrad*), a fiery verse narrative in the style of Rilke's *Duino Elegies*, conveys the meaning of his three trips to the destroyed and rebuilt city, first as a German soldier, then as a Soviet prisoner of war, and finally as a member of a GDR writers' delegation. Next he wrote novellas, almost in the classical mode, about his experiences as a boy at home and as a German soldier at the front, including *Stürzende Schatten* (1959; *Falling Shadows*) and *Das Judenauto* (1962; *The Car with the Yellow Star: Fourteen Days out of Two Decades*, 1968). Willingly, but to his own frustration, in the late 1950s he submitted to the demands of the Bitterfeld movement and worked in a plant, but did not write the great "factory novel" that many people expected of him.

Fühmann greatly changed in the mid-1960s, when the Party once again expressed its displeasure with authors loyal to their own imaginations. He began to rework texts of the past, quietly opposing any demand for propaganda, seeking only "the truth of the day, the week, or the year." In 1964 he wrote a letter to the minister of culture deploring the dominance of the didactic element in contemporary writing and suggesting that he, like many other authors of the republic, would write better books by following his own instinct rather than fulfilling the constantly changing orders of the functionaries of culture. He avoided publishing his more important texts in the official organs and left the Writers' Union by his own decision. Possibly as a response, he was promptly removed from the Central Committee of the National Democratic Party, of which he had been an active member, because of his "political mistakes." Friends missed his poetry and his prose narratives about contemporary issues; instead, he retold "Reineke, the Fox" and "Androcles and the Lion" for children, edited some fairy tales about animals (1965), and published prose versions of Homer's *Iliad* and the medieval *Nibelungenlied* (1971) for children and adults. Yet his turn to the old stories was more than mere escapism: alone among the writers of the GDR, he rediscovered for himself the revealing force of fairy tales and the anthropological meaning of ancient myths. While carefully avoiding any allusions to the interpretive possibilities of psychoanalysis, he went far in studying and using Karl (Károly) Kerényi, and occasionally Lenin and Thomas Mann, to define the dialectical message of the fairy tales, that true wisdom of the people in which "the most modest things were always the grandest," and the potential of myth, which enables human beings to measure their lonely individual experience against models of what mankind has experienced as a whole. In a lecture addressed to students and faculty of Humboldt University (published in a more complete version in 1974), he cited Molly Bloom's interior monologue in Joyce's *Ulysses* as one of the instances in recent literature where old mythical thinking about the opposition of body and soul, sexuality and eroticism, "God and the animal" had resurfaced triumphantly. He defended myth in Kleist and Kafka against the misuse of myths by the fascists, suggesting that myth was at the core of great literature because it resisted reduction to what was merely useful for the day.

In his collection of stories *Der Jongleur im Kino; oder, Die Insel der Träume* (1970; *The Juggler at the Movie Theater; or, The Island of Dreams*), Fühmann returns once again to his experiences as an introverted boy of eight or ten and explores his prepubescent feelings of revolt, escapism, and submission to the rules of living set by his middle-class parents. He ironically calls his four stories "studies in bourgeois society," and offers fragments of a self-analysis rather than cohesive thoughts about a small-town society close to the borders of the Nazi Reich. The most impressive story is the one about the poor juggler who, offering a brief performance when the local movie theater is opened, turns out to be a hapless amateur who leaves the hall quickly but proudly. To the boy, the juggler has become a symbolic figure incarnating everything denied to his childhood by his middle-class upbringing: "adventures, magic, ghosts . . . , the mysterious Other"; he feels the burning desire to run away with the man to a realm of freedom hardly imaginable.

Twelve years later and only a short time before his untimely death in 1984, Fühmann stood his ground firmly in the long essay *Der Sturz des Engels* (1982; *The Fall of the Angel*), which clearly revealed how a GDR writer of his background and intention really felt. Looking back on his experiences with people and poetry in their historical contexts, he radically corrects an earlier image of the self originally conceived in the age of Socialist Realism and meant to be "used" by the people. He tells us about abrasive inner conflicts, increasing bitterness, welcome self-illusions, and daily repressions and their psychosomatic consequences (the affirmative writer who seeks refuge in heavy drinking, ultimately destroying his health). Here Fühmann tries, as he says, to "think through" a failure—his failure to feel more deeply and think harder. As a young prisoner of war suddenly without a name or a past, he found himself in the harbor of Novorossisk (a glimpse of glaciers and the putrescent sea) and longed for something "new and unheard-of." In the camp school he encountered the "new" in the person of the party instructor who taught doctrine as relaxedly and firmly "as if he were a cowboy handling the lasso." Fühmann excoriates himself for his "proud delusions" of judging everything from a class point of view not really his own, and deplores his past perspectives of black-and-white contrasts, without traditions, without mysteries. As a soldier he bought a small volume of Georg Trakl's poetry only a few days before the Reich was destroyed; when the prisoner, in whose mind remembered Trakl poems now combined with his own verse, returned to Germany, he was told that Trakl was proscribed by Socialist Realism. At that moment, Fühmann remembers, he felt as if "struck with a whip."

Among the GDR writers, Fühmann strikes me as a loner lost between generations and interest groups. He belonged neither to the older group of dedicated Weimar Communists who reestablished antifascist writing in the Soviet zone of occupation, nor to the younger group born and trained in the new republic.

There was always something visionary, fiery, and yet vulnerable in his imagination (whether committed to the "regeneration" of Europe by force or to the building of a new socialist society of utopian equality). I believe it was his most personal tragedy that, confronting his past and the future, he felt compelled largely to forego writing poetry for other genres and modes, first because he wanted to serve the social demands of the new society in a private act of atonement, and later because he wanted to find a sphere for himself relatively untouched by the authorities. He combined a distinct and occasionally provincial traditionalism, respectful of older poetry and classical prose, with a productive eagerness to remind his readers and GDR critics of modern authors long neglected, including Georg Trakl, James Joyce, and T. S. Eliot; going back, or rather forward, to fairy tales and myths, he established himself on firm ground from which he fought against the literary utilitarians. Traveling to Hungary and to his own Bohemian homeland, he studied both older and contemporary literature, and published many exquisite translations of Hungarian and Czech poetry largely neglected by readers in the West. He says much in his particular choice of favorite poets: Miklós Radnóti, a Hungarian Jewish poet who was killed after his concentration camp was evacuated by the SS; the Czech František Halas, long loyal to communism but later involved in growing conflicts with the Party; and Halas's contemporary Konstantin Biebl, a veteran Communist who killed himself when the party censors disparaged his exquisitely romantic verse, sustained by visions of distant islands of a serene and exotic life. Knowledgeable GDR poetry readers did not need any further explanations of why Fühmann translated poetry that was so dark and different.

AN AMERICAN IN BERLIN (GDR): STEFAN HEYM

Stefan Heym once said that as journalist and writer he learned his important lessons from Mark Twain and Ernest Hemingway, not from Theodor Fontane or Thomas Mann. Residing now in a suburb of East Berlin, he continues to rely on "the strict syntax of the English language," which demands clear thought, and writes most of his important novels in English before they are (or are not) published in German. Heym was born into a middle-class Jewish family in Chemnitz (today Karl-Marx-Stadt) in Saxony in 1913 and involved himself early in causes of the Left. He was dismissed from the local school for writing a poem against a general of the Reichswehr. He studied German and history, but when Hitler seized power he immediately left Germany, going first to Prague and later to the United States, where he received a fellowship at the University of Chicago. In New York City he edited the *Deutsches Volksecho* (1937–39), an antifascist weekly of Popular Front orientation that was not supported by democratic socialists or liberal Jewish exiles. He directed his effective polemics against the German Nazis in New York, the functionaries of their Bund, and Leni Riefenstahl, when she appeared on the American scene to peddle her Olympics movies. In 1943 Heym joined the U.S. army, got his American citizenship while in basic training, and in army camps in Missouri and Maryland received special instruction as an interrogator of German POWs. A year later he fought his way from Normandy to Germany, writing leaflets on the way that were delivered by artillery shells to their uniformed German readers. In 1945 he joined the illustrious group of writers who edited the Munich *Neue Zeitung*, published in the office building of the former *Völkischer Beobachter*, the newspaper of the Nazi Party. He believed that the U.S.-Soviet wartime alliance was important for the future. As tension between the Allies mounted, he resigned his job and returned to the United States, where he was not to stay for long.

Heym's early novels, including *The Crusaders* (1948), a largely autobiographical novel about his experiences in the army, and *Goldsborough* (1953; *Goldsborough, oder Die Liebe der Miss Kennedy*, 1954), a social romance about striking miners, may well belong to the recent history of the American novel rather than to German literature, since they were written in English for American readers. Heym himself has said that in the early 1950s he made his mind up to leave the United States, following the example of Thomas Mann, Charlie Chaplin, and Bertolt Brecht. After a long wait in Prague, where a show trial against veteran Communists of Jewish origin was just then being held, he received permission to enter the German Democratic Republic. He settled there just in time to witness the workers' rising of June 1953, a totally unexpected and shattering experience for many reasons, revealing to him as it did the conflicts between citizens and the Party and, to the experienced journalist, a media system totally dependent on directives from above and incapable of accommodating intelligent responses from below. After the rising Heym thought that the best response would be to write a regular column entitled "Offen gesagt" ("Frankly Speaking") in the *Berliner Zeitung*, in which he tried to combine—at least until political measures following the Hungarian revolution interfered—his loyalty to the historical intents of the republic with personal honesty in small matters of prime importance to a growing number of readers totally disgusted with abstractions. Heym's vicissitudes in the GDR have always been related to political changes of climate: during the few seasons of welcome thaw, he could plead for a freer press and publish some of his novels (after Honecker came to power in 1971, three in a row); but during the long frosts, he published more abroad than at home.

In 1965, Heym was prominently included in the party catalogue of literary sinners; consequently, he had little chance to publish *Der Tag X* (*X Day*), which discusses the events of June 1953 not altogether according to the party line. When the novel, now entitled *5 Tage im Juni* (1974; *Five Days in June*), appeared in West Germany, it turned out to be an entertaining potboiler conforming more or less closely to the requirements of Socialist Realism, but advancing a number of ideas in conflict with the authorities. Heym tells us how the working people in an important East Berlin plant responded to the oscillations of the "New Course" proclaimed by Party and government in early June, and to the concurrent demand that productivity norms be increased by 10 percent everywhere. Two forces fight for the souls of the restive working people: agents from the West who want to bring down the government by manipulating the workers' ire, and a heroic and thoughtful functionary of the Party who, being close to the plant workers, wants to convince the party organization that the increase in norms should be canceled, as other measures have been recently. The agents (paid mostly by the Office East of the Social Democrats in the West) are active, trying to make an old worker the spokesman of protest. But the party functionary, although nearly expelled by his organization, tries to carry his message to his comrades in the highest party offices and to the officers who edit the daily newspaper, published by the Soviet army. On his way downtown he confronts crowds of demonstrators who escalate their economic protest into political demands for free and secret elections—for him, the end of the world. He also witnesses the (historical) scene in front of the GDR Ministry of Labor, where the beleaguered bureaucrats agree to rescind the increase in norms. He returns with the good news, but his fellow workers are on the march too, all hell breaks loose, criminal elements (no doubt) loot the nationalized food stores, and Soviet tanks have to restore law and order. Shattered to its foundations, the party organization recognizes that the loyal functionary wanted to do his job (being ahead of the Party, the novel insists) and ships him off to an ideological training school, where he will qualify for further high positions in the political hierarchy.

I am afraid that my paraphrase of the plot sounds more ironic than it should; it would be wrong to misjudge Heym's combination of structural and ideological elements. The story moves fast, each section being defined by the date and exact hour, so as to bring it closer to the documentary mode. Individuals tend to be utterly typecast, including the agents from the West, who have thin moustaches and watery eyes and beat their girlfriends, and the loyal functionary or positive hero, who is a Communist from way back and suffered a long time in a concentration camp. I do not believe that party censors would have had any objections against the method of narration, but Heym advances two views radically incompatible with the prescribed line. In a brief dialogue among Soviet officers, he suggests that the waverings of Party and government may have been caused by the shift of power in Moscow after Stalin's death in March 1953. Also, equally unacceptable to the ideologues, he suggests a variation on the official conspiracy theory, saying that we should distinguish between the trigger of the events, which was the conspiratorial work of the agents, and the events' actual cause, the legitimate frustrations of many working people. "Thousands of workers do not conspire; these were movements of different dimensions." The final message theatrically affirms "that there is only one Party and only one flag," with "the logic of history" on their side.

The late sixties were not particularly propitious for the publication of Heym's novels in the GDR, but when Honecker came to power in 1971 and announced his change of cultural policies, conditions eased at least for a while. Heym's biographical novel about Ferdinand Lassalle (London, 1969), the first founder of a

German workers' association (shown to be as egotistic as Stalin), and his Defoe novella (Zürich, 1970) both appeared in the GDR, though with some delay (1974). His novel *The King David Report* (*Der König David Bericht*) was published in the Federal Republic in 1972 and in the GDR in 1973; like the original American version (1973), it received the critical acclaim of most reviewers. In *The King David Report* Heym, who is not usually interested in Jewish traditions, takes his cue from the biblical books telling the story of Saul, David, and Solomon. Trying to reconstruct from his own point of view how these texts have been compiled, he produces a "historical" novel of contemporary meaning, especially for readers disturbed by the official revisions of historical records in tightly controlled societies. The intellectual Ethan, son of Hoshaia, finds himself involved, against his better instincts, in the efforts of King Solomon to legitimize his absolute power by the "One and Only True and Authoritative, Historically Correct and Approved Report" about his father, King David, but feels dissatisfied with the glib, cautious discussions of the royal commission charged with editing the document. Eager to discover what really happened, Ethan searches for old tablets and questions many witnesses, including a few surviving unpersons, only to discover David's horrible deeds of murder and betrayal. Heym handles Ethan's first-person narrative with allusive wit (using an ironic imitation of the biblical style, exploded here and there by modern terms and idioms), but his linguistic inventions strengthen rather than lessen an utterly melancholy story. Ultimately, Ethan is called before the King and "silenced to death": no word of his will ever reach the ear of the people, except for one short psalm that the King finds particularly trite. There is no hope; "we seem to be living," Ethan muses, "in two worlds: one that is described in the teachings of the wise men and judges and prophets, and another one which nobody speaks of but which is real."

Stefan Heym has remained the antifascist of the German 1930s who continues to believe in the enlightening power of the spoken and written word. As a practicing journalist and author of many best-sellers, he wants to write challenging, effective, and relatively uncomplicated texts and novels attracting wide audiences rather than just the intellectual elite. Largely unconcerned with questions of narrative structure, he prefers to work with typified characters in the old vein, the love intrigue, and a melodramatic turn of events. Torn between seeing himself in the tradition of Joseph Conrad, using a language that is not the one of his earliest years, and his political interest in being easily accessible, he does not always avoid the fast and the glib. His political attitudes are equally ambivalent. He won a U.S. army commission and a Bronze Star (later demonstratively returned to President Eisenhower) on the field of battle, and left the United States in the McCarthy era because he did not believe that the country had enough strength and intelligence to change, yet he stubbornly endures his conflicts with the GDR authorities, believing that "in socialism, transformations happen every day." His changing views of Czech political events suggest something about his basic loyalties: in the 1930s he courageously defended the Czechoslovak democracy as a bulwark against Hitler, but twenty years later he asserted that history was on the side of the Communists who had done away with the bourgeois republic. After the Russian invasion in 1968, he suggested in a conversation with an American interviewer that "some of the Czech things had gotten out of hand," adding that "the invasion was a panic reaction—but an understandable one." Moving closer to the international peace movement, Heym, like others, may disagree with many of the demands of the GDR, but he firmly adheres to Marxist ideas of history and the working class, believing in a Party superior to all others in its privileged interpretation of the true meaning of history and of what is to be done in the future.

THE SEVENTIES: ULRICH PLENZDORF; THE BIERMANN AFFAIR AND ITS AFTERMATH

The post-1971 years are often described by official interpreters as a period of "shaping the developed socialist community," but these interpreters qualify, or rather obliterate, the optimistic label by adding that, at least for the time being, GDR society still has to be characterized as a "nonantagonistic class society" constituting a complex scene of pressures and group tensions. The average consumer is certainly better off than in any time in the past, though the economists have abandoned the goal of catching up with the Federal Republic. By 1977, for every 100 households there were nearly 36 cars, 85 TVs, 95 refrigerators (compared with 0.4 in 1955), and 78 washing machines (0.5 in 1955); but whenever the functionaries proudly stress such material progress, the intellectuals intimate that it is foolish to define the success of socialism in terms of something that capitalism has offered to its societies anyway. In the spring of 1971 the aging Walter Ulbricht was replaced as first secretary of the Party by Erich Honecker, who had started on his way to the top in the old party youth organization among the miners of the Saar region. In June 1971 the Eighth Congress of the SED immediately announced that, in a time of détente, increasing international acceptance of the GDR (especially among Third World nations), and excellent production results at home, Honecker favored a useful combination of orthodoxy and pragmatism, and he himself assured writers that the Party was willing to develop a "full understanding of the creative search for new forms." On a later occasion he again confirmed that, according to his view, there could be "no taboo in the spheres of art and literature," if artists and authors were proceeding "from the firm position of socialism." The subsequent Writers' Congress of 1973 attested to a new course of tightly supervised liberalization: the Bitterfeld way was unobtrusively discarded; party authorities ceased to excoriate writers publicly and shifted discussion to professional organizations; and some challenging books appeared, as for instance Christa Wolf's *Nachdenken über Christa T.* (1968; *The Quest for Christa T.*, 1970), which had first been printed in a relatively small edition but was now republished for a wider audience. Following the Helsinki Accord, however, when one hundred twenty thousand GDR citizens petitioned the government for the right to emigrate legally, the authorities had second thoughts about the incipient liberalization. By the mid-1970s they had again reduced their intellectual allowances, as clearly seen in their ritual exclusion of the talented poet Reiner Kunze (b. 1933) from the Writers' Union in early 1976.

The work of Ulrich Plenzdorf would have come to public attention much earlier, had he not insisted on putting his ideas into film scripts, which were even more rigidly controlled than fiction. Coming from a family of Berlin working people, Plenzdorf (b. 1934) studied the Marxist classics at the Franz-Mehring-Institut, worked for three years handling stage props, and served in the GDR army before being admitted to the Babelsberg State Film School (1959–63), where he began writing scripts of a lighter kind. In 1972 the periodical *Sinn und Form* (*Meaning and Form*) published his story *Die neuen Leiden des jungen W.* (1973; *The New Sorrows of Young W.*); within months, the story went through many editions in East and West. Courageously produced as a play by the theater in Halle in the GDR, it was taken over by most theaters in German-speaking countries (in West Germany, it was the most popular play of the 1974–75 season) and was finally made into an East German movie [1976], as Plenzdorf had hoped it would be when he wrote it seven years before. When the august Academy, somewhat disturbed by the popularity of the story and the play, convened to discuss its sources and merits, Plenzdorf dryly remarked that he was kept writing by "external pressure," even during the years in which he could never do what he really wanted to do, and by the "repeated rejection of the script." Pretending not to hear these words, the Academy members went on discussing how Plenzdorf had used Goethe's *Sorrows of Young Werther* in his text.

Distrusting the Olympian narrator of traditional realism, Plenzdorf presents his story of the life and death of eighteen-year-old Edgar Wibeau in a combination of voices. The young man has accidentally electrocuted himself while carelessly working on an invention, and his father, who did not care much for the boy when he was alive, tries to discover what really happened and why. The father talks to neighbors, comrades, and friends who were close to Edgar during the last months of his life, and Edgar himself speaks somewhat disrespectfully from "beyond the Jordan," or the realm of the dead. Quoting from Goethe's *Sorrows of Young Werther* (a copy of which he found in the W.C.) and from Salinger's *Catcher in the Rye*, his real favorite, Edgar comments on what his father hears about him and, in his engaging way, tells us the truth about his experiences. Edgar, a somewhat unruly apprentice in a provincial factory, left his home and job after quarreling with his foreman ("accidentally" dropping a heavy metal plate on his toes) and traveled to East Berlin to hear good jazz and have more fun than he could have back home. Penniless but ingenious, he finds shelter in a decrepit gazebo in the backyard of an old house scheduled for bulldozing to make room for new housing developments. He goes hungry for a while, but makes himself useful as the "external concierge" of a kindergarten next door and promptly falls in love with big-eyed Charlie, who is in charge of the children. (He always waits for the moment when she sits down on the garden bench, because she raises her skirt to sit on her panties.) Instead of writing letters as Goethe's Werther did, he produces tapes to describe his new way of life to a buddy. Mostly to please dutiful Charlie, he joins a brigade of workers who restore old apartments, and clumsily paints window sills and walls. But when Charlie's friend Dieter returns from the army and marries her, Edgar is really desperate. He quarrels with Addie, the brigade foreman who is obsessed with constructing an economical spray machine for house paints. Withdrawing to his gazebo, he builds his own spraying contraption from second-hand materials and instantly goes "over the Jordan" when he pushes the 380-volt button. Technologically he had the right idea: the brigade constructs the spray machine according to his plans, and the dropout Edgar will be remembered officially as the "technical innovator" whose idea will benefit the many comrades moving into restored apartments newly painted, or rather sprayed, in record time.

Edgar is a good kid who, like his buddies in the GDR and elsewhere, is simply sick and tired of the rules, slogans, and ossified precepts of adults obsessed with achievement and success. In his particular case his mother, who efficiently runs a vocational school, incarnates socialist law and order, while his father, who prefers to stay on the fringes painting abstract pictures that few people understand, represents the demands for individual self-realization (one of the reasons why father and son are in search of each other). Plenzdorf has taken great care to show that Edgar does not secede from communism but merely from unimaginative Communists. Edgar is explicit about his loyalty to communism: he is a pacifist by nature, but after seeing snapshots from Vietnam, he would gladly join the National People's Army. It is of ideological importance that the only member of the working brigade whom he really likes is a seventy-year-old proletarian named Zaremba who (straight out of Brecht) has all the wisdom of the people, still drinks and loves hard, and instead of spouting party slogans when the tempo lags, sings old songs from the Spanish front where he fought Franco. Yet Edgar's imagination thrives on the ideas and fads of the American sixties generation. Hash may not be readily available, but the young people try to smoke at least dried banana skins (with little results), and like to get "really high" (always using the American term) on pop and rock. Materially and symbolically, jeans are of fundamental importance. Edgar has written a song that he obligingly plays to us from "over the Jordan"—"Black jeans? no/ Blue jeans, oh/ Oh, Blue jeans, yeah"—and tells us the story of how three thousand East Berlin teenagers create havoc when the government decides to sell a batch of jeans, but switches the sale to a back-street shop lest a sale in one of the big department stores turn into a public demonstration (which happens anyway).

Public discussion of Plenzdorf's Wibeau story moved in irrelevant if symptomatic directions in both East and West. In the East, critics asked whether or not Edgar was a "typical" figure (letters pouring in from schools indicated that young people identified overwhelmingly with him). In the West, commentators promptly overrated Plenzdorf's willingness to challenge, at least at that time, the basic premises of East German social life. Plenzdorf had the unusual courage to put on public view the new subculture of the young working population, but he did not argue against Marx or Lenin and rather optimistically suggested that the new youth culture, whatever it was, would produce a welcome revitalization of prematurely sclerotic socialism. Plenzdorf did not really break with tradition: Edgar the dropout turns into a technical innovator (a detail particularly stressed in the first East German version of the story) and regrets his self-willed isolation from the people, while his brigade comrades confess that they should have tried to understand his personal problems better. Plenzdorf's skill in combining different idioms has been much less discussed than the political implications of the text, as if these implications were not constituted by the way Edgar uses his idiom, made up of pop slang, Goethe (in particular moments of emotional intensity), and Salinger, to express feelings and perceptions totally different from those articulated in the official language of the older generation. In the Wibeau story Plenzdorf, a sophisticated explorer of different idioms in their social functions, is far ahead of ideologists who lightly toy with the possibilities of a communism made more humane by imported jeans, electric guitars, and daringly long hair.

In his popular movie and subsequent film story "The Legend of Paul and Paula" (1974), Plenzdorf continued to express the desires of a younger generation frustrated by the codes of the adults. He recounts the vicissitudes of a pedantic official in the State Ministry of International Trade (attaché case and all) who is miraculously transformed into a young man of fine emotions by his love for Paula, a somewhat disorganized cashier in a supermarket. The charming Paula (played by film star Angelika Domröse) turns down the advances of aging Herr Saft, who owns a well-appointed dacha and makes good money buying and selling old tires on the side. She laughs when she embraces Paul, and rips his shirt (that old Tennessee Williams gesture imbued here with new socialist meaning). The lovers dream of putting their great white bed on a riverboat that floats gently down the Spree River while they make love, enchaining each other with innocent flowers, but Paula later dies giving birth to Paul's child.

Plenzdorf does not lack the talents of a socialist Erich Segal, but he surprised most of his readers by publishing, in the West only, a cryptic short text entitled "Kein runter, kein fern" (1978; "Not Down, Not Far"). It is an experimental montage of different texts, or rather a combination of contradictory "voices." We hear the interior monologue, haltingly, stutteringly, of a psychologically disturbed East Berlin teenager who hopes to attend a concert by the Rolling Stones on the other side of the Wall but is beaten up by the People's Police when they attack a crowd of young people. We also hear the voice of his father, who wants to impose upon him an ideological and repressive education, and that of a journalist reporting on the state radio, in the most appalling clichés, the military parades celebrating the twentieth birthday of the GDR. We suspect that the psychotic boy will be put in a state institution. There is total loss of hope, and we are left shattered by a searing experience far more disturbing in its final implications than anything Plenzdorf has written before.

In 1976 the fragile combination of political control and a small measure of literary spontaneity was destroyed almost overnight, when the authorities resolved to deprive the poet and ballad singer Wolf Biermann of his GDR citizenship and thus exile him to the West. Many intellectuals and writers, among them numerous loyalists, asserted themselves in protest outside channels prescribed by the party organization. Wolf Biermann was born in 1936 to a Hamburg working family loyal to the Weimar Communist Party. (His father was arrested by the Gestapo and after eight years in prison was murdered in Auschwitz.) He joined the Communist Young Pioneers after the war, moved to the GDR in 1953, briefly worked as an assistant in the Berliner Ensemble after Brecht's death, and spent many years studying political economy, philosophy, and mathematics. Encouraged by the composer Hanns Eisler, he began writing and performing his own songs in the early 1960s. When he tried to establish a Berlin Workers' and Students' Theater, however, the authorities interfered; by 1963 he was forbidden to perform in public, and the SED expelled him from its ranks.

Biermann considers himself a radical poet and maker of ballads, revolting against the ossification of thought and the misuse of power in capitalist countries and in the "real" socialism of the GDR. His public stance often conceals from his audiences a fragile and romantic sensibility easily wounded by too much reality. Programmatically cultivating the heritage of François Villon (pursued in one of his ballads by the GDR police under the name of Franz Villonk), as well as that of his "cousin" Heinrich Heine and Bert Brecht (whom he does not entirely trust), Biermann wants to remind young socialists everywhere of the authentic revolutionary traditions that he finds symbolized in his father, Rosa Luxemburg, the Black Panthers, and the Freedom Movement in South Vietnam. He also wants to reveal what is wrong with GDR orthodoxy, with rapacious capitalists and their Social Democrat allies (viewed strictly according to the German Communist party line of the late 1920s), and with puritanical functionaries unwilling or unable to drink, dance, love, or live. His poems and songs—collected, for instance, in *Die Drahtharfe* (1965; *The Wire Harp*, 1968), *Mit Marx- und Engelszungen* (1968; *With the Tongues of Marx and E/Angels*), *Für meine Genossen* (1972; *For My Comrades*), and *Preussischer Ikarus* (1978; *Prussian Icarus*)—were published in West Berlin and Cologne and circulated in samizdat copies on the GDR side of the Wall, where they reached wide audiences, often on West German long-playing records copied by eager young GDR listeners. "They who once bravely endured in the face of machine guns," Biermann tells the aging officials, "are afraid of my guitar. . . . The smell of terror can be sensed on the snouts of bureaucrat elephants/ When I treat a concert hall to my songs."

By 1965 Biermann was considered the supersinner among the "skeptics." He was forbidden to publish, perform, or travel. His little apartment in East Berlin, not far from the one where Brecht had lived, became the goal of many pilgrimages of intellectuals among the late 1960s generation. He made his first public appearance in the GDR ten years later in a Protestant parish house in a Berlin suburb. The Party now wanted to get rid of him as quickly and quietly as possible. When the West German Metal Workers' Trade Union (traditionally close to the Old Left) invited him to West Germany, he received immediate permission to go and performed in Cologne on November 13, 1976, before thousands of students and working people (documented on CBS 88 224, double LP). Three days later the GDR official news service announced that the "proper authorities of the GDR" had denied him the privilege of "further residing in that country" and had deprived him of his citizenship. In a commentary of November 17, 1976, the party newspaper added that at the Cologne concert, visible on TV on both sides of the Wall, Biermann had committed "crimes against the GDR and against socialism" by attacking the state and, "lapsing into the dark morass of anticommunism," had transgressed against his citizen's loyalty obligation (*Treuepflicht*).

Twenty-four hours after Biermann had been deprived of his citizenship, some of the most prominent GDR writers of both younger and older generations closed ranks and communicated to the Western news services a protest statement addressed to the GDR authorities. The text stated that although Biermann was an "uncomfortable poet," the socialist republic should be able to bear with such discomfort "calmly and thoughtfully." The authors of the statement stressed that while they did not identify with every position Biermann took, they protested against his loss of citizenship and requested the authorities "to reconsider the measures taken." The number of signatures increased with the force of an avalanche: among the first-day signers were Jurek Becker, Volker Braun, Stephan Hermlin, Sarah Kirsch, Günter Kunert, and Christa Wolf and her husband Gerhard; on the second day twenty-five more writers and artists signed (among them Plenzdorf and the popular film star Angelika Domröse), on the third day twenty-three including de Bruyn, and on the fourth day thirty-three. All this was quite apart from the open letters directly addressed to the first secretary of the Party by the poet Bernd Jentzsch (who was on a reading tour in Switzerland and stayed there) and the aging physicist Robert Havemann who, quoting Rosa Luxemburg, suggested that Biermann was a dyed-in-the-wool Marxist who was merely opposed to a "dictatorship by a handful of politicians." The Party organized the usual ritual of public loyalty statements, but the results were rather meager and unedifying: the composer Paul Dessau delivered his text without ever mentioning Biermann's name; Anna Seghers published a brief and utterly confusing statement; Hermann Kant, soon to be president of the Writers' Union, condemned his colleagues for using a capitalist news service (they evidently wanted their statement to be known); and Peter Hacks attacked Heinrich Böll, "that landlord of traveling dissidents," who on West German television "had made big eyes like a big dog drawn by Thurber," and once more expressed astonishment at "counter-revolutionaries being published in socialist countries."

While the protest gathered force in West Germany, where the German Communist Party nearly split over the case, the SED broke off public discussion. This revealed a deep rift between the intellectuals and the Party and left the first steps of punishing the dissidents to the local branches of the Writers' Union, which promptly declared that signers of the statement had "objectively given support" to the class enemy, and within a short time reprimanded and excluded a number of dissidents, whether they had signed or not, depriving them of the right to publish and to participate in the old-age pension system. It was just the beginning of a wide-ranging and systematic new action against intellectual and political dissidents. While the party authorities had learned to live with a literature of modest formal experimentation, they were mortally afraid of Czechoslovak or Polish infections and were totally unwilling to accept the continuing possibility of a united front of intellectuals dispensing with the blessing of the Party as the only "vanguard" of political life. Suspect actresses, musicians, singers, poets, and novelists were told to leave the country or were offered quick approval of their petitions for exit permits (often forced on them by the state security services); some were given passports of long validity to stay abroad, while others were arrested and then expelled directly from prison to West Germany. For those staying at home, publication abroad was made even more difficult. The currency laws were changed to make it impossible to sign individual contracts with West German publishers and to receive royalties from abroad. Then a further change of the law, made in August 1979, threatened people who transmitted statements or manuscripts to organizations or people outside the republic with imprisonment of from five to eight years. Between 1976 and 1981 more than three hundred intellectuals and artists left the republic for the West. It has become impossible to speak, as one legitimately could in the early 1970s, of a unified GDR literature, since much of its development now occurs in the West.

6

CHRISTA WOLF: A QUESTION OF LOYALTIES

Alone among the GDR writers of the middle generation, Christa Wolf (b. 1929) has written increasingly difficult and rewarding novels, each of which triggered prolonged discussions in East and West. She is a reticent, strongly emotional, and reflective person, given to abrupt changes rather than strong continuities in her career as critic and writer. It is not easy for an outsider to speculate about the transformations of her political and literary commitments, which are characterized by an early loyalty to Stalinist orthodoxy (to expiate, I believe, her willingness to believe the Nazis); by an unhesitating insistence, somewhat later, on critically reconsidering her experiences as woman, author, and citizen of a socialist society; and more recently, by a turn toward the ideas of the Greens, the feminists, and the peace movement. In contrast to de Bruyn and Plenzdorf, who both come from families of Berlin working people, Christa Wolf, née Ihlenfeld, was born in the small town of Landsberg (Warthe), now Gorzów Wielkopolski in Poland, into the lower-middle-class family of a grocer. From her own writings we know a good deal about her school years and early crushes and her escape, with some members of the family, to Mecklenburg when the Soviet armies advanced from the east. After working as secretary to a village mayor in Soviet-occupied Mecklenburg, she completed her *Gymnasium* education in 1949, joined the SED in the same year, studied German literature in Jena and Leipzig (1949–53), where the critic Hans Mayer was among her teachers, and wrote a master's essay on problems of realism in Hans Fallada, a socially committed novelist of the late Weimar Republic. After finishing her studies, she worked as reviewer, critic, and editor in East Berlin and Halle. In 1962 she moved with her family to Kleinmachnow near East Berlin and continued to write her narratives, but after the mid-1960s she wrote them in a changing mode, skeptical if not weary of the power of fiction and distrustful of any slogans, past or contemporary. In 1976 she was among the writers who signed the Biermann petition. She has been exempt from the sanctions suffered by many others, however, and in her recent writings prefers, like many of her colleagues, to confront and interpret situations and characters from German Romanticism or Homeric Troy rather than of her own time. She has received many awards, among them the Heinrich Mann Prize of the GDR Academy of Arts (but only a meager GDR State Prize, Third Class) and has traveled widely, first in the Soviet Union and later in the United States, where she taught as writer-in-residence at Oberlin College in 1974 and, in the spring of 1983, as visiting professor at Ohio State University. Reticent as ever, she has yet to write about her experiences with American undergraduates and colleagues.

Recent interpreters rarely mention *Moskauer Novelle* (1961; *Moscow Novella*), Wolf's first published story. Certainly it would be easy to start a discussion of her literary achievements with her later novels and to forget her active and occasionally aggressive involvement as critic and author in asserting the doctrine of Socialist Realism and the Bitterfeld movement. In her story a German pediatrician, a member of a GDR delegation on an official trip to Moscow, meets a Soviet translator (the delegation guide). They recognize that they had met fifteen years earlier in Mecklenburg, when he was a lieutenant in the Soviet army and she worked (as had Christa Wolf) as the new assistant to the village mayor. They both know that they loved each other, but her memories are burdened by the dark knowledge that she neglected to warn the Soviet authorities of two fanatical Nazis setting fire to a Soviet army magazine (fighting the blaze, the lieutenant permanently injured his eyesight). The Soviet linguist, still wearing his protective green glasses, and the German physician feel renewed tenderness for each other, but both know in their hearts that they have to go back to their families and the workaday world; the woman breaks off her stay in Moscow and returns to Berlin. In my retelling, the story sounds more intimate than it is allowed to be: the prescribed positive hero, an old Bolshevik functionary who is understanding but of firm ideas, is not missing; in a Ukrainian kolkhoz, an epic feast is arranged with folk dances and medals in abundance; and the brief encounter of the lovers lasts for only a few confused days, since both know they must sacrifice their sudden passion to the work-ethic superego of revolutionary puritanism. Fortunately, the lovers do not have bodies; to indicate that something is wrong, they smoke more cigarettes than usual.

In 1959 Wolf joined the Mitteldeutscher Verlag in Halle as editor. Eager to fulfill the demands of the Bitterfeld movement, which urged writers to share the experience of the people, she worked for a time in a railway factory. In her novel *Der geteilte Himmel* (1963; *Divided Heaven: A Novel of Germany Today*, 1965), relying in part on these experiences, she awkwardly combines a sentimental love story with sustained attention to contemporary problems of industrial production. The book provoked wide-ranging discussion of an ideological rather than a literary nature in both the GDR and the Federal Republic. Within months, ten editions were sold, and one year after its publication (it was soon translated into fifteen languages) a movie of it was made in the GDR that was welcomed internationally.

Rita Seidel, who is training to become a teacher, works during vacation time (as does every student) as a member of a production brigade, putting windows into railway coaches. Almost without knowing it at first, she finds herself deeply involved in the collective drama of the working people and the organizational problems of their nationalized factory, which is trying to increase its output in spite of old equipment and the disarray caused by the disappearance of key personnel to the West. She lives with Manfred, an ambitious young chemical engineer committed to advanced research and his university career, in the dark villa of his middle-class parents. However, admiring the active party members in the factory, she feels increasingly incapable of agreeing with Manfred's skeptical ideas about history and his personal pride in his research. One day the state planners disregard a technical innovation that Manfred has worked out; he leaves for West Berlin with the blessings of his mother (who dislikes the country girl Rita anyway) and has little trouble finding himself a convenient job in West German industry. A week before the Wall goes up, Rita travels to West Berlin, where the lovers walk through the dusty streets, but something essential has changed. Rita, remembering her comrades in the brigade, leaves Manfred to his personal ambition and buys herself a return ticket to Halle and socialism. Yet she cannot forget easily: one hot afternoon when she wants to commit suicide, she is nearly killed by rolling stock. She needs a long time in a rest home to sort out her feelings and fully renew her commitment to communal life. "She saw how inexhaustible supplies of kindliness used up during the day were renewed each evening. And she was not afraid that she would miss her full share of kindliness."

Rita's story was probably discussed in the GDR more widely than any other book in the early 1960s, and it is instructive to know who participated in the debate and what was said or ignored. The first responses were enthusiastic, but the party comrades in Halle, the actual locale of events, felt less than satisfied with the importance that Wolf, in telling a love story, had assigned to the party organization. The local Halle party paper mobilized an entire group of critics and correspondents (including one Werner Rainowski, whom Wolf had once panned), to attack the aberrant way in which she presented the question of everyday party discipline. She was accused of explaining the division of Germany from a national rather than a socialist point of view; of underrating the leading role of the Party in organizing social and political life; of characterizing party members as suffering administrative punishments and disciplinary job relocations; and ultimately of presenting a "decadent" view of life. The publication of these aggressive articles may have been a local vendetta of provincial officials. Shortly after the building of the Wall, however, more important issues of political commitment were at stake in the republic. The Party and the government, eager to have their policies confirmed by a successful book read widely by the younger generation, turned against the local critics and had their top literary functionaries confirm that Wolf's novel was of fundamental importance as "the first attempt to write about the immediate present." Even the Soviet writer Konstantin Simonov contributed a remark, widely quoted in the publicity campaign, to the effect that the book, though of somewhat complicated construction (flashbacks), was very interesting. In a 1963 discussion of Politburo and cabinet members with a delegation from the Writers' Union that was publicized by the media, Wolf's *Divided Heaven* was officially recommended as truly constructive. Hans Koch, first secretary of the Writers' Union at the time, was speedily dispatched to Halle to tell the locals that Wolf may have underrated the role of the party organization, but that it was politically wrong and potentially harmful to call her way of writing decadent. (I wonder what Professor Koch thinks of her today.)

The narrative skillfully defines the skeptic Manfred and his burned-out father, once a Nazi and now an SED party member, as people truly alive. Manfred especially, who in his emblematic dialogues with the positive functionary Wendland comes close to quoting Nietzsche, does not appear villainous at all, but rather the spoiled child of an ambitious mother, or a proud young man trying to define himself in a historical situation of the "not yet and the not any more." He feels deeply hurt when, in the moment of decision in West Berlin, Rita shows that she is far stronger than he because she has the courage, while he is choosing the more comfortable way out, to return to a "harder and more severe life." It is the narrative procedure of sustained flashbacks that compels us, unfortunately, to share a surfeit of melodramatic memories in Rita's bland mind. Constantly looking up to the stars, sniffing the fragrance of the budding flowers (if not mercilessly prevented from doing so by the Halle smog), and clutching at her Manfred, she may embody all the social issues of the moment (as Jack Zipes suggests in his effective defense of the novel), but she is intellectually incapable of an analytic view of the situation. She may have chosen the harder life, but she has done it for the softest of reasons. In the West, she believes, everybody is alone "in the most terrible way," whereas in the East everybody is so "hot and near." She has chosen the womb again, perhaps in the dark guise of the locomotive factory, and reenacts the age-old German cry for a *Gemeinschaft* that gives full bliss and stills all doubts once and for all. We are closer to the German past than the new terminology might suggest.

It is not unfair to say that for nearly ten years Christa Wolf was an activist among writers, but that in the early and mid-1960s she changed quietly and radically. A short piece, "Juninachmittag" ("Afternoon in June"), appearing in an anthology of new prose in 1967, suggested to her friends that she was moving away from prescribed realism. Then her second novel suddenly revealed her restless gifts, long repressed by too many dogmatic beliefs and now engaged in the intense self-examination of a writer distrustful of any word that can be said or written. *Nachdenken über Christa T.* (1968; *The Quest for Christa T.*, 1970), far from being a traditional novel with massive representations of society and a concerted group of characters, courageously if somewhat belatedly shared the experimental attitudes of German prose writers after the *nouveau roman.* Instead of despairing over the difficulties of cohesively dealing with experience, her thoughtful text makes an essential virtue of playing with possibilities and explorations. We are confronted with a controlled process of trying to remember, rather than an attempt to write a linear story, and, in trying to remember, the writer explores authentic ways of speaking about people, society, and writing itself.

Wishing to recapture the image of her friend Christa T., who died of leukemia, the narratrix gathers letters, diaries, and manuscripts (for the other Christa wrote poetry and fragmentary stories, too) in order to reconstruct, often against the strong evidence of her memories, how her friend lived, worked, dreamed, and died. She reconstructs their first encounter in school during the war years; their meeting again in a classroom at the University of Leipzig seven years later; Christa's relationship with a serious fellow student; Christa's painful experiences as an elementary school teacher; her marriage to the veterinarian Justus; the birth of her children; an affair, or rather "the thing," with Justus's friend; her insistence on building a house for herself and the family on the seashore; her illness; and her death one cold day in February. Events, facts, and documents recede in time, absorbed in an incessant and compassionate stream of reflections about a young woman who by her own instinctive decision withdraws from society to realize herself in joy, fullness, and purity, and who continues beyond her death to challenge her biographer and readers, though in different ways, perhaps, in East and West.

The loyal biographer, who goes on reconsidering her own life while exploring that of her friend, feels deeply attracted, in an elective affinity, to Christa's attempt "to be herself." Christa T. feels incapable of being intoxicated, as others are, by "the waving banners, the deafening songs, the hands clapping rhythmically over our heads"; when a group of students prepares collectively for an examination in order to get the highest marks, she absents herself innocently to read Dostoyevski. Christa's friends assure us that she was as enthusiastic as everybody else of her age in expecting the new society to bring a surfeit of freedom, but when her fellow citizens began speaking about new socialist people, she was looking into herself. The pedants among her colleagues feel that she had her distinct reservations about a collective without imagination, built by the GDR Gradgrinds who were eager for quick success but incapable of "gazing, dreaming, letting it happen." Yet Christa T. was not only an introspective or laid-back socialist who, wanting to be left alone, was ahead of her generation by nearly fifteen years, but also a writer who early confronted questions of increasing interest to her biographer. If Christa did not go on writing, it was because she felt the difficulty of handling words that ceased to fit things: "She was doubtful, amidst our toxic swirl of new name giving; what she doubted was the reality of names. . . . She strongly felt that naming is seldom accurate and that, even if it is accurate, name and thing coincide only for a short time." In a highly regulated society that prided itself on the exact correspondence of big words with great events, Christa T. made a disturbing discovery, and her biographer, who in the experiences of her friend (if she ever existed) explores aspects of her own life, is not unwilling to see the radical consequences of her insight. If referentiality itself is in doubt, we all have to start communicating and living in a different way, socialists or not.

There is an almost incredible gap of attitude and literary quality between Wolf's early writings and her search for Christa T. in herself, with her reflections about what we can or cannot do in a world where almost everybody believes that language can be easily used in naming people, ideas, and things. In her earlier writings Wolf offered abstract solutions, but here she thinks about tentative approaches to problems that seem as insoluble as ever. While the text is far less radical in its narrative procedures than Uwe Johnson's *Mutmassungen über Jakob* (1959; *Speculations about Jacob*, 1963) or Fritz Rudolf Fries's *Der Weg nach Oobliadooh* (1966; *The Road to Oobliadooh*, 1968)—Johnson left the GDR early and Fries can publish only selected narratives at home—it is rich in illuminating literary allusions. For the first time in her experience as a writer, Wolf has moved from submissive enthusiasm to asking simple questions, yet she has not given up her intense feelings. In trying to avoid the assertive, ideologically melodramatic, or doctrinaire formula, her narrative tends too often to be sweetly serene. Her inclination to remove fragile Christa, or her other self, as far as possible from the massive pressures of industrial society (which in her case happens to be socialist), ultimately results in her relegation to a shadowy sphere of inwardness where she cultivates her kitchen garden and her emotions. A GDR commentator once complained that Wolf reduces the problem of power to a question of feelings—a criticism incapable of grasping the implication that strong feelings in a socialist system without a human face constitute a form of resistance. But the question is not farfetched whether Christa T., by taking on the role of a Mecklenburg housewife, really resists or rather capitulates by leaving the organization of society to those whom she cannot tolerate—in some contrast, perhaps, to Christa Wolf herself, who takes the risk of publishing her book. In one of her interviews Wolf has suggested an important distinction between sensitivity and sentimentality, but I wonder whether the distinction defines her practice everywhere. "The air," she writes of Christa T.'s agonies, "would be full of the cries of geese. Sometimes, rarely, she'd write a letter, or listen to music. The moon rose over the lake, she could stand for hours at the window and watch its reflections in the water." On the printed page, sincere feelings have their own way of deteriorating into the most traditional German kitsch, whether derived from Theodor Storm or anybody else.

In *Kindheitsmuster* (1976; *A Model Childhood*, 1980), Wolf continues her self-examination in another mode, looking closely at her own childhood and youth during the Hitler years and immediately after the Allied victory in Gemany. Watching her younger self from considerable distance, Wolf wants to answer the difficult question of how people of her generation have become what they are, and rightly believes that a traditional exercise in literary biography would not do. We are confronted with three strata of time, thought, and experience that will illuminate each other: an account of a family excursion from East Berlin to her birthplace on July 10, 1971 (the hottest and dustiest day of the year); the actual narrative of the young girl, here called Nelly, from the early 1930s to the early postwar years; and, on a more abstract level, literary and political reflections dating from November 3, 1972, to May 2, 1975, on the process of writing the book, including disquisitions on memory, forgetting, battles in Vietnam, and Nixon's speeches. Wolf asks how it happened that Nazi rule was accepted and supported by the small-town families (among them her own, who had voted Social Democrat for years). Fleeting moments of domesticity, seemingly unpolitical, reveal how people came to ignore, forget, and neglect what others did or said, as long as the rituals of middle-class order were upheld. She is ambivalent about her first role model (a demanding teacher and almost ascetic functionary of the Nazi Women's Organization), but is frank in trying to explain to herself why Nelly joined those shouting for the Führer and was eager to be trained to lead a group of the Nazi girls' Bund. Perhaps, she suggests, it was not merely the desire to be somebody, but a kind of exchange transaction in which the young girl offered her submission and her strict performance of duties for the guarantee of being respected by others and for relative freedom from angst.

Stephen Spender, who reviewed *A Model Childhood* for the *New York Times Book Review* (October 12, 1980), says that the book reminded him of Elsa Morante's great novel *History* because, with "both books, one is convinced of the lives of ordinary people described, but a bit dubious of the interpretation of history imposed upon them." I am more disturbed to see a self-searching writer reproducing the party line about opposition to the Nazis being sustained exclusively by organized Communists and, when she ponders the vicissitudes of modern socialism, to hear her speak about Vietnam and Chile but not about Poland or Czechoslovakia on her doorstep. Yet it is also true that Wolf writes eloquently about the dangers of self-censorship threatening the writer from within. I believe that, ultimately, her memories are a tragic book which, given her circumstances, has to repress a good deal about contemporary problems in order to reveal the forgetfulness of others in another age.

It has often been said that Christa Wolf always writes about women, but only in recent years has she removed her characters to centuries long past. In *Kein Ort. Nirgends* (1979; *No Place on Earth*, 1982) and *Kassandra* (1983; *Cassandra*, 1984), both translated by Jan van Heurck, she risks being misunderstood in her intentions by audiences both in the GDR and elsewhere. In the GDR most readers assume that writers, in moments of intense ideological pressure, escape to the realms of history and myth (as happened in Nazi Germany), while readers in the Federal Republic are particularly fond of contemporary issues clad in old costumes, because the historical articulation satisfies their middle-class desires for *Bildung*, once so marvelously provided by Thomas Mann. In the short novella *No Place on Earth*, Wolf turns to the Romantic authors Karoline von Günderrode and Heinrich von Kleist. In prose more allusive than descriptive, and relying a good deal on interior monologue, she tells about a party of friends and two solitary people who talk to each other on a walk. The year is 1804, and even if we do not know much about German Romanticism, we grasp from conversations over teacups (as the Rhine rolls past the windows) that times have changed rapidly since the French Revolution, pushing people into particular jobs, as for instance writing the history of laws, the concern of the scholar Savigny, or selling perfumes wholesale, the occupation of the party's well-to-do host.

Karoline von Günderrode, a sensitive writer of lyrical poems, and the playwright Heinrich von Kleist, two guests who cannot stand party talk on grand matters, take a walk together and, in a sudden moment of trust and openness, reveal to each other their frustrations and desires, so close in loving and hating. Impoverished and driven by an implacable thirst for absolute self-realization, sharply aware of the androgynous elements of their sensibilities, and despising the "unlivable life" in modern society, they both deplore the reductive existence determined by the new distribution of labor; intone the old German idealist dirge about the totality of serene life lost; and see only an intolerable future in which people of action and people of reflection will be separated forever from each other. (Both Günderrode and Kleist died by suicide.) Wolf's fiery accusations of the execrable state, guilty of seeking values only where they can be figured out in percentages and of tolerating ideals only for utilitarian reasons, are readily understood by readers in the GDR. But American reviewers, not needing to consider the political context of the original publication, as usual enjoyed the considerable advantage of being able to discuss the novel on its own, as far as it can be done. Writing in the *New York Times* (September 6, 1982), John Leonard would obviously have been much happier if Wolf wrote like Günter Grass, yet he "also wished that American writers were as serious about the intimate . . . relationship between literature and history" as the difficult and daring German writers "insist on being."

In her 1983 Frankfurt University lectures, in which she surveyed her recent work, Wolf called *Cassandra* a "key story." She told her students how, in her readings of Homer, Aeschylus, and ancient myth (all in preparation for a journey to Greece), essential concerns deeply troubling her in the 1970s came together in a firm configuration: the question of war and peace; the demand for the autonomy of women; and her hope that a counterepic would bring to light what the literary genres of patriarchal society had long obfuscated. In the accounts of her childhood memories, Wolf had spoken of her mother as the Cassandra of a provincial grocery store who had dark forebodings about the future of warring Germany while putting fresh loaves of bread on the shelves, but it was Wolf's reading of Aeschylus's *Agamemnon* (lines 1,256–1,330) that overwhelmed her with a sudden, compassionate feeling for Priam's unfortunate daughter. Wolf takes her narrative cue from the dramatic moment when, after the destruction of Troy and her family, Cassandra is brought among Agamemnon's spoils to Mycenae and waits in front of the forbidding palace to be slaughtered. Cassandra believes that this is the last time span allotted to her (while Agamemnon is being murdered inside), and in an ultimate act of defiance wants to assert her consciousness of what compelled her to live as she did. She recounts her life for us and herself in an interior monologue of many time shifts and extraordinary poetic power that is not even seriously vitiated by Wolf's insistence on using a few modern terms of politics and bureaucracy. Cassandra remembers how she grew up as the king's most beloved daughter, but by choice separated herself from her own kind and the city and joined a community of women of all ages and origins, assembling in friendly togetherness on the slopes of a mountain at some distance from the palace. She thinks of her father, who was unwilling to see the brutalities of the war and to make peace; of Aeneas, the only man she ever truly loved (because of his quiet strength and unhesitating tenderness); of the Amazon queen Penthesilea, whose merciless hate of men she did not share; of her brother Hector, senselessly butchered by the Greeks; and of the last day of burning Troy, when she was raped by Ajax at the altar of Athena before being dragged away to the ships of the victors. She does not fear death and yet, in a desperate moment of foolish hope, wishes that the gods would allow a woman slave to hear what she thinks and transmit it to her daughters and granddaughters, so that "side by side with the stream of the heroic epic, her tiny thread of water would reach laboriously the distant and perhaps more happy people who might be alive in future centuries." She cannot die without praying that her words be given permanence.

In her Frankfurt lectures (later published in the GDR with minor deletions approved by the lecturer), Wolf comments on her interpretation of Cassandra and how she came to write the book. She conceives of Cassandra as an early, if not the earliest, example of a lively and intelligent woman seeking her "autonomy" and anticipating, three thousand years ago, the modern battle against "degrading women to objects." Being of royal blood, she knows that, in order to learn and to be herself, she cannot be trained for any profession other than that of priestess and prophetess. Her family expects her to fulfill her duties according to prescribed tradition, but she cannot sacrifice to tradition the truth that arises from her ability to "see" without illusions or lies what is really happening. Inevitably she provokes her family and the community into explaining away her warnings as madness while trying to silence her by imprisoning her in a subterranean cave (a punishment particularly welcome to the chief of Trojan internal security, who will survive all disasters). Since Greek and Trojan men are allied against women, Cassandra comes to see war as a universal consequence of patriarchy (though Wolf the commentator tells us that in some parts of the world, Europe excepted, wars of liberation are thoroughly legitimate).

I have considerable difficulties in squaring Wolf's view of ancient matriarchies with the story itself. In the narrative, the women on the slopes of Mount Ida gather in the ancient cult of Cybele, sustained by ritual dances that exhaust the rational mind; but Wolf the critical commentator, upon encountering two young American feminists in search of Minoan matriarchy, does not hesitate to express her qualms about potential regressions. In her review of the novel and the accompanying essays in the *New York Times Book Review* (September 9, 1984), Mary Lefkowitz said that Wolf's "research methods" were "eclectic, unsystematic, and intuitive" (as if Wolf had set out to compete with professors of classical philology), and suggested that her "random thoughts about life and literature" did not really constitute "informative discourse," but only "the mental anguish of a woman trying to understand the world around her, but lacking the knowledge and mental discipline to offer persuasive and practical solutions." The philological expert may have reasons to complain, but perhaps Wolf should be judged only on her own ground. What she has written is a feminist essay in which old Marxism gives way to new thought, not an old-fashioned historical novella based on archaeological facts.

Christa Wolf first appeared on the GDR literary scene as a young and eager defender of the Stalinist doctrine of Socialist Realism. The less said about her intolerant reviews written in the 1950s, the better. It may be more important to speculate about the moments of fundamental change (her switch of allegiance from the Nazi girls' Bund to the Stalinist apparatus did not affect the structure of her thought), and to ask whether these moments perhaps occurred in the mid-1960s or, to be more precise, were brought to public awareness when the Ninth Plenum of the SED Central Committee renewed its battle against "skepticism" in 1965, censored many writers for deviations of one kind or another, and prompted Wolf to defend one of the younger novelists accused of being too "subjective." In 1963 the Party had hoped to co-opt Wolf fully by making her a candidate for membership in the Central Committee, but her name was deleted from the list in 1967, and her writings unmistakably suggest that she was no longer enthusiastically doing what the apparatus required her and others to do. In her subsequent essays she stresses the need for an intense consensus of literature and socialist society, since both desire "to help people to attain self-realization"; precisely because socialist society turns against the past and toward the future, literature must liberate itself from unchanging conventions and "relate to intellectual developments and social movements so as to open a future to human beings, free of age-old and brand-new magic formulae of manipulation." At a time when the student radicals in the Federal Republic wanted to do away with any writing uncommitted to collective concerns, Wolf, who had gone through her own experiences, passionately suggested that socialist society was more complex than ever, and asked for a new way "of expressing the finest nuances of emotional life" and "the specific differences between individuals." It was emblematic of her changing sensibilities that, in the mid- and late 1960s, she combined her longtime admiration for Anna Seghers, the "teacher of the entire nation," with close attention to the Austrian poet Ingeborg Bachmann, in whose writings Wolf hears "the bold and plaintive voice" of a woman broken "but not defeated, full of sadness yet without self-pity, suffering but not in love with pain" (1966). Somewhat later, Wolf even praised Max Frisch, that analyst of the most private feelings.

In the late 1960s Christa Wolf talked about her rediscovery of the creative self mostly by speaking about other writers. In the early 1970s, however, she defined her views (all the while stressing her Marxist studies as an essential experience) in a more personal and less camouflaged way, asserting that the "inward" or "subjective authenticity" sustained by the sensitive self is essential to a "genuine" and "believable" literature. Arguing against "linearity" and the sequential plot of the well-made novel of realism, and for "depth" of storytelling that is not afraid to fuse time perspectives, she suggested that reality and literature actually embrace each other in the writer's consciousness, rather than confronting each other like a mirror and what it reflects (as she herself and an earlier theory had maintained). Of course she was eager to put her rediscovery of the creative ego, and of the "writer as an important person again," into the full context of developing socialist society; combining a bit of Brecht with a good deal of Schiller, she insisted that only the creative self could "intervene" in the social world, seize the readers' most hidden emotions, and "enhance their sensibilities." Yet in the late 1970s, in both her narratives and her essays she pushed further and radically separated the creative self from the pragmatic world, hinting that such a separation, if not opposition, offered one of the few remaining possibilities for bringing to life values and aims more humane than those projected by technology, economic expectations, and everyday politics; the new enemy was the industrial distribution of labor, both in capitalist societies and those socialist societies where mere usefulness is preferred to self-realization. Wolf had at first argued against her younger and doctrinaire self, but now, liberated from her most private burdens, she felt free to warn against "reified dreams" in all societies driven by pressures for material and technological achievements, to define her writing as "doing research for peace," and to ally herself with those people in the GDR and elsewhere who want to achieve autonomy for women and not merely change them into men. She has come within inches of being the most thoughtful writer of the Green movement on either side of the Wall.

7

SHAPES OF POETRY

In the sixties, younger critics often suggested that the destruction of Hitler's Reich had not really changed the writing of poetry. It is true that lyrical tradition, nourished by classical and romantic forms, was strong in the forties and fifties, but tradition functioned differently for different people. Conservative Nazi collaborators used older forms to demonstrate their allegiance to the national heritage, while others at home or in exile used these forms to show that it was one of the fundamental tasks of the antifascist writer to rescue poetic tradition from Nazi infection. The end of World War I and the founding of the Weimar Republic had explosively strengthened expressionist art and Dada protest against traditionalism, but the last days of World War II and the final victory of the Allies did not trigger a similarly exuberant creativity. If, among the melancholy and hungry people writing poetry, literary conflicts emerged, they were mostly of a retrospective kind. These conflicts ranged against each other, at least by implication, those who went on believing in the regenerative power of the classical idiom (among them Johannes R. Becher in the Soviet zone of occupation and Ernst Schönwiese in Austria), and those who wanted to renew the memories of Georg Trakl, expressionism, and the French surrealists—memories very much alive in the Vienna cafés as well as in Paul Celan's earliest verse and Karl Krolow's later poetry.

Some of the most exquisite poems of the late 1940s and 1950s were written by the "Salamanders," as authors resuscitating lyrical closeups of nature were called by their adversaries, who insisted that poetry had above all to confront people in their social and historical involvements. The new nature poetry, which was to absorb many war memories, provided its own strong element of continuity going back to the later Goethe and to the harsh and exacting lyricism of Annette von Droste-Hülshoff (1797–1848). Wilhelm Lehmann (1882–1968) in the West and Peter Huchel (1903–81) in the East, who emerged as the new masters of the nature poem, had both begun writing in the 1920s, as had Oskar Loerke and Elisabeth Langgässer, who was forbidden to publish in Hitler's Reich. Lehmann, a teacher in a North German prep school, published his first collection of poetry (after writing many more or less expressionist narratives) at fifty-three. His volumes *Entzückter Staub* (1946; *Enchanted Dust*), *Noch nicht genug* (1950; *Not Yet Enough*), and *Abschiedslust* (1962; *Joy of Parting*) were eagerly read and imitated by a middle generation haunted by German history and thankful for his rediscovery of humble herbs, leaves of grass, and weeds in ditches, always named by the poet with the precision of the loving botanist and linked, as he had learned in his studies of Gaelic folklore and W. B. Yeats, to old legends and myths. Huchel, who returned to the GDR from a Soviet prison camp, had been closer in his childhood to poor people working the land. In his *Gedichte* (1951; *Poems*) and his later collection *Chausseen Chausseen* (1963; *Roads Roads*), he returned more often than Lehmann to the life of peasants and fishermen, but combined his pastoral scenes with threatening images of persecution and the war. For many productive years (1948–62) he edited *Sinn und Form* (*Meaning and Form*), the most distinguished literary journal of the GDR, but lost out against the doctrinaire functionaries. In his old age he left for the West and died in a little village near Freiburg im Breisgau, revered by many on both sides of the Wall.

Discussions of postwar poetry were quickly dominated, at least in the West, by the astonishing comeback of Gottfried Benn (1886–1956) and the sudden inclination of German intellectuals from at least two generations to share his aversion to history and to the false consolations of metaphysical beliefs. Many people shared his melancholy passion for pure form and articulate expression, created to triumph over change, vicissitudes, and fleeting events. A physician by profession, Benn had been one of the early expressionists, shocking readers with his *Morgue und andere Gedichte* (1912; *Morgue and Other Poems*), which spoke of disfigured corpses and the "wombs that decayed in the cancer wards." Not much later, he had shocked them again with his anti-intellectual desire to escape from the ugly world of "the brain," commerce, and mass civilization into a luminous realm "of nihilism and music," intensely blue seas, and the "sultry luxuriance of sunburned flesh." In 1933, much to the disgust of his avant-garde readers both in Germany and in exile, he briefly supported the "New State," of which he spoke in biological terms of rejuvenation. But the Nazi functionaries expelled the former expressionist from their literary organization as well as from the medical association, whereupon Benn chose, as he said, the "aristocratic form of emigration" and had himself reactivated as an army physician who was kept busy compiling suicide reports. Immediately after the war he was blacklisted by the Allies, while again working as a physician in the ruins of Berlin. His *Statische Gedichte* (1948; *Static Poems*), published in Switzerland and a year later in the French zone of occupation, overwhelmed readers by their sonorous negation of all human history, their defense of Nietzsche's concept of the world as an aesthetic phenomenon, and the precision of images designed, like stones or flute songs, to survive whatever was happening in human time. Benn, who died in 1956 in Berlin, was anathema to the activist sixties, but he was well on his way to being rediscovered in the late seventies and early eighties by young poets thoroughly disappointed in their utopian expectations.

In the years after the war, Karl Krolow (b. 1915) developed his own distinct and inimitable mode of the late modernist poem, absorbing the legacies of Rilke and the nature poem and the lessons of the French surrealists and Federico García Lorca. In *Auf Erden* (1949; *On Earth*) his images are finely honed: the moon moves from the "armpits" of the clouds, the summer air hits the landscape like "a blue whip," and as we picnic under the trees, we hear "sickles hiss like snakes" in the wheat. In later verse collections, including *Die Zeichen der Welt* (1952; *The Signs of the World*) and *Fremde Körper* (1959; *Foreign Bodies: Poems*, 1969), Krolow rapidly moves away from the limitations of German botany, liberates himself from concentrated attention on the rustic, and expresses a glowing feeling of transience that is radiant rather than dark, yielding a serene knowledge about the limitations of being human. The poem "Verlassene Küste" ("Lone Coast"), published in 1948 and justly renowned for its exact ambivalence, anticipates much of his finest writing with its images of "sailboats and laughter long past"; the endurance of melancholy "made of black honey"; and memories of card-playing sailors "alone in the flesh" with their mysterious knives "nicked by the sharp wind of eternity, watching." Krolow was not remiss in defining his idea of the supreme poem, fundamentally opposed to that of Gottfried Benn: if Benn wanted to create a self-enclosed text as an objet d'art "set off from experience and history," Krolow wanted his poem to be "open" to all "encounters and resistances" with which it is inevitably confronted, a "porous" structure capable of yielding something of itself to the exterior world and of absorbing something of that world in return. Krolow is a master in husbanding his wiry poetic energies. Never raising his voice but willing to irritate readers, he has done more to bring the German poem closer to French and Spanish writing than anybody among his contemporaries. His verse of the late 1950s is of rare cosmopolitan distinction, and there are many first-rate poems, often elegiac in mode, in his work of the late 1960s and 1970s, which responds ironically to public demands for social relevance. Few in German writing are capable of speaking of our pleasures and burdens with such thoughtful ease.

The reemergence of political poetry on the postwar German scene is less easily described. Even Brecht's incipient lyrical renascence in the late fifties and early sixties compelled his new readers, far more interested in the poetry of his middle life than in his earlier or later manner, to go back to German folk songs and late medieval ballads, which had been among his most useful source materials; the poet Brecht, unlike the playwright, was definitely a conservative revolutionary. The first young German who published political poems in a contemporary idiom was Hans Magnus Enzensberger (b. 1929), who belonged to the new generation of angry young people of the Adenauer period. Brilliantly combining his rhetorical gifts with an astonishing literary erudition, he aggressively faced in the periodical *Kursbuch* (which he founded) and in his poems the rapacious new market society of high technological requirements without making any detours into recent or more distant history. Enzensberger's early volumes of poetry, *verteidigung der wölfe* (1957; *in defense of wolves*), *landessprache* (1960; *language of the country*), and the somewhat more subdued if not elegiac *blindenschrift* (1964; *writing for the blind*), reveal an extraordinary richness of forms, allusive wit, and contradictory speech patterns reminiscent of or parodying Benn or Brecht and unparalleled in their Alexandrian brilliance anywhere in the writings of his contemporaries. With condescending irony and cold furor, he attacks those wielding military and economic power and those sheepishly willing to feel at home in the oppressive structure of capitalist society, sustained by poisonous technology and obfuscated by media verbiage. Condemning generals, professors, managers, and "fat widows" busily accumulating useless commodities, he does not spare their helpless and inarticulate victims (buying, consuming, watching TV) and, rather paradoxically, praises the serene and fulfilled existence of a few rare animals (as long as they have aesthetically pleasing names) and a selection of trees, modest vegetables, and humble plants, among them cherry trees, celery, and the northern lichen.

In 1968, however, Enzensberger turned ferociously against his own literary past and demanded that intellectuals immediately assume the burden of educating their fellow citizens politically. A short time later he theatrically resigned his fellowship at Wesleyan University in Connecticut, paid out from capitalist monies, in order to depart for Cuba. He devoted himself to pure "factography," as for instance his documentary text *Das Verhör von Habana* (1970; *The Havana Inquiry*, 1974) on the Bay of Pigs prisoners. Yet one cannot accuse Enzensberger of being doctrinaire: his collected *Gedichte 1955–1970* (1971; *Poems 1955–1970*) anticipate a general turn to lyric meditation; his epic poem *Der Untergang der Titanic* (1978; *The Sinking of the Titanic*, 1980) reveals ominous feelings of ontological catastrophe; and in the new poems collected in *Die Furie des Verschwindens* (1980; *The Fury of Disappearance*), he comes close to writing like a student of Gottfried Benn, showing anew his despair of universal history.

His expectations of doom have not prevented him more recently from editing *TransAtlantic*, an imaginative West German periodical modeled on *The New Yorker* that is perfectly appropriate to his personal combination of intellectual sophistication and radical chic.

The sixties were an age of protest poetry of at least three kinds that occasionally influenced each other: the poetry of political activism (increasingly serving the collective cause by producing texts for posters, songs, or agitprop documents); concrete poetry radically exploring the functions of language in its social contexts; and a new wave of Beat writing following the example of the San Francisco school. Among the activists, younger poets in the West were again eager to function as mouthpieces of the masses (that dream of every lonely writer waiting for the mail), while their contemporaries in the GDR, sick and tired of being voices of progressing history, longed for a chance to articulate some of their private desires. The experiences and writings of Erich Fried and Günter Kunert, both gifted lyrical poets in the older sense, distinctly suggest the contradictions of intentions and context: Fried turned from the difficult idiom of his early poems to a simple and more epigrammatic mode, while Kunert moved from affirmations of the new socialist order, expressed in verse according to the Brecht tradition, to a restlessly meditative verse relying on its own freedom beyond all formal restraints.

Erich Fried (b. 1921, Vienna) left home when his Jewish father was killed by the Gestapo, settled in London in the late 1930s, and in his hermetic early poetry revealed a longing for the Austria of his youth, forever lost, and his great admiration for Joyce, Gerard Manley Hopkins, and Dylan Thomas. (Fried is one of the great and, unfortunately, unknown German translators of Shakespeare's plays in our time.) In the mid-1960s he committed himself to political action, gave up the BBC job that he had held for sixteen years (1952–68), and published *und Vietnam und* (1966; *and Vietnam and*) in his new mode of short stanzas and sharp statements, rarely allowing for lyricism (except perhaps when he writes about his Vienna childhood). Yet in another way Fried has not changed at all: in his *100 Gedichte ohne Vaterland* (1977; *One Hundred Poems without a Country*, 1980), awarded the International Publishers' Prize and simultaneously published in seven languages, he suggests as convincingly as ever that he continues to write in the tradition of Karl Kraus, the imperious Viennese satirist who never ceased to believe that spoken and written language reveals the abominations of people as social beings. Fried's most effective poems of the recent kind take up words or a slogan used by his adversaries and mercilessly show the full inhumanity of their implications.

Günter Kunert (b. 1929) barely survived the war in Berlin, being half Jewish according to the Nazi lists. After 1945 he studied applied art, published his first satirical poems in Brecht's manner, and also wrote widely for GDR media. In *Tagwerke* (1961; *Works and Days*) he had high hopes for the noble cause of humanity advanced by poets, explorers, and technicians, yet his affirmations of a glorious socialist future were shot through early by a growing awareness that people, being frail, dive into the light "like snapshots, for one hundredth of a second," then fall into "dark eternity again." As early as 1960 he was attacked for his bourgeois attitudes, allegedly close to those of Rilke (though Kunert actually preferred to study Carl Sandburg, Edgar Lee Masters, and Edgar Allan Poe); a few years later, his poems were condemned as "existentialist" by a member of the Politburo. He was allowed to go to the University of Texas at Austin and also to a British university as resident writer in the early and mid-1970s, but, like so many of his generation, he signed the pro-Biermann petition and so was expelled from the SED. In 1979 he received a government visa to move to West Germany, where he resides today. In his poems of the 1970s and early 1980s, including *Warnung vor Spiegeln* (1970; *A Warning of Mirrors*), *Abtötungsverfahren* (1980; *Process of Mortification*), and *Stilleben* (1983; *Still Life*), he presents fragmentary views of landscapes, and ossified and sclerotic people threatened by violence, bureaucracy, and the withering away of their own bodies. In his many essays, above all in his *Verspätete Monologe* (1980; *Delayed Monologues*), published shortly after his move to the West, he has turned to an archaeology of our culture (often taking his cue from the later Freud) and exposes the mythical patterns in our concepts of history, Marxist and non-Marxist alike. His hometown Berlin has become the final emblem of change: once "happiness lay in ambush" there, but now "everything is surveyed, filed away, and torn down/ and there is nothing left/ to describe."

In the late 1960s the predominance of the poem committed to

social action was increasingly challenged by many writers, or rather artists, of "concrete texts" that were widely discussed internationally at the time. Concrete poetry was created to show and explore the particular materials of speaking and writing, and inevitably implied theories of anthropology and semiotics, as well as new ideas about the qualities of phonic and graphic signs in communications of meaning. The first signals that a younger generation was eager to resuscitate some of the concerns of the European avant-garde of *entre deux guerres* came from Vienna, Sweden, and Switzerland. It was the Swiss writer and industrial designer Eugen Gomringer (b. 1925) who, in a sequence of publications including *konstellationen* (1953; *constellations*, 1968) and *ideogramme* (1960), produced an astonishing kind of visual poetry in the traditions of Mallarmé, Marinetti, and the rational Bauhaus. Intent on making a poem a "well-functioning, beautiful object in space," and believing that the traditional expression of feelings no longer had a legitimate place in the rapid tempo of communication, Gomringer revived arguments against the burdens of the sentence and of syntax in general. He scattered isolated words (often of the most homely kind, like "tree," "child," and "flower") over the white page in aesthetically effective patterns or in strictly regulated configurations, and hoped to suggest, by the most restricted basic vocabulary, "a considerable number of semantic relationships" and a good deal of psychological tension. Later, in *das stundenbuch* (1965; *the book of hours*, 1968), he revised his concept of the spatial poem as individual object and, taking his cue from more recent ideas of environmental design, developed texts to function in entire systems, working with inventive permutations. Gomringer may have been rash in assuming that his contemporaries would prefer a functional idiom as symbolized in the stark semiotics of international airports, but his spare exercises with the visual elements of texts, classicist in orientation and of reflective wit, have aged more gracefully than his theories of technological mankind.

Helmut Heissenbüttel (b. 1921), a North German of strongly didactic habits and unusual literary erudition, calls his "concrete texts" (whether poems, narratives, or radio plays) "agrammatical" exercises; certainly they are closer to the legacy of Gertrude Stein than to Ezra Pound's ideograms or Kurt Schwitters's phonetic experiments. Heissenbüttel's *Kombinationen* (1954) and *To-*

pographien (1956) were documents of poetic conflicts in his own consciousness, mobilizing against each other the emotions of his early poetry, often Rilkean, and a harsh constructive intention that rearranges traditional verse in skeptical collages or in structures of repetition. Heissenbüttel knows the history of the European and American avant-garde from Kandinsky to John Cage better than anybody else in Germany. His theories of writing, defined in *Über Literatur* (1966; *About Literature*) and *Zur Tradition der Moderne* (1972; *On the Traditions of Modernity*), are at times far more convincing than the practical repertory of his wide-ranging linguistic experiments in *Das Textbuch I–VI* (1960–67; *Texts: Selections*, 1977); his witty quasi-novel *D'Alemberts Ende* (1970; *D'Alembert's End*), about a group of Hamburg intellectuals; or the epic games with the morphology of folk tales in *Eichendorffs Untergang und andere Märchen* (1978; *Eichendorff's Demise and Other Fairy Tales*). Heissenbüttel believes that language has changed rapidly in our age, losing internal cohesion so as to isolate individual words and accentuate "vocabulary." Individuality itself has withered away; the speaking subject is being reduced to a "batch of speaking habits"; and closer attention to modern articulation reveals its "hallucinatory elements," triggered by the irritations of the world.

Paradoxically, defenders of language experiments were most innovative when competing with political activists, rightly arguing that an advancing analysis of linguistic "materiality" radically contributed to knowing the true functions of verbal communication. By the early 1970s, however, readers and publishers were getting tired of emancipatory experiments, so that most practitioners of concrete poetry, among them Franz Mon, Heinz Gappmayr, and Diter Rot, retired to small, highly specialized magazines. Even Heissenbüttel has not entirely resisted the new temptation of writing autobiographical poems and timely stories that can be read and pondered with much intellectual pleasure and few irritations.

The poetry of political activism and the revealing demonstrations of concrete writing were not entirely balanced by a third kind of protest poem, the Beat writing advanced by Rolf Dieter Brinkmann (1940–75) and a few of his allies, including Wolf Wondratschek and Uwe Brandner. Brinkmann, who came from a North German town, settled in the early 1960s in Cologne and, guided by Dieter Wellershoff, tried his hand at a few prose texts and a novel that were read as "new realism" in the wake of the French *nouveau roman*. In the intellectual unrest of the late 1960s, he was one of the few younger people who reached out to the writers of the United States counterculture rather than to the European Marxists of the thirties. He admired and translated Frank O'Hara, Charles Bukowski, and William S. Burroughs, and edited the much-discussed anthologies *ACID* (1969) and *Silver Screen* (1969). In his own collections of poetry he wanted to quicken the demise of old forms and metaphysical attitudes by a new kind of imagism "catching momentary impressions" in "snapshots," precise, firm, and "translucent"; he advocated "no more big emotions," but "small momentary excitations." Whatever was alive in the world lived in the solitary moment; in his publications *Godzilla* (1968) and *Die Piloten* (1968; *The Pilots*), Brinkmann combined text with photos, occasionally pornographic, and with comic strips in a desperate effort to stop time as it flowed away in linear writing by stills transfixed on surfaces. In his anarchic rage he kicked, screamed, went through the entire drug repertory of the "scene," and within three or four years, as the radical floods subsided, found himself without friends, publishers, or means of subsistence, being dependent on handouts, or on fellowships in Rome and at the University of Texas at Austin, which always welcomes new German talent. He was killed in a car accident in London on his way home in 1975; his posthumous collection *Westwärts 1 & 2* (1975; *Westward 1 & 2*) was praised by many critics stunned by his death. *Westward 1 & 2* balances formal experiments of many kinds; rich meditative poems sustained by their own rhythms of sorts (often articulated in the synchrony of two columns on the page) and more traditional quatrains; idyllic tales from far countries ("Oh, peaceful noon"); and snapshots of the foggy, crumbling cores of American cities. He was ever aware of "sunflowers and express trains speeding through dark flatlands," which reminded him of American poetry.

From the frustrations and defeat of the late sixties protest movement, a new lyrical attitude emerged, more or less shared by younger writers in the Federal Republic, Austria, and Switzerland. Changes were not abrupt, and the defenders of the new kind of writing, firmly coalescing in the mid-1970s, cited Walter Höllerer's programmatic demand (1965) for a "long" and "republican" poem open to timely interests and using everyday speech, and the achievements of R. D. Brinkmann's later poems, seen as initiating an exemplary way of confronting experience. Jürgen Theobaldy (b. 1944) defined the new assumptions as critic, editor, and practicing poet in his *Veränderung der Lyrik: über westdeutsche Gedichte seit 1965* (1976; *The Transformation of the Lyric: On West German Poetry since 1965*), a collaboration with Gustav Zürcher; in his remarkable anthology of contemporary verse, *Und ich bewege mich doch* (1977; *And Yet I Move*), gathering contributors from virtually three generations; and in his own verse collections, which deviated more and more from his own theoretical norms.

Theobaldy's poetry, as seen in *Blaue Flecken* (1974; *Bruises*), *Zweiter Klasse* (1976; *Second Class*), *Schwere Erde, Rauch* (1980; *Heavy Earth, Smoke*), and *Die Sommertour* (1983; *The Summer Tour*), clearly shows the virtues and limitations of the new sincerity, proudly insisting on a modest thematic range and distrustful of fantasy and all antiquated ideas of art. Having worked as an apprentice in an industrial plant before studying to become a schoolteacher, Theobaldy describes how in the factory he secretly escaped to the men's room to write poetry about boxing matches, fairs, and lovers lost under the arches of bridges. Theobaldy's poems of the seventies are above all urban snapshots (or Brinkmann mellowed); nature is highly suspect (unless the sea can be revealed as "tourists' piss"), and trees grow only in backyards. His poetic consciousness productively enjoys a certain claustrophobia while thriving in small apartments, desolate parks with empty beer cans in the bushes, and corner *Kneipen*. The poet takes hopeless train rides from one city to another (carefully dated to confirm authenticity) and nurses sober feelings of love: "I would wish to write a short poem, one in four or five lines . . ./ one that says everything about both of us/ and yet betrays nothing/ about you or me." In his collections of the early eighties, Theobaldy does not avoid the artful, in the traditional sense, as programmatically as he did earlier. There are stanzas, rhymes, and poems indubitably resembling sonnets. Going back to Catullus and the great modernists of his own century, Theobaldy now impresses by a new finesse of perception (the "warm handles" of knives in the sun) and develops a compressed, allusive speech that combines hopes for a new serenity with the lyrical power of epigrammatic evocation, "smiling, smoking, hanging around with each other/ lust for beauty, sometimes, ancient pictures." In the best of his dry poems we are close to an almost Anacreontic enjoyment of the "big chill" of our social failures, sustained by an elegiac memory of the late sixties, and by the ascetic praise of small daily things and events—not, of course, Rilke's "jug" and "threshold," but a can of tuna, a dish of ravioli, and above all old Westerns, however reactionary their ideological implications may be.

The years from the mid-1950s to the mid-1960s were, in all German-speaking countries, the most productive time for poetry energetically recuperating from earlier devastations. The student revolt, by transferring imagination to the streets and proscribing it in writing, turned almost an entire generation of writers and readers to other genres and, by preferring spontaneity and sincerity to art and technique, made it difficult for the poets of the seventies to go beyond a reportage idiom without metaphors and allusions. Yet by defining the literary expectations of a whole age group, the student revolt was also responsible for a radical democratization of poetry in the early 1970s. Writing poetry ceased to be the privilege of the elite; women and men of all ages were encouraged to write and publish; handmade little volumes were typed and xeroxed; and people were not afraid to start from scratch. (Unfortunately West Germans, unlike American or GDR writers, do not accept the unromantic idea of poetry workshops.) At the same time, poetry in local and regional dialects (once cultivated by elderly schoolteachers on the conservative side) made a strange and surprising comeback everywhere. Local dialects were first rediscovered, as special phonetic material, by many experimenters in Austria and Switzerland more than twenty years ago. Later, however, they were used by younger people eager to communicate with close friends in their neighborhood or with fellow participants in regional protests against nuclear plants, U.S. military installations, or other enemies of the environment. (Once a sign of the Right, dialect now indicates the populist Left, whether red or green.) These are years of slow poetic rejuvenation rather than moments of great poetry to compete with that of Robert Lowell, Yves Bonnefoy, or Joseph Brodsky, but gifted younger poets are certainly in the making. Michael Krüger, Ursula Krechel, Peter Salomon, Ulla Hahn, Fritz Deppert, and Michael Buselmeier (not to mention the many gifted GDR writers whom I consider elsewhere) have gone far in writing poetry of independence and originality.

NICOLAS BORN

Among the younger poets and writers of the 1970s, Nicolas Born (1937–79) went far beyond the self-imposed limitations of the everyday poem without metaphors; his untimely death from lung cancer deprived German writing of a distinct voice of unusual promise and independence. Born in Duisburg in the Ruhr, he was trained as a technical expert in chemigraphy (a process involved in the printing of books), but then went on long journeys to Greece and Turkey and by the mid-1970s settled in West Berlin. Though he never studied at a university, he actively sympathized with the students' demands, and while he later stressed that he was not a Marxist, he shared his friends' opposition to corporations and multinationals. Believing in a friendly socialism without "bureaucracy and symbols," he at times felt close to anarchist ideas, yet in the years of terrorism told his radical friends that the republic was definitely not a police state of the fascist kind. As a writer, he first joined the young authors affected by the *nouveau roman* (under the guidance of Dieter Wellershoff), then later participated in the activities of the Berlin Literary Colloquium organized by the critic Walter Höllerer. He survived precariously on occasional fellowships until the success of two novels, *Die erdabgewandte Seite der Geschichte* (1976; *The Far Side of History*) and *Die Fälschung* (1979; *The Deception*, 1983), somewhat eased his lot. (The first novel is about the difficulties of loving; the later one, made into a remarkable movie, relates the private and professional experiences of a West German reporter in war-torn Beirut.) Between 1967 and 1972 he published three volumes of poetry that were increasingly independent of his predecessors and friends R. D. Brinkmann and Jürgen Theobaldy. His collected *Gedichte 1967–1978* (1978; *Poems 1967–1978*) include a number of lyrical sketches and scattered fragments clearly showing that he was well on his way to a new kind of hermetic poetry, in full and productive sympathy with Pablo Neruda, Ernst Meister (the lonely West German survivor of the difficult poem), and Sarah Kirsch. In 1979 he told a friend that he hoped to live one or two more years, but his days were cut short.

Knowing industrial production from firsthand experience rather than from theories about it, Born, in his many essays and reviews, rises against the "world of the machine" like a Luddite, but his arguments are far less simple than those of many of his contemporaries. He sees social life as dominated by the "megamachine," which mercilessly determines the lives even of those who possess its tremendous power, and he believes that it has transformed our experience into a "labyrinth." We live in a "psychedelic space of collective stimuli, devices, and vibrations in which we respond by reflexes, signals, and slogans," and are condemned to live in a pseudonature of "unbreathable air, undrinkable water, and sterile soil." In his early collections *Marktlage* (1967; *Market Conditions*) and *Wo mir der Kopf steht* (1970; *I've Got My Head Screwed On*), Born theoretically accepted the ideas of his generation about what a simple poetic text should do, but in actual writing he was, from the beginning, far more relaxed than his irritated age group. In his poem "Berlin 1966," whose title announces timely political interests, he surprises us by anticipating much later moods of self-ironic contentment: "tired of truth/ we praise the gardens again/ turn to girls and visit people/ we like." Talking perhaps of his own life, he speaks of "diseases, quiet, and definite/ with the sweet smell of used cars and churches"; yet cafés and the rain invite thoughtful moments, and "an especially beautiful flower" triggers associations of happiness and solidarity: "tonight the lamps will be burning brighter/ good news will arrive/ and kind acquaintances." In the second collection, Born's resistance to the activist poem perceptively stiffens: he suggests that it is foolish to demand that poets either write socially effective verse or none at all. In the long poem "Da hat er gelernt was Krieg ist sagt er" ("There he has learned what war is he says"), he returns to memories of his father, who returned late from the war and was "successful in giving his children the wrong education." He sees himself in the new role of father watching his own child ("sometimes you look at me/ as if you knew everything already"), and more than once considers what it means to write a poem instead of committing oneself to social action like so many others: "I believe this poem cannot be used for anything/ I believe that it is just a poem for me."

Born accompanied his later writing by postscripts and remarks in which he suggested that, in the process of "losing illusions," the poem itself turns out to be the "reliable" thing, retaining something of the "primal," the "mythical" element of language not yet totally mobilized for everyday functionality. Impressions of city life and the usual "snapshots" have become rare or are taking on a symbolic reference long denied. The descriptive and narrative poems change to meditations that another decade would have called philosophical. Single lines and poems stretch out into resonant questions about how individual consciousness differs from that of others in the contemporary moment of history. In restlessly pressing monologues often organized rhetorically as litanies, Born probes the possibility that his self consists of what it could have been in many shapes and of what it actually turned out to be: "you are all the colors and races/ you are the widows and orphans/ . . . you are alone and you are everybody/ you are your death and you are the Big Desire/ you are the plan which you unfold and/ you are your death." Mere facts, once so important, are now disqualified as "painful" and "boring." Yet an honest search for ourselves has become more difficult than ever: ". . . did we question ourselves enough?/ shall we be a question radiating far/ an end/ is everybody a question/ and is every question a question about everybody?" In the last years of his life, Born for the first time gladly confessed that he wanted to write "beautiful poems" and that, against all expectation, some of them indeed turned out to be beautiful. Among them I would include many of his poetic fragments: "When I die I want to be alone/ untouched, unblurred/ not a word/ everything should look genuine."

SARAH KIRSCH

Sarah Kirsch, born Ingrid Bernstein in 1935 at Limlingerode in the southern Harz Mountains, began to write in close touch with the gifted sixties GDR generation of Saxon poets, including Volker Braun and Karl Mickel, but later went her own way. She worked in a sugar refinery before studying biology at the University of Halle, and continued her training at the Johannes R. Becher Institute, a school for writers where she worked with the poet Georg Maurer in 1963–65. Later she lived in Halle and East Berlin. After joining other party members in petitioning the GDR government to reconsider its measures against the poet Wolf Biermann, she received permission from the authorities to leave for West Berlin, where she lives today, like so many other GDR writers of her generation, in an uneasy state of abeyance, not quite in exile but not at home either. She has published seven collections of poems and poetic prose texts (difficult to separate from lyrical poetry) but also, in her early years in the GDR, tales for adults and children, reportages from industrial experience, and translations from Russian. In her documentary prose text *Die Pantherfrau* (1973; *The Panther Woman*) she transcribed, from authentic tapes, the lively memoirs of five women: a trainer of wild animals in a state circus; a political functionary (actually, the *Kaderleiterin* supervising political work in Brecht's Berliner Ensemble); a member of parliament; a plant manager; and a factory worker. These are texts in the tradition of Oscar Lewis, Studs Terkel, and (in West Germany) Erika Runge, but Kirsch prefers the example of Maxim Gorki and his efforts to preserve revolutionary experience "realistically" and without fear of everyday dialect used in moments of true excitement.

Kirsch published her first verse with that of her husband in 1965. In *Landaufenthalt* (1967; *A Stay in the Country*), the first collection of her poems published independently, she continues the romantic tradition with a strong dash of self-irony, firm rhythms rather than soft music, and the striking precision of the expert who knows every tree, bird, and flower by a specific and often marvelously allusive name. Her nature poems are never distant from German history and the realities of the "little neighborly country" in which she lived; from train windows she watches "the translucent trees/ easy to wound" and praises the little flower gardens, carefully tended by signalmen and station masters, as welcome signs of friendship and humanity. But Kirsch, who changed her first name from Ingrid to Sarah in sympathy for the victims of Nazi persecution, has not forgotten the past. The snow is always black in the cities, she suggests, but white on the graves of the Jews. In her poem "Der Milchmann Schäuffele" ("Milkman Schäuffele"), somewhat reminiscent of Paul Celan, she confronts us with the spectral figure of a survivor who has buried his dead and many other corpses and now dispenses milk from his covered wagon, hoping (in a dialogue with the writer) that Kirsch will give him a family again by the sheer power of her imagination. The poet thinks of fairy tales as if they could happen now (mounting her nylon coat to fly over the countryside and land in the bed of a handsome blacksmith who gives her a piece of fragrant soap) and celebrates the opulence of each season: "sweetly, the summer in my window reaches/ his hand spread out like linden trees/ offering honey to me and leaves, swirling." A strong, proud sense of her body strengthens her ironies: she smokes a lot, likes her drinks and her men strong, and confesses an inclination "to lie down on her desk, to drink red wine until the morning birds scream."

Kirsch's *Zaubersprüche* (1972; *Magic Spells*) was discussed more often by friendly critics in the Federal Republic (where the general turn to private affairs coincided with the intimate tone of much of her new poetry) rather than in her homeland, where official reviewers grew weary of her independence. Many of her new poems still speak of trips to Soviet Georgia, a writers' conference at Lake Okhrid (aging Viktor Shklovski nimbly jumping ashore from a fishing boat), or Lenin's white cat, but she hints at having lost many friends: "in the beginning my nature was carefree and happy/ but what I have seen pulled my mouth/ down to my feet." She misses a collective audience: only "sailors and drivers" nod when she speaks, and later even they fall silent. The most impressive of her new poems are about the hopes and treacheries of love. She delights in witches' incantations, curses, and spells to punish the unfaithful ("frost, rain, and mire on your feet, you of the thin skin"), and enjoys magic formulas to attract a disloyal lover to her red sofa, where they could test again their powers in the struggles of love. An inveterate and restless traveler, Kirsch has continued her habits in the West. Although many of her American poems in *Erdreich* (1982; *Earth Realm*) strike me as merely descriptive and lacking in her earlier intensity, she has a strong voice and an irrepressible imagination, only strengthened by her allegiance to Mayakovski, Annette von Droste-Hülshoff, and occasionally Celan and Brecht. As a writer, she has always belonged to that ancient Green party which hopes that forest, lilac trees, and sea will offer us protection from the onslaught of history, newspapers, and bulldozers of every kind.

8

AUSTRIA: SOCIETY AND LITERARY LIFE

When the Hapsburg monarchy withered away in the fall of 1918, German-speaking Austrians did not believe that an Austrian republic could survive economically and politically. On November 12, 1918, the new republican parliament, dominated by the Socialists, unanimously declared that German Austria (Deutsch-Österreich) considered itself an integral part of the revolutionary Germany emerging from the Wilhelmine empire. The Allies insisted on independence and in the early 1920s contributed, surely too little, to strengthening the faltering Austrian economy. They were unable to change the new economic patterns of central Europe (the key industries of the former monarchy were now located in Czechoslovakia) or to solve the problem of structural unemployment, which resulted in mounting social and political conflicts. In the civil war of 1934 the "Blacks" defeated the "Reds" by shelling the housing developments in Vienna-Floridsdorf (once the pride of socialist urban planning), by keeping the railways running, and by easily shifting police and regular army units from one region of Austria to another. Growing Nazi pressure in the mid-1930s compelled Austrians of the Right and Left to think again about what was unique in their cultural heritage and political hopes. The "Christian corporate state," whatever its many unchristian vices, defined itself by a strong patriotism, with emphasis on ideas of the "Austrian people" and a "Christian-German civilization" distinct from German National Socialism. Only a few days before the Germans marched in, Austrian Conservatives and Socialists, who suddenly emerged from illegality, were unanimous in wanting to defend Austrian political and intellectual integrity against Nazi violence. It was too late: in Salzburg and elsewhere, the German army was welcomed by happy girls in freshly ironed dirndls (historic scenes somewhat understated in *The Sound of Music*), while the Viennese turned out in force to listen to Hitler raving on the Heldenplatz, and the Viennese Jews, including Chief Rabbi Israel Talglicht, were forced by many of their fellow citizens to wash the dirty pavements on their knees. In early April the first special train left Vienna to deliver Austrian patriots, arrested by advance units of the Gestapo, to German concentration camps. These camps turned out to be the most important training institution for an entire generation of the Austrian political elite that would take over in the spring of 1945.

Among the writers, the endemic conflicts between the few organized Nazis, their many nationalist collaborators, and the liberals (everybody else, including the many Jewish intellectuals of Vienna) had been articulated on the international scene at the P.E.N. Club congress at Ragusa, Yugoslavia, in 1933, and at a subsequent Vienna meeting during which the hard-core nationalists left the organization. The corporate state offered a fragile and brief respite. After the civil war of 1934 a first wave of militant Socialists left the country, to be at first welcomed in the Soviet Union and then killed off in the Stalinist purges. Many writers who had to leave Germany in the late winter and spring of 1933 settled in Vienna (where they were occasionally invited to Alma Mahler-Werfel's soirées) or in pleasant Salzburg villages, before having to escape again overnight in March 1938 to Switzerland, France, England, Israel, or the United States. During the war the Nazis and their allies, including the gifted poet Josef Weinheber (who killed himself when the Soviet army came close to his home in Lower Austrian Kirchstetten, where W. H. Auden later resided for many years), ruthlessly controlled literature and the arts, and the authorities pushed their favorite rustic writing of "Blood and Soil," long anticipated by many Austrian peasant novels. Hitler hated "red Vienna," where he had spent many years in restless obscurity learning his anti-Semitic and pan-German lessons among the Viennese *Lumpenproletariat*, but Baldur von Schirach, leader of the Hitler Youth, Viennese Gauleiter, and maudlin poet, wanted Vienna once again to be the center of the arts. During the *Kristallnacht* in early November 1938, forty-two Viennese synagogues were burned to the ground. Eichmann's Zentralstelle (Central Office) forced more than 100,000 Jewish citizens to emigrate before the beginning of the war and later organized the deportations to the death camps. (In November 1942 the old Jewish community of Vienna was dissolved by the authorities; only five hundred Jews survived in hiding.) In the city theaters, performing until the fall of 1944, local actors and producers tried to make a living at some distance from official Berlin. A few sophisticated Willi Forst movies celebrating imperial Vienna, with a dash of Busby Berkeley added, were often interpreted—at least by some people in the audience, myself included—as exercises of independent Austrian art in disguise. Imaginative writing persisted elsewhere: in a Geneva garden house, the impoverished Robert Musil continued writing his novel *Der Mann ohne Eigenschaften* (*The Man without Qualities*), which was never to be finished; in London Erich Fried, later a radical voice of the 1960s generation, wrote patriotic Austrian poetry and studied James Joyce; in an English school Theodor Kramer, who had written verse for the poor and inarticulate "who had no voice," survived as a librarian; and in New York State, Ernst Waldinger taught at Skidmore College and thought of the "cool farmhouse rooms" of Austria with bitter nostalgia.

Austrian resistance inside the country thought of future independence more firmly than the exiles, at least those in the Western world. The Western Allies, belatedly reflecting on what they had not learned in 1918, vaguely discussed a future confederation of south German Catholic states. The Soviet Union, and Austrian exiles in Moscow and among Tito's partisans, held on to the idea of an independent republic without any confederation (more easily to be swallowed up by international communism), and in the Moscow Declaration of October 1943 the Soviet viewpoint more or less prevailed. In Austria the Germans themselves were the most effective teachers of Austrian independence. In 1942, when delegates of the German conservative underground came to Vienna to explore the future, hoping that a conservative Germany without Hitler would include Austria, they were told by representatives of the local resistance that the Austrians were again thinking of a republic entirely their own.

A NEW BEGINNING; THE VIENNA GROUP

The Soviet army, which in the early spring of 1945 was closer to Vienna than a few advance units of the Western Allies, came with detailed plans to organize an Austrian government. The Austrian resistance group 05 had been active in Vienna and the Tyrol shortly before the Allies marched in, but for a while the Soviets incarcerated the independent 05 leaders, who had conveniently gathered at the Vienna Auersperg Palace. In their temporary absence, while the SS still fought on the other side of the Danube, the Soviets established a provisional government entirely along old party lines, with a few important jobs going to Communist functionaries flown in by special plane. But the Communists overrated their popular support, and when the first elections were held in November 1945 (from which old Nazis were excluded), the conservative People's Party (ÖVP) won 85 seats in the parliament, the Socialists (SPÖ) 76, and the Communists, actively supported by the local *Kommandaturas* and the Soviet occupation forces, only 4 (174,000 out of an electorate of 3.4 million).

Austrian independence was again won at a propitious moment shortly after Stalin's death in 1953. Although the local Communists in the late 1940s and early 1950s tried to change the government structure by infiltration (mostly of the Vienna police), their attempts to cripple the elected government through massive street demonstrations, secret negotiations with Conservatives, and (in the fall of 1950) barricades in the streets failed because the Vienna workers, traditionally organized by the Socialists, worked together with students and loyal police to clear the streets. The elections of 1949 had not much altered the predominance of Conservatives (77) and Socialists (67), and the Soviets decided that it was much more useful to have a permanently neutral independent Austria than a minute people's democracy in Vienna and its environs. On May 15, 1955, the new state treaty (*Staatsvertrag*) signed by the Soviets and all the other Allies was shown to the Viennese from the balcony of Belvedere Castle by Leopold Figl, the minister of foreign affairs. By the fall of 1955 all foreign troops were gone from Austrian soil, and a central government ran the country without interference from either side of the demarcation lines that had once separated Soviet and American occupation forces and two distinct ways of life.

As long as money did not have much value and there was nothing to buy on the official market, *Kultur* was favored by nearly everybody. The Allied administrations installed their learned cultural officers, who brought in new plays and arranged tempting buffet suppers for impressionable and hungry artists, and if one nation's cultural officer did not like a play or new manuscript, another might. Hans Weigel, Friedrich Torberg, and Hilde Spiel, influential critics for years to come, returned from exile, and Vienna's ancient attraction for young writers from the Balkan regions (now dominated by Socialist Realism) was undiminished: Milo Dor, a young Serb who had come in a forced-labor contingent during the war, decided to stay on and write in German, and Paul Celan, after leaving his native Bukovina, briefly settled and published in Vienna before going on to France, where he had studied before the war. There was no dearth of cultural information, as long as the Allies provided the newsprint, and the intellectual periodicals *Turm* and *Plan* expressed respectively a more conservative and a more progressive or rather experimental view of the arts. *Turm* was more committed to exploring the great past of Grillparzer and Hofmannsthal, whereas *Plan* (which had first appeared shortly before the Nazis moved in) was loyal to the legacy of the European avant-garde that had survived in the Vienna underground as stubbornly as it did in the shabby cafés of Prague, Bucharest, and Budapest. The rediscoveries of these years were above all Kafka and Hemingway (as in Germany). At the same time the writer Otto Basil and the painter Edgar Jené, coeditors of *Plan*, resuscitated the surrealism of the 1920s and 1930s, which now all but overwhelmed a whole younger generation that had grown up in intellectual isolation. In January 1947 the Vienna Art Club was founded by younger painters and writers, and a pattern of conflicts between traditional and experimental artists was initiated that has yet to disappear from the Austrian scene.

The currency reform of November 1947, making the Austrian schilling more valuable, and the state treaty of 1955 substantially changed the cultural scene. Most of the early periodicals disappeared, the avid reader again became an eager consumer, and the joyful national restoration yielded somewhat ambiguous results. Once again, much energy was expended in exploring the distant or recent past; Joseph Roth, the melancholy Jewish monarchist, had his belated renascence; and unknown novels and stories by Herbert Zand, a remarkable writer in the expressionist tradition, were edited by Wolfgang Kraus, himself a cultural critic of note. Fritz Herzmanowsky-Orlando, who combined the elegiac and the grotesque, was published for the first time, and Friedrich Heer, historian, editor, and later dramaturge at the Burgtheater, in many brilliantly written volumes reconsidered the function of Austria in European intellectual and political developments. The grand old men and undisputed masters of the modern Austrian novel, George Saiko, Albert Paris Gütersloh, and Heimito von Doderer, rather belatedly came into their own and were read with deserved attention. (In the United States few readers know about Doderer's thoughtful exploration of the ideological age in his massive work *Die Dämonen* [1956; *The Demons*, 1961], a novel that competes in technique and substance with Thomas Mann's *Doktor Faustus*.)

The younger generation of Viennese artists felt increasingly frustrated by the constant conjurations of the old monarchy as paradise lost and by glib speeches about Austria's cultural mission in the world. In West Germany, Group 47 was developing as an almost professional organization of politically committed writers, but in Vienna at that time writers, musicians, painters, and producers stuck together in their little jazz cellars and, for better or worse, were more interested in systematically experimenting with their materials than in supporting political parties not particularly interested in their aesthetic pursuits. It is difficult to define the program of what was later called the Wiener Gruppe (Vienna Group), a loose and shifting gathering of friends that attracted public attention by the late 1940s but dispersed in 1964—mostly to West Germany, where rich radio stations and more courageous publishers were eager to support experimental literature.

All these people had studied Dada and Wittgenstein, cybernetics and Gertrude Stein; they disdained what they called "mystification, symbolism, and metaphysics" and were fond of challenging the traditional and irrational assumptions of the arts. In April 1953 H. C. Artmann (superbly talented in producing any style of writing at will, in German and in a number of other languages, some rather obscure) published the "Acht-Punkte-Program des poetischen Aktes" ("The Eight-Point Program of the Poetic Act"). In the mid-1950s the Group was fond of organizing surrealist processions through downtown Vienna, declaiming decadent poetry to shock the solid citizens and then quickly disappearing into their jazz cellars again. Among the Vienna Group, Friedrich Achleitner (b. 1930) combined an interest in architecture with work in Concrete Poetry; Konrad Bayer was a gifted playwright who later committed suicide (1964); Oswald Wiener (b. 1935), a jazz musician, linguist, and mathematician, later wrote *Die Verbesserung von Mitteleuropa* (1964; *The Correction of Central Europe*) to show the problems of narrative language from a linguistic point of view, then went to Berlin to become an innkeeper; and Gerhard Rühm (b. 1930), the true Renaissance artist of the group, produced electronic music, phonetic poetry, and collages, and with admirable erudition theoretically defended what others did more unreflectingly. Within the European context, the Vienna Group had its indisputable importance because it renewed the legacies of the old avant-garde in a new phase of experimentation, at least ten years before the eager West Germans rediscovered Dada and surrealism. By exploring the phonetic richness of local dialects, as H. C. Artmann did in his best-selling *med ana schwoazzn dintn* (1958; *with a black ink*), the members of the Group, in imitation of Federico García Lorca, substantially widened the range of literary idiom. The Group still preferred surrealism to Herbert Marcuse, craft to Hegelian concepts; in spite of what German radicals now say, it is only fair to argue that the Group kept alive a restlessly analytical bent of mind essential to new art and good politics.

THE FIFTIES AND EARLY SIXTIES

Austrian life in the fifties and early sixties was shaped by an almost uninterrupted economic boom, and by a progressive ossification of political experience caused by the joint government of the conservative People's Party and the Socialists in the absence of an active opposition (the Independents, including many nationalists, were occasionally of local importance, but the Communist Party had lost its parliamentary representation by 1959). Austrians assert that by 1974 the standard of living, measured in terms of the individual's buying power, was three times higher than in 1950 or 1937, but economic advances were also based, often paradoxically, on policies of the past and on investments from abroad. The corporate state of the mid-1930s had built up a net of hydroelectric power stations to cover all internal needs; the Germans had systematically created key industries around Linz and Styrian Erzberg; early nationalization laws (1945–46) had protected other German plants from expropriation at least by the Western Allies; and the Marshall Plan, originally approved in Austria even by the weak Communist Party (in some contrast to Czechoslovakia), made possible new investments in industrial production as well as in important tourist services. In the late 1950s there were still striking differences between the east of the country, originally occupied by the Soviets, and the western regions. The population of Vienna decreased substantially and later stagnated, while in the Burgenland industries, once supervised by the Soviets, the average wages by 1961 were still 60 percent below the Austrian average. (These differences have been obliterated now, with the possible exception of the tourist industry, in which the western regions far outdo the eastern landscapes of Lower Austria, that last summer paradise of Western Europe, especially for impecunious American travelers.) After the hungry years, economic advances were ultimately based on sustained productivity and, in turn, on the willingness of the employed to collaborate with the employer. While the Socialists for some time went on paying theoretical homage to their Austro-Marxist past—relinquished, more or less, in the party program of 1958—in practice they were the coarchitects of an elaborate and finely honed system of mutual discussions and institutionalized agreements (*Sozialpartnerschaft*) that have made strikes a rare event in Austria. The institutionalized process of negotiating and keeping the social peace, guaranteed by both employees and employers, reflected, in the economic sphere, the decision of Conservatives and Socialists not to renew the suicidal conflicts of the 1920s and 1930s. Many of the political representatives of both Right and Left had gone through the same Nazi camps and so, once in power, developed a legitimate idea of necessary collaboration. Within a few years, however, this collaboration deteriorated into the much maligned *Proporz*, an ossifying system of totally unconstitutional interparty agreements about issues and people, outside and above parliament. From about 1952 to 1966, when the discredited consensus finally broke down, for every "black" village postmaster there had to be a "red" assistant, or vice versa. People began to speak about a "democratorship" (*Demokratur*) and a red-black state party running everybody's life from the cradle to the grave.

The postwar economic boom and the sharing of political power by the ruling parties did not inevitably strengthen the arts. In spite of official pronouncements, matters of *Kultur* were not of prime importance to either individual citizens or the budget planning of the ruling parties. On March 25, 1954, three thousand Austrian artists, among them the most popular actors of the Burgtheater, marched in protest through the center of Vienna. Ten years later the universities were restive. Yet only after demonstrators had clashed in the streets in the city center, and an old man (who happened to be a former concentration camp prisoner) was mortally wounded by a rightist student, did the government begin to pay more detailed attention to university matters. Most older functionaries of the ruling parties, especially those in the middle ranks, were for a long time unable to grasp the political implications of cultural affairs, if not the essential function of the arts in a civilized society. The absence of the Jewish intellectuals was felt acutely; the last remnants of the old middle classes, with their literate inclinations, had not survived the postwar inflation; and the new, all-absorbing middle strata, of uncertain tastes, was not ready yet for difficult books. Most of the newspapers, especially those published by party headquarters, were unreadable, and a 1972 survey indicated that two thirds of the populace did not read books at all, while those who did preferred the current best sellers of the West German market and (a surprise to Americans) the novels of Pearl Buck.

As in West Germany in the decade of material restoration, in the Austrian fifties and early sixties poetry dominated literary modes. In the writings of Christine Lavant and Ingeborg Bachmann, alternate potentialities of the lyric distinctly emerged. Christine Lavant (1915–73), the ninth child of a poor miner in a forlorn Carinthian valley, used Christian images and thoughts in intensely personal meditations, or rather prayers, articulating inherited religious traditions and burning feelings that alternated between a mystical love and a ferocious hate of God. Unschooled, half-blind, tubercular, and lonely in her village, Lavant wrote for a long time on her own. When she discovered Rilke in 1945, she fell victim to his sweet temptations (as so many writers do) and needed many years to speak again with her own brittle and, as it were, cracked voice, unhesitant in confronting ugliness, evil, and spiritual exhaustion. Her major verse collections—*Die Bettlerschale* (1956; *The Beggar's Bowl*), *Spindel im Mond* (1959; *Spindle in the Moon*), and *Der Pfauenschrei* (1962; *The Peacock's Cry*)—do not suggest an increasing refinement of language, but stations of despair. She rarely uses the social or technological vocabulary of our age, but fills her world with reminiscences of fairy tales, peasant lore, and church hymns. She is not at all a poet of nature ("moon, wind, and birds have done nothing for me"), and often sees herself as a "she-wolf" or "she-fox," "chewing" the weeds of sadness and "barking" her prayers through the cold night. In her later poems, which are all untitled and structured as questions and answers, she concentrates her metaphysical frustrations (as did Paul Celan at the same time in Paris) in a series of compound nouns and adjectives often resisting interpretation (e.g., *Zitterbaum*, *Erz-Angstschrei*, *herzverzwergt*), and defines her art, though suspecting that it is Lucifer's gift, in opposition to God's demands: "crucified on the stones/ I cannot carry a rose-tree." Before she died she studied a good deal of Thomas Merton and Teilhard de Chardin, whose works were provided to her by well-meaning friends. But her best poems always came from a desperate certainty untutored by literature or theology—from her involvement alone, unceasingly, in a dialogue with Abraham's God, powerful and cunning: "you shall have to negotiate with my ashes/ talk to my whining bones/ and discover the password of the smoke . . ."

For a few years Ingeborg Bachmann (1926–73), who is now being rediscovered by a new generation of feminists, overshadowed Austrian and German poets of the time; her two slim volumes, *Die gestundete Zeit* (1953; *On Borrowed Time*) and *An-*

rufung des grossen Bären (1956; *Conjuration of the Great Bear*), were lyrical best-sellers considered representative of the historical moment. She satisfied many expectations: the philosophical friends of literature admired her knowledge of Wittgenstein and Heidegger, demonstrated in her dissertation, and the lyrical existentialists, not exactly rare in the fifties, felt attracted by her cool prophecies of eschatological disasters to come. Bachmann started with Hölderlin, Rilke, and Benn, and often with Hugo von Hofmannsthal's skepticism about what language can do, yet she insisted on her own difficult and often harsh articulations in which images of Austria (rarely specific) blend into heroic and archaic Mediterranean landscapes, while her hymns to the sea and the sun reveal a sharp consciousness of the end of time, demanding that we be cool, stoic, and free of all illusions. There are foggy beaches, rocks, and ships, yet other poems toy with the fashionable vocabulary of city bars and, initiating a strategy later widely imitated, take up tags of everyday idioms, advertising slogans, and lines from old songs and, unmoved by sentimentality, analyze the hidden implications of history that these language fragments preserve. In contrast to Lavant, Bachmann was a cosmopolitan writer who traveled widely, lived in Berlin, New York, and Rome, and moved easily on the international scene with a proud sense of style and, at times, febrile energy. In the 1950s and 1960s she turned to writing radio plays and short stories, gathered in the impressive volume *Das dreissigste Jahr* (1961; *The Thirtieth Year*, 1964).

In her novel *Malina* (1971), which came close to being an intensely personal confession, Bachmann distinctly parted ways with those of her contemporaries who wanted literature to be of only social relevance. Here she withdraws to a little street in the Third District of Vienna (somewhat arcadian); lives with Malina, a meditative man of the past who appropriately works in a museum; yet passionately loves Ivan, who is actively committed to the contemporary world. The volume presents self-revelations and self-tortures in a narrow world of intense and wounded sensibilities, yet has an effective structure: in the first part, the rituals of happiness with Ivan; in the second, terrible dreams of a powerful, fascinating, and brutal father; and in the third, the loss of Ivan and anticipations of death—counteracted throughout by comedy scenes from Viennese cafés, a poetic fairy tale, a philosophic parody of a press interview, and precise observations of how the Austrian aristocracy converse on their *Salzkammergut* country weekends. Hermann Broch once suggested that the true romantics in our age of relativity are those obsessed by the absolute; Bachmann, who said in her 1960 Frankfurt lectures that we should attend "the perfect, the impossible, and the unreachable . . . whether it was love, freedom, or other values," was one of the most resolute, and perhaps desperate, romantic minds of her time. When she died in Rome in 1973, not even her friends knew whether she burned to death in her bed by accident (falling asleep with a lighted cigarette) or whether she committed suicide in the most gruesome way.

OPPOSITION TO THE VIENNESE ESTABLISHMENT: THE GRAZ GROUP

It was no coincidence (the Marxists would say) that the new protest against the *Proporz* culture, organized in Vienna, was articulated in Graz, the Styrian capital close to the Yugoslav border. In 1958–59 the first attempts were made by resident artists to change the old and unused Stadtpark Café into a place for new art and literature. In 1958 a club, the Forum Stadtpark, was established to push the project, and on November 4, 1960, a first public reading was presented which (somewhat reminiscent of the first Dada evening in Zürich in 1916) was a rather conservative event, gathering, among the participating authors, Heimito von Doderer, by then the patriarch of the Viennese novel, and Franz Nabl, a distinguished resident writer of the realist school. By 1961, however, an entire new generation had gathered around the Forum Stadtpark, only later (in 1968) to be called the Grazer Gruppe (Graz Group), though not everybody was from Graz and most, after a brief Graz stint, moved elsewhere, preferably to West Berlin, where the socialist city government was eager to distribute Ford Foundation money to young writers in order to resuscitate the literary life of the burned-out city. Among the younger people emerging from the Forum Stadtpark was Alfred Kolleritsch (b. 1931), a gifted novelist who from 1960 on edited the periodical *manuscripte*, the most important voice of new Austrian writing; Barbara Frischmuth, a learned philologist and sensitive prose writer interested in Lewis Carroll, Virginia Woolf, and renascent feminism; G. F. Jonke (b. 1946), intent on turning the traditional *Heimatroman*, the novel of peasants and hometowns, inside out; and last but not least, Peter Handke, who made his brief appearance here while pursuing his studies of law at the university. All statements about the Graz Group are equally true and false; while the Vienna Group published occasional manifestoes, each of the Graz artists and writers followed his own star; what they had in common, at least in the early years, was unusual talent, a suspicion of the Viennese for becoming enmeshed with Establishment power, and a shared commitment to undermine traditional forms and genres by new practices.

Barbara Frischmuth's *Die Klosterschule* (1968; *The Convent School*) seems far more radical to Austrian readers than to outsiders, who may be inclined to admire its tender qualities. It is an ingenious attempt to show how students live in a Catholic educational institution. It shows middle-class girls brought together in dormitory, chapel, and dining hall; busy sisters who supervise, teach, pray, and talk; erudite teachers of English and Latin; and the ecstasies of puberty and more or less innocent games behind the bushes in the garden. Frischmuth works with three voices that she artfully combines: her own (or rather that of a young girl who willingly submits to religious and educational discipline); the "we" of the girls as a group; and the collective voice of the sisters, who transmit their wisdom to their wards so as to protect them from the snares of the devilish world outside. It would be easy to interpret these prose pieces as an anti-Catholic tract, but even an ideological reading cannot underrate the particular problems of narrative technique: the author absents herself, and what we hear is language, or rather languages, as they reverberate and reassert themselves. As a literary structuralist, Frischmuth isolates language systems and holds them up to us, showing how they function and what kind of clichés they transmit. Paradoxically, the autonomy of language protects speakers and listeners; the issue of truth and untruth resides in communication itself, while girls and nuns move in a world of almost speechless feelings. In spite of their overused and hackneyed language, people come through as warm, innocent, and deeply concerned with each other.

In some contrast to Barbara Frischmuth and Alfred Kolleritsch, G. F. Jonke's *Geometrischer Heimatroman* (1969; *Geometric Home Novel*) shows that some younger writers of the Graz Group (though Jonke comes, like Handke, from Carinthia) continued the more radical efforts of the old avant-garde, heroically kept alive in Austria by the Vienna Group of the late 1940s and 1950s. Jonke's first important novel was a linguistic anatomy of a traditional narrative genre particularly favored by the Nazis—the *Heimatroman*, or village or small-town novel, richly praising the unshakable virtues of the peasants, with blue-eyed maidens (in dirndls according to the region) and, at least in the pre-Nazi phase, a teacher or village priest with a social consciousness seen in soft focus. Jonke tries to construe the abstract genre model (sometimes using pen-and-ink drawings), but ultimately he relies on parody to reveal what is most typical in the recurrent characters, situations, and ideas. Yet parody does not easily transcend what it parodies: negating one text, Jonke simply creates another text with strong affinities to the one negated. While he constantly corrects his own assertions by counternarratives, he succeeds most convincingly when he dons the mask of the local teacher or old-fashioned priest who records, in the community chronicle, how artists visit the place and then leave again, like the hippie visionary who recites something in the village square that sounds surprisingly like modern Austrian phonetic poetry. The "geometric novel" wants to reveal the shabby conventionality of a cherished genre but, with a burst of epic energy unforeseen by theory, and occasional wit, it creates another *Heimatroman* of the reverse kind, entertaining at least for long stretches to the trained reader.

The increasing importance of the *Länder* (provinces) corresponds to the diminishing power of Vienna in federal Austrian politics. The Styrian border regions, which lie close to Hungary and Yugoslavia, have become the home of many gifted writers, whatever their age and literary loyalties. In the late 1970s Klaus Hoffer and Matthias Mander published extraordinary narratives, or rather prose texts, intensely marked by Styrian landscapes and experiences without being in the least provincial. Klaus Hoffer's *Halbwegs: Bei den Bieresch* (1979; *Halfway: At the Biereches'*), the first volume of a larger project, unexpectedly combines the simple story of an outsider in a village community with the most erudite, if cunningly disguised, allusions to contemporary world literature (including Borges, Joyce, and Walter Benjamin) and a distinct concern with the function of language and myth in individual and social life, reflecting a wide range of semiotic and poststructuralist thought without ever, miraculously, sabotaging the reader's interest in the narrator's luminous idiom. A young man travels from the city to the region of the Biereschs, an impoverished clan in a fictional corner of Styria. Following the complex local customs, for a year he takes the place of his deceased uncle, so as to make death more reassuring to the dead. While he sleeps in his aunt's bed and works (like his uncle) as a mail carrier, he encounters many members of the tightly knit Bieresch community, in which small groups and sects are deeply committed to their own particular myths and an incessant effort to understand the true meaning of the inherited stories and parables. Much in the Bieresch conversations sounds like attempts to come to terms with the burdens of Austrian history ("we do as anyone would do who has gone through a terrible shock"), but many of the myths, at times reminiscent of Hasidic legacies, take on linguistic and ontological issues far beyond the local sphere. Hoffer continues Kafka's work, but he has emancipated himself from what may have triggered his imaginative quest, and freely moves in a cryptic world of independent illuminations.

Matthias Mander's *Der Kasuar* (1979; *The Cassowary*) surprised and challenged many readers, for it is not every day that an experienced middle-aged corporate manager writes a substantial and thoughtful book reflecting his personal and professional experience in a restlessly precise prose reminiscent of the best experimental writing of his time. Mander's reflections have a complicated and yet mathematically simple structure composed of what he calls catalogues, preliminaries, reports, complaints, affirmations, letters, and stations, each neatly subdivided as in a filing system; he does not tell a cohesive story but articulates his paragraphs "atom by atom, without center, of crystalline nature, an ordered net." There is nothing naive or homespun about Mander: he is a highly educated engineer who has been active in his corporation (a producer of steel and chemicals) for many decades, yet has a precise knowledge of the masters of the modern novel (Austrian and otherwise). The quiet insistence with which he accumulates bits and pieces of memories, biographies, impressions, and reports about his life creates a convincing image of human relationships in industry that is largely absent from the writings of his younger contemporaries, who do not (as he does) conceive of "strength in one's profession as a symbol of human resilience" in an "inhospitable" world. Thinking of the many file clerks, stenographers, fellow engineers, and administrators with whom he has worked closely for years, he provides a colorful corrective to the schematic projections of the corporate world advanced by many left-of-center writers and certainly demonstrates more radical self-irony than do his younger colleagues. Mander's speaker, or rather writer, is called Rausak, and we have to read his name in the manner of a palindrome—that is, backward—to discover his symbolic self-portrait in the image of a *Kasuar* (cassowary), a large bird incapable of flying and yet armed with sharply shafted wings, a fast runner through the thickets and underbrush, "a strong animal of the flat country, and yet a winged soul." Readers over forty will discover much to consider seriously here.

A THIRD REPUBLIC?

The stationary *Proporz* system obfuscated rather than revealed incisive changes in the Austrian demographic and social structure, but by the mid-1960s the results of these changes were affecting the entire range of public life with rapid force, and even the political parties began, if rather belatedly, to adjust. Many observers now said that the Second Republic, founded in 1945 to restore Austria after the ravages of the Nazi dictatorship and the war, had come to an end and that, as a result of the popular referendum of 1964 (making the media more independent of the political functionaries), the breakdown of the *Proporz* system (1966), and revived tensions between the government and a genuine opposition, a Third Republic, truly modern and genuinely expressive of an industrial society, had come into being. Political life was affected not only by the striking increase in population and industrial productivity in the southern and western regions of the republic, but also by the change in the composition of society itself whereby, following the general pattern in Western European societies, the primary sector was rapidly losing strength while the tertiary or service sector was gaining. By 1974, 50.3 percent of the work force was employed in the service sector.

The structural changes in Austrian society should have strengthened the Socialists, but in the 1966 elections the People's Party won a resounding victory (85 seats to 74 for the Socialists) and constituted its own government for the first time in the history of the postwar republic. The Socialists found themselves suddenly in the opposition and, above all, in dire need of a party reorganization. For many reasons, the Conservatives had effected their own party reform earlier in the 1960s and now were able to project a more timely image to the younger electorate. After the death of Chancellor Julius Raab (Austria's Adenauer), a new generation of party reformers, including the Jesuit-educated lawyer Hans Withalm (b. 1912), the labor functionary Alfred Maleta (b. 1906), and the future chancellor Josef Klaus (b. 1910), took over the organization. These men tried to cope with the insoluble problem of the conflicting interests of peasants, employees, and employers; organized their own groups within the party; and, at least for the time being, convinced the electorate that they constituted an expert team ready to take Austria from wine and waltzes into the electronic age. The Socialists, forced by defeat to reevaluate their policies, elected Bruno Kreisky (b. 1911), who had long been Austria's foreign minister, as their new party chairman. Within four years, by mobilizing the managerial intelligentsia and the strong younger Socialist electorate outside Vienna, Kreisky assured the Socialist Party of an absolute majority for the first time ever (1970: Socialists 81, Conservatives 78; 1971: Socialists 93, Conservatives 80) and became the most popular postwar Austrian chancellor, whom citizens ironically called their "Emperor Bruno." An eminently intellectual politician, he appealed to the young technical and economic intelligentsia, whom he asked to collaborate in defining his program. A man of many contradictions, he is loyal to his friend Willy Brandt but also keeps in touch with a few liberal Democrats in the United States. For reasons best known to himself, he understands Arab aspirations more willingly than Israeli policies (as foreign minister he visited Cairo but not Israel, where his older brother lives). He delights in reading Sigmund Freud, but his favorite book is Robert Musil's novel *The Man without Qualities*. Almost single-handed, and with telegenic elegance, he made

Austrian politics attractive even to intellectuals, yet he has never really aroused much sympathy among the younger writers. Willy Brandt had Grass, but Chancellor Kreisky, who resigned the chancellorship in 1983 to make way for a Socialist/Liberal coalition, always had to be his own best friend.

In the early 1960s, the political functionaries and managers had begun to discover the prestige of *Kultur*, and some efforts were made by successive governments to extend the material advantages of the new welfare state to writers and artists. In the 1970s, literary discussion often deteriorated into polemics about who received subsidies and how much, and the techniques of writing grant proposals were as much a topic in Sankt Pölten or Linz as in the United States. Austrian writers cannot hope ever to have enough readers at home, and West German publishers, especially Suhrkamp in Frankfurt, were important in feeding young Austrian intellectuals. But in the late 1960s the Austrian way of granting public subsidies developed into a complicated system raising many expectations not easily fulfilled. Professional Austrian writers go on making a living mostly by writing for the state-run radio and the TV stations; by the mid-1970s there were forty-two literary periodicals in the small country, ranging from the radical *Wespennest* (*The Wasp's Nest*) to the more balanced *Literatur und Kritik*, all of them at least to some degree supported by the government or other public institutions that also support school readings, Austrian publishers (to help them compete with the West Germans), and younger authors committed to special projects. Authors are right, I believe, in arguing passionately that the support of the arts is skewed in favor of music, opera, and the theater, those traditional darlings of the Austrian sensibility. In the mid-1970s each of the small periodicals received about 20,000 schillings, but at the same time the government paid 388,000 schillings for a new *Don Giovanni* set to be created in Italy and more than 200,000 schillings for transporting the set to Vienna.

In the early 1980s questions of social security, in the wider sense, were of prime importance to writers of both the older and the younger generation. The writers feel that the welfare state should protect working people of uncertain livelihood—in their case, one gained by selling their texts to the media—as effectively as steelworkers and policemen. Following the practical example of their West German colleagues, who systematically began discussing questions of income, taxation, and pensions in the late 1970s, they believe that writers should unionize, just as other working people do, and perhaps constitute their own section in the Austrian Federation of Trade Unions. Close observers believe that, within a short time, 70 percent of all Austrians will depend on wages and salaries. The trade unions are the real power in the country today, and the traditional parties have reason to de-emphasize their "black" or "red" past and compete, in a more or less pragmatic way as Democrats or Republicans would, for the votes of a large but unified petit bourgeois electorate, among which unemployed masses are as absent as picture-book capitalists (in 1982, Austria had the highest density of car ownership in Europe). Even the question whether or not Austria exists as a spiritual idea does not provoke the violent arguments of a generation ago. The older, Herderian cultural idea of Austria, centered on monuments, older literature, and cemeteries, is giving way, at least among the younger generation, to a functionalist concept—Austria as a society operating in a particular way. When Austrians travel, they do not like to be confused with Germans, whatever their views of the Austrian idea might be.

West German radicals are bothered by the absence of a real Austrian student revolt in 1968 (not until the mid-1970s did Austrian Socialists strengthen their position in student organizations). Ulrich Greiner, who himself went through the West German student movement, has written an intelligent essay, "Das Ende des Nachsommers" (1979; "The End of Indian Summer"), in which he tries to define Austrian literature. The title of his essay alludes to the nineteenth-century Austrian novelist Adalbert Stifter, considered by many to be a defender of escapist serenity. Greiner characterizes Austrian literature, in some contrast to German writing, as "unpolitical and artificial, or in other words lacking in relevance." He believes that Austrian "artificiality" is the result of the social resignation and political impotence extending in Austrian history from the late eighteenth century down to at least 1918, but he grievously underrates the great flowering of liberalism after 1866 (recently discussed by Carl J. Schorske) and the Austro-Marxist tradition. Political commitment is not a West German monopoly, and it is a different question entirely whether or not Austrian writers have sustained the traditions of art and imaginative writing, when many of their West German colleagues succumbed en masse to the temptations of liquidating imagination in the name of social utility.

A STRONG PRESENCE

Austrian writers, especially those old enough to have friends among the Vienna Group, have been loyal to continuing language experiments for a longer time than their West German colleagues, who made experimental noises in the late 1960s but were tired of the whole thing five years later. Ernst Jandl and Friederike Mayröcker, the two superstars of the aesthetic revolt (as one of their colleagues called them) have been responsible for sustaining many avant-garde impulses far into the 1980s, but it would be deceptive to suggest that they do not differ in range and intents. In his many recent text collections, from *Laut und Luise* (1966) to *Der gelbe Hund* (1980; *The Yellow Dog*), Ernst Jandl (b. 1925) has been developing a rich and surprising repertory of phonetic, pictorial, and semantic language games proceeding, as it were, from inside tradition and never abandoning a hidden respect for the formal assumptions that such games demonstratively disregard. Traditionalist readers can understand what these games are about without much training, and Jandl's books and LP records (he is a first-rate performer of his phonetic texts) have sold well in Austria as well as in West Germany. His friend Friederike Mayröcker is less accessible. Jandl plays his many games with disarming skill, whereas she has more intensity than range. While it is true that, at least typographically, her recent collections *Je ein umwölkter Gipfel* (1973; *A Clouded Summit Each*) and *Die Abschiede* (1980; *The Partings*) come close to what we call prose, she has never relinquished her fundamental impulse to articulate a contemporary consciousness and the compact togetherness of its conflicting perceptions. Being closer to the legacy of Gertrude Stein than to Dada, she does not exactly invite the reader to share her thought-and-language sphere, which consists of fragments of feelings, impressions, and images, if not the bric-a-brac of contemporary living.

Jutta Schutting (b. 1937, Amstetten, Lower Austria), who studied photography at the Academy of Arts and trained for teaching at the University of Vienna, published her first poetry in the early 1970s and within a decade emerged as a writer of intellectual importance. Her *Liebesgedichte* (1982; *Love Poems*) is for many reasons a central event in Austrian poetry of the 1980s. These long, cryptic, and syntactically complex verses do not indicate whether they are addressed to a man or a woman, but achieve a true balance of unrepressed emotion and a bitter certainty about language spoken between lovers in moments of bliss, but also in the terrible time of alienation and loss. Serenity and fear clash abruptly: "In these two doves, put there on the shoulder of the road, we shall remain together, white on white." Yet the lovers are torn apart when the shadows fall, and like children on a campground "stumble over cords of tents and don't know where to go." Schutting also renews Gertrude Stein's belief in the power of irrevocably naming what is loved, and invents baroque chains of compound nouns to appear in litanies closely related in rhythm to the rituals of the church—"you paw of heaven, clutch of velvet, thorn of silk"—or indulges in a new combinatory language of her own: "You mymyyou, you thousandtimesbelovedeternallyandonandon." Words quickly change, "sentences and clouds are only quotations/ and we, looking into beautiful clouds . . . try to speak of what dissolves and what has shifted/ like our clouds." To speak in a language that we distrust about feelings of uncertain permanence may have become nearly impossible, but Schutting's love poems sound strikingly honest even after Wittgenstein and nearly eighty years of Austrian skepticism about what language can or cannot do.

The strong interest of younger Austrian writers in language experimentation possibly delayed the emergence of a new, socially committed realism of the working people for nearly ten years (at least in comparison with the West German Group 61 and the *Arbeitskreise Literatur*). Michael Scharang, Franz Innerhofer, and Gernot Wolfgruber have written novels of an intensity often absent in the writings of their counterparts in the Federal Republic. Scharang (b. 1941), who comes from a Styrian working-class family, is the intellectual among the new realists and now deliberately writes far below his theoretical sophistication for mass audiences. After completing a Vienna Ph.D. dissertation on Robert Musil, he first tried to use experimental texts in radically criticizing capitalist society. Then, in the early 1970s, he joined the Austrian Communist Party (undeterred by its anti-intellectual bias after 1968) and turned to writing novels about young workers who do, or do not, learn their political lesson on the production floor. In *Charly Traktor* (1973) he tells the story of a confused young worker who, after venting his rage against management in blind violence, comes to see that he can be more useful to future society by banding together with other members of the working class (preferably organized in the CP). *Der Sohn eines Landarbeiters* (1976; *The Farmhand's Son*) offers the corresponding narrative about a proletarian rustic who does not want to learn about solidarity and finally commits suicide.

Franz Innerhofer, born in 1944 at Krimml near Salzburg, profoundly shocked his Austrian readers by an honest and brutal autobiography recording how he grew up as a farmhand and apprentice mechanic in a Salzburg village. In his volumes ironically entitled *Schöne Tage* (1974; *Beautiful Days*, 1976), *Schattseite* (1975; *Shadowside*), and *Die grossen Wörter* (1977; *The Big Words*), he showed what it means to be a modern serf in the countryside (visited by unsuspecting tourists), and what immense courage and strength it takes gradually to develop an articulate self-consciousness unwilling to submit any more to daily coercion and degradation. (The first volume, in which he speaks of himself in the third person, is more powerful in its impersonality than the other volumes, but it is hardly possible to say what is "good" or "better" in these authentic nightmares.) For literary reasons, I prefer the narratives of Gernot Wolfgruber (b. 1944) showing working-class experience in small towns, and especially his *Niemandsland* (1978; *No Man's Land*), describing the attempts of a young working man to acquire higher qualifications and to rise to the white-collar offices, where he finds himself a near alien among the salaried employees. Wolfgruber is a sociological stickler for revealing detail; he concentrates on the different codes of the two worlds in food, dress, cars, language, and lovemaking, and leaves his *Aufsteiger* or "career guy" unhappily suspended between the social realms. I know of no other novel closer to the microscopic, corrosive, and overpowering pressures of what is called central European mobile society.

Among the many gifted writers of the middle generation, Gerhard Roth (b. 1942, Graz) has shown great independence of mind and a fine sense for the virtues and possible limitations of working with inherited genres of writing. Roth wanted to become a physician like his father but later studied computer technology. While leaning toward Peter Handke's ideas of the late 1960s in his early work, he emancipated himself from the burdens of the avant-garde and preferred a more serene mode of narrative close to shared contemporary Austrian experience. He began by exploring schizoid characters and, after a trip to the United States with the playwright Wolfgang Bauer, wrote two "American" novels triggered by his intense identification with Raymond Chandler's Philip Marlowe. In his more recent writings he takes a close look at the difficulties that Austrians of his age have in finding a place, or meaning, in the community. In Roth's later novel *Der stille Ozean* (1980; *The Pacific Ocean*), introduced by a quotation from Herman Melville, we are closer to daily life in the Styrian provinces; from recurrent images of grayish landscapes, aging people, and hunted animals, a paradoxically slow and strong affirmation of neighborly bonds between simple people in the village communities emerges. A surgeon, married and the father of an eight-year-old daughter, has been involved in a malpractice suit; though it is not made clear whether he was found guilty or not, he seeks refuge alone in a village near the Yugoslav border and finds himself, rather reluctantly at first and more willingly later, drawn into the seasonal activities and traditional rites of the country. He is invited to pheasant hunts and marriage dinners; meets the priest, the doctor, and the undertaker (who has made it a practice to buy old things from the bereaved for a small discount in the price of the funeral); and comes close to happiness when he can give medical help to a worker hurt in an accident. Precisely because of the tender and recalcitrant clarity of its humane vision, it is one of the most important novels of the decade. Austrian readers cannot complain about an absence of energy on their literary scene.

9

THOMAS BERNHARD: THE DARK SIDE OF LIFE

In his native Austria Thomas Bernhard has long provoked stock responses from those who intensely love or bitterly hate what he writes or says, and English-American translations of his writings have been publishing flops more often than not. He has asserted that he wanted to irritate people, and since he is a man of absolute ideas and never admits any shades of meaning or nuances of value, we are asked to take him as we find him, with his important novels, more or less trivial plays, and Austrian quirks, or to keep away from him altogether. Commuting between his old farm at Ohlsdorf near Gmunden in Upper Austria and his favorite spot on the terrace of the Café Sacher in the center of Vienna, he has been his own best public relations agent, an expert in biting the hands that feed: when he received the Austrian State Prize as early as 1968, he made headlines with his nasty remarks about literature, culture, and the Austrian nation at large. These recurrent performances tend to hide the complex ways in which a writer of unusual power and devastating independence has been developing since the mid-1950s, when he first published sweetly melancholic verse imitative of his compatriot Georg Trakl and regularly contributed to a local Socialist newspaper without, of course, being a Socialist at all. His early writings clearly culminated in *Korrektur* (1975; *Correc-*

tion, 1978), a disturbing masterpiece that, in spite of George Steiner's fervent pleas, few people have tried to read and even fewer finished. Subsequently, he was content to write plays that at best offered magnificent roles to star actors, and a series of autobiographical narratives very much in the mode of Thomas Wolfe. Only in the early 1980s did he again gather his most productive energies and publish, in close sequence, fictional and autobiographical narratives in which the tragic and the grotesque startlingly combine. Like so many contemporary Austrian authors, he is a rough provincial but an important writer, driven by the most searing intensity of vision and language, and closer to Joseph Conrad and Thomas Hardy than anybody writing in German today.

Bernhard was born in 1931 of Austrian parents in a Dutch home for unwed mothers. His early family frustrations, somewhat reminiscent of those of Peter Handke, may have left their mark on his epic world devoid of happy moments, love, and the true togetherness of women and men. He never knew his father, who later married in Germany and was killed late in the war in Frankfurt an der Oder under circumstances never clarified. For a long time his mother left her son to be brought up by his grandparents. When she returned home with a new husband and the husband's children, she sent Thomas to City Hall every month to pick up the five marks paid out by the state for the support of illegitimate children, "to show him how much he was worth." His childhood and youth in Vienna and in some Bavarian villages and towns close to the Austrian border was blessedly lightened by the presence of his maternal grandfather Johann Freumbichler (1881–1949), who, of Salzburg peasant origin himself, had traveled widely and published a number of novels well received by local audiences. The grandfather was Bernhard's first role model, and the young man wrote his first novel on the decrepit American typewriter that the old man had left to him. During the later years of the war and immediately thereafter, the young student commuted from Bavaria to Salzburg, where he attended a boarding school run by a militant Nazi, and spent much time in the rock galleries that had been drilled by forced labor, where the Salzburgers sought refuge and often died of suffocation during Allied air raids. After the Americans arrived he went on attending his old school, nearly destroyed, which was now run by the Catholic clergy.

By 1947 Bernhard, feeling totally frustrated by his academic training, dropped out of school, began working as a grocer's apprentice, and was happy for the time being because the grocer's shop was located in the most plebeian neighborhood of the city, where he felt at home among the lonely and underprivileged. When his dying grandfather was transferred to the hospital, Bernhard was taken ill himself (he is quick to explain his experience in psychosomatic terms) and spent three years in hospitals and TB sanitaria definitely unlike the elegant place in Mann's *Magic Mountain*, being shabby hells peopled with emaciated ghosts scurrying around with fever charts and sputum bottles. In the early 1950s he studied music and acting at the Vienna Academy and the famous Salzburg Mozarteum, wrote an examination paper on "Artaud and Brecht," published three volumes of poetry, and for the Salzburg *Demokratisches Volksblatt* wrote mostly court reports but also many news items about official cultural events and local poetry readings. In 1963 his first novel was welcomed by Carl Zuckmayer, the grand old man of German drama, as a first-rate achievement. After a good deal of restless traveling in the Balkans and Poland, places not fashionable then among his contemporaries, Bernhard settled on his farm in Upper Austria, where he still resides today. He hates Austria, or so he says, but he has never tried to live or write away from the landscapes of his early youth.

Bernhard's first novel, *Frost* (1963), counteracts his own lyrical beginnings and all the rustic affirmations of traditional Austrian literature in general. Early critics praised Bernhard's power in showing the dark forests high up in the craggy Salzburg mountains (as if he were a writer of the peasant life like his grandfather), but it is closer to the truth to say that he stares, and forces us to stare with him, at a landscape of death suddenly revealing itself like a massive black summit. A young medical student is sent up from the valley, where he is being trained in the hospital, to a mountain village to check on a painter who has withdrawn from the cities, his art, and his friends into utter loneliness. What he discovers up there goes far beyond medical textbook expectations. He explores, he says, what cannot be explored: the painter takes him on his daily walks through fogs, forests, and ravines, and he listens to the desperate man's raging monologues, nurses him when he is exhausted, and learns from him about the people in the villages, all treacherous, ugly, sick, or doomed. Through the artist, the medical student learns about death in every shape and kind: he is shown the stinking poorhouse, where old people die on the floor; the place where the village animals are slaughtered; and the spots in the forest where, during the last days of the war, hundreds of horses were killed, and slain soldiers were found, their tongues cut out and their penises stuffed in their bloody mouths. The student is spared nothing: the painter drags him to the funerals of those whose skulls were crushed in accidents or who were burned in bonfires, and talks relentlessly of the great frost that will ultimately destroy the world: "People will freeze to death in midsentence, . . . in the midst of crying for help . . . and the stars will shine like nails with which the heavens have been shut closed." One day the painter disappears in the forest; the gendarmerie looks for him listlessly, then after a few days gives up the search because of the fog. Did the painter commit suicide or was he killed in an accident? The medical student cannot answer the question, not even to himself. He decides to leave this world of valleys and darkness and goes to Vienna to conclude his studies there.

In *Frost* Bernhard early defined most of his central interests of an ontological kind (or rather their radical negation), his narrative procedure, and a few stock figures and leitmotivs. It has been argued that, within the Austrian context, he was among the first to create a "black" *Heimatroman* and to subvert the traditional novel of noble peasants and eternally blue skies above majestic mountains, yet he was not content to merely end a literary genre; his real purpose was to relentlessly sabotage any possible affirmation of life itself. The painter despairs of art, love, Austria, communism, the world. In one overpowering gesture, a curtain is flung open and life, human existence, nature, and the flesh are revealed as mere forms of something indescribably indecent and rotten. Writing turns out to be a way of showing the destructive forces of being, disguised as disease of body and mind, the instinct of murderers, the last confessions of people about to kill themselves. Bernhard's narrative procedure, first established in *Frost* and used later for more than twenty years, involves the report of a willing or unwilling witness who observes and listens closely. In *Frost* it is the medical student who for twenty-seven days takes down in his notes what he hears of the painter's monologues. In later books there will be others, sons, acquaintances, and friends, who let the author avoid an unmediated encounter with the protagonist by relating his thoughts and sayings in indirect speech, and only rarely in direct quotations. These witnesses, and those speaking, will all be men because, in Bernhard's narrative world, intimacy, trust, and what is called friendship are possible chiefly among men, rarely among men and women. The landlady in the decrepit inn is a slob who buys dog food from her lover to serve to her guests. She anticipates a whole chorus of dubious women, unkempt, with open blouses, smelly, of pitiful intelligence but rapacious desires—unless, of course, they are sisters, and their brothers are bound to them by deep feelings, open or repressed. The structure of these relationships comes close to resembling those in spaghetti Westerns, with their archaic tribal laws.

In his novels of the late 1960s and early 1970s, *Verstörung* (1967; *Gargoyles*, 1970) and *Das Kalkwerk* (1970; *The Lime Works*, 1973), as well as in some of the accompanying shorter narratives including *Ungenach* (1968) and *Watten: Ein Nachlass* (1969; *Watten: A Legacy*), Bernhard does not necessarily expand his range but trains himself in concentration and intensity; narrative procedure does not essentially change, and the witness report and untrammeled speeches continue to constitute the basic parts of the texts. In *Gargoyles* Bernhard works with a curious story of ascent and revelation. A country doctor takes his son, a mining student, on his daily rounds in a Styrian valley; on the way he visits a few friends, then finally ascends a high mountain to see old Prince Saurau in his castle of Hochgobernitz. The prince's monologues, disordered and despairing, fill nearly two thirds of the book and suddenly break off without a distinct conclusion. It is a quest novel in disguise or, better still, in reverse: in a letter to his father, the young mining student has asked him to be more open in their relationship (especially in regard to his sister, who is on the brink of madness); the father's decision to take his son along may well be, as the critic Bernhard Sorge suggested, an oblique way of answering the son's letter by showing him what the world, unfortunately, is all about. In the valley they encounter the dying, the crippled, the diseased, the murderers (an innkeeper's wife has been killed by a drunken miner), and a few absurd attempts to resist the curse burdening all humanity (a Jewish real estate agent has settled there in his "private hell," and an industrialist busies himself writing a philosophical treatise that he revises day after day). Meanwhile, high on the mountain, the schizoid prince surveys the landscape from his turrets and deplores the decay of Hochgobernitz, which, like all Austria, was once a center of arts and aesthetic pleasures, "a high point of its history in history," and now has no future at all. The prince has doubled the estates of his forefathers but fears that his son, returning one day from his sociological studies abroad, will mercilessly disperse and destroy the great property, since he has been "trained for destruction" and has no more use for what once was "the most precious, the most demanding, the most astonishing." There is not much consolation that the young mining student may take home: history ultimately lacks meaning, and if we look for a human being, it is, the prince believes, "as if we were looking around constantly in a giant morgue."

In *The Lime Works* Bernhard resolutely works with narrative indirection and recurrence; the result is a grim book that disinvites rather than welcomes the resilient reader. A loner has shot his ailing wife at Christmas, people in the neighborhood talk about his strange ways, and a busy insurance agent who never forgets to pride himself on his sales gathers what is being said in the local inns and by those who have known the murderer from his earlier days. For a long time, it seems, Herr Konrad wanted to buy the lime mill, because he desired nothing more than total isolation in order to concentrate on his studies. After living in the big cities of Europe, he squandered much of his inheritance to buy the decrepit mill, moved in with his crippled wife, and transformed the old lime mill into a fortress of solitude: new locks were bought, iron grills installed, a gun collection started, and high bushes planted around the walls. For ten years or more, Konrad had planned to write an exhaustive study on the auditory sensibilities; he had excerpted hundreds of books, and in his isolation terrorized his helpless wife with daily experiments according to the Urbantschitsch Method developed for the hard of hearing, only to recognize that his experiments were useless. When his wife wants him to read to her from a

Romantic poet, he responds by forcing her to listen to his readings of the Russian nihilist Kropotkin. Totally obtuse about what he is doing to her, he calls marriage "the means of nature to achieve torture by nature." (It may have some etymological meaning that his terror mill is located near Sicking, which phonetically resembles Silling, Sade's castle of unspeakable horrors in *The Ten Days of Sodom*.) Konrad tells himself that he is ready to begin writing his study, but every day there are new reasons why he cannot do so. Told by the local bank that he has exhausted his credit and the mill is to be sold off, he uses one of his guns to kill his wife and then hides in the manure pit, where after two days he is found by the state police. Like Konrad, Bernhard drives here too hard and too far: what we discover about these gruesome events is filtered twice or three times through provincial minds of limited perception; the helpless reader (who finds himself too often in the role of Konrad's crippled wife) cannot endlessly cope with a piece of repetitious prose that works on him with the relentless whine of a dentist's drill.

One might say that Bernhard's first three novels, however different in achievement, were training exercises for *Korrektur* (1975; *Correction*, 1978), his fourth novel, which, in spite of the most urgent insistence of critics on both sides of the Atlantic, has not yet attracted the wider audience that it fully deserves. Compact and yet paradoxically rich in characters and situations, it is the record of an intense thought process rather than a story. The narrator or rather biographer, by profession a mathematician, tries to reconsider the life and death of his friend and colleague Roithamer, a Cambridge philosopher of Austrian origin who has recently committed suicide, and to grasp the meaning and the horrors of his friend's experience. Psychologically and geographically, we are imprisoned in narrow space with the narrator, who has settled in the garret of a taxidermist's house in a bosky glen in Upper Austria, near a swift mountain river incessantly dashing against the rocks. This is the same room where Roithamer, whenever he came from Cambridge to his native country, worked on his most productive ideas and studied Hegel, Schopenhauer, and Ernst Bloch with attentive abandon. The biographer sits at Roithamer's desk, listens to the river, attempts to edit the philosopher's complex biographical manuscript about his childhood and youth at nearby Altensam, the parental estate, and as his work goes on, immerses himself and us through scattered notes and obsessive memories in Roithamer's own mind. For ten years the philosopher made plans to build a perfect forest house in the shape of a cone, designed out of hatred for all traditional architecture, for his sister, whose spiritual being it was to express in exact correspondence. Roithamer did not foresee, however, that the perfection of his concept could not be matched by imperfect mortal flesh. We are forced to believe that the ideal beauty of the cone house triggers his sister's terminal illness. After she has been buried, he hangs himself in the forest—correcting the life force in his own way—and the cone dwelling will turn to earth again, since nobody is allowed to enter it.

Bernhard's narrative procedure here is distantly reminiscent of Mann's *Doctor Faustus*, of the humanist who wants to understand the life of his friend, the composer of fatal genius. In Bernhard's novel, which stresses intellectual essentials, we are spared the symbolic bric-a-brac of German cultural history, and I am not certain that it really helps us to know that Bernhard modeled his Roithamer, at least at times, on his famous Austrian compatriot Ludwig Wittgenstein, who moved between Cambridge and Austria in both academic and private life and astonished students and colleagues by his aversion to prescribed rituals. There are, of course, striking analogies between Bernhard's Roithamer and Wittgenstein, including the scattered notes and the perfect house for the sister (the real Wittgenstein built one for his own sister in the middle of Vienna), but it would be a mistake to read *Correction* as a kind of fictionalized biography. It is a narrative contemplation about the limits of philosophy, taking a few imaginative clues from Wittgenstein's life, memorable more for its invisible melodrama than its visible events. As in some of his earlier narratives, Bernhard uses some of his belligerent energies to show us the dark side of Austrian society, but it is not just the concern with stifling Austrian tradition that pushes Roithamer close to Wittgenstein. Bernhard looks to his compatriot because he loves his pristine drive to think what nobody else has thought in the history of thought, his desire to move to the border situations of philosophical inquiry and to correct all potential answers in an ever-renewed engagement. From the ultimate correction, or the radical negation of life, the solitary human being emerges, tortured but triumphant, as a judge who does not hesitate to pronounce sentence on himself. Whether Bernhard undertakes a philosophical quest in the guise of fiction or uses fiction as an instrument of philosophy, the narrative has memorable force and, contrary to what Bernhard has done before, does not lack a distinct balance between aversion and compassion. Figures like Roithamer's terrifying mother (Bernhard's revenge on motherhood in general) and those of the taxidermist Höller and his family, who have been peacefully present in Roithamer's life, give it unexpected consistency of epic power.

Bernhard is not a writer to keep still. While producing his important novels of the early and mid-1970s, he went on writing plays year after year (or rather one every six months), and a series of autobiographical narratives in which he sees himself as a ruthless partisan fighting against his family, his diseased body, the country, and society at large. In his plays, which have been widely disseminated by television, his Jacobean imagination combines with a sure sense of sparse theatrical effects. While some critics have suggested that he always rewrites the same play, it would be much fairer to say that he works like a thrifty director on a limited budget, using the same stock characters (belonging to his mental repertory company), props, and leitmotivs over and over again. All his plays feature monstrous monologues of one or two protagonists who appear in the changing costumes of dictators, writers, cripples, politicians, mad philosophers, and contemporary misanthropes; these characters all share the disturbing habit of wanting to dominate the scene absolutely, of merely taking cues from others while never responding to partners in dialogue, and of inevitably needing a sidekick, more often than not a mute and dehumanized woman, to order around, hate, and torture. Bernhard's more impressive plays, including *Ein Fest für Boris* [1970] (*A Feast for Boris*) and *Der Präsident* [1975] (*The President*, 1982), are about power and art. Since he despises power of any kind yet is tremendously fascinated by it, his monster monologues at times speak critically about his own desires to manipulate and dominate people. In *Vor dem Ruhestand: Eine Komödie der deutschen Seele* [1979]; (*Eve of Retirement: A Comedy of the German Soul*, 1981), Bernhard tries to sketch the portrait of a concentration camp commander (who later becomes a West German judge) and his two sisters, one sharing his bed and the other, a cripple, studying Rosa Luxemburg. The play is an unmitigated disaster that survives only because of audiences eager to see Nazi melodrama in endless variations.

In his autobiographical narratives of the middle and late 1970s, including *Die Ursache* (1975; *The Cause*), *Der Keller* (1976; *The Cellar*), *Der Atem* (1978; *The Breath*), *Die Kälte* (1981; *The Cold*), and *Ein Kind* (1982; *A Child*), Bernhard reminds me of Maxim Gorki or Thomas Wolfe in his massive, stubborn attempts to give a true account of his early years, without sparing himself or his readers. Bernhard, of course, needs time to rid himself of a nearly hysterical attitude toward his student life in Salzburg, the city of suicides, so as to arrive at a more sober view of himself and others, and to develop a deeper commitment to understand sufferings not his own. He is aware of the difficulties of speaking the truth about himself, and not only about himself. "The love of truth," he writes, "is like any other love, the quickest way of falsifying matters. . . . We want to speak the truth, and we do not speak it." There are dark and devastating images, seen as it were from hell, of his postwar experiences, the streets of Salzburg, the German border villages, the dust of Vienna. Other writers might have felt totally exhausted after exploring their youth in five volumes (and writing a dozen plays in addition), but Bernhard only felt strengthened for having freed himself of past burdens. He has learned to command the breathless circular syntax of his autobiographical complaint with skill and force. In *Holzfällen: Eine Erregung* (1984; *Timber: An Irritation*), he returns to his experiences of the 1950s, when he arrived in Vienna as a lonely Salzburg student eager to be part of the literary and musical scene. Observing a dinner given for a famous actor (unfortunately on the very day on which a dear woman friend has been buried), he has ample opportunity to denounce the city, after twenty and more years, as a "machine for the destruction of genius," and the Burgtheater as an "institute of screams and absolute brainlessness."

Bernhard's short piece *Alte Meister* (1985; *Old Masters*) once again irritated the Austrian establishment by mercilessly attacking the great artists of the past, including Anton Bruckner and

Gustav Mahler, but the Austrian government official who thought it necessary to defend traditional culture did not read closely enough. He ignored Bernhard's discussion of German philosophy at large (which calls Heidegger the "petit bourgeois of German philosophy" and Schopenhauer "a tonic for survival") and totally misjudged the purpose of the book. Far from wanting to be purely destructive, Bernhard asks existential questions about art and pain and discusses a human suffering that cannot be mitigated by aesthetic consolations. Both *Timber* and *Old Masters* are enraged, paradoxically witty, and strangely moving books of genuine self-exploration.

It is too early to define the particular quality of Bernhard's new achievement in the 1980s (we are just witnessing its initial moments), but I suspect that it will be a matter of a new distance and perhaps even of nascent self-irony. The usual leitmotivs are there, but they are handled firmly and without sentimentality. In addition, more often than at any time in the past Bernhard provokes the legitimate question of whether he is moving from the tragic toward grim comedy. In rare moments he even sounds like Johann Nestroy, the great Viennese master of metaphysical wit emerging from the clash of the noble and the earthy, of the stern language of philosophical aspirations and the more relaxed idiom of daily life.

In *Wittgensteins Neffe: Eine Freundschaft* (1982; *Wittgenstein's Nephew: A Friendship*), Bernhard returns to the autobiographical narrative, but one far less concerned with his own vicissitudes than those of Paul Wittgenstein, a Viennese relative of the renowned philosopher. Bernhard calls his narrative an esssay in friendship and has magnificently succeeded in rescuing for us the memory of a close friend and an unusual human being whose life and miserable death in many ways reflect Bernhard's own ideas about what, in our age, an existence of true meaning should be. The two are brought together by a Vienna musicologist (who later "degrades" herself by dropping out and going to the provinces to grow her own radishes), but the friendship has its real beginning when both are patients in the Vienna hospital on the Baumgartner Höhe, Bernhard in the pulmonary compound and Paul, on the other side, in the Steinhof asylum for the insane. (The two compounds are separated by a decrepit wire fence, giving Bernhard the opportunity to offer Breughelesque descriptions of mutual visits, the mentally disturbed among the lung cancer patients, and vice versa.) The writer and Paul, a decided nonwriter, share many attitudes, ideas, and inclinations, but clash in others. They are both "experienced patients" who usually get tolerably well by mobilizing their vital energies against the physicians and the medical establishment. They love opera intensely and can talk about it to the point of exhaustion (though Paul is anti- and Bernhard pro-Karajan), and they share a violent distaste for cultural institutions, local newspapers, and Austrian governments. While Bernhard prides himself on distrusting all plebeians, Paul has a soft spot for them in his heart, gives away much of his money to the poor (as did his uncle Ludwig), and ultimately finds himself dependent on the Wittgenstein clan, one of the three or four richest families in Austria, and, as far as clothes are concerned, on hand-me-downs from Prince Schwarzenberg (tailored, one assumes, by Knize). Bernhard is much attached to Wittgenstein's nephew because Paul is one of those who dare to live against their family and the world. Ludwig Wittgenstein, Bernhard suggests, "was perhaps more of a philosopher, and the other, Paul, perhaps more insane," but we possibly believe that Ludwig was a philosopher "because he put down his philosophy on paper and not his madness," and we think of Paul as insane because he "suppressed his philosophy, did not publish, and exhibited his madness alone." Bernhard assumes that both Ludwig and Paul were human beings of the greatest distinction. However, knowing Bernhard's assumptions, I suspect that he puts Paul a notch higher because he refrained from writing and insisted on being a thinker of the greatest potential who would never finish anything that would immediately, by virtue of being turned into a finished and printed product, become part of the massive, cold, resistant world (publish and perish). Konrad in his fictional lime works, ever preparing to write about the auditory senses, and Paul Wittgenstein, the unpublished philosopher, have much in common.

Der Untergeher (1983; *Going Under*) again sustains itself by the nervous and meandering energy of an interior monologue, or rather a monologue about monologues. The speaker, or thinker, of the *monologue intérieur* is a middle-aged Austrian pianist who comes from a well-to-do family, against whom he rebelled by turning to art. He, together with Glenn Gould and the music student Wertheimer, who survived the Nazi time in England, was trained by Horowitz in the early 1950s; the three were good friends (or so we hear), roomed together in Salzburg, and listened to one another's exercises. Glenn Gould, long before he died of heart failure while playing, excelled all others in his dedication to art and the purity of his renowned performances. Now Wertheimer too is dead (by suicide), and the friend, examining his memories, tries to discover why Wertheimer chose to kill himself in the most horrible way, by hanging himself on a tree in front of his sister's house. Wertheimer himself may have left a clue by putting J. S. Bach's *Goldberg Variations*, as performed by Glenn Gould, on his record player before traveling to Switzerland to kill himself. The text breaks off abruptly when the friend, in Wertheimer's empty rooms, starts listening to Gould's translucent record.

It is important, I think, to mistrust the friend and to read his monologue against the grain. The breathless confession reveals much that the friend wishes to hide, and actually undermines, from within, his constant assertions of a close friendship with Wertheimer. He cannot but confess that he did not do everything for him when help was needed: when Wertheimer, shortly before his death, wrote him letter after letter, he did not respond, pretending that he was too busy, and in his self-centered concern for his studies of art and music, always *in statu nascendi*, did not want to "yield" to his despairing friend. Ultimately, *Going Under* is not only about the moral failure of a musician to help a Jewish friend intent on self-destruction, but also about the ideas of art they both share. Both believe in perfection of technique as if it were art itself, identifying the perfect virtuoso, no longer among the living, with the creative artist, and confound the precision of reproduction with the initial act of composition. If perceived in the light of their ideas, Bernhard's virtuosi are grotesque figures who compel us to ponder and revise our ideas about art and art's perfection.

Among his Austrian and German readers, there has been a certain dearth of perceptive criticism of Bernhard's contradictory writings. Responding in kind to the stubborn absolutism of his views (which admits only superlatives on the negative, and more recently on the affirmative, side), readers are either infatuated, if somewhat reluctantly, with his prose narratives and a few plays or have ceased to read them, arguing that there is no reason why they should pay for texts that try to offend them, especially if they are women. Within the context of ideologies the loner and, more recently, the snob Bernhard is more appreciated to the right of center than by the Left. No wonder: being an elite anarchist, he despises "the people" as much as he does the political organizations of Socialists and Conservatives, and the readers and critics who were instrumental in building up his image (among them the aging playwright Carl Zuckmayer and Peter Handke) were not necessarily speaking for the Left. It is not difficult to accuse Bernhard of a distinct monotony of recurrent figures and motifs, for instance, the breaking up of the large estate reminiscent of imperial Austria, or the theoretical treatises not yet written or never to be finished, but it would be more important to ask, I think, how and in what context Bernhard uses the recurrent elements of his imagination. Bernhard as unrepentant macho (who once suggested that one of his intelligent feminist critics should go to a Mexican mountaintop and meditate there in the nude) is another matter entirely. The whore/madonna opposition recurs in his writings in the configuration of the slattern (mother, innkeeper, etc.) and the sister to whom all adoration is due. A psychoanalytical view (not yet attempted), by going back to his autobiographical narratives and allusions, should tell us more about the desires and neuroses that shape his epic world, which in the full sense of the word is strongly disfigured. (In a cryptic passage of *Wittgenstein's Nephew*, he remarks that the real *Lebensmensch* of his existence has been a wise woman who, thirty years older than he, has guided him in all decisions of his later life.) The writer Bernhard cannot be defined by formula; he has written novels and narratives of the first rank, including *Correction* and *Wittgenstein's Nephew*, and while he has often trivialized himself in plays, interviews, and public performances showing his disgust for the social world, he has a strong voice that reminds us of the darkest side of our lives, and of our utter helplessness in spite of all social and technological consolations. Perhaps the German critic Günter Blöcker was not far from the truth when he praised Bernhard as a writer "keeping alive our sense of astonishment."

10

PETER HANDKE: A FRAGILE WITNESS

Peter Handke was three years old when World War II came to an end and therefore belongs to an age group totally different from that of Günter Grass or Heinrich Böll. In one of his early essays he remarks that literature was his real teacher, "making him attentive to true reality," and offering to him the possibility of "being aware of his consciousness." Sketching the story of his life and achievements, I do not have to speak about POW camps, the Eastern front, or resistance to the Nazi dictatorship (which determined much of the experience of the older generation), but rather about conflicts concerning literary techniques and forms, the media (including German talk shows), and whether Handke represents the ideas of the '68 generation or actually anticipates the inward turn of many younger people after the withering away of the student revolt. Radicals of the Left have had a particularly difficult time rejecting or praising what he has written. In the late 1960s Handke wavered between calling himself an unorthodox leftist and a writer of anarchist leanings, but not many critics on the left were pleased with what they called his "formalist" interests or his obscure texts, evidently not written for the "people." After the publication of his Paris notebooks in the late 1970s, they had even more legitimate reasons to feel troubled about his solipsist attitudes, if not about the almost mystical tone of his most recent writings. Handke, who comes from a poor rural family, has never given up fighting for the emancipation of individual perception from everything that may force it into prescribed molds of tradition, but critics who insist on the inherited norms of the Left or the Right cannot see that he articulates one of the central concerns of our age. Demonstratively showing off his Beatle haircut and dark glasses, he started out as a young law student undermining traditionalist language and the inherited forms of literature, because they kept him from expressing the true nuances of his feelings. After twenty years of going it absolutely alone, he has reached a preliminary moment of surprising and visionary pride in the radiance, uniqueness, and strengths of living his own life. If a new religiosity of the earth, family bonds, and the right of every individual to define an appropriate space of inalienable experience could have its modern saints, he certainly would want to be among the first of them.

EARLY EXPERIMENTS: NARRATIVES AND PLAYS

Many of Handke's commitments and idiosyncrasies of the personal and aesthetic kind are the results, often hidden, of traumatic childhood experiences in southern Carinthia, and his best writing obliquely or openly returns to his early life with his grandfather, mother, and siblings. He loves to remember his grandfather, a craftsman of Slovene origins who was terrorized by his German-speaking village neighbors because he wanted to see the region under Yugoslav rule. Handke was born out of wedlock in 1942 in the hamlet of Altenmarkt, near Griffen; his mother fell in love with a German soldier (actually, a rather unheroic and balding savings bank clerk who had a wife at home) and, after giving birth to her child, quickly married a German noncommissioned officer (in private life a tram conductor) who did not object to the baby and was transferred to the front anyway. Mother and child went to live with the husband's parents in Berlin for a while, returned to Austria to escape the air raids, and after the war went back to Berlin to wait for the return of the husband. In 1948 all three traveled from East Berlin back to the little place in southeastern Austria, where the growing family lived in utter penury in an attic, Handke senior being employed in the modest carpentry shop of his in-laws. There followed a provincial childhood among the poor, regulated by the thousand stringent rules of permissible behavior. Alone among his siblings, Handke was fascinated by stories, learning, and books. After elementary school in the village, he was sent to the Marianum near Klagenfurt, a boys' school preparing most students for the priesthood, and later to a public *Gymnasium*. When he was fifteen or sixteen, he began reading Faulkner and Bernanos, two writers excluded from the conservative canon of literary instruction; later he said that the world of these books was far more real to him than the world of his actual experiences.

In 1961 Handke went to Graz to study law. Although he attended some of the lectures (he later parodied the Austrian legal idiom), he wrote a good deal for himself and the Graz radio station, and was early encouraged by Alfred Holzinger, the learned editor of literary broadcasts there. In the early 1960s Handke participated for a short while in the activities of the Forum Stadtpark Group and published his first story in *manuskripte* (1964). When Suhrkamp published his first novel a year later, he married Libgart Schwarz, a young actress of the Graz theater ensemble, and with rare courage decided to concentrate on his writing entirely. Critics of his own generation, and others, have never forgiven Handke for being the first media personality of German literary history, not so much because his first novel was a success (it was not) but because, they say, he was a master of aggressive and meretricious self-dramatization. A nobody, at the 1966 Princeton meeting of Group 47 he derided the art of the current writers, among them Günter Grass, as impotent literature of mere description (which was certainly to be found in his own early texts as well). Supported by the considerable marketing expertise of the Suhrkamp publishing house, he became a public figure almost overnight, watched by aging avant-gardists with envy and by the radicals with ideological suspicion; even the legitimate international success of his plays, or rather his theatrical experiments, of the late 1960s did not appease his adversaries. Like so many young Austrian writers, Handke lived for a while in Frankfurt, Düsseldorf, and Berlin and traveled in the United States. When his mother committed suicide in her Austrian village in 1971, he had separated from his wife at least for the time being. He moved with his daughter Amina (born in 1969) to the Paris suburb of Clamart, where he kept himself out of all groups and cliques and experimented with making movies. His narratives and notebooks indicate that he began enjoying the firmness and serenity of classical and realistic texts, including Goethe, Adalbert Stifter, and his modern Austrian compatriot Heimito von Doderer. By the late 1970s Handke felt ready to make his separate peace with the country of his origins. He wrote a short novel entitled *Langsame Heimkehr* (1979; *Slow Homecoming*, 1985), and by 1979 settled with Amina in Salzburg, where he lives and writes today.

In his earliest texts, written mostly during his student days in Graz, Handke protests against inherited genres and forms that limit our possibilities for authentic perception. Unmasking these forms as mere "schemata" that have long falsified what we feel or think, young Handke, willingly or unwillingly, argues like the Russian formalists. He too believes that it is possible to make our experience more genuine and intense if we learn that our inherited ways of storytelling, or rather realism, and the theater, or rather the well-made play, interfere with and block our spontaneous and unique perceptions. Handke's first novel *Die Hornissen* (1966; *The Hornets*), unfortunately reads like second-hand Faulkner compiled by a third-rate Robbe-Grillet, yet paradoxically it hides, perhaps too successfully, moving and illuminating memories of the narrow world in which Handke grew up. Even in radical negation he creates an epic situation, if not a kind of story close to the Austrian village novel: there is the lonely hamlet, the forest, the moors, the inn, and the village cinema as always in Handke, and his provincial contemporaries, the Benedikt family, the father, the other woman (of strong sexual attraction), the sister, and the brothers Matt, Hans, and blind Gregor, whose name has reminded many critics of Kafka's young man who changes into a despicable bug.

The sixty-seven segments of the narrative mosaic can be read as revealing Gregor's attempt to explore his responsibility for Matt's death (by drowning in a brook) and his efforts to suppress his guilt feelings; his memory, often presented as that of a man who remembers a book he has read, continually returns to that bleak day in November when Matt did not return from the forest and Gregor lost his eyesight, as if to punish himself. "In his brain," the narrative says, "the spot in which he believes to have remembered something, blends into others without order," but he also knows that he tries to lie when shifting the responsibility for the accident to his brother Hans (who reappears in later narratives). The blind man has the power of intense recall because the visible world does not affect him any more; things, sounds, and remembered fragments attack his consciousness like vicious hornets; and whenever memories turn into well-shaped sentences or pretentious stories, Gregor, the blind teller of tales, challenges himself to be more precise, even at the risk of epic stutter: "I tell you . . . I begin once more to tell you . . . one could go on in the following way. . . ." Though he regresses into description, he wants only the present awareness, unspoiled by the verbal means of presentation. There are many luminous passages about past experience in the forest and around the family table, yet narrative precision, as in the *nouveau roman*, often disintegrates into a mere staccato of ceremoniously chronicled detail. In his second novel, *Der Hausierer* (1967; *The Peddler*), young Handke pushes his experiments further, and with far less success. As he himself has explained, he wants to use the exemplary form of a whodunit to express feelings of sorrow, anger, and rage, and splits each of his chapters into a theoretical and a practical part. In the first part he suggests a general and spirited theory of the thriller as interesting as that of Tzvetan Todorov, whom he might have studied closely; in the second part, however, in which he offers us narrative clues for our own investigations, he mercilessly bores us. Handke's first novel was at least sustained, as the Austrian writer Michael Scharang remarked, by a conflict of two forces ranging freely against each other—memory and formal discipline; but it is difficult to argue with H. C. Buch, who said that Handke's ironic exploration of the thriller never overcomes its own "clinical sterility."

In his insistence on a lone act of formal revolt, Handke underrated the long history of opposition to the traditional novel in modern writing; in his early efforts to bare the conventionality of inherited narrative forms, he revealed himself as a somewhat grim epigone of an entire generation inimical to the traditions of realism. Handke is far more ingenious, witty, and effective in shaking the foundations of the theater, so important to Austrian and German ideas of *Kultur*. Turning against the naturalist traditions of the stage (trying to imitate something that really happened elsewhere) and against Brecht's epic theater (which needs illusions to destroy illusions), Handke wrote in rapid sequence half a dozen speech-plays or *Sprechstücke* which, boldly and without attention to messages, reveal the theatrical process itself, and ask how language actually functions in imposing law and order on our spontaneity and how it disfigures the integrity of the individual. Against a "theater of mediation" eager to offer a story, a plot, or an ideological message, he wants to create a "theater of immediacy," based on the pure presence of the theatrical event itself—a signifier not referring to something else, but working with an "intensity of sound" finely honed to make the audience "more attentive, keen of hearing, and wide awake." (Even Handke cannot quite rid himself of the Schillerian idea of the theater as an educational institution, though this time it is our sensibility that has to be trained.) In *Weissagung* [1966] (*Prophecy*), four speakers recite tautologies; in *Das Mündel will Vormund sein* [1969] (*My Foot My Tutor*) [1971], for a change not a word is spoken, but a rustic guardian is decapitated by his ward on the darkened stage; and in the baffling *Ritt über den Bodensee* [1971] (*The Ride across Lake Constance*) [1972], actors and actresses wearing masks of the most famous performers of the modern German theater, including Elisabeth Bergner and Heinrich George, explore the powers of acting (no wonder it is a favorite of theater schools). In Handke's notorious *Publikumsbeschimpfung* [1966] (*Offending the Audience*, 1969), the wittiest of his early speech-plays, his argument against fable, imitation, and semantics changes into first-rate theatrical entertainment of a particular kind. The performance, if it is one, starts with the audience entering the theater, and the usual expectations are intensified by the whispers of ushers and elegant program notes. The stage is empty, and four speakers (who, according to Handke, should train for their performance by listening to the Catholic liturgy, the noises of cement mixing machines, and the Rolling Stones) condescendingly and sternly address the audience; after they have presented a theory of Handke's theater, opposed to that of Stanislavski and Brecht, they commence their sustained abuse of the assembled audience in all the idioms of politics, criticism, and the gutter. There are a few carrots, but teacher Handke uses a big stick to "change our consciousness," and not only as momentary members of an audience in the theater.

In *Kaspar* [1968; 1973], his most impressive speech-play, Handke goes far beyond his explorations of literary and theoretical conventions and fastens on language itself, not only as material of literature but as basic instrument of communication, of shaping experience and enslaving the mind. As a reader of recent anthropologists, Wittgenstein, and the linguists, he raises questions about the function of language in human experience and, pushing beyond Austrian fin-de-siècle skepticism about language, suggests that language, or rather the structures inherent in language, enslave the speakers because they shape their thinking and their perceptions of what is in the world (the Humboldt-Sapir-Whorf theories radicalized). The central figure of the play recalls the historic Kaspar Hauser, who as an adult was found nearly speechless on a Nuremberg square in 1828 and later was closely watched by Europe's scientists as he slowly acquired language. Handke admits that he studied Anselm von Feuerbach's contemporary legal and psychological work (1831) about that famous German foundling with more profit than the poems written about him, but he is not interested at all in sketching a portrait in historic costumes, as Werner Herzog did in his film. Essentially, Handke sees his Kaspar as a timeless human being, incarnating the potentialities and the dangers of language; the original title of the play was *Speaking*. Kaspar is forced by language to produce language and to submit his thought and experience to its structures, which ultimately deprive him of his individuality; the fundamental question is whether he can keep alive a spark of resistance against its powerful and depersonalizing laws. Handke directs Friedrich Schiller's famous cry "*In Tyrannos!*" against the rules of language operating in his own mind.

Handke has long opposed plots and the presentation of causalities on the stage, but in *Kaspar* he is compelled by the idea of language training to return to a presentation of psychological developments, however fragmentary, and to show us how Kaspar begins to be dehumanized as soon as he starts speaking a shared and a shareable language. In the conventional intermission the audience itself turns into a tortured Kaspar, being forced to listen to taped collages of political speeches and sheer noise "piped through loudspeakers into the auditorium, into the lobbies, and even the outside streets if that is possible." Handke works with black-out techniques to show the stages in Kaspar's fatal language training. In stepping forth through the folds of the theater curtains, Kaspar experiences his new birth and glares like Frankenstein's monster at a world not understood (parts 1, 2, and 3). He tries to repeat the only sentence that he is able to say ("I want to be a person as somebody else was once") in different voice modulations abstracted from the historically documented sentence that the real Kaspar Hauser repeated again and again. The mechanical voices of the Prompters, articulating the impersonal system of language, tell him that even his first sentence was ruled by order (parts 8–16) and commence to torture him by a flood of speech, while he desperately tries to defend his own personal sentence against the grammatical exercises and formulas (17–18). When they offer him useful new sentence models (19–25), Kaspar repeats them and, submitting to the language rules, inevitably begins ordering his own small world, his dress, and the furniture on the stage, so that suddenly he resembles a "dummy in an interior-decorating exhibition." But the training goes on relentlessly; the voices continue the brutal prompting; and five silent Kaspars appear on the stage (possibly denoting projections of Kaspar dehumanized) to demonstrate order as conformity of behavior (33–50). Finally overwhelmed, Kaspar speaks his great, largely rhymed, festive, and foolish monologue, now fully identifying with order, property, and reason, as praised by the Prompters: "I am calm, dutiful, and receptive. . . . I would like to be a member. I would like to cooperate."

In the second part of the play, Handke has to say whether or not the use of shared language undoes our individuality, but his answer is ambivalent, and his textual changes (the second version of the play, translated into English by Michael Roloff, differs somewhat from the first) demonstrate his legitimate difficulties. If it is possible to use language, as he does, in writing a protest play against language, Kaspar, who stands for the playwright Handke, too, cannot be simply lost to conformity and enslavement. (The rules about order that the Prompters recite are taken from Nazi language but also from Chairman Mao's little red book). Once again (62–63), Kaspar recites a hymn of stupidity and clichés in which he fully agrees with the brutal Prompters, but then, almost abruptly (signaled by a hidden quote from the playwright Ödön von Horváth and a door that refuses to stay shut), Kaspar articulates a deeper insight, the thoughtful self-exploration of what has happened to him, and the bewildered intimation of an attempt to revolt. As the five other Kaspars, his reflections, increasingly produce inarticulate noises to ridicule and negate language, he begins to see through the impositions of grammar and morphology and thinks of happier times when he "laughed as an individual." Before his mind disintegrates, he quotes Othello, a fellow victim of social codes, but he also recognizes his false pride in mastering language, for it was language that mastered him. *Kaspar* may not be a play to please members of the Modern Language Association of America, unless they are willing to question what they are doing, or traditional audiences, who are usually repelled by the stern laboratory scene and the total absence of stage realism; but it is a courageous theatrical undertaking for the more philosophical friends of theater. Avoiding all rigidity of ideas, Handke shows Kaspar as a "Chomskian baby in a Skinner box" (to quote Linda Hill) and suggests that we cannot do with or without language: if we rely on it unquestioningly, we run the danger of submitting to its conventional structure of law and order, but if we reject shared and traditional language, we risk turning back into inarticulate King Kongs. It is a difficult choice, and not only for the professional writer.

Six years after *Kaspar*, Handke's two-act play *Die Unvernünftigen sterben aus* [1974] (*They Are Dying Out*) [1979] indicated how quickly he had moved away from his analysis of theatrical genres and language to concentrate attention on how people live in industrial society. The Yale Repertory Theatre explained the play as a "wry comment on the cult of mass marketing and its creators," and many people in the New Haven audience left during the first act, possibly unwilling to watch an exploration of their own way of life. Handke's combination of Swiftian irony and Strindbergian symbolism puzzles and disturbs; instead of the "matching sofas and armchairs," the conventional props, he puts onstage in act 2, among other things, "a large, slowly melting block of ice . . . and a large boulder with changing inscriptions." Most critics, used to finding virtue among the underprivileged rather than at the top, were particularly perturbed by Handke's Herr Quitt, a most successful and intelligent (Shavian) capitalist with an extremely fine sensibility, who destroys his competitors, sees through the process of alienation, longs for a language close to genuine experience, and enjoys reading Adalbert Stifter's novella *Der Hagestolz* (1854; *The Loner*). Quitt's friends have a good deal to say about advertising, which "animates the world of goods" and "endears to us the objects from which we have been alienated by ideology," but they lack Quitt's piercing and elegiac intelligence, so close to Handke's own, and do not understand his longing to escape his role by smashing his head against the big rock in the living room. The women in the play reflect the alternatives almost allegorically: Paula, a savvy manager, successfully and rationally operates in the corporate world, but Quitt's wife (left nameless) warns us distractedly, uttering disconnected words like "Ammonites" throughout her husband's parties, and constantly flushes the toilets (her way of indicating what should be done to the world). It is not Paula but the disconsolate wife, Handke believes, who is on the right track.

WRITINGS OF THE SEVENTIES

Handke recently remarked that "not even a pig" would try to reread his early prose experiments. Fortunately, most readers have formed their opinion about him from his short novels and other texts of the 1970s, which offer as many distinctive features as did his plays of the late 1960s. In the 1970s Handke, putting aside his linguistic experiments, uses rather sparingly what he has learned in writing about the possibility or impossibility of achieving self-realization in a world constituted by habit, recurrence, exchange, repression, and loss of genuine feelings. His narratives, whether fictions or quests for fulfillment or autobiographies, are strangely fragile (that is, devoid of dense realism), yet they do not lack the intimate insights of the finest perception and are all curiously calm in tone, never yielding to irritation, rage, or melodrama. *Die Angst des Tormanns beim Elfmeter* (1970; *The Goalie's Anxiety at the Penalty Kick*, 1972) is still close to a literary exercise, in spite of its strong story, but in *Der kurze Brief zum langen Abschied* (1972; *Short Letter, Long Farewell*, 1974) and *Wunschloses Unglück* (1972; *A Sorrow beyond Dreams*, 1974), two narratives of painfully autobiographical substance, Handke frees himself from his inhibitions, while in *Die Stunde der wahren Empfindung* (1975; *A Moment of True Feeling*, 1977) and *Die linkshändige Frau* (1976; *The Left-Handed Woman*, 1978) he speaks freely about a man and woman trying to understand and live what they feel is inalienable in their individuality. Perception and feeling, unbent and unenslaved by habits and social requirements, may be the new key words. In his journal *Das Gewicht der Welt* (1977; *The Weight of the World*, 1984) Handke, to the dismay of his political readers, offers us in brief and luminous notes what he learned by training his sensibilities on long walks through the streets of Paris before, as it were, preparing for his slow return home to a new appreciation of the simple things in life back in the country of his birth.

In his short novel *The Goalie's Anxiety at the Penalty Kick*, Handke tells the story of the mechanic and onetime soccer star Joseph Bloch, employing the epic imperfect tense as any traditionalist would, while using Kafka's narrative perspective. Just as Kafka constantly watches his "K.," so Handke loyally stays with Bloch when he wakes, dreams, and kills, while all other figures are seen from the outside, uttering words and making gestures without an inner life. Handke, who has studied Klaus Conrad's treatise on the early stages of schizophrenia (*Die beginnende Schizophrenie*, 1958), shows Bloch's mental disintegration stage by stage: progressively he loses his willingness to speak and his ability to live in a real world shared with other people. Fired from his job (or so he believes), he wanders aimlessly through a shabby Vienna of espresso cafés and railway stations, seeks peace at a movie, sleeps with the movie cashier who sold him the ticket, and kills her after spending the night with her in her suburban apartment. After wandering around Vienna again, he takes a bus to a village near Austria's southern border, where a former girlfriend runs an inn in the shadow of a castle (intimations of Kafka again). There too he experiences only restlessness and disgust: the people who speak to him remind him of his own distrust of language, and the newspapers reporting about the murdered cashier do not surprise him at all. Handke does not want to offer us a psychiatric report, but the story of a schizophrenic killer who actually wants to be caught. This story lets him explore a process of perception totally out of the ordinary: the less Bloch speaks, the more strikingly immediate the environment emerges from the context; ultimately, the world completely falls apart into details without number. In the end Bloch merely regurgitates instead of trying to communicate with words, and escapes to the village football field to be overwhelmed by an elemental anxiety. The things of the world have now changed into mysterious hieroglyphs, while in the text itself archaic pictures of isolated objects replace the usual typographical symbols for words. Bloch's schizophrenia may be a last desperate chance to withdraw from a conformist world of shared semiotic and social rules into a realm of absolute nonconformity (a romantic thought, were it not for the woman murdered on her shabby bed).

From his very beginnings, Handke above all feared falsifying perception, particularly the falsification caused by ossified habits of literature. He himself said that he wished to use "every possibility" of writing only once, because otherwise any possibility would deteriorate into a habit of writing. Since, in the 1960s, he had exhausted the possibilities of protesting against procedures of imitation and meaning no less radically than had Hans Arp or Kurt Schwitters, he was prepared for the turn to the personal, confessional, and newly meaningful. His *Short Letter, Long Farewell*, which somewhat surprised the critics by its intimate intensity, combines, in the mode of a personal narrative rather than a novel, a report on an American tour, a chronicle of his marital difficulties, and a kind of literary self-analysis of striking serenity and basic resolution. His breathless, aggressive, and polemical intonations have disappeared, while his oldest memories of family, childhood, and the Austrian landscape return. He begins his American tour, with an appropriate if hidden compliment to the author Patricia Highsmith, in a small hotel in Providence, Rhode Island, knowing that Judith (his wife, whose laconic parting letter reaches him in the hotel) watches his every move from a distance. He travels alone to New York, where he admires Lauren Bacall, and to Philadelphia, and later drives with the young college teacher Claire, whom he had met on an earlier American trip, and her daughter Benedictine to Saint Louis, where a traveling German theater group performs Friedrich Schiller's *Don Carlos* to a loyal ethnic audience. But Judith has remained on his tracks from New York to Missouri and beyond; in Tucson he discovers her luggage on the airport conveyor belt. After an excursion to

Xavier del Bac he is roughed up by a gang of local youths (all arranged by Judith, he believes). Acid drips, he thinks, from the faucets in his motel room, and when he confronts Judith on a lonely promontory on the West Coast, she pulls a gun that he takes away from her and throws into the surging sea. Her hate is burned out, and he has learned patience; after a visit to John Ford, relaxed in his California home, they are finally "ready to part in peace."

The trip to California to hear John Ford's teachings is a voyage of change and quest as in the classical German *Entwicklungsroman*, with Handke's narrator looking deeply into his past to find out more about his burden of panic and fear. His childhood days in Carinthia, blessed and threatening, and unforgettable family scenes are painfully present. Transatlantic telephone calls to his mother run, as it were, through the umbilical cord, and his intent to visit his brother, cutting lumber in Oregon, brings back primal conflicts that we know from his first novel. Yet the traveler distinctly feels that he is freed of his narcissism by his conflict with Judith, by the experience of the American landscape (still reflecting the collective and moral efforts of the pioneers), and by the traditions of the great realist literature of the German nineteenth century that looks away from the frustrated ego to the harmony of the world. He even ceases to feel his usual disgust with everything that is not his own self and believes that it has now become easier "to rid himself of the need to get attention by showing off." He closes his *Great Gatsby*, and on the Greyhound bus to New York opens Gottfried Keller's *Der grüne Heinrich* (1854; *Green Henry*, 1960), learning patience, openness to nature, and acceptance of the world as it is given to the senses. As he proceeds on his quest for something more than the life that he had in the past, he often quotes the Austrian Catholic Adalbert Stifter, whose language begins to color his conversations and his views of clouds and mountains, and he listens closely to Claire, who explicates to him, after the Schiller performance, the difference between European heroes, "with the hand on the sword belt" and a good deal of talk, and American historical figures who really act unequivocally to fulfill a moral task and go through physical, not abstract, adventures in the wilderness. To complete his *éducation du coeur*, he finally visits John Ford, whose movie *Young Abraham Lincoln* emerges as counterstatement to Schiller's *Don Carlos.* He questions Ford about his film stories, and what he hears from him ultimately confirms that he was right all along to break through the prison chamber of his sensibilities. "We don't long to be alone," Ford says, speaking from American experience as seen by Handke, "when a man's alone, he's contemptible . . . and when he hasn't anybody but himself to talk to, he dries up after the first word."

Seven weeks after his mother had committed suicide in the little Carinthian village where she was born, Handke began writing a tentative memoir of her life; fortunately, the conflict between the son who was deeply hurt and the self-conscious writer attentive to his literary task was won by the saddened son. *Wunschloses Unglück* (1972; *A Sorrow beyond Dreams*, 1974) is Handke's most simple, intimate, and moving piece of prose, though he may be constitutionally unable to lapse into totally unreflective writing. From his jottings, memories, anecdotes, and notes, a portrait of Marie Handke emerges that clearly tells us about her attempts, and final failure, to create a life of her own in her country, her job, and her marriage: "She was, she became, she became nothing." Handke does not want to deal with mere biographical facts but, loyal to his inclinations, seizes and tests the cliché by which people usually talk about their mothers, trying to explicate the true meaning of these almost automatic utterances. He is particularly illuminating when he examines the way people without much interest in politics, including Marie and her friends, talk about the annexation of Austria by the German Reich, the war, and the party conflicts of the Second Austrian Republic. But Handke is far from the obscurities of his early writings here; in the ways of realism, he shows what it means to be a girl in a closed Austrian village community. To have been born into such surroundings was itself deadly for a woman, "for all was settled in advance"; even her Slovene father did not sympathize with her desire to learn something, and for economic reasons merely accepted the fact that she left the house at fifteen or sixteen, to be trained as a cook in a fashionable resort hotel. She had her moment of "eternal love" with the bank clerk, and when she moved with the other man to war-torn Berlin, "she carried her head high and acquired a graceful walk." When she came back to the village with her husband and growing family, the rules of village life to be "neat, clean, and jolly" caught up with her—more children, three abortions, submitting to the husband who drank and was tubercular. Late in life she regained something of her independence of mind and liked to sit in a little café and talk to people. The villagers thought that she was strange and "skittish." When prolonged headaches made her daily chores intolerable, one day, after having been to her hairdresser, she took an overdose of sleeping pills, "put on menstrual pants, stuffed diapers inside, put on two more pairs of pants, and an ankle-length nightgown, tied a scarf under her chin, and lay down on the bed."

Short Letter, Long Farewell and *A Sorrow beyond Dreams* compelled many German critics to change their view of Handke and to remind the reviewers in the United States that Handke, who had been discussed as a brilliant young playwright, was a highly gifted prose writer as well. Handke's probing and highly personal way of recording his experiences in post-Vietnam America did not necessarily endear him to the West German Left, which was slow in coming to see how legitimate it was to look at language from a social point of view. It was characteristic of contemporary German criticism that it discussed his American book by stressing that he had not only created a serene image of a country made up of pure consciousness, but told the reader much of "bloody America" (as for instance an episode of a veteran's epileptic seizure). To recommend *A Sorrow beyond Dreams*, one German critic said that the suicide of Handke's mother clearly showed how people suffered in "late capitalist society" (late feudalism would possibly have been more appropriate). American critics were somewhat ambivalent about *Short Letter, Long Farewell* but far less hesitant about *A Sorrow beyond Dreams*. I believe that it was the tentative success of *Kaspar* (in spite of the usual bunch of people leaving the performance) and the sincerity of *A Sorrow beyond Dreams* that made Handke known on the American scene, at least among the younger intelligentsia of the universities and in New York and California.

Die Stunde der wahren Empfindung (1975; *A Moment of True Feeling*, 1977) and *Die linkshändige Frau* (1976; *The Left-Handed Woman*, 1978) continue Handke's impressive achievement of the 1970s. I would put the story of *The Left-Handed Woman*, first published in America in *The New Yorker* (November 7, 1977), above the earlier story, because it does not simply want to shock the reader and combines piercing insights with a shyness of narrative attitude difficult to define. Both are slim but subtle narratives about people who insist on suddenly breaking with the routine habits of their lives and on searching painfully for a distant and unclear way of authentic experience, close to hidden feelings that they decipher slowly. These people go through a self-willed and violent shock of leaving, or of being left by, their marriage partner, and grope toward peace and serenity for their sensibilities; though they do not necessarily know what road to choose, they begin to feel moments of hope of achieving what they ultimately desire. In *A Moment of True Feeling*, a young press attaché of the Austrian embassy in Paris wakes up one day in his apartment and knows that his old life has changed. (His first name, Gregor, is again that of Kafka's young man who changes into a bug.) He has dreamed that he has killed an old woman and tells himself that he can continue his former existence only by pretending that nothing has happened. The story of *The Left-Handed Woman* (the title is derived from an American song) moves somewhat less abruptly and its world, a Frankfurt suburb of prefabricated ranch houses with picture windows, lacks the French romantic aura. (Handke's 1978 movie shifts the narrative back to the Paris suburb where he himself lived, and with good results.) One day after Christmas the young woman Marianne resolves that she wants to live alone with her child, asks her husband to leave her alone in the house, and tries to make a living doing free-lance work for a Frankfurt publisher for whom she worked before her marriage. People warn her that it will be difficult to survive in utter loneliness, but she does meet other loners, among them an unemployed actor and a saleswoman in a boutique. After an improvised party at which old and new friends gather and reveal their true selves to each other, early spring comes; in the first warm sunlight Marianne feels, or so she believes, that she is opening up to true experience.

These two stories are told in a supremely detached way, without a trace of accusation or rage, yet they differ widely in their narrative perspectives. The narrator closely watches Gregor's consciousness, and though he does not give us any ultimate reasons or motivations for his protagonist's change of attitudes and desires, he describes clearly what goes on in his strange mind.

In *The Left-Handed Woman* we are confronted by far more cryptic figures and events, because the narrator looks at everybody from the outside and, like a professional behaviorist, does not tell us anything that he does not see or hear; since Marianne is a woman given to long silences and pregnant stares, we do not really know whether she has a profound soul or none at all. These lonely people who are setting out on a quest of self-fulfillment are not rare in German writing, but Handke's figures differ from Novalis's or Hermann Hesse's by their unwillingness or inability to believe that religiosity or philosophies of the past or present offer hope or consolation. They are enclosed in their emotions, and feminist critics are right in suspecting that Marianne's unwillingness to participate in the rites of the church or the rituals of a women's meeting (which are juxtaposed, like the killing of the pig and a description of holy communion in Handke's early *Hornets*) suggests something of the narrator's assumptions, somewhat softened in his movie version of the text. Gregor and Marianne are really on their own in an existential sense, and cannot accept anything but their own values, which emerge from their intimate sensibilities.

A SLOW RETURN

Handke's short novel *Langsame Heimkehr* (1979; *Slow Homecoming*, 1985) suggests a new change in his thinking and writing affecting the narratives, essays, and other publications of the 1980s, including such divergent texts as a translation (1980) of Walker Percy's *The Movie-Goer*; *Kindergeschichte* (1981; *Child Story*, 1985); and the play *Über die Dörfer* (1981; *About the Villages*), which, to the astonishment of most younger critics, was staged at the Salzburg Festival, a center of affirmative arts and dinner-jacket crowds, in the late summer of 1982. It is not difficult to see that he is moving away from ruthless experimentation to a yearning for the truth of the great masters of past centuries, from his narcissistic fixations to a new willingness to look at the world outside the ego, and from his recurrent anxieties about living (still strikingly visible in Gregor's attitude in *A Moment of True Feeling*) to a firm acceptance of experience, however painful and grim. What is still missing in his fictions, and perhaps in his life, is a trusting workaday love for a woman or a man, a gap filled in his fiction by Amina, his adored daughter, who slowly emerges as a mystical child illuminating the darkness of our world. Handke's *Slow Homecoming* indicates, and not by its title only, the range of changes to come. It is, literally, the study of a scientist who has been working in Alaska, the frozen fringe of the world, and prepares to return to Austria, the country of his origin. We are to see only his departure and the intermediate stations of his trip, among them Berkeley and Manhattan, rather than the final destination, hidden under the clouds when his plane finally prepares for landing. Valentin Sorger, the geologist who wants to go home in a more than geographical sense, is the first central figure in Handke's fiction who has a job and is proud of it; if he had not been trained, the serene narrator suggests, "to read the landscape" and to transmit his results "in strict order," he would be totally useless to people (not a good thing in this particular book). Sorger, whose name means "worrier," is a philosopher of science or rather of human existence in a world examined by science, and though he uses his instruments carefully and rationally, he feels a "desire for salvation" that "burdens his eyelids." He tries, wherever he goes, to be a "conscientious observer of landscapes," because it is his pet idea that all landscapes merely hide a particular "space," the actual dimension of the history of mankind and of the individual, the secret of life, as it were. There are moments when the shapes of the earth are closer to his mind than the humans who surround him, but he is determined to give up brooding about himself and to go on looking for "harmony, synthesis, and serenity" at large.

Die Lehre der Sainte-Victoire (1980; *The Lesson of Mont-Sainte-Victoire*, 1985) emerged from Handke's ruminations and readings after the return to his homeland, and it reads like a text written by the philosopher and geologist Sorger. It is not fiction at all but rather a narrative bringing together, in a kind of ingestive motion, personal memories, comments about his recent studies of art and aesthetics, and glimpses of his wanderings in Provence and the Salzburg mountains. For instructive contrast, it should be read immediately after his autobiographical *Short Letter, Long Farewell* of a few years earlier. The Mont-Sainte-Victoire in Provence constitutes, quite appropriate to Sorger/Handke, a central symbol that unifies the most divergent aesthetic materials (it is duplicated, in the last pages, by a view of a mountain range near Salzburg). While Handke wearily circles around the mountain range and finally makes his ascent to the top of the ridge, he has a chance to reflect on life and art, his new master Cézanne (who loved the mountain), Courbet, and Edward Hopper, and to consider his recent qualms about being a writer who wants to seize "the structure of things." It is a curious book of tentative approaches and, often, half-baked ideas about aesthetic issues. In the absence of any self-irony Handke can be rather pompous, yet it is difficult to distrust the intensity of his desire to grasp the functions of color and form in the world of art. On his ascent he has his epiphany of evil (a half-mad bulldog behind the wire fence of a Foreign Legion installation bares its teeth and reminds him of a world of exploding grenades and destruction), but he has made up his mind to search for what is radiant, and in moving passages denounces his own past art linked to the unfortunate assumption that evil has more reality than good. The mountain teaches him that the supreme art is one that shows "being in peace" (*Sein in Frieden*); we are again close to Stifter and Goethe.

Handke's later work *Der Chinese des Schmerzes* (1983; *The Chinaman of Pain*) continues the narratives of coming home to Austria by quietly celebrating the city of Salzburg, its landscape of hills and mountains, and the villages of the surrounding plain. Critics did not write kindly about *The Chinaman of Pain*, mistaking it for an unsuccessful novel rather than a poetic Salzburg ode in prose. The Left, of course, had reasons to quote ironically some maudlin sentences, but it is not easy, at least for the sensitive reader, to resist the serene rhythm of rich perceptions offered to eye and ear, and the ceremonious prose praising the city and the surrounding region as a "refuge" to be defended. Handke's unexpected love poem to Salzburg responds to Thomas Bernhard's ecstasies of hating the old city that, unlike any other in Austria, triggers the strongest feelings one way or the other.

The first performance of Handke's *Über die Dörfer* [1982] (*About the Villages*), staged in the Salzburg Felsenreitschule by the well-known filmmaker Wim Wenders, left the critics confused rather than stunned, and the fashionable audiences rather tired after listening for five hours straight to a "dramatic poem," rich in lyrical and prophetic moments but entirely lacking in dramatic tension. Handke uses the tortured memories of his family constellation for a mystery play reminiscent, in its passages of long rhymed lines and choric arrangements, of an expressionist oratorio. Family problems assume ontological proportions; a prophetic woman calls on the humble and humiliated to assert their dignity; and a child is crowned, possibly to rule the coming realm of sun, earth, and sky. The play is simply uneven: the merely pompous elements (lines in which Handke wants to reinvent Hölderlin or, worse, Heidegger) alternate with surprising moments of overwhelming intensity and genuine poetic power. German and Austrian critics have said rightly that many verses of the play sound like beautiful quotations from political speeches made by people of the Green movement, revealing their diffused populism and antitechnological return to nature. The play touches a nerve of the age and paradoxically fascinates by its combination of ideological mush and occasional poetic energy.

Sober views of Peter Handke's writings have long been distracted by his early belligerence and the manner in which the German mass media responded to his self-dramatizations. He both used and rejected many of the ideas of his contemporaries on the left in his early writing, and inevitably found himself for a considerable time embroiled with the Marxists and the partisans of the student revolt. As the wunderkind of new Austrian writing, he rejected the realist genres as well as Brecht's ideas, which were rapidly turning into the opiate of the younger German intellectuals. By insisting on his fundamental privilege of interpreting his own ego above all else, he came close to anticipating a fundamental change in the German intellectual climate at large. In the late 1970s and the 1980s he learned to look away from himself, turned to the classics, and wooed the given world of luminous things and landscapes harboring the secrets of people. He himself said that he considered *Slow Homecoming* and the subsequent texts, among them *The Lesson of Mont-Sainte-Victoire* and *About the Villages*, to be a record of his return to his roots. He has again baffled many readers of the younger and older generations by his earnest willingness to substitute a new way of trying and groping for what was, in the 1970s, an assured mastery of narrative touch. He is on the road once more, leaving behind a remarkable achievement as he sets out on that old Parsifal quest for fulfillments more felt than known.

11

PROBLEMS OF THE THEATER

In the intellectual life of German-speaking countries, the theater has long fulfilled a fundamental function by articulating and pressing questions of philosophical import and public relevance. German playwrights were blessed and burdened by an awareness that they were teachers, not merely entertainers, of society at large; audiences expected them to provide meaningful views of present and future. Friedrich Schiller, later the favorite playwright of the liberal middle classes, proudly declared in the age of the French Revolution that the theater legitimately competed with religion and the law, offering "visual presentations" instead of "abstractions"; whenever justice was corrupt or yielded to the blandishments of vice, the theater was to seize the sword of justice and drive "the vicious before a terrible court of law." During their years in power, the Nazis, after abortive attempts to renew old Germanic rituals theatrically, preferred a staid repertory of Viennese operettas and the classics done without much verve (unless Gustaf Gründgens was performing). Schiller's stern ideas and the innovative advances of the Weimar Republic survived only in some of the theatrical undertakings of German exiles scattered about the world, and in some of the small Swiss theaters offering refuge to German producers and actors expelled from home for reasons of race and political loyalty. In September

1944 all theatrical activities within Germany were halted, but even though at least half of all theater buildings were destroyed by air raids, regular performances began almost immediately after the Allied military governments took over in the summer of 1945. The most popular new play was Carl Zuckmayer's *Des Teufels General* [1946] (*The Devil's General*, 1962), about an air force general torn between his instinctive honesty and his service to the Nazi war machine. Others, written by returned soldiers, prisoners, and exiles, included *Die Illegalen* [1946] (*People in the Underground*) by Günther Weisenborn, who had been liberated from a German prison by the Soviet army; *Draussen vor der Tür* [1947] (*The Man Outside*) [1952], an expressionist dirge for young soldiers by Wolfgang Borchert, who died of war wounds before the play was produced; and last but not least *Der Flüchtling* [1955] (*The Refugee*) by the Austrian playwright Fritz Hochwälder, who resolved to stay on in Zürich, where he had settled in a garret during the war. Brecht was quick to leave the United States in the fall of 1947 (one day after being commended by the House Committee on Un-American Activities as an exemplary witness), but he was in no hurry to return to Berlin, preferring instead to stay with friends in Switzerland, renegotiate his contracts with his West German publisher, and discuss the possibility of acquiring Austrian citizenship (which he did). Of the four thousand German-speaking theater professionals who lived in exile in forty countries, nearly 60 percent returned to German or Austrian stages after the war.

In its modest way the Zürich Schauspielhaus, and perhaps the Basel theater as well, did more than any other theater within the range of Nazi power to employ refugees, produce new plays written in exile, and encourage young local authors to write their own plays boldly and in competition with dramatists from the "outside." It was Kurt Hirschfeld, himself an exile and dramaturge of the private Schauspielhaus, who was responsible, in spite of strong resistance by Swiss conservatives, for hiring refugee professionals, including the actress Therese Giehse (1898–1975), the producer Leopold Lindtberg (b. 1902), and the stage designer Teo Otto (1904–68), and for incorporating, into an otherwise traditionalist middle-class repertory, disturbing new plays of political import like Brecht's *Mutter Courage und ihre Kinder* [1941] (*Mother Courage and Her Children*, 1955); *Leben des Galilei* [1943]

(*Life of Galileo*) [1947]; and *Der gute Mensch von Sezuan* [1943] (*The Good Woman of Sezuan*, 1948).

Max Frisch and Friedrich Dürrenmatt, whose plays predominated in the German repertory of the late 1940s and 1950s, had a unique opportunity to learn something about their craft from the plays of Thornton Wilder, often performed in Switzerland, and from those of Brecht. While Frisch (whose works I discuss in a separate chapter) long vacillated between private and public plays before preferring prose narrative to the mechanics of the stage, Dürrenmatt's achievement is more purely dramatic (in spite of his extraordinary skill as an author of detective novels). Dürrenmatt's early plays were metaphysical in orientation, historical in costume, and occasionally reminiscent of expressionist mysteries, but in his famous plays of the 1950s, including *Der Besuch der alten Dame* [1955] (*The Visit*) [1958], he moved closer to Wedekind and Brecht, then in the early 1960s wrote his macabre comedy *Die Physiker* [1962] (*The Physicists*) [1964], radically doubting the projects of modern science and revealing his anxieties about a future world without meaning or life. Dürrenmatt shared Brecht's thoughts about tragedy, but if in Brecht's Marxist universe tragedy has no place (everybody is to be happy in communism; Aristotelian catharsis is but a "massage of the soul"), Dürrenmatt believed that in the age of the "butchers" Hitler and Stalin, and of growing impersonal bureaucracies, tragedy in the traditional sense, as a matter of individual responsibility and particular suffering, was impossible: "Creon's secretaries deal with the case of Antigone." In an age without tragedy, the tragic playwright Dürrenmatt himself nearly fell silent; though he has written adaptations of Strindberg (1969) and Shakespeare (1970), he has not produced any more major plays.

In the Soviet zone of occupation and later in the GDR, the inherited structures of the German theaters were quickly used by new organizations of Party and state to advocate their interests. In the beginning the repertory was as inclusive as that in other zones of occupation, but the new republic was increasingly firm in demanding that Soviet models and the precepts of Socialist Realism be followed. Brecht arrived in the last possible moment of Popular Front tolerance. On occasion, having discovered that the authorities were not quite ready to provide him with his own theater, he spoke angrily of "the stinking breath of the provinces," but he was unaware, I think, of the rapid changes of cultural policies yet to come. On January 11, 1949, his Berliner Ensemble performed *Mother Courage and Her Children*, but he was unable to move into his own theater on the Schiffbauerdamm until 1954. In the meantime the Party had committed itself to Socialist Realism (in theatrical practice, to the legacy of Stanislavski) and Brecht, in spite of occasional compromises, ran into considerable difficulties, being accused of formalist tendencies. The Berliner Ensemble, advancing Brecht's plays and ideas, was an international success, making the "epic theater" of critical alienation the *dernier cri* in Munich, Paris, London, and later even Moscow, but in the GDR, Brecht's activities were limited for a long time to his East Berlin showcase. (He himself complained that his plays were performed nearly everywhere except in the GDR.)

The GDR establishment theater developed in far more conservative ways, relying on "regular" plays by Friedrich Wolf or Hedda Zinner (still of the Weimar generation), or Helmut Baierl and Erwin Strittmatter, who did not prevent their audiences from emotionally identifying with heroes ultimately embodying Party demands. Among the writers who moved from West to East was the gifted young playwright Peter Hacks, who in 1955 was at first welcomed by the authorities, since he provided artful satires of old Prussian militarism. But Hacks was immediately condemned when he staged contemporary GDR problems, as for instance in *Moritz Tassow* [1965], a witty verse comedy about a rustic swineherd who, in his enthusiasm for communism, rushes ahead of the party program, then loses out in a conflict with party functionaries and decides to become a poet in order to be less burdened by reality. Under pressure, Hacks turned to adaptations of the ancients, as did many of his colleagues, but his ingenuity and wit have not prevented him from joining the Establishment; he was one of the few GDR intellectuals to support the government in the Wolf Biermann affair. It is not his ideology, I suspect, but the attitude of the snob who wants to be different that has separated him from the many dissidents and compelled him to side with the few conformists.

After its long isolation, the German theater was nothing if not eagerly cosmopolitan (though stages in the West preferred French and American fare, and those in the East, inevitably, Soviet authors). Ionesco and Beckett were quickly translated, at least in the West, and performed in the early 1950s. But the German theater of the absurd developed slowly and did not have a prolonged or massive chance to contradict the traditionalist attitudes of an audience expecting the theater to dispense noble meaning of metaphysical import or social dignity, since a society that only recently had returned from hell was constitutionally unable to welcome spectacles adamantly refusing to yield ideological consolations. Yet the theater of the absurd restored imagination and the arbitrary images of poesy, at least scenically. Distrusting prolonged argument, causality, and psychological determinism, it reminded audiences of the older art of the mime, the acrobat, and the magician, and knowingly or unknowingly rediscovered forgotten links to the splendors of surrealism. Wolfgang Hildesheimer (who later turned to his own versions of historical plays and innovative fiction) provided an appropriate defense by suggesting, in his Erlangen speech of 1960, that the theater of the absurd was of course philosophical too in that it categorically *refused* to deliver messages; he wisely argued that the absurdist stage actually used the impotence of the theater, which had never changed or transformed any human being, as a wonderful subterfuge for acting and playing. Many playwrights were affected, but none yielded totally. Max Frisch, Friedrich Dürrenmatt, and Peter Weiss briefly toyed with absurdist stage techniques, while Günter Grass and Wolfgang Hildesheimer, each in a spate of plays, expanded the potentialities of the absurdist stage, Grass for instance in *Die bösen Köche* [1961] (*The Wicked Cooks*) [1967] and Hildesheimer in *Nachtstück* [1963] (*Nightpiece*, 1967), the latter effectively pitting against each other an intellectual burdened by his aversion to history, art, and religion, and an extroverted and happy criminal who copes easily with the exigencies of life. The absurd was quite fashionable for a while, and a number of plays by Slawomir Mrozek, Václav Havel, and Milan Kundera, all taken to be vaguely absurdist, were imported from Poland and Czechoslovakia to extend the repertory of German stages.

In the early and mid-1960s, when the younger generation began asking radical questions, the theater turned to presenting the social and political facts of recent history (or so the playwrights believed) and, somewhat later, to analyzing how the underprivileged, whether on farms or in big cities, went on living without really knowing who manipulated their language and expectations. Documentary theater and the new "folkplay" (*Volksstück*) of the sixties were intimately linked to theatrical developments in the Weimar Republic that had never been fully realized because of Nazi intervention. The ground for the second phase of documentary theater (phase one occurred in the Weimar mid-twenties) was prepared by the delayed trials of Nazi functionaries and concentration camp guards, and TV reports about the recent past. It was Erwin Piscator who, returning to his commitment to historical documentation, produced Rolf Hochhuth's *Der Stellvertreter* [1963] (*The Deputy*, 1963) and immediately challenged the conservative establishment, encouraging other playwrights to study contemporary history and present the pertinent texts, reports, and files on a stage that was thus transformed into a stern courtroom and, occasionally, into an agitprop meeting. Documentary theater included a wide range of stage procedures, all based on the assumption that the author should submit to the authority of historical texts. While Hochhuth used documents to elaborate postscripts or quotations in long stage descriptions, others, including Heinar Kipphardt in *In der Sache J. Robert Oppenheimer* [1964] (*In the Matter of J. Robert Oppenheimer*, 1968) and Peter Weiss in *Die Ermittlung* [1965] (*The Investigation*) [1966], used the texts of court protocols and investigative hearings more consistently, without being able, or willing, entirely to sacrifice their own partisan interpretation of events. (Oppenheimer protested against Kipphardt's "reading" of his motivations.) In the years of the student revolt, documentary theater created its own new legends about the Vietcong, the revolutionary history of the 1920s, or Hölderlin, then in the mid-1970s gave way to the new folkplay and a renewed aversion to history itself. Gaston Salvatore's *Büchners Tod* [1972] (*Büchner's Death*) was a dirge, many observers believed, for the student revolt as well as documentary theater at large.

The new wave of the mid-sixties folkplays continued the Weimar theater's eagerness to contradict what affirmative celebrations of the *Volk* had obfuscated for social and political reasons. It was a matter no longer of material needs (alleviated to some degree by the welfare state), but of the miseries of impoverished minds haplessly filled with inherited prejudice and borrowed ideas, and of the dearth of genuine language, condemning the inarticulate to imitate the sham vocabulary of the media, if not to express their speechless desires in senseless violence. If, in the great social plays of the turn of the century, compassionate writers like Gerhart Hauptmann had still believed that even poor weavers and peasant girls were able to express, however strenuously and poetically, something meaningful about their burdens, the new naturalists had long ceased to believe in these possibilities of articulation. They studied the close interrelationship between a restricted vocabulary, social deprivation, and the lack of hope, and created a stage of inevitable clichés and long silences. In spite of its interest in Harold Pinter and Edward Bond, the new folkplay was largely a Bavarian and Austrian affair, strengthened by the traditions of the *Volksstück* in the Catholic provinces and by the belief of most of its local practitioners that in the South an older, perhaps precapitalist, form of experience strongly persisted. (This belief was not really borne out by sociological evidence, which showed that the Catholic South, formerly agricultural, had gone through a rapid and effective industrialization with a vengeance, whereas the North, with its old coal and steel industries, was regressing into an anachronism of its own.)

Martin Sperr was the first to shock the public with his *Jagdszenen aus Niederbayern* [1966] (*Hunting Scenes from Lower Bavaria*, 1972), and the young playwrights of the Graz group, including Wolfgang Bauer and Harald Sommer, were not long in exploring the world of provincial outsiders and dropouts. Not only in Austria but all over the Federal Republic, theaters were reviving the extraordinary plays of Ödön von Horváth (1901–38) about the innocent and vicious petty bourgeois of the early 1930s, as for instance his *Geschichten aus dem Wienerwald* (1931; *Tales from the Vienna Woods*, 1977). Rainer Werner Fassbinder, who had not yet resolved whether to work with his Munich *antitheater* or to make movies, rediscovered the Ingolstadt plays of Marieluise Fleisser, a gifted woman playwright of the Weimar years close to Brecht, who had promptly exploited her as a friend and fellow artist. Peter Turrini and later Franz Xaver Kroetz carried the folkplay far into the seventies and restored a stark stage realism absent in the immediate postwar years.

Fleisser's *Pioniere in Ingolstadt* [1928] (*Sappers in Ingolstadt*) and

Sperr's *Hunting Scenes from Lower Bavaria* clearly showed the historical continuities of the folkplay and perhaps a change of tone. Fleisser's play, once produced with Brecht's assistance and with Peter Lorre in a major role, shows Bavarian small-town life almost calmly, working with the depressing implications of spare language rather than with explicit argument. A regiment of (mostly North German) sappers arrives in town; hard pressed by their sergeant, the soldiers look for quick adventures with servant girls; and the girls yield to money, a means of emancipation, or to their own maudlin feelings, not shared at all by the men, who do not want to be trapped in emotional involvements. The sergeant drowns because his men do not want to save him, and a young girl learns how easy it is to be exploited by men, whether employers or lovers.

In *Hunting Scenes from Lower Bavaria*, Sperr paradoxically combines a more radical attitude, merciless in its accusations of an intolerant village community, with a dramaturgy close to the late nineteenth-century naturalist tradition. He tries to present the entire social structure of a typical village, from the rich *Bürgermeister* and the local priest down to the farmhand and the gravedigger (needless to say, the local philosopher), and explicitly relates his individual figures, insiders and outsiders, to property, labor, and the political context following World War II. Sperr shows how the village community angrily persecutes those who do not belong: Silesian refugees, who are foreigners in Bavaria; a retarded young man afraid of being shipped off to an institution by his widowed mother, who is eager to marry a younger farmhand; and Abram, unsure of himself, unemployed, and gay. Abram tries to conform to village expectations, but when a girl pregnant with his child demands that he marry her, he kills her, and the entire village sets out to hunt him down in order to deliver him to the authorities and collect a reward. He is sentenced to life imprisonment; the retarded man, his only friend, hangs himself; and the villagers, who celebrate at the inn and sing an old hunting song, make plans to use the reward money to buy a new church organ, while suggesting that another Hitler is needed to deal with such people.

The traditions of stage naturalism, the Bavarian peasant theater, and the radical critique of society sustain F. X. Kroetz's scenes of the bitter life of south German country and city plebeians, factory workers, and inarticulate petit bourgeois on the edge of instinctive violence. Kroetz (b. 1946) is not really one of them (coming from a middle-class family and the Munich *bohème*), but he has an exceptionally fine sensitivity, strengthened by many years in odds jobs, to what people say or rather are incapable of saying. While students of Marcuse in the late 1960s considered the fate of the underprivileged in neo-Hegelian terms, Kroetz put these people directly on the stage and fearlessly uncovered continents of speechless misery in a self-satisfied society priding itself on material success.

His play *Heimarbeit* [1971] (*Home Industry*) consists of twenty short scenes, or "takes," and operates with a merciless economy of character and props. He scorns naturalistic decorations à la Stanislavski; a table or a bed suffice, and idiomatic language alone, or rather the predominance of silence, creates a world of incessant want. A working couple, a father and mother with two children, live in a little town in south Germany. Willy, fortyish, has been injured in an accident (actually, he fell off his Moped while drunk), and in his convalescence earns his living by filling little seed packets while his wife Martha cleans apartments. In bed, Willy demands his marital rights, but tired Martha refuses; she tells him that she has become pregnant by somebody else while Willy was in the hospital—"not meaning to," she says. Willy explains to her how his mother aborted unwanted children with a knitting needle. She clumsily tries to follow his advice (onstage) but does not succeed; when the child is born, it has a disfigured forehead. Willy tries to kill the baby by exposing it to cold night air (the old peasant method of population control). When Martha leaves him in disgust, he spends his evenings masturbating (onstage) and kills the baby (onstage) in hot bath water. The little corpse is buried. Willy, who will be charged with child neglect rather than with murder, brings Martha home again. She tells her children that "now order has been restored," and when Willy wants to come to bed again, she simply tells him to wash first: "cleanliness is the most important thing." *Home Industry* shocked the Munich audiences because it was a radical play without radical politics. The stark concentration on the two people excludes dramatic analyses of economic and social background. The playwright in no way suggests that his Willy and Martha will ever change: outside, there may be revolts or emancipations, but inside, in crowded silence, there live people condemned to re-creating an order of mendacious rules and false cleanliness, nor is it at all clear whether their restricted idiom causes their poverty, or whether poverty condemns them to the utter lack of lucid speech.

We can read *Männersache* [1971] (*Men's Business*, 1976) only in a revised printed version, because Kroetz himself insisted that the play no longer be shown on the stage in its original form. Even in its new printed version, it is a nasty, claustrophobic story of power, role reversal, and violence. Martha, who continues to run the butcher and tripe shop that she inherited from her parents, falls for a working man, challenging all his traditional assumptions about "submissive women." After a good meal she suggests that they go see an X-rated movie. Then, shifting awkwardly to more literate High German, she confesses to him that she has started to write a diary that he should read, in order to learn how irrevocably "he stepped into her life." To humiliate her, Otto demonstratively pages through a pornographic magazine before telling her to undress (not completely, he implies, because he does not want to see all her ugliness) and complains about her whining dog, which, he says, distracts him from his usual feats in bed. Woman and man are caught in the belief that dignity comes only with dominance; he accuses her of sodomy, and she accuses him of having pissed on her in bed instead of demonstrating his virile powers. Pride, pain, and hate are fused in their mutual taunts, and since she wants a man equal to her stong feelings, she fiercely challenges him to a "match" where they will take shots at each other in turn with his gun. She shoots first and is pleased to see that he stands up to her, a true man, but in the continued exchange of fire (in which both fastidiously stick to the rules of the game, as if it were ping-pong) she is killed first and he, fatally wounded, staggers over her corpse. *Men's Business* has suffocating intensity and will provoke disturbing questions for many years to come (though Kroetz's American version is in effect a different play).

Stallerhof [1972] (*Farmyard*) [1981], the best of Kroetz's plays before he committed himself in the early 1970s to direct political action in the service of the German Communist Party (DKP), suggests many directions of his future work. The scene is a small

Bavarian farm, but Kroetz insists on revealing the realities of contemporary peasant life camouflaged by colorful folklore arranged for the tourists—the narrowest code of beliefs and traditions, and the most intolerant attitudes of those who have a little power over those who have less or none at all. It may be difficult to speak here of a love story in the usual sense. Sepp is a hired hand, fiftyish and hoping to retire soon (he thinks he will have enough money to live in Munich), and Beppi is the retarded fourteen-year-old daughter of a family of farmers who do not hide their disgust for her. Sepp is a lonely man (again, his only friend is his aging dog), and Beppi has nobody but Sepp, who listens to her questions, works with her in the stables, and tells her stories from the Wild West about the happiness of a white man and an Indian squaw, the parable of a happiness the two will never find. Sepp takes Beppi to the fair; when she defecates on a scary ride, he tenderly cleans her body, and then has intercourse with her without a word or thought. When the parents find out how she became pregnant, the father takes his revenge by firing Sepp and poisoning the dog, while the mother tries "to wash out" the baby with a solution of lye—without success, so that Beppi speechlessly enjoys her motherhood. In *Geisterbahn* [1975] (*House of Horrors*), a continuation of the play, she is ordered by the authorities to surrender the child to a state home and kills it rather than give it up. *Farmyard* was more popular with theatergoers than was *Men's Business* (the more powerful play), but of course Kroetz made it easier to grasp what brings Beppi and Sepp together. It is certainly the most "silent" of his plays: there are utterances in approximate Bavarian idiom, but the sweetest moments of innocence and love are articulated in gestures and in blissful pauses that constitute the essence of communication. The scene showing Sepp and Beppi in the garden of an inn (2.3), happy together without being able to say so, has an incredibly spare force strongly reminiscent of Büchner's *Woyzeck*, without being imitative at all.

In 1980, when Kroetz publicly announced that he had left the German Communist Party, he stated in an interview that he felt more attentive than ever to "his own existential ruins," which he wished to grasp as social phenomena, confirming his old aversion to bringing the "masses" onstage: he preferred individual characters whose experience and language were close to his own. Kroetz's play *Nicht Fisch nicht Fleisch* [1980] (*Not Fish Not Fowl*) suggests that his newly won intellectual independence has made him a more thoughtful and ambivalent writer; he keeps to his habitual realism of working-class characters, now articulate because they are Munich typesetters, and does not hesitate to work with an element of sudden expressionism, reminiscent of the young Brecht and his *Baal*. The environment is strictly contemporary: a printing shop is being modernized by the introduction of computers, and Kroetz wants to show how the lives of the workers and their wives are affected by the irrevocable change. Hermann eagerly represents his fellow workers as a glib trade union official and tries to convince them that technology should be used by the workers to build a better future. Edgar, his old friend, has difficulties being retrained because he refuses to accept the new abstract process, longs for the feeling of the lead letters in his experienced hands, and suspects that the new method is depriving him of qualifications that he acquired over long years of arduous experience. But Kroetz never looks at men alone: Hermann, who in the workshop utters all the trade union clichés, demands of his wife Helga that she abort their third child because they cannot afford further expenses, while Edgar, after he has given notice because he does not want to rely on a "trade union pittance in a featherbedding job in which he is not really wanted any more," feels emasculated by his successful wife Emmy, who rises from supermarket clerk to branch manager and at home talks about changing her outlet into a "nonrepressive sales environment," combining the profit advantages of the old-fashioned family store with those of a big supermarket. The men, who have left their homes, meet in a spectral lake landscape of existential despair and, like figures in a German expressionist drama, bare their souls to each other in language close to poetry. Hermann has been humiliated by his comrades, who are tired of his empty words (they applied a bicycle pump to his anus, so that he defecates blood), and Edgar, a lover of fish, takes off his clothes in preparation for a long swim, intending never to reappear from the freedom of the waters. Yet there is a semblance of earthly resolve: shivering and sick, both men return to their pregnant wives, and Helga prepares a warm and nourishing soup that they eat obediently. The title of the play refers to an existential condition of human beings deprived by nature of the airy and watery elements of untrammeled or instinctual living.

Inside and outside the political organization, Kroetz has gone through his own process of self-realization. The characters in his early plays were condemned to absolute solitude by their physiological drives and their inability to talk to others, but in the later plays they have learned that they are lonely in a shared world of love of work and marriage, closely interconnected, and do not expect a solution offered by any classic, socialist or otherwise. Kroetz, who has learned more from popular peasant farce than he himself admits, no longer tries to shock his bourgeois audiences with somber scenes of masturbation, sodomy, or abortion, but rightly insists that his working couples are closest to revealing the truth to each other when they go to bed after work. He continues using a more or less local dialect, not as an obstacle to communication but, in his own words, as a dignified "expression of work, landscape, and society." It is less clear whether his advancing sympathies for resolute, pregnant, soup-dispensing women, in contrast to foolish, unthinking males, mark a regression to a *Kinder und Küche* view of femininity long abandoned by others. The critic Georg Hensel once said that Kroetz was the only true Christian among contemporary German playwrights, and Kroetz's sustained compassion for the underprivileged among his fellow citizens certainly does not lack any of the virtues of a soul Christian by nature.

By the mid-1970s the renaissance of Weimar realism on the documentary stage and in the new folkplay was rapidly giving way, as sooner or later in other literary genres, to a new interest in private experience and individual feelings. Abandoning its spare courtroom sets and fake haystacks, the theater changed into an open space of intimate confession, strange mysteries, shows of the bare body, and cryptic fantasies. The old and the new subjectivity had been long sustained on the stage by Max Frisch and Peter Handke, who paradoxically and perhaps prematurely ceased to work for the theater, but younger playwrights of the political sixties had a difficult time disengaging themselves from the traditional idea of the stage as pulpit and tribune (a notion never totally abandoned in the GDR). In the West, Botho Strauss was almost the only dramatist to consider the quest of the individual for self-realization, but even in the GDR voices of lovers and husbands were increasingly heard onstage. New playwrights were largely absent. The directors emerged as the new masters of the stage and created their own theater of unfettered, intense, visionary performances, occasionally learning from the Living Theater (which had emigrated from the United States and was traveling in Europe) and from Jerzy Grotowski's rituals, but insisting on the absolute sovereignty of their interpretive fantasy, unwilling to submit to meanings sought by an earlier generation in inherited texts. If the sixties was an age of playwrights, the seventies was a decade of self-willed directors repelling those who wanted to hear the voices of authors, yet attracting audiences eager to see the emotional frustrations of the time played out by theatricality itself. New productions by Peter Palitzsch, Claus Peymann, Peter Zadek, Klaus Michael Grüber, Luc Bondy, and Peter Stein were discussed with an attention reserved in earlier times for new plays. Performances were shifted from the old stages to garages, factories, empty film sets and, in at least one trying instance, to the Berlin Olympia stadium. Georg Tabori of the older, and Pina Bausch of the younger, generation experimented with theatrical modes reducing the verbal element or using the pure motion of expressive dance.

In some contrast to the highly centralized theater in France, England, and (to a lesser degree) the United States, the traditional German decentralization of theatrical life, historically related to the regional autonomy of principalities and territories, makes the cultural landscape more varied and unpredictable. After the achievements, and much of the personnel, of the antifascist Zürich Schauspielhaus had been absorbed by the new postwar beginnings of the German and Austrian theater, it was Brecht's Berliner Ensemble that developed supreme standards of staging and acting in memorable performances widely imitated all over the world. Originally, the Ensemble was established by a 1949 decree of the SED Politburo naming Brecht as artistic manager and making his wife, Helene Weigel, a magnificent actress and disciplined party member, director of the enterprise. Brecht's successors Erich Engel (1881–1966), whom he had first met in Munich in the early 1920s, and Manfred Wekwerth loyally continued Brecht's work under rapidly changing conditions, in their own republic and internationally. In the late 1960s the most innovative younger people again congregated in West Berlin, where the city government was willing to support experiments of a radical kind, provided they brought back something of Berlin's glory of the 1920s. On August 1, 1970, the Berliner Schaubühne am Halleschen Tor was formed by directors, actors, dramaturges, and theater enthusiasts; for nearly ten years, by virtue of its courage, collective commitment, and intensity of performance, it was first among German theaters. The productions of Peter Stein, and also of Klaus Michael Grüber, were watched as eagerly all over Europe as Brecht's Ensemble had been twenty years before. Brecht's and Gorki's revolutionary play *The Mother* was the first production, but immediately after Brecht, Stein turned to Peter Handke, to be followed by Kleist, Botho Strauss, and magnificent stage "studies" of ancient Greek tragedy and Shakespeare. While the dispirited Left again mobilized its arguments against the new "culinary theater," the Schaubühne, now housed in the famous Erich Mendelsohn building on Lehniner Platz, developed, at least until the late 1970s, a magnificent art of the theater far surpassing the concepts of the fifties or sixties.

The entire structure of the theater, in German-speaking countries West or East, rests on a complicated system of public subsidies that have been provided for nearly three centuries, first by kings, princes, dukes, and archbishops, and later by cities, towns, and the administrations of cantons and regions; if the subsidies suddenly stopped, only a few metropolitan theaters, a scattering of private enterprises (abolished in the GDR since 1953), and a few traveling troupes would survive. In the postwar years the costs of running theaters—all of them repertory companies in American terms—have steadily increased: in 1958–59 42.8 percent of costs was covered by income from the sale of tickets in the Federal Republic, but in 1968 the figure was only 30 percent and in 1972 only 19 percent (even in theater-loving Austria, only 21 percent in 1972). The number of people attending theatrical performances fluctuates. Changing generational preferences and the new media keep some younger and older people away, and even in the *Kultur*-conscious GDR the number of people attending plays declined between the early 1950s and the late 1970s by one third, while attendance at children's plays nearly doubled.

In the Federal Republic, the sixties' cry for the destruction of "bourgeois theater" by radical actors, dramatists, and directors (all paid by allocation of tax money) alienated or offended theatergoers, who were mostly middle-class anyway. Between 1962 and 1972, West German theaters lost 12.8 percent of their audience, and the question was seriously discussed whether attendance should be free for everybody. The question was dropped quickly, however, not so much for budgetary reasons but because experts argued that German audiences, well trained in their traditional pieties, would not believe that something of cultural importance could be offered free and would therefore stay away completely. Professionals assume that, in the Federal Republic, on the average only 16.7 percent of all expenses (1984) are recovered by income, though Hamburg audiences contribute 24 percent to their theater budgets, audiences in Bavaria 20 percent, those in West Berlin 17.6 percent, and Hessian audiences as little as 11 percent. German theater has remained, in more than one sense, an eminently public affair.

BOTHO STRAUSS AND THE NEW SUBJECTIVITY

In any conversation about the changes of German literary sensibilities in the mid-seventies, or about the *Neue Subjektivität* that replaced the collectivist temper of the late sixties, Botho Strauss will be mentioned early, especially by those who for one reason or another underrate what Peter Handke has done in rediscovering that individual human beings have thin skins and suffer from terrible anxieties. In the plays and prose pieces by Strauss, the New Subjectivity has triumphantly established itself on the Berlin scene, once the birthplace of the student revolt and now the home of radical countercultures. While even playwrights like F. X. Kroetz and Heiner Müller at one time or other still face the necessity of defining themselves against Brecht's legacy, Strauss, who alludes to Jacques Lacan as easily as he does to Michel Foucault or Claude Lévi-Strauss, relegates Brecht and his epic theater to a past almost as distant as that of Marlowe or Sophocles. The son of a pharmacologist, Strauss was born in 1944 in Naumburg/Saale (later occupied by the Soviet army) and went to school in the Federal Republic, though his writing rarely alludes to his childhood experiences and the *Gymnasium* in the West where he was called the *Schnelldenker* ("fast thinker") by his classmates. His biography is that of a professional who does not say much about his private life. We know that he studied literature and sociology at the universities of Cologne and Munich, contributed to *Theater Heute* (*Theater Today*), the most important stage journal in the Federal Republic, and early participated in the creative work of the Berlin Schaubühne, assisting in the renowned productions of Kleist, Ibsen, and Gorki and staging a witty production of a nineteenth-century Labiche farce on his own.

In his first play, *Die Hypochonder* [1972] (*The Hypochondriacs*), Strauss writes for stage practitioners rather than for the audience. The young dramatist shows off his artful ability to construct a play in which traditional expectations are systematically disappointed and pretends to search for a higher meaning that is absent. We are told, ironically, that the mysterious events happen in Amsterdam in 1901, but the definitions of time and space seem no more than a useful cue to the set and costume designers to remove the characters, if such they are, from the present, though not too far. The complex "dark" plot (replete with at least three corpses, a cunning maid familiar from the French "well-made play," and a few philosophical discussions) develops in an aesthetically attractive milieu of seigneurial splendor with a leisurely pace that is almost Victorian. Nelly, a young woman, has killed a pharmacologist. Released on bail, she tells her husband Vladimir, a hypochondriac who seems to have great difficulties with living in general, that she murdered the man because he demanded that she leave Vladimir, whom she loves. It may be closer to the truth, however, as Vladimir's mother assures her son, that Nelly killed him in the service of a pharmaceutical corporation eager to get hold of a new TB antidote developed by her victim. Then Vladimir's father Jacob, who looks astonishingly like his son, give or take a few white hairs, announces in a great revelation scene that it was he who manipulated everything. Struck with terror, Nelly recognizes that she never acted of her own free will, since every one of her decisions was mere semblance, falsified by his mastery. The great manipulator also explains why it was necessary to kill other people; confesses that his old love for Nelly had its ultimate fulfillment when she recognized that she was always utterly dependent on his will; kills her, too; and leaves with the treacherous maid, who was in the know all along, or so she believes.

Here Strauss almost succeeds in isolating his theater, rich in literary allusions to Walter Benjamin and Borges, from his potential audiences. It is witty and self-involved Grand Guignol that makes good use of Friedrich Dürrenmatt's claustrophobic comedies of the 1950s, Frank Wedekind's disturbing frankness in revealing the darkest side of human affairs, and Georges Feydeau's nineteenth-century bedroom farce pressed to absurd extremes. Yet the playwright is so concerned with undercutting habitual assumptions that the play tends to break up into episodes and moments of emotional insight, funny confrontations, and self-assured gags. The final revelation scene comes almost in the shape of another play entirely, and leaves us with the unanswerable question as to whether the play is about father power or, anticipating Strauss's later writings, about people in search of their true selves.

In his subsequent plays Strauss moves deliberately toward people sadly reaching out for faint possibilities of true feeling in an age in which all cherry orchards have long been replaced by cement cities. He takes one step at a time, and his melancholy comedy *Bekannte Gesichter, gemischte Gefühle* [1975] (*Well-known Faces, Mixed Feelings*) cannot do without a sweet magical interlude, and flickering neon lights indicating that, for a moment at least, everyday causality has been suspended again. In a shabby hotel near Bonn, the capital of the Federal Republic, a few middle-aged couples and a permanent guest who happens to be an amateur magician of some accomplishment have been living together like characters in a Russian play about guests on a country estate. The hotel owner hopes to make a deal with the Ministry of the Interior to change the hotel into a vacation home for civil servants and so assure himself of a quiet bureaucratic job, but everybody, including the overage bellhop Günther, who does all the service jobs, opposes his plans. The guests do not see any reason to abandon their "astonishing memory of passions," or rather the memory of affairs involving everybody with everybody else. There are hobbies, fortunately, and all the guests watch Günther and Doris, the hotel owner's wife, train daily for the grand German tournament in ballroom dancing. When it becomes obvious that Doris lacks the requisite finesse, she suddenly disappears and, thanks to the magician, her place is taken by an idealized, ravishing, and accomplished Doris who dances with perfection and kindles new passion in her husband. When he insists on making love to her right away, the neon lights flicker again, the ideal Doris disappears, and the real Doris returns with a terrible hairdo, lots of food for the starving guests, and the announcement that she is pregnant. Next morning Stefan, her husband, is found dead in the hotel freezer: incapable of facing the new situation, he has committed suicide. While Doris foolishly hopes that he will come to life again by thawing, the others are happy that now they will be able to go on living in the hotel as before, with the old roof over their heads.

It may take some time before we grasp the mutual involvements of all the characters, but desires and relationships past and present are blurred in their own consciousness, and we somewhat confusedly participate in their gray life, until the other Doris appears to confront drab routine with the splendor and perfection of art. Stefan is the sensitive human being predestined to cruel disappointment; he wants to get rid of his musty hotel and mounting debts, and longs for the serenity of a steady job because he "feels sick" owning property. All he aims for is to become, in an ironic Arcadia, "a conscientious civil servant, a reasonable man: in a quiet modern office, with a view of some greenery, fully air-conditioned and with light, much light." When the magical Doris assures him that she is his wife, he has his legitimate doubts, yet wants to embrace her because he feels that a moment of love will change his life: "Passion, in me, hits an unsuspecting man." The mere possibility of that perfect and fulfilled moment makes it impossible for him to go on living.

In his *Trilogie des Wiedersehens* [1977] (*Three Acts of Recognition*)[1982], Strauss sketches a scenario about the contemporary disillusions of the new professional classes, including a few Yuppies, who make their first appearance on the German stage here. I would feel easier speaking about a return to late nineteenth-century stage traditions of realism and psychology, if the actual scene was not an art exhibition called "Capitalist Realism," ironically unmasking even the theater of realism as an event of calculating art. There is as little plot as in real human affairs. On the day before an official vernissage, members of an art club, weary habitués and hangers-on, congregate and talk about art and, more intensely, about themselves. They accuse each other of utter insensitivity, rehearse potential romances that are immediately discarded, and deplore their solitude: "Now, I'll be staring in the morning for a long time from my window, walk among alien people through the streets of the city, and so get a slight taste of life, without really noticing." These conversations and monologues take nearly five hours to perform, but since everybody talks about *Beziehungen* (relationships) and the impossibility of *Beziehungen*, German audiences usually attend in rapt concentration.

The scenes are arranged in cinematic sequences resembling a new and more inclusive version of Arthur Schnitzler's *Reigen* (1903; *Hands Around: A Cycle of Ten Dialogues*, 1920), with the contemporary difference, of course, that people do not consummate their affairs with constantly changing partners but for many reasons find it impossible to commit themselves at all. Everybody feels a recent loss, has been left by a lover or friend, lives alone, and deplores the lack of communication; only the invalid exhibition guard does not seem to have any difficulties at all, tells ethnic jokes (anti-Italian circa 1943) and, as an amateur broadcaster, talks easily on assigned wavelengths to his friends in Hartford, Connecticut. Feelings are burned out, tentative, in abeyance; two women console each other by saying how *glückstraurig* ("happily sad") they are. The play does not suggest that the arts offer a counterworld of meaning and purity, but the idea is not totally absent either. Pictures are at least capable of creating cracks in reality (where the sign dominates, somebody says, the thing to which it refers cannot be), and the young writer Peter tells us in moving soliloquies, clearly in the service of the playwright, that art, in an age in which human capabilities of enjoying and suffering are withering away, should help "resuscitating tears, lost laughter . . . and the great agitations" of the heart.

Six years after the premiere of his first play, many critics considered Strauss the most gifted and provocative playwright in the Federal Republic, and believed that he had come closest to reflecting recent transformations, public and private. After his "scenes" *Gross und Klein* [1978] (*Big and Little*) [1979] had appeared in print (four editions within two years), most of the important theaters competed to be among the first to produce the new play. It shows a woman's haunting quest for something she herself would have difficulty naming exactly. If, in earlier plays, Strauss moved from an element of countercausality and magic to everyday conversations in a bleak space totally our own, he now strongly communicates a feeling of how unbearable our world would be without transcendence of some kind or other. Lotte, thirtyish, not particularly intellectual but not particularly foolish either, wants to be involved in the lives of others. Incessantly trying to listen, to talk, to share, and to help, she is unable to find responding kindness, a tender gesture, a place that welcomes her. Her journey without fulfillment takes her from North Africa to the north and the industrial west of Germany. Though she may have learned something about herself (for her understanding of what happened to people seems less and less tentative), people shut her out, warn her against involving herself too much, and condescend with a smile when, almost looking like a bag lady, she begins to rummage in rubbish heaps, insisting that she is looking for newspaper articles written by her husband. In the last scene she sits, disconsolate and alone, in the waiting room of a physician, but since she has not made an appointment and cannot say what is wrong with her, she is asked to leave, like so many times before.

Never has Strauss worked with so many divergent and colorful figures and yet created such drab regions of solitude, dearth of willingness to understand, and despair hidden in the most inconspicuous idioms of small talk. There are dozens of characters of many age groups and regional origins, but they no longer appear in large and cozy congregations: at most, they come in hapless pairs, or they have lost something of their humanity, as for instance the family of the Frisian dentist who, terrified by the thought of potential losses, has even his garden furniture cemented into the infertile ground. Lotte remains cut off from other people by our conditions of life, technological and otherwise; she listens behind drawn blinds, talks in front of windows that are shut in her face, lingers at the gates of apartment blocks to find the right buzzer, wanders through long corridors (individual rooms being shown in short scenes), and writes a letter, never to be mailed, in a vandalized telephone booth. Any apartment, any office, any human space has become as distant, forbidding, and unreachable as the castle was to Kafka's sad K.

In *Big and Little* Strauss productively uses the expressionist or Strindbergian dramaturgy of a quest proceeding by stages, but offers little hope of ultimate solutions or salvations. In spite of the epic sweep of her journey, Lotte does not really progress anywhere, unless one measures her progress in eighths of inches. Against her will, Lotte asks metaphysical questions and, to the astonishment of many, speaks of God, "who is simple and who does not change." In one of her extended monologues, distinct in its density of metaphor, she suddenly confronts a giant book that oozes blood, and earnestly tells the Creator that she does not want to be his "vessel" or "chalice," since mere existence is difficult enough; she refuses to sustain his burdens, too, in addition to everything else. She knows that He is at work: He first made everyone abandon her and then headed straight for her. Saying her "No!," Lotte tries to stop the blood dripping from the pages of the book, which may incarnate her life, and on an impulse cannot but embrace it as her very own. Thus, in spite of qualms and indirections, a young German playwright shows us a human being, wounded and seeking, quarreling with a power above and beyond humanity.

By profession and early commitment, Botho Strauss is a dramaturge and playwright, but his stories and novels are not mere comments on his plays. His first stories express a sharp consciousness of loss, rehearsing the possibility and impossibility of living in a void created by a sudden absence, estrangement, or departure: there is nothing left to do but die slowly or defend oneself by writing, with uncertain results. In *Marlenes Schwester* (1975; *Marlene's Sister*) a middle-aged schoolteacher suffering from an elusive blood disease parts ways with her sister, who refuses to be annihilated in a vampiric relationship, and wastes away in a country commune where she is gently tolerated by the workers, who believe that her feelings belong to a past age of society. In *Theorie der Drohung* (1975; *A Theory of Threat*) a young author commits himself so intensely to what he writes about a mysterious woman (who suggests that she is the one who left him recently) that he loses the consciousness of his own self, making it impossible for us to separate his own thoughts from those of the woman and the text he writes about her. Both the schoolteacher in her agonies and the author in the process of writing are "zero persons" or tremendously porous personalities; inside and outside merge, love changes into the "burning passion to observe each other constantly, from changing distances in space," and death and writing emerge as the ultimate destructive and creative powers respectively.

In his novel *Die Widmung* (1977; *The Devotion*, 1979), Strauss has not yet freed himself completely from the compulsion of his earliest stories, yet he assures himself of an ironic distance by alternating a third-person narrative about a young man abandoned by his woman friend with long excerpts from a manuscript of his ruminations. Once again, in a deteriorating Berlin apartment, we encounter "the implosion of desire in a vacuum, consisting of longing, waiting, the emptiness of the I, stillness, and a lack of hope." The young man, a bookseller who has given up his job, spends seven or eight hours a day on his "conscientious and terrible protocol of separation," hoping to present his pages to the woman and compel her, by the power of his writing, to return to him. When she finally calls, he takes the manuscript and, even though he is told that he is no longer wanted, leaves it with her in a cab. A new life begins: expecting her to return soon after reading his protocol, he cleans the apartment, takes a new job, and prepares exquisite food, only to be told by an innkeeper that a cab driver has returned an unopened manuscript left behind by a woman. The unread manuscript, an anatomy of solitude, is rich in insights for any reader.

Strange, powerful, and of far-reaching implications, Strauss's novel *Rumor* (1980; *Tumult*, 1984) closely explores a father-daughter relationship in a technological society functioning by psychological repression. Fortyish and uncertain about his future, Bekker, a frustrated communications and planning expert, returns from the north of Germany, where he tried in vain to find a university job, to Frankfurt, where he hopes to get work in a research institute where he was employed once before. He now suddenly becomes aware that Grit, his daughter, has grown into a self-assured woman who runs a travel agency and complicates her life by wanting to separate from her lover, a survivor of the late sixties. Vegetating in the brutal city, Bekker feels tortured. Father and daughter decide to go for an Austrian vacation, but it turns into a unmitigated disaster. Bekker begins to drink, and Grit, who has long suffered from cysts and circulatory problems, falls ill and has to be taken back to Germany, where the surgeon suggests that subsequent operations may or may not ease her afflictions. While Grit recuperates, her father feels closer to her than ever. On their return to her apartment, however, where Bekker serves as nurse and cook, she feels threatened by his growing emotional demands. Precariously balancing his willingness to help and his sexual desires, she relegates him to a dark little room from which he undertakes restless walks through the city, where he encounters the forlorn and lonely. Crying out for closeness, he tries to masturbate in her presence, but Grit resolutely packs his bags and exiles him to a small hotel. For days, her telephone keeps ringing and when she answers, she hears "nothing but the heavy, lascivious, forest-deep breathing of a man who must have the lungs of a giant."

In one of his ghastly nighttown encounters, Bekker meets his old teacher Bongo standing in front of his old house, from which Bongo has been evicted by his son, who makes money in real estate. Hurt and without a future, the two men compete with each other in violently deprecating all the fundamental ideas on which traditional humanism was once built. Bongo, a biologist, declares that human beings appeared in history as mere "typos of genetic transmission, pure coincidences, mistakes, disturbances in the process of duplication," while Bekker intones a semiotic dirge on humanity at large, once the pride of philosophy and history: "we are filled to the brim with microtexts, codes and alphabets, nothing but the dominance of laws and alien structures—where should space be left for an I?" Yet before life yields totally to code systems, says Bekker, things will triumph over human beings: one day, in the garden, the abandoned grill will suddenly speak to a piece of chewing gum, "while we human beings stand there stiff and speechless, and thinking of the falling snow."

Strauss obliquely warns us against attributing a character's opinions to the author. Taking our cue from his argument against "certain and foolish assumptions," we should strictly separate Bekker's complaints against humanism, in the wake of the younger Barthes and Michel Foucault, from what the entire novel wants to say. Bekker may describe the disappearance of the individual, to be superseded by information codes, but the book certainly makes a stand for individuality, since it is peopled by human beings of the most diverse kind: eager insurance agents, a funny Austrian waitress, a fearful woman proud of her pregnancy, and Grit herself, shaken by the pains of her sick body and weakened by her illness (described in full physiological detail)—all individuals demanding compassion and needing charity. As in some of Strauss's plays, sensitive people are driven to look beyond the material confines of their social condition for something more substantial, different, strong, and difficult to name. If Lotte in *Big and Little* believes herself involved in an involuntary struggle with a transcendent power, Bekker listens intently and furiously to the diffuse voices and rumors of what the social codes silence and repress; deep down, he believes he hears the disruptive noises of an approaching earthquake or terrible geological dislocations, mad desires, the "communications of the universe," a "grand river" majestically running under the brittle crusts of the earth. It is the ultimate, the anarchic voice of undisciplined life; in his heavy breathing, if it is indeed his, all repression, all suffering, all the power of nature invincibly resound.

It has become one of the basic ploys of Botho Strauss reviewers to say that he speaks for a generation disappointed by the failures of the student revolt, but I personally believe that the issues of the late sixties have become, for the people of his dramatic and narrative world, as meaningless as last year's snow. There may have been an age of collective rage, but his men and women were never a part of it; they are no longer aware of history, German or any other, or for that matter of any future for which to work and live. Strauss shows the lives of these people but does not necessarily sympathize with them all. Anguished by the terrible presence of all perceptions in the modern consciousness dominated by total synchrony, he demands that the true poet write against the "freaks of presence" (*Gegenwartsfreaks*) by "breaking with his time and by unchaining himself from the totality of presence." He has called one of his most rewarding collections of prose pieces *Paare, Passanten* (1981; *Couples, Passersby*), and his characters in plays and narratives are true loners, hermits, and *flaneurs* who constantly think about their failing relationships with other women and men. Even if, as in his witty (and somewhat frothy) play *Der Park* [1984], Titania and Oberon come to West Germany to resuscitate, in a new midsummer night's dream, love and lust in the minds of the people and to "awaken deeply buried desires," they cannot but grotesquely fail in their effort to discover a genuine reflection of their own erotic powers in the "feeble souls" of the new urban professionals, continually discussing their confused "logic of feeling."

Families, clans, the solidarity of people working in the same office, political organizations—none of these exists any longer in a universe of self-enclosed, shabby city apartments, while the sociological language of yesterday has totally yielded to the fern-bar idiom of psychotherapy, marvelously parodied in his *Kalldewey Farce* (1981). To say that Strauss is one of the first postmodern German writers really means that he admires Georges Bataille, Rilke's *Duino Elegies*, Celan, or Cassavetes rather than epic theater or the German classics. He needed a few years to rid himself of his own clever handling of Wedekind, Dürrenmatt, and the French well-made play before turning into a kind of Chekhov of the German welfare and singles society, and it is characteristic that many of his people, above all Lotte and Bekker, reveal an intense longing for something that may be transcendent, a strong power above or a threatening tumult below. It has been a long time, at least in German writing, since we have heard of such desires.

HEINER MÜLLER: A LOSS OF FAITH

Heiner Müller was known for a long time to theater professionals rather than to mainstream audiences, and only after collaborating recently with Robert Wilson has he been more widely discussed in the United States. He does not write for the commercial theater, trying to create a consensus of affirmative pleasures. Müller learned a good deal from his father's political experience; the older man, an organization Social Democrat from way back, was put in a concentration camp in 1933, released, and imprisoned again because he refused to accept the Nazi regime; later he was expelled from the GDR Party of Socialist Unity because of his "Titoism" (i.e., unwillingness to acknowledge Stalin's supremacy) and avoided persecution by the new authorities only by escaping to the West. Müller, born in 1929 in Saxon Eppendorf, served in the Reich Labor Service and in the Wehrmacht. After the liberation he worked in offices and cultural organizations until he was hired by the East German Maxim Gorki Theater (1958–60). After many conflicts with the hierarchy, he became dramaturge of the post-Brechtian Berliner Ensemble (1970–76), and later of the East Berlin Volkstheater. He began writing short scenes about his war experiences and the life of people building the new socialist industries. His impressive scenarios included a dramatic version [1956] of John Reed's *Ten Days That Shook the World*. In his early sketches he preferred the radical agitprop style of the Soviet late 1920s and of Brecht's sparse *Lehrstücke*, considered "formalist" by the GDR authorities in the mid-1950s, and in his burning thirst for a Communist absolute found himself far to the left of the Party's intentions. His "industrial" plays *Der Lohndrücker* [1958] (*The Scab*), *Die Korrektur* [1958] (*The Correction*, 1984), and *Der Bau* (*The Construction Site*)—the latter written in 1963–64—appeared in print rather than in frequent performance and were publicly criticized by the functionaries. His "agricultural" play *Die Umsiedlerin oder Das Leben auf dem Lande* (*The Refugee, or Life in the Country*), completed in 1961, was performed once and did not reappear on the stage until ten years later in revised form.

In 1965 the Party's Central Committee renewed the fight against "skepticism" and "immorality," seen as ultimately serving the capitalist class enemy, and Müller together with Wolf Biermann figured prominently among the chief sinners. (Müller's wife Inge, who had often collaborated with him, committed suicide one year later.) Like other GDR playwrights, Müller responded to party criticism by turning to adaptations of the ancients, Shakespeare, and venerable Soviet classics, but each of his adaptations turned out to be a contemporary play in camouflage, raising the most disturbing questions about what communism had promised and what it was delivering to the people. His quasi tetralogy—*Philoktet* (completed in 1966; *Philoctetes*, 1981), *Herakles 5* (1965), *Der Horatier* (1968; *The Horatian*, 1976), and *Mauser* (1970;1976)—ingeniously sets the ancients and Brecht against each other, and in a language more intense and poetic than that of any other living German playwright, confronts head-on the issue of ends and means, and of human beings manipulated by one another in the name of history or truth. If Müller had lived in the age of the Inquisition, he would long since have been burned at the stake as a heretic, but the GDR functionaries try to deal with his radical plays by using the carrot and stick: he has received some of the highest literary awards that the government distributes, but has been expelled from the Writers' Union (1961) and banned from the stage many times. (*Mauser* was first performed in 1980 by students and faculty of the Austin Theater Group at the University of Texas, with the author attending; *Philoctetes* was performed in the GDR only in 1977.)

In his plays of the late 1970s and early 1980s, if they are still plays and not explosions of nervous energy aimed at the constrictions of the stage and of life itself, Müller has gone far beyond his dispute with the Party and the technical possibilities of the stage, epic or otherwise. Though not wanting to relinquish entirely his belief in the emancipation of human beings, he has lost his faith in a rational future and sees history as a whore. Torn between faint memories of hope and black despair, he tramples on tradition and, as in *Hamlet Maschine* [1979] (*Hamlet Machine*, 1984), tears old plays impatiently to pieces. In his *Germania Tod in Berlin* [1978] (*Germania Death in Berlin*), he grotesquely heaps together the horrors of the German past, creating collages of betrayal, torture, and death; in more recent plays, returns to the world of the French *ancien régime* to excavate images of power, errant reason, and sex. It is paradoxical that Germany's only present-day metaphysical playwright should be a disenchanted Communist who long dreamed of the revolutionary Soviet Union as Utopia lost, and now is obsessed by images of people torturing each other, as if performing a tableau by the Marquis de Sade.

Müller's early "industrial" plays differ from those of his East German contemporaries in their aversion to conventional stage realism. *The Scab* and *The Correction* are plays about the changes people undergo in a socialist society—imperceptible, painful, and often against the comfortable habits of their fellow workers who are still deeply rooted in the past. *The Scab* goes back to the economic and ideological problems of the immediate postwar period, when the authorities tried to increase productivity by richly rewarding exemplary worker "activists" who, imitating the early Soviet miner Alexei Stakhanov, far surpassed required production norms. In those years the East German mason Hans Garbe became a national hero, and even Brecht, at least for a fleeting moment, thought of writing a play about him. Müller, however, takes a closer look at what was involved in pushing workers to superproductivity. He tells the story of one Balke (Garbe) who in his brickyard and ceramics plant (actually Siemens-Plania in East Berlin) outperforms everybody else and challenges his buddies, more interested in wages and a few extra bottles of beer, to productive competition. Contrary to regulations, one of Balke's coworkers uses wet stones to speed up repair work on the factory kiln and causes it to burst. Construction almost stops, and the technicians are helpless because they assume that the kiln has to cool down before fundamental repairs can be made, but Balke says that he can work on the kiln chamber by chamber while the fires are going.

Yet Balke is not a man without a past: the local party secretary, who has to decide whether Balke's ideas are feasible, knows for many reasons that Balke can do the job effectively. They had worked together in an armaments plant during the last years of the war, and when the secretary systematically sabotaged the production of grenades for the Wehrmacht, Balke, though not a Nazi, denounced him to the authorities in order to save his own life. Yet the party secretary also knows that fulfillment of the production plans requires that Balke's offer be accepted, that there is no room for revenge. Balke, more hated than ever by his fellow workers, is roughed up after work, but he tries to do his job nevertheless, even after stones have been put in the heat ducts and repair work has to be halted for some time. Balke (again) tells the authorities, or rather the party secretary, who the saboteur is. Work has to go on; one of Balke's helpers is felled by the intense heat; another assistant is needed and, surprisingly, one of Balke's enemies volunteers for the job. Balke first hesitates but then accepts his offer, not out of friendship but because he needs help. Balke has learned his lesson from the local party secretary: he and his adversary set out to complete an important job.

Even friendly critics complain that, in *The Scab*, Müller tries to deal with too many complicated issues at once. The compression of interests is not diminished by the sparse and laconic mode, closely related to the expressionist theater and Brecht's *Lehrstücke* of the early 1930s. Yet absence of realism does not exclude the presence of social realities: Müller, who above all believes in the perfection of the absolute idea, does not shy away from showing the imperfections of human beings, which will be healed by progressing history. The local party secretary (Müller's positive hero, exactly as prescribed by the Soviet traditions of Socialist Realism) knows that communism has to be built by people here and now, not by saints; it is precisely the strength of nascent socialism, he believes, that it can and does use the energies of middle-class engineers, former Nazis, drunks, and rowdies whose only interest is the weekly paycheck, booze, and fornication. There are few consumer goods to be had, workers are frustrated, and when the comrade who used the wet stones is sentenced to seven years in prison for sabotage, they go on a rampage and destroy the food sold by the state at exorbitant prices in the factory shop. The party secretary clearly sees the contradictions in the construction of socialism in a country only recently dominated by fascists. Balke's energy triggers, as critics have suggested, a process of learning in the minds of people around him, but he himself is one of those who first have to learn the difficult lesson of giving up self-regard in his work for the future of society. *The Scab* wants to be a spiritual exercise, or a play about transformation of consciousness: to condemn the activist Balke as a scab reveals an obsolete way of thinking; to see that his dedication to work contributes to the general well-being of everybody is to gain a new perspective on material production.

The trouble is that Müller uses a story of double sabotage to prepare for Balke's enlightenment: when Balke denounced a co-worker to the Nazi authorities, he was a despicable informer, but when (after some hesitation, for he does not want to be pushed into his old role again) he tells the party secretary, his former victim, who has sabotaged the kiln repairs, he turns out to be a loyal and admirable defender of the new republic. There is too much ideological melodrama in such a dialectical reversal to prepare for Balke's willingness to go back to the defective kiln with somebody who hates his guts. Balke repeats in his own way what the local party secretary has himself done in accepting Balke as an activist, but the experience of the two men—the one imprisoned by the Gestapo, the other one kicked by his buddies on a dark street corner—cannot be compared easily, and the disparity threatens to make the play's structure of motivations totally mechanical and abstract.

After the party conference of 1965, Müller was not the only author and playwright to turn from contemporary issues of industrial and agricultural production to the classics (so did Peter Hacks, among others). Müller used the older texts more radically and with greater distrust than any of his colleagues, in order to explore questions of principle—of lying and speaking the truth, of manipulating people and respecting their spontaneity, of fighting for a grand cause by using villainous means. It is of only limited usefulness to compare the Sophoclean original of *Philoctetes* (409 B.C.) and the Müller version, first performed in Munich [1968], and much later in the German Democratic Republic [1977] and off Broadway [1980]. Sophocles' *Philoctetes*, a somber play with a happy ending, is rich in changing emotion, from lyrical feeling to the tortured cries of the diseased hero; it is peopled by merchants and humble sailors, all ultimately guided by the gods, and in the end is illuminated by the splendor of divine Heracles, appearing ex machina, who will bring Philoctetes and his famous bow back to Troy, where the hero will be healed of his festering wound. Müller has cut the story to the bone, banished the gods, excluded the extras, and transformed the melodrama into a searing disquisition about war, deceit, murder, and untruth. The initial situation may be that of Sophocles, but Müller has changed the characters and aims. As the Trojan War drags on, Ulysses and Neoptolemus, Achilles' son, land on the lonely island of Lemnos, where diseased Philoctetes, master of the invincible bow, had been left by the Greeks ten years before. It is not really the bow, however, that Ulysses wants but Philoctetes himself, whose appearance before Troy may be the only means of driving Philoctetes' listless men to battle again: "There is no life on Lemnos which the war/ does not need before Troy." Ulysses knows that Philoctetes hates him, for it was he who had left the "useless" hero, incapable of fighting, on the island. He tries to convince young Neoptolemus that Philoctetes cannot be taken by force from the island, at least as long as he has his bow, but that a "net" of arguments would do the job more effectively. Ulysses suggests arguments that Neoptolemus can put before Philoctetes more convincingly than anybody else—namely, that Neoptolemus himself was offended by Ulysses when deprived by him of his father's weapons (true), that he has left the alliance against Troy (false), and that on his way home he wants to rescue the suffering Philoctetes (also false). Neoptolemus at first refuses to dishonor himself by telling lies, however useful, but Ulysses reminds him that he is bound by supreme duty to win the war and therefore cannot refuse to serve the cause.

Philoctetes, who initially distrusts the young stranger, feels moved, after so much solitude, by the presence of a human being who speaks his own language. Against his better instincts, he believes what Neoptolemus tells him and, after one of his terrible seizures, in a mellow and almost lyrical moment of anticipating his return home, hands over his bow to the young man. But honest Neoptolemus does not want to hide the truth any longer and tells Philoctetes why he has agreed to tell Ulysses' lies. In the final confrontation Philoctetes and Ulysses compete for the allegiance of Neoptolemus. While Ulysses and Neoptolemus rage against each other, Philoctetes seizes his weapon and brings down a vulture to serve as Ulysses' last meal. To protect Ulysses, his ally for the duration of the war, the impetuous Neoptolemus kills Philoctetes, and Ulysses, totally unmoved, has to think up another repertory of lies in order to use at least the dead Philoctetes in the service of the cause. He carries the corpse to the waiting ship and plans to tell Philoctetes' men that vicious Trojans invaded Lemnos and killed their leader, because he had refused their offer to change sides: "They killed him for his loyalty/ because they could not change it/ with their gold." It is a good propaganda story, Ulysses hopes, and will renew the anger of Philoctetes' men waiting before Troy.

Müller's *Philoctetes* is a cryptic play because it unfolds, in spite of its concrete images, on a high level of abstraction. Critics in East and West have tried for years to define their divergent understandings of what the events on the stage actually mean, and their efforts have not been made easier by the author himself, who at different moments has offered his own interpretive contributions, somewhat inconsistent with each other or with the play, or seemingly so. When the play was first published in the GDR in 1965, Müller's friends defended *Philoctetes* as an "anti-imperialist play" showing a barbarous society greedy for spoils and war; Ulysses was simply the older and Neoptolemus the younger nihilist, and Philoctetes a truly tragic hero who was killed because he did not want to fight. Meanwhile Müller's inquisitive adversaries at home stressed the pervasive pessimism of the play (GDR functionaries like their tragedies optimistic), and at least one of them ominously mentioned that a few readers felt that the play was "inimical to the Party." In West Germany an intelligent attempt was made to interpret *Philoctetes* philosophically in terms of a perfect Hegelian tragedy: Ulysses was inevitably both right and wrong to represent the overriding interest of the state, and Philoctetes both right and wrong to insist on his individuality. But more recent discussions in the GDR, after the play's first performance in 1978, show that Müller's fellow citizens have a difficult time dwelling with pure abstractions, even Hegelian ones, and want to interpret the play in a way relevant to their experience: it is a question of how far ancient myth can be used to illuminate issues "internal to socialism," as the interpreters coyly say, or whether history, as an ever-renewed presence of people tortured and manipulated, stops outside the Berlin Wall.

Müller himself is rather shrewd in his suggestions: when queried recently, he told his audiences to read the text closely and insisted that events of the play were taking place in the "prehistory" (*Vorgeschicte*) of mankind, but as early as the mid-1960s he also said that *Philoctetes* offers "a discussion of problems and wrong developments, connected, e.g., with the person of Stalin." More recently, Müller returned to the difficulties of *Philoctetes* in a published letter (1983) to Mitko Gotcheff, his Sofia director, voicing continuing worries about the play, which, he thought, should not be produced in the abstract mode of Brecht's *The Measures Taken*; the actors, as they did in Sofia, should bring to the play "the accidental, the unnecessary, the 'pebbles,' " and show "the resistance of the bodies to the rape by the objective necessity of ideas, the word that has turned into murder." Turning against "fashionable" interpretations, Müller calls *Philoctetes* "the negative of a Communist play" and argues that the relationship of theater, reality, and audience is more complicated than Brecht believed: "the theater can rediscover its memories only by forgetting its audience," or by asserting theater as theater in which the actor contributes *to* the emancipation of the audience by his or her emancipation *from* the audience.

Müller has surrounded *Philoctetes* with a number of short choral scenes and a farce (or rather a potential postlude), and these texts may be helpful in defining the range of his ideological interests, at least in the late 1960s, and the special way in which he combined fragments of ancient myth and the formal idiom of Brecht's *Lehrstücke* at its most disturbing and skeletal. Close readers of Soviet and Communist history may understand these texts more readily than other audiences, but even the ideologically disengaged will be challenged by the precision of these chilling pieces. In *The Horatian* a Roman hero returns home and kills his sister as she weeps over the corpse of a slain enemy, after which the chorus of judges demands that, in public events, the full truth about the hero/killer be made known to all future generations: one part of the truth should never be sacrificed to the other. In *Mauser* an experienced comrade who has meted out revolutionary justice in a Soviet city to defend it against outside and inside enemies in the civil war is put to death by his own comrades, because he has continued to kill people in his rage for blood and without painfully reflecting in each case. *Herakles 5* (written in 1964–65) reveals Müller's unsuspected sense of broad humor. Heracles, rather tired after completing four of his gigantic labors, confronts labor number 5, the cleaning of the Augean stables. Suddenly feeling his vital strength incarnating the energies of all working people, he decides to challenge his father Zeus: "Allow me/ to change your world, Dad!" Müller's interpreters and critics in East and West have always preferred to analyze his ideas and, understandably, have rarely given full attention to his admirable poetic idiom. In the plays of the late 1960s, above all in *Philoctetes*, Müller proceeds from and refines Brecht's method of creating an irregular, grating, roughed-up blank verse that compels listeners to think about what is being said, rather than immersing themselves in emotional empathy sustained by the sweet deceit of regular beats. The verse itself, with its sudden inversions, postponements of key nouns, and harshly arranged accents, operates as a fundamental alienation effect that makes the audience, or so the playwright hopes, reflect the total situation of the speakers, however dense their utterances. In the recent development of German dramatic verse, a straight line runs from Brecht's early version of Marlowe's *Edward II* to Müller's *Philoctetes.* While there may be German playwrights more willing to accommodate the theatrical desires of their audiences, there is none who can compete with Müller's noble and disturbing scenic verse.

Müller has said that he wrote *Germania Death in Berlin,* which is characteristic of his later work, between 1956 and 1971, but, as so often, he may well have used older scenes and scattered materials to complete a discordant, desperate, and provocative spectacle closer to absurdist theater and Antonin Artaud than to Brecht. It is a gory and grotesque vision of German history, eschatological in its frustrated hopes, presented as a collage of the most divergent materials, theatrical styles, encounters, and episodes—a dance of death in which dismembered Wehrmacht soldiers, Hitler, old Communists, whores, young workers with illusions, children, and kings move like puppets, deliberately showing their strings. The fourteen scenes or parts constitute a panorama of German history from the mid-eighteenth century down to our own days, but dramatic attention clearly concentrates on events of basic importance to German communism: the end of World War I, the 1919 Spartacus rising, Stalingrad and its consequences, the establishment of the GDR, and the revolt of June 17, 1953, when construction workers on the East Berlin Stalinallee struck against their own government. Many scenes are paired and comment on each other. *Brandenburg Concerto One/Two* presents Frederick the Great as a talented clown and then, two hundred years later, shows a reception in his Potsdam castle (in which he still appears as a funny feudal vampire) to honor an exemplary worker who appears with a bandaged head, because his fellow workers almost killed him out of hate for his socialist fervor. *Brothers One/Two* offers first a reading of selected passages from Tacitus's *Annals* about two inimical brothers among the restive German tribes on the Roman border, and then a glimpse of a GDR prison cell in which two other brothers meet: a former Nazi specialist in torture who was first tortured by the Gestapo himself and then deserted by his former friends on the left, and a loyal Communist now being purged by his own comrades, who is killed by the other inmates. German history has changed into a Grand Guignol: dying soldiers returning from the Russian plains encounter heroes of the *Nibelungenlied* who masturbate onstage, while in his *Führerbunker* Hitler drinks gasoline, chews on rugs, and clutches the tits of Goebbels, who has become pregnant. Yet there is a story, though a faint one, implying something like a message for the last and true believers. This message is cast in heroic blank verse that separates it from the prose and rhymed couplets of the rest of the play. The characters who speak such meaningful language (earlier reserved for kings and queens) are Hilse, an old worker and believing Communist; a young mason; and a prostitute whom the young mason deeply loves. Old Hilse (reminiscent of the fatally wounded weaver in Gerhart Hauptmann's famous naturalist tragedy written in 1892) had been hurt by a stone-throwing gang of young thugs when he continued working while others went on strike against the GDR government, but in the hospital he has been shifted to the cancer ward to die there; the young worker and the prostitute visit him to be with him during his last moments. In his agony, he proudly tells about the coming victory of communism, anticipated by the Moscow metro built by the people for the people: "If you had eyes/ to see through my hands translucent/ red flags over the Rhine and the Ruhr."

Müller's loss of belief in salvation by history results in the progressive atomization of his plays. In the absence of promised meaning, the later plays fall apart into brief scenarios, fragments, manipulated quotations from classical drama, caricatures, or puppet shows. In *Das Leben Gundlings Friedrich von Preussen Lessings Schlaf Traum Schrei* [1979] (*Gundling's Life Frederick of Prussia Lessing's Sleep Dream Scream*, 1984), the incoherent title itself indicates the discontinuities of the historical montage, which concentrates on bits and pieces from the lives of J. P. F. von Gundling (Leibniz's successor as president of the Prussian Academy of Science), the Prussian philosopher-king (who was as brutal with his troops as his father Frederick William had been), and the enlightened playwright G. E. Lessing, to whom Müller feels particularly close, precisely because Lessing failed in his self-chosen task of creating a theater of national significance. West German audiences usually leave the theater in protest when the scenario is performed, but the Dadaists would have loved it, perhaps deluding themselves about the abyss of rage and personal despair from which these brief scenes of brutality and destroyed hope emerge.

Heiner Müller's achievements are among the most important of the German stage, and his conflicts with the GDR Party and its cultural policies have long hidden from many Western audiences his radical change of beliefs and techniques. He is the only playwright in the Communist world who, so far, has successfully combined personal allegiance to the past of socialism with the most challenging exploration of despair and hate of history, which he shows to be a torture chamber in which human flesh is torn and burned. He came to distrust Brecht's new version of the old Schillerian idea of the theater as a moral institution, and by the early 1970s felt compelled to articulate his loss of ideology in the idiom of Beckett and Artaud, and, in *Das Quartett* [1982] (*The Quartet*, 1984), his recent play about language, acting, power, and sex, in the idiom of Choderlos de Laclos and Sade. His early plays are still peopled by thoughtful party secretaries, hard-working peasants, and proletarians eager to learn a rational lesson about the future of socialism, but he went on to create a theater of blood and domination, injury and betrayal, increasingly mingling people with monstrous puppets on the stage. Possibly he has not given up all hope for the emancipatory changes of mankind (since he continues writing), but Hegel and the classics of dialectical materialism are faint memories; he believes that the real transformation will come, if ever, from the "anarchic and absurd" risings of the Third World. Though he once wrote plays to advance the Five-Year Plan, today he speaks of the "orgasmic structure" effective in all major plays of world literature, including his own.

12

SWITZERLAND: BITTER CHOCOLATE

Switzerland is a poor and, at the same time, a very rich country. The dearth of raw materials forced the Swiss, after they had ceased to sell themselves as professional soldiers to popes and kings, to invest their exemplary ingenuity in producing labor-intensive commodities, and to welcome eager tourists to those magnificent mountain ranges on which the *grands hôtels* are still more profitable than precarious farming and a few goats. The image of Switzerland as a blessed and peaceful country of sturdy peasants and honest burghers banding together in their Alpine villages and proud medieval cities to defend their orderly and clean way of life (democratically established, at least in the oldest regions, since 1291) has been fully established in the historical consciousness of many Swiss generations and their neighbors. The mobilization of the Swiss citizens' army to defend the country, or at least its mountain heart, against a possible German invasion in the early 1940s fully reaffirmed the inner cohesion of the Swiss federation, composed of different linguistic groups, and defined political and intellectual attitudes of citizens and intellectuals alike at least until the early 1960s.

The country is not exempt, however, from sociological and intellectual change. The Swiss traditionalists now face a younger generation that distrusts the defensive and introverted Swiss ideals of the war years, and at the same time, as in many other European countries, the constituent groups of society are being transformed rapidly. If, in 1960, 146 persons out of 1,000 were still active in the primary sector of the Swiss economy and 389 in the tertiary, twenty years later (1980) only 73 out of 1,000 persons continued to work in the primary sector, while the number of persons in the tertiary sector rose to 530. As in neighboring Austria, Heidi joined the work force of the urban service industries some time ago.

The high performance of the Swiss industries, including textiles, chemicals, electronics, and tourism, cannot be sustained without the massive import of foreign labor, and the presence of hundreds of thousands of workers from Italy (in 1982, 300,000), Spain (100,000), Yugoslavia (70,000), Portugal, and Turkey in traditional communities proud of their old codes of behavior, has changed the resident populations and created many problems for everyone. (It shows Swiss common sense that, in the national referendum of 1970, a majority voted against tight-fisted proposals aimed at the foreigners.) The presence of so many workers from the Mediterranean regions has changed the relationship among the various religions and linguistic groups: after the Protestants had been dominant for centuries, by 1980 the Catholics outnumbered them, while the number of native speakers of Italian had risen more rapidly than that of the other language groups, including (in 1980) nearly four million speaking a variety of German or rather Germanic idioms, more than a million French speakers, and more than 50,000 speakers of Romansh, mostly in the mountains of Graubünden. There were other problems, mostly ignored by the tourists: in the late 1950s the dominant political parties, among them the Liberals, the conservative Catholics, the Social Democrats, and the Peasants, Artisans, and Citizens' Party (recently renamed the People's Party), had agreed to a proportionate representation in the Federal Council, but there were disturbing problems to be solved. In the 1960s inflation was rampant; the separatists of the French-speaking Jura regions (traditionally part of the canton of Bern) bombed railway stations and courthouses and were granted the privilege of creating their own canton (1979), the first such constitutional measure since 1848; and West German terrorism at times spilled over the Swiss borders in bloody shootouts with the border guards.

Swiss direct democracy in the villages, towns, and cities of the cantons often resembled New England town meetings, except for denying the vote to women, but in the 1960s and early 1970s the franchise was finally extended to women locally and federally. Yet in 1981, male voters in three cantons still held out against women.

Throughout German-speaking countries, the spoken idiom and the written language differ in some degree, but Swiss writers who belong to the German language group labor under particular burdens and have to work out their own response to the challenge of a linguistic schizophrenia from which they cannot easily escape. The mountains and the history of Switzerland are both responsible for a sharp division between the dialect used in everyday life and the formal language employed on ceremonial occasions. The writers, like everybody else, find themselves speaking a local dialect ancient in phonology and geographically restricted to a small region. (In Basel one distinguishes even between the idiom spoken in the city and the one spoken in the surrounding countryside.) But they encounter *Schriftdeutsch*, as they call High German, in schools and universities, listen to it in the theater, and read it in the newspapers. As children, lovers, parents, and consumers, Swiss citizens use their ancient dialects, but as soon as the citizens want to write, they have to decide whether to use the local and intimate dialect or to employ *Schriftdeutsch*, which immediately implies the question of how they feel about and relate to the great literary traditions to the north and east. Swiss literature in German cannot be described simply in the unifying terms of nineteenth-century literary history, which assumed a fusion of language, society, and state. Language levels and generational preferences shift and change, and even Max Frisch and Friedrich Dürrenmatt (long considered by readers abroad as incarnating Swiss German writing) cannot be read simply as symbolic representatives of a complex community of richly talented writers who have remained largely unknown, even if they write *Schriftdeutsch*, as for instance Meinrad Inglin and the poet Albin Zollinger have done. In recent years the literary use of local dialects has greatly increased. In our century, as in earlier times, there were many popular writers, among them the Bernese Rudolf von Tavel (1866–1934) and the Schwyzer Meinrad Lienert (1865–1933), who wrote stories and novels in their local idiom and for their own audiences. In the sixties and seventies, however, local dialects have been rediscovered as a truly democratic means of communicating with one's friends in the neighborhood, the valley, or the community, and many young poets and singers of socially committed rock tunes prefer to speak or to perform in the local idiom.

The intellectual conflict between the older generation, committed to the traditional Swiss virtues and the defense of the spiritual heritage of the country (*geistige Landesverteidigung*), and the younger people who were born in the last years of the war and later, emerged in the 1960s and 1970s in many shapes and variations. In his essay "Heimat oder Domizil" (1962; "Home or Place of Residence"), Kurt Guggenheim, who belongs to a distinguished Jewish-Swiss family, appealed to readers willing to honor the revolutionary traditions of 1848 and disparaged the loss of patriotism, the disregard for roots, and the growing skepticism about Swiss law and order, which separate harmonious Switzerland from its restive neighbors. Among the many responses to Guggenheim's affirmative and melancholy essay, I find Kurt Marti's *Die Schweiz und ihre Schriftsteller—die Schriftsteller und ihre Schweiz* (1966; *Switzerland and Its Writers—The Writers and Their Switzerland*) of particular importance. At a relatively early moment Marti, a Bernese Protestant minister and author of note, articulated and often anticipated the feelings of the younger generation and combined historical insight and range of argument. He fully recognizes the virtues of those who wrote the liberal constitution of 1848, but argues that it is exactly the unchanging insistence on these achievements that has relegated writers and intellectuals, if they happen to be critical, to the periphery of society. Arguing against the exclusive idea of a patriotic and traditionalist literature, including Meinrad Inglin's distinguished novel *Schweizerspiegel* (1938; *A Swiss Mirror*), widely read as a statement of Swiss liberal traditions in an illiberal time, Marti sketches the countertradition of Swiss writers who wanted to go their own way and were forced to escape: the poet Hans Morgenthaler to the Thai jungles; the novelist Jakob Schaffner to Nazi Germany, where he was killed in an Allied air raid; Ludwig Hohl to a dank cellar in Geneva. Or there were those who killed themselves, like the playwright Caesar von Arx and the poet A. X. Gwerder, or those who sought refuge in madness, such as Friedrich Glauber, a kind of Swiss Raymond Chandler, and above all Robert Walser who, having been read and praised early by Franz Kafka and Walter Benjamin, turned into one of the archetypical figures of the European avant-garde.

The spiritual defense of the country had its time, but a few years after Marti's seminal essay Peter Bichsel, one of the few younger writers whose concise prose was widely read beyond the Swiss border, defined the ideas of his particular age group in much more ironical terms. The real enemy was not a fascist or a Communist, Bichsel said in his newspaper articles "Des Schweizers Schweiz" (1966; "Swiss Switzerland") and "Sitzen als Pflicht" (1966; "Sitting as Duty"), but the perverse attitude of those Swiss citizens who remain content to parrot an official point of view rather than to participate articulately in political life. The Spartan times of the war, he added, strengthened Swiss self-consciousness because everything worked out well for the country: "With our attitudes, our army, and the beauty of our country, we must have deeply impressed God Himself."

The growing European and later transatlantic fame of Max Frisch and Friedrich Dürrenmatt, read and performed far beyond the Swiss frontiers in the late 1950s and early 1960s, partly obfuscated the rapid emergence of a new generation of writers who felt close to one another in their eagerness to work with closeups of individual fellow citizens and little places, however provincial, rather than to raise large questions about Switzerland or the world in general. Their intellectual interests differ widely: Otto F. Walter in *Der Stumme* (1959; *The Silent Man*) told the powerful story of a young worker in search of his father, whose death he causes by accident; Hugo Loetscher in *Die Kranzflechterin* (1964; *The Florist*) sketched the plebeian life of a German working woman in Zürich; and Walter M. Diggelmann in his polemical novel *Die Hinterlassenschaft* (1965; *The Legacy*) unmasked sentimental ideas about the Swiss in World War II, showing how Jewish refugees were treated with disdain if not sent back whence they came. Erika Burkart (b. 1922) somewhat belatedly came into her own as a strong voice among the poets, and Jürg Federspiel, in *Orangen und Tode* (1961; *Oranges and Shapes of Death*), began experimenting with short stories before confronting the inimical forces of New York for the first time in *Museum des Hasses—Tage in Manhattan* (1969; *Museum of Hate—Manhattan Days*).

The growing alienation between the established and the younger generation was confirmed in the so-called Zürich feud of 1966. Upon accepting the literary prize awarded by the city of Zürich, Emil Staiger, a professor of literature at the university, reminded his audience that it was the duty of the historian to reveal the "dark spots" of literature, unfortunately abounding today with "psychopaths, criminal characters, the awful in grand style, and calculated perfidy." Referring to the serene consolations of Horace, Goethe, Schiller, and Mozart, he excoriated the "cesspool" of modern writing unwilling or rather no longer able to reflect "altruistically active man, a mother quietly working day by day, the risks of a great love, and the silent loyalty of friends." Staiger's trouble was that he generalized his deprecations, naming only Peter Weiss among the specific sinners, and inevitably irritated even his friends of the middle generation, not to mention the younger writers, who suggested that he represented the anachronistic view of an elite public that had ceased to exist. Max Frisch remarked that, unfortunately, his friend's speech would have been welcomed among the Moscow functionaries, and Peter Handke from across the border observed even less charitably that he felt reminded of a speech by Grandma Moses deploring the perversions of modernity, except that Grandma Moses would never have made such a speech. In a postscript published in a West German periodical, Staiger reminded his many critics that they did not really confront the fundamental question raised, namely, whether a poet who wanted to endure through the changes of times could do so without an ethical attitude of one kind or another. He also sadly confessed that he once suggested Thornton Wilder as a candidate for the Nobel Prize, only to hear "untrammeled laughter among the friends of modernity."

The Zürich feud was, at least on the surface, of a literary kind, pitting against each other defenders of the classical/romantic canon and the partisans of contemporary writing. The wider ideological implications of the conflict emerged about three or four years later when a group of younger writers and critics gathered (as the Graz group of younger Austrian writers had done in the early 1960s) to secede from the established writers' organization, which they viewed as too deeply involved in sustaining the dominant powers. In the late summer of 1969 a little red book on *Zivilverteidigung* (civil defense), put together by an army officer and a professor of geography, was distributed by the authorities, or rather by the Department of Police and Justice, to all Swiss households free of charge. Many critical readers, among them the authors Kurt Marti and Adolf Muschg, were quick to say that it was written in a martial way not exactly corresponding to the spirit of participatory democracy, and when a TV commentator discovered that the French version was edited by Maurice Zermatten, president of the official Swiss writers' organization, many German- and French-language intellectuals protested against this "harmful" publication introduced by a member of the Federal Council. The executive committee of the writers' organization discussed the matter with the president, expressed its loyalty to him, and asked the membership whether an extraordinary meeting should be scheduled to discuss the issues at hand. Of 483 members, only 43 insisted on the special meeting. But after a small group of dissidents recommended to their colleagues that they leave the organization collectively, twenty-two prominent writers and a few who had never belonged to any organization met in the town of Olten to consider the situation. Within a short time the dissidents organized what was called the Olten Group (1970) and began to publish almanacs and anthologies to which many gifted younger writers, as well as Max Frisch and the erudite critic Gerda Zeltner-Neukomm, contributed. Perhaps it is only fair to say that the great majority of writers in the Olten Group use German rather than French, Italian, or Romansh.

Young writers differ from the older generation to a large degree in their doubts about the existence and legitimate function of a Swiss literature, but the continuing discussions confirm that it is not easy to push the question aside. Of the post-Frisch generation, Adolf Muschg has been most vocal in saying that, for cultural and political reasons, there should be no "Swiss" literature, the existence of which would allow the Germans beyond the border to condescend to the "small" and indulge, in whatever revived form, in a more or less subtle "cultural imperialism." Assuming, for the sake of argument, that he was speaking to an Australian observer, Muschg called the idea of Swiss literature a "foolish kind of self-assurance," denied any important feeling of mutual closeness among Swiss writers of different languages, and argued against the traditional view that Swiss literature was always strong in all kinds of sober didacticism and realism but insufficiently articulate in romantic or expressionist writing. In an interesting discussion held at the Darmstadt Academy in 1980, Muschg was answered by Hanno Helbling, an erudite cultural editor of the *Neue Zürcher Zeitung*, who, referring to examples of Swiss writing in French and to the Bernese tradition, concluded that, in spite of all protests and doubts, there were "common features" in all Swiss writing of whatever language. "A Swiss writer," he said, "writes in the social situation of a state federation" to which many of his readers elsewhere do not belong, and Swiss writers have particular "difficulties in communication that can be solved in many different and even contradictory ways." These difficulties, he insisted, are approached by Swiss writers "consciously" and in a manner that differs from that of writers living in the midst of a social and linguistic region untroubled by the pressing question of who their actual readers are. (If a Swiss writer designates his bicycle by saying *"Fahrrad"* in *Schriftdeutsch* and not *"Velo"* in the idiom, he has taken a definite stand on the question.) Muschg reluctantly accepts a concept of "Swiss literature" in order to express his radical doubts about its usefulness, but Helbling, who does not have the novelist's ax to grind, suggests that a Swiss literature exists without really being one in the traditional sense of nationality or a union of patriots.

WRITERS OF THE SEVENTIES; THE ZÜRICH YOUTH REVOLT

The young writers who published their first important books in the seventies shared the critical views of the sixties generation. They too were stubbornly unwilling to say "yes" readily in social and private affairs and cultivated the habit of speaking about themselves in a tone of solid, if not stolid, seriousness. These writers (eight out of ten were schoolteachers) loved to cling to small villages or lonely hamlets (while spending their ample vacations in Greece or Sicily). Many introspective novels, the privileged form of the young, tell the story of someone under thirty returning from the outside world (often Manhattan) to a mountain valley to think life over again. Erica Pedretti (b. 1930), a writer, artist, and mother of five, began publishing later than others in her age group. She came to Switzerland as a German-speaking refugee from a small town in northern Moravia and spent some time in Paris and New York before settling in the Grisons and later in the Bernese region. In her mind, past and present coexist violently: traumatic early experiences in war-torn Moravia brutally interfere with any later moment of serenity in a different and more peaceful world. In *Harmloses bitte* (1970; *Something Harmless, Please*) and *Heiliger Sebastian* (1973; *Saint Sebastian*), a remarkable montage of prose pieces, she reconstitutes a contradictory record of her life, setting against one another the memories of a sensitive girl who was not consulted when she was put on a Red Cross transport train to Switzerland; impressions of a Manhattan jewelry workshop on Forty-seventh Street, teeming with exiles from all corners of the world; and scenes from married life in a fragile Swiss Arcadia. She carries the heavy burden of not being able "ever to live in the place in which she finds herself," and of being compulsively driven to return, to recuperate, to seize things "which want to escape memory" in disconnected staccato sequences. Pedretti has had difficulties in writing cohesively, but in her more recent novel *Veränderung* (1977; *Stones*, 1982), which tells the story of a friendly Swiss neighbor, she convincingly shows that she has learned to look away from herself and to listen more carefully to what other people say about their own lives.

E. Y. Meyer's novel *Die Rückfahrt* (1977; *The Return*) confronts questions on the minds of many younger intellectuals but does so quietly, without shrillness or melodramatic turns. It is one of the characteristic stories about going back in search of a fuller understanding of one's own experience, in psychological or psychotherapeutic terms. A young teacher who thinks of becoming a writer has been found culpable in an accident in which his friend was killed when their car, driven at high speed over a foggy mountain road, went over the edge. The three distinct parts of the narrative are not arranged in chronological sequence. Rather, they move from the weeks in a Lucerne sanitarium where the teacher is being treated, to an Easter excursion in the Ticino where he visits his friendly nurse and her mother, a painter of some distinction, and from there to much earlier events that include his first experiences as a teacher, the admiration for his friend (a state-appointed curator of historical buildings), and the fateful day in the rainy mountains. Self-exploration never deteriorates into narrow solipsism, but Meyer demonstrates rare skill in showing his characters: the young teacher, who is involved in rather long but thoughtful conversations; the somewhat enigmatic nurse whom he loves for a fugitive moment; her mother, who tells him much about contemporary art; and the custodian, who enlightens him about the Swiss past on trips to old churches and castles now endangered by the industrial destruction of landscapes. Meyer is precise and often circumstantial in writing about landscapes and objects of art, streets, and restaurant menus, especially of the more rustic kind. Some of the conversations about the preservation of older architecture and the issues of modern intellectuality (prompted by his reluctant musings about his role model Hermann Hesse), and an account of newly discovered rock paintings near Italian Bergamo, sound like graceful imitations of Adalbert Stifter and Thomas Mann, perhaps deliberately so. It is an intense novel of insight and range and yet, trying to rediscover "sensuous individuality in the abstract mass society," it reveals its own dearth of sensuality, too energetically repressed to be evident in the soberly controlled text.

A few reviewers have suggested that Gertrud Leutenegger, born in the small town of Schwyz in 1948, was spoiled by early praise, and it is easy to see that she differs from many of her somberly introspective colleagues by her striking vivacity and her spirited ease of tone. In her first publication, *Vorabend* (1975; *The Eve*), she showed a certain fashionable flair for combining political interest and lyrical articulation by exploring, in a collection of experimental prose pieces, eleven streets of a city through which a demonstration will move on the following day. In *Ninive* (1977), which she calls a novel, she tells a plausible love story with a firm touch and a good deal of whimsical literary allusion to please more knowledgeable audiences. It too is, in its own way, a narrative about a return. A young small-town girl of local bourgeois background and a teenage Italian whose mother works in the textile mill fall in love and, after a long self-willed separation (she working as a custodian in a Swiss museum and he selling newspapers in Berlin), they decide to return to where it all started. In their hometown the biggest whale in the world is being shown, embalmed, as a sight-seeing attraction, and they believe this to be as good an occasion as any to mingle with fellow citizens and sightseers and rediscover "the severe plot of their own history." They spend the night huddled together in the light of the flares, as do their fellow citizens, and talk about the past and their present experiences. Then, after the whale has been dismembered in the morning (it was the last station of the exhibition), they are again certain of themselves and of their feelings and walk away "on a white surface unrolling like the wind, before them." Leutenegger, who comes to writing by way of the theater rather than the university seminar, directly and indirectly refers to Herman Melville, naming a few of her chapters according to the anatomical parts of the decaying whale, but does not indulge in heavy-handed allegory and spends her narrative energy in presenting her contemporary lovers who, blue jeans and all, resolve to commit themselves to each other in the future. If she deleted the occasional cliché from her prose, she would be a sophisticated writer of high standing.

There is nothing haphazard or facile in the novels of Hermann Burger, who is the most forceful of the new writers of the seventies and without equal in his unerring and inventive discipline of language. Writing in the traditions of Swift, Kafka, and, as he himself asserts, Thomas Bernhard (perhaps with a dose of surrealism added), he has attracted more astute critical attention than any of his colleagues, who lack his obsessive erudition and his insistence on what is of aesthetic interest to him and hardly anybody else. He calls his prose volume *Schilten* (1976) a "school report to be submitted to the conference of inspectors." It consists of twenty quartos in which, in ingeniously bureaucratic language, a lonely schoolteacher defends before the school authorities of the canton his pedagogical methods and his way of living, each inseparable from the other. His school, where he lives on the upper floor, stands next to the village cemetery, and the gym is used for wakes conducted by an evangelical sect dominant in the valley. Haunted by the closeness of the dead, the teacher has conceived a systematic pedagogy of death and dying that he prefers to teaching about life, without noticing, in the growing confusion of his mind, that his horrified pupils stay away and that he teaches his necromantic lessons to an empty classroom. His quartos are organized as a kind of encyclopedia of his life and mind, concentrating respectively in ironic circumstantiality on a funeral rite, a room in the school, his predecessor, the school collection of birds (as dead as doornails), the history of the harmonium (which he plays) in general and in particular, and chapters from the history of the valley, including its postal and bus services. The reader of the quartos is not surprised that a coda, written by the cantonal inspector of schools, reveals that the author of these manuscripts has been committed to an institution for psychiatric treatment, all costs to be paid by the tolerant authorities. Burger slyly subverts the Swiss assumption that writers have to be serious, since he, or rather the teacher, is marvelously inventive in describing the "scriptification of his existence," indulging his "cemeterial bagatelles," or describing the daily four o'clock crisis in the life of any teacher upon returning from his class to his empty room (though in his case, of course, the class is as empty as his garret). *Schilten* is a book of remarkable power and macabre art that firmly establishes Burger as an author of superb promise.

It was symptomatic of the Swiss, but not merely of the Swiss, situation in the 1970s that the literary publication most widely discussed was an authentic, not fictional, autobiographical essay in which a young man of thirty, dying of an incurable cancer, argued about society and himself. (He received the news that his manuscript would be published in the agonies of his last hour in a Zürich hospice.) In his bitter and violent *Mars* (1977; 1981), a teacher of Romance languages who calls himself Fritz Zorn ("rage" in German) rather than reveal his real name Angst, commences his self-analysis by saying, "I am young and rich and educated, and I am unhappy, neurotic, and alone." He adds that of course he has cancer, as should be evident, he notes, from his first sentence. Zorn describes his youth in one of the villas on the Zürichberg "Gold Coast," the hilly shore of Lake Zürich where the upper middle classes reside: in family life "harmony" reigned supreme, and everybody was to strive for the "higher things" represented by Goethe's works in the library, and to repress anything that might be disturbing, whether it was a matter of religion, politics, or sex. In school Zorn was well-behaved and, being highly gifted, had little trouble in his university seminars; while complaining about his loneliness, he actually spent most of his day sipping coffee in the university courtyard and writing short plays for the graduate student club. He traveled a good deal in Spain and Portugal without companions either male or female and, after passing his examinations, lived in an expensive apartment in the center of Zürich and taught school, an underground man on the penthouse level. When a neighbor died, Zorn felt that death had finally entered his own life; a tumor developed on his neck consisting, as he says, of his "suppressed tears," and a physician told him that he had cancer. (Zorn, turning to Wilhelm Reich's fuzzy ideas, suggests that it was caused by being "nice" and "neat" all his life.) In his self-analysis, Zorn develops a social and psychological etiology of his disease: he accuses his parents of having avoided happiness, meaning, and clarity, and of having infected him with their own fatal repressions. It is the family, the environment, Switzerland, the "system" that has caused his disease. Raging against the "anonymous superpower," Zorn finds himself "in a concentration camp, and gassed by the parental legacy in himself," and therefore declares "total war" against father, mother, and society. Many young Swiss readers believed that these confessions revealed much that was wrong in a contemporary society in which they were compelled to find a proper place and, disregarding Zorn's *viva la muerte* mysticism, deeply felt that he expressed their own radical negation, soon to be expressed in the streets of Swiss cities.

Zürich police and restive young people (not students but apprentices and the unemployed) fought each other in mid-1980 and then again in the spring of 1981, and in many of the demonstrations against the Establishment, clowns danced, skin was bared, and the black flags of anarchy appeared. Many Zürich youth groups had long demanded living space for themselves in an "autonomous youth center," but the city government was not exactly eager to negotiate seriously. In the early spring of 1980 a recommendation to appropriate sixty million francs for the renovation of the city opera was discussed and approved by the city government; on the evening of March 30 a small group of young people went to the opera house to demonstrate against the appropriation and for a subsidy to establish a youth center. The police were ready in the foyer of the theater, and a pitched battle, in full view of the first-night audience, developed in front of the "cultural temple of the bourgeoisie" (to quote the terms of the young), later to be joined by the audience from a rock concert nearby. The battle lasted all night, was sporadically renewed on subsequent days, and spread to Bern, Basel, Lausanne, and Geneva, polarizing political opinion as it did so. The writers of the Olten Group sympathized with the young people; the Zürich Social Democrats, said to be more flexible than their colleagues elsewhere, took it upon themselves to work out a solution; and a modest amount was approved to renovate an old factory that soon opened as a youth center. After it had functioned more than ten months, it was closed again by a concentrated attack of the Zürich police force, who claimed that it had become an asylum for drug pushers, dropouts, and criminals. After a relatively quiet winter, on March 21, 1981, the intransigents among the young gathered again to retake the building but were repulsed by the police. In his essay *Zürich, Anfang September* (1981; *Zürich at the Beginning of September*), the young writer Reto Hänny, who participated in the opera demonstration and was later arrested by the police, tells about the clashes in the streets and what went on in the police precincts; he reveals much of the malaise of younger people in a well-ordered society not inclined to tolerate distrust of hard work, discipline, and competition. The Swiss paradise has become a rather fragile affair.

13

ADOLF MUSCHG: BODY AND SOUL

Adolf Muschg (b. 1934) shares many of the interests and views of a middle generation; he is much younger than Max Frisch and yet too old to identify fully with the theories of the late sixties. He believes that the pscyhological energies liberated in the revolts of 1968–69 were far more productive than the political ideas of the time. Insisting on his own psychosomatic problems, he has little difficulty in convincing those who went through a moment of radical commitment and, later, a time of intricate self-examination, that he speaks with a voice close to their own recent experiences. Muschg's father was a schoolteacher and the editor of a little local newspaper who in his advancing years married his young nurse. Though family life was frugal, young Muschg was sent to a private country school on a community fellowship, and went on to an elite Zürich *Gymnasium*. Muschg has said of himself that he was marked early in life by his mother's expectations: she wanted him to be a pastor or physician, a distinguished member of the community, but he preferred to study German, English, and philosophy at Zürich and Cambridge and to fulfill her wishes by becoming a man of letters. He wrote a dissertation on Ernst Barlach, the writer and sculptor persecuted by the Nazis, and then in true Swiss fashion spent his *Wanderjahre* traveling widely, teaching in Tokyo, at Göttingen, and at Cornell

(1967–69) before returning home to a position as professor of literature at the Zürich Federal Technical University (ETH). Muschg is not a retiring scholar but, perhaps against his grain, a public personality who combines teaching, writing, frequent TV appearances, and political activities with apparent ease. Whereas writers of the older generation often debate how far to go in practical commitment to everyday politics, he joined the Swiss Social Democratic party, ran for a seat in the Ständerat (Lower House), and was appointed to the commission charged with rewriting the Swiss constitution. In the mid-1960s the thirty-year-old Muschg wrote his first novel, which was immediately praised as the beginning of a significant achievement. As he continues publishing novels, short stories, plays, and radio features, the reviewers mix the most legitimate respect with some qualms about the epigonal component of his sensibilities. Whenever West German broadcasting stations or Modern Language Association sections in America need a sober and enlightened view of Swiss or central European intellectual affairs, Muschg is inevitably invited. It is the task of literature, he once said, to offer "a detailed view of truth and a large vision of hope," and it would be unfair to say that he did not try to live up to his own exacting demands.

In his first novel, *Im Sommer des Hasen* (1965; *In the Summer of the Hare*), Muschg surprised his reviewers by the civilized amplitude and fine discretion of his narrative art; there was little to suggest the beginner. The intricate narrative structure closely relates to those German Romantic prose compositions that consist of concatenations of individual stories illuminating each other, but there is nothing antiquarian about Muschg's concerns. We are reading a report addressed by the public relations manager of an important Swiss corporation to its president, a descendant of the founder. In celebration of the centenary of its active involvement in Japanese commercial affairs, the corporation, at the suggestion of the PR department, has offered to send six young Swiss writers to Japan, each one to write an essay or story "about Japan in the widest sense," to be gathered in a *Festschrift* inscribed to the memory of the firm's founder. The PR manager has now withdrawn to a little country inn near Zürich to report about his travels and his encounters with the six writers, who have related to him their separate experiences "in the summer of the hare." The manager's report is rich in divergent images of Japanese life and letters, humble, charming, and of intense aesthetic attraction. Ultimately, a highly intimate communication emerges in which the middle-aged manager resigns from his job and recommends, as his successor, the one writer of the six who did not write anything at all. After the experiences in Japan, his own and those of the six writers, the manager wants "freedom" and an intensity of life that he has long missed in his job.

The novel attests to the many gifts of the author, but it by no means ushers in a radically new stage of Swiss or German writing. After Muschg had taught at the Christian university in Tokyo, he returned home with a collection of travel impressions and Japanese sketches; the confessional report of the PR manager skillfully provides a unifying framework concentrating many but not all of the elements. The writer of the report is at first not much more than an impersonal voice, but from chapter to chapter he acquires more of an individual sensibility. In talking about the texts produced by the six Fellows (rather than directly quoting them) Muschg has his chance to indulge in parody and satire, especially if a Fellow parades his productivity in a collage of tapes. There is an effective touch of the sadly grotesque, possibly reminiscent of some renowned nineteenth-century Swiss novellas by Gottfried Keller, in the quest of Adalbert Huhn, a Fellow who wants to learn about Zen from monastic sources and acquires nothing but persistent digestive troubles, or in the problems of his colleague Florian Distel, who cannot bear the idea of returning to his father, a Swiss preacher of the Apocalypse, and so kills himself in a hot bath. Yet there is much to admire: a fashionable essay, for instance, about the best qualifications for a successful PR manager—who, the narrator insists with a good deal of self-irony, should come from the lower-middle classes, receive a good academic training in the humanities, and be kept simmering in a frustrating minor teaching job for a long time before finding a liberating opportunity in corporate services; or the many purple passages about Tokyo and the charms of Japanese landscapes, the material of the original travelogue. The most impressive part of the novel is the story about the brief encounter of a young married Swiss writer and the Japanese student Yoko, who meet on a bus, do not speak each other's language (they use a kind of esperanto English), and yet love each other gloriously, though it is a love without a future. Muschg and all his writing contemporaries usually shy away from love stories, but his tale of the young Swiss and Yoko, a student of theology who wants to become a social worker, combines the sober, the chaste, the lascivious, and the fragile in an unforgettable way. "It was a marriage in every respect: except that it was built on taking leave and being transient."

Of his second novel Muschg himself said that it was an overambitious project that failed, and though most reviewers agreed with his view, I am less inclined to deal harshly with *Gegenzauber* (1967; *Countermagic*), because it is closer to Muschg's own early experiences than his first novel and fully reveals the contradictions of his remarkable gifts. To discover something about the balances, or rather imbalances, of fable, genre, and language in his sprawling second book is to learn a good deal about his particular problems as a contemporary writer. The story itself recalls the structure of his first narrative, but he insists on creating playful complications: a young student, just a few months before his final examination, decides to write a truthful if somewhat defensive report about a group of his friends who hang out in the old country inn Soldanella (the name of a tender Alpine flower), and about their efforts to save the old place, at least for a while, from being destroyed by road builders eager to link the village (really a suburb) with the center of metropolitan Zürich. The student's manuscript is written in response to a book on the same subject by a member of the group who has betrayed all its ideas of decency; since the false friend is an experienced film critic (especially proud of reviewing movies that he has not seen), the student does not have an easy time doing a better job. The colorful Soldanella group resists all the pressures of contemporary society in a somewhat vague but highly effective way, denouncing the rat race, commercialism, the city, and everything that is "not of the mind, and without a purpose." When demolition threatens, the young people conceive the idea of making Soldanella a registered landmark. When they are on the verge of success, their strategies are unmasked by the traitor. The village, deprived of its last refuge for the creative, becomes a legal part of the city of Zürich, and the young student decides, in an ironic reversal, that it might be a good idea to study road construction in a leisurely way.

If Muschg had resisted the temptation to show what can be done with such a mildly entertaining story, he might have written a comfortable little novel about breaking away (the young narrator does go through his pubertal confusions while writing the story), perhaps enlivened by a few lashes against meretricious critics and the news-mongering media. The novel's excess yields its own surfeit, though mostly of the satirical kind: Friedrich Dürrenmatt and Max Frisch, biting on their pipes and being mostly inarticulate, make their cameo appearances; the Zürich publisher Peter Schifferli, who published the novel, looks disheveled, and behind him, party guests observe "a young Swiss writer with gray hair" who "has written a heartfelt book about Japan" (Muschg himself, of course). Portrayed at a time when the West German students were ready to take to the streets, Muschg's young Soldanella group is more or less averse to politics and dreams intensely about its lost childhood and a rustic paradise far away from the city and from the exertions of labor and making a living (the narrator's father is a prosperous car dealer who takes care of all that). The Soldanella people are traditionalist Greens fifteen years ahead of their time.

In his novels of the early 1970s Muschg increasingly concentrates on how psychological lesions, accompanied by somatic afflictions, relate to particular social pressures emanating from the Swiss establishment. In *Albissers Grund* (1974; *Albisser's Reasons*) Muschg succeeds in writing a highly intimate, disturbing, cryptic, and largely uneven book in which bold psychological and social analysis has not entirely pushed aside his readiness to please the reader, at least in passing, by predictable situations and Swiss stock characters. Albisser, a teacher (once again of vaguely emancipatory drives) shoots and almost kills, after many expensive sessions or rather conversations over tea, one Constantin Zerrutt, a graphologist, a self-appointed therapist, and allegedly one of Freud's last disciples. Zerrutt, whose eyesight is imperiled, has to be hospitalized, and the authorities begin their investigation right at his bedside. Deeply distrustful of this intellectual vagrant without a working permit, they quickly push the victim into the role of the accused, who will soon be expelled from the country. Zerrutt may have been a father figure or a superego to Albisser, who desperately wants to go his independent way, but the authorities are not really interested in his reason for shooting his friend, which they define as a "psychological compulsion," but in his return to the folds of conforming society. Zerrutt reappears in Muschg's *Das Licht und der Schlüssel* (1984; *The Light and the Key*), a rather dissolute Dracula narrative concluded by thirteen letters about still lifes, Vermeer, and the art of looking at old paintings. The trained explorer of psychosomatic mysteries and "dubious graphologist" Zerrutt changes into a therapist who, being from Transylvania, renews the lustful techniques of bleeding (especially the wives of cardiologists whom he consults about his circulatory problems), and finds himself involved with a KLM flight attendant who suffers from a particularly vicious form of leukemia. The shift from Zürich to a kind of blurred Amsterdam, with the required *Grachten* and other showplaces, does not add any unexpected materials, and the odd combination of hematology and old art is far too diffuse to sustain my interest from beginning to end.

Baiyun, oder, Die Freundschaftsgesellschaft (1980; *Baiyun, or The Friendship Society*) constitutes Muschg's first true masterpiece of undisputed rank. He has used the ploy of the committed, or rather involved, narrator reporting on the experiences of a group of people in unusual circumstances before, but here he controls his "fatal gift of always saying too much" (to quote a critic) with resolute energy. Even his growing interest in exploring the potential of the traditional murder story strengthens rather than diffuses the narrative, since he uses it with literate irony. A group of more or less prominent Swiss citizens has been officially invited to visit China. One of the group, a loudmouthed and overbearing Zürich professor of agronomy, is found dead one morning in his hostel room. The other people in the group—a renowned Swiss author (somewhat resembling Max Frisch at his morose best); an expert in international trade; a retired pesticides specialist; a bookseller from Schaffhausen; a frustrated upper-middle-class woman named Gaby; and a professional psychologist, who tells the story—at times suspect the Chinese of having killed the agronomist (who on one of his solo walks ventured into a forbidden military zone), and at times suspect each other. The schedule of visits to agricultural communities, hospitals, and steel factories goes on relentlessly; the members of the group find themselves increasingly involved with provincial officials in highly personal conversations that may be part of a police investigation conducted with rare *politesse* (or far less so in the case of the trade expert, who expressed an interest in the Cultural Revolution); and a hapless attaché of the Swiss embassy tells them that diplomats cannot interfere with a murder investigation. Even the accompanying Chinese translators, who have become close to the group, now keep their cool distance, but a short time before the return from the provinces to Peking, one of the officials reports that medical analysis has shown that the professor suffered from a kidney condition increasing the presence of adrenalin in his body, and that an antidepressant caused a fatal adrenalin shock. It could have been a perfect murder, but it was really a "coincidence with fatal results." It is one of the literary ironies of the novel that Muschg ascribes its actual program to a writer of Max Frisch's habits and physiognomy; more successfully than ever before, he shows in sober and provocative detail how a group, dislocated in time and place, copes with increasing doubts about itself. Since it is not clear whether the daily ritual of sightseeing has not become a way of keeping the group under close observation, the country itself appears at a double or triple remove. There are all the usual visits to new archaeological sites, ancient temples, clinics practicing acupuncture, and new industrial centers, yet everything appears in the sparse images of an alien life, close in its humanity and yet unapproachably strange—thin lilac bushes, soldiers in old-fashioned buses, peasants on the road, and young women in surprisingly colorful blouses. If an alienation effect can turn prose to melancholy poetry, it happens here, and more than once.

As a reviewer and critic in periodicals and in other media as well, Muschg has come to work with assumptions found in early Marx and late Freud, and above all in the intimate and public experience of the Swiss intellectual of his own time. He certainly has more respect for the grand literature of the distant and recent past, including Kleist, Hölderlin, Rilke, and Gottfried Benn, than most of his West German contemporaries. Being convinced that the generation of '68 ignored the intimate origins of the arts and incapacitated itself by leaving the arts to the "class enemy," Muschg wants to test a combination of social and analytical ideas for interpreting the creative process, including the use of "body feelings" for "words," and bringing into play his own perceptions in responding to the emotional charges of a text. His study of Gottfried Keller, in stark contrast to recent abstractions of West German university writing, confronts the Swiss poet, novelist, and public functionary in a highly personal way; in a somewhat conservative analysis, still insisting on illuminating the writings from the life, rather than vice versa, it convincingly shows how in his fiction Keller succeeds in fulfilling his secret wishes to possess his own mother and how, at the same time, he tries to expiate the act. It is a lively and speculative monograph that tends to deteriorate only when Muschg tries, in vain, to revitalize some older concepts from Georg Lukács, freely translating them into more recent semiotic terminology. Muschg knows a good deal about contemporary American writing, including that of Donald Barthelme and Susan Sontag (whose essay "Against Interpretation," he believes, should be obligatory reading for all teachers of literature). And yet, surprisingly enough, he defends Hermann Hesse (whom he, like everybody else in his generation, once deprecated as "a rose gardener with a Ticino straw hat") in his role as a political writer who challenged "political power" by his "aesthetic honesty."

Muschg's theoretical and autobiographical essay "Literatur als Therapie?" (1981; "Literature as Therapy?") concentrates on discussing the mutually sustaining potentialities of writing and psychoanalysis without undue simplification. While he explains in some detail why he did not complete his own analysis (it was inefficient in coping with his somatic condition and threatened his pain, to which he owes so much as a creative writer), Muschg separates art, useful for moving toward an encompassing theory of the self, from therapy. Yet he does not want to miss either, because both art and therapy "contribute to a sense of balance, of a humanity that has come to threaten itself." Ultimately, he pleads for order, flexible and alive: "We do not live without moving but it is not motion itself for which we live."

Swiss conservatives tend to think of Adolf Muschg as an intellectual of the restive Left, but in other contexts he may seem to be a socialist of amply liberal leanings, eager to separate the legacy of the Stalinists from an emancipatory Marxism without dogma, and increasingly concerned with the social mechanism of psychological repressions, and its dehumanizing results, in modern industrial society. Muschg has come to psychotherapy somewhat later than his West German colleague Dieter Wellershoff, who involved himself in the study of Freud almost immediately after he returned from the war. While Wellershoff has retained a didactic and scientific interest in analytic theory (his novels lack the openly confessional element), Muschg does not want to abstract writing, whether of novels or essays, from his own experience, and often speaks about his own childhood or youth when developing a fictional character or theoretical concept. As a writer, he has certainly moved close to the "me generation," although he does not care to view the ego, his own or others', outside the specific pressures of the Swiss establishment. (Max Frisch's middle-class intellectuals move mostly in their own separate space of experience.) Critics of the orthodox Left and other traditionalists are fond of discussing their continuing distrust of the artist Muschg, who has adopted almost any style at will and exhausted a diverse repertoire of formal possibilities. It is true of course that Muschg, before ever approaching Marx or Freud, went through his bourgeois moments of admiring Rilke and, even more revealingly, Albrecht Schaeffer, now unknown, but renowned a generation or more ago for his subservience to Stefan George's *l'art pour l'art* views. Muschg differs from many of his contemporaries by ascribing an important function to literary form, which, he says, being more than mere content or "what is said," generates the possibility of communication between author and readers. His best writing, including many of his short stories, *Albisser's Reasons*, and *Baiyun, or The Friendship Society*, increasingly shows that he is a gifted writer who has learned important lessons about going the more difficult rather than the more pleasing way. He sees himself as writing against the Zürichberg—the residence of the educated, the rich, and the powerful. It may be his real burden that, as an author of inherited forms and civilized language in the tradition of Thomas Mann and Max Frisch, he continues a mode of writing not totally unwelcome in that bastion of traditional taste.

14

MAX FRISCH: THE LAST ROMANTIC

I have long been tempted to call Max Frisch the last Swiss romantic, and his recent publications have convinced me that I would be grievously wrong to use the term in an ironic way or not to employ it at all. Frisch wrote his first play as a high school student in the late 1920s, when Brecht was working on *The Threepenny Opera*, and in 1945, when many young German writers of a new generation appeared on the scene, as artist and citizen he entered yet another stage of his career. His achievement has more continuity than that of most of his German contemporaries (he was spared an immediate involvement in the "Third Reich" and the war), yet there is nothing more characteristic in his own story than striking discontinuities. He has been restless and often longed for change; though often comfortably settled in personal relationships, commitments to particular ideas, and literary forms, he has never failed to break out of stifling self-definitions, to seek new tasks for himself, to escape from and destroy his chosen genres (many of his texts, especially his plays, exist in three or four revised versions). There were times when he joined the many writers and intellectuals who resolutely turned against their society (whether in its Swiss, West German, or Austrian form), but he always hesitated to go all the way in radical politics, and ultimately preferred to fall back on his liberal skepticism. He may have been a romantic in the traditional sense when, in his earliest writings, he longed to be where he was not, but later he certainly tended to be a romantic in a more substantial meaning of the word—that is, someone who relentlessly explores the ways in which a fragile consciousness reflects, transforms, or perhaps creates what we call the real world.

A VIEW OF HIS LIFE; EARLY WRITINGS

Max Frisch was born in Zürich in 1911 to a lower-middle-class family; he would say later that he had repressed all memories of having once been poor and underprivileged. There were relatives in Germany and Austria; his mother was employed for some time as a governess in Russia before she returned home to marry; and his father was a craftsman who worked without a professional degree as an architect and wanted his son to have the proper credentials. Young Frisch studied (1930–33) modern literature, art history, and psychology (under Heinrich Wölfflin and C. G. Jung, among others), but when his father died he had to make a living and began to write sports pieces, travel feuilletons, and short stories, often published by the *Neue Zürcher Zeitung* (whose conservative views he would later attack). Yet he felt frustrated by free-lancing, and when a friend from a rich family underwrote the cost of further studies, Frisch decided to give up writing, dramatically burned his manuscripts (or so he says), and began to study architecture. It was only the first of many changes of mind. In 1941 he received his architecture degree, and a year later, while Soviet and German armies clashed at Stalingrad, he won the first prize for a city swimming pool project, opened his own office, and married a young woman from the well-to-do patriciate (her parents had welcomed Churchill on their country estate). For some time he worked on architectural projects as well as new stories and plays, but in 1946 he went again on a trip to Germany (where he had traveled occasionally with a Jewish girlfriend in the 1930s), and radically changed his mind about what he was writing. Increasingly restless, he traveled a good deal, spent a year in the United States on a Rockefeller Fellowship in the early 1950s, and in 1954 published his novel *Stiller*, which for the first time made him better known to an international audience. He closed his architectural office in 1955, never to reopen it again, then separated from his wife (they were divorced somewhat later), lived again as a free-lancer in a small place near Zürich, and went on extended voyages to the countries of the sun: Mexico, Cuba, Greece, and the Near East.

I am describing Frisch's earlier years in some detail because they suggest a characteristic pattern that recurs in his later life and in his writings—one of settling and escaping, dwelling and longing, involvement and separation. If some critics speak about his experiences in terms of marriages and divorces, it is only because he himself, more than any other older writer in German, felt attracted by the intimate questions of love, loyalty, marriage, betrayal, and renewed loneliness, especially in his later years.

In 1960 Frisch settled in Rome to be close to the Austrian writer Ingeborg Bachmann (1926–73), an erudite student of Wittgenstein's philosophy and a woman of intense feelings, but three years later, exhausted by jealousy and self-torture, he left her and lived with and later married Marianne Oellers, a gifted translator of American fiction thirty years his junior. He bought an old house in the forlorn Onsernone valley near the Italian border, acquired an apartment in Berlin, and traveled widely with Marianne in Eastern Europe, the Soviet Union, America, and the Near East. After his second marriage ended in divorce in 1973, he moved to New York and bought a loft in Soho. His friends remember his time of serene happiness with a young woman whom readers know from his narrative *Montauk* (1975; 1976). But idylls do not last, in New York or elsewhere: in the early 1980s Frisch once more returned alone to his native city of Zürich and settled in a little penthouse apartment in the city center. A recent snapshot shows the septuagenerian in his usual corduroy jacket, standing in front of the James Joyce Pub, not unhappy at all, a citizen among citizens who, after so many restless voyages, reveals an ultimate sense of permanence at home.

The sixteen-year-old Frisch submitted his first (late expressionist) play by mail to Max Reinhardt. But he really began writing in the early 1930s as a traditionalist if not eclectic poet, brooding over issues characteristic of German writing from the time of the Romantics down to Gottfried Keller, the most important Swiss writer of the nineteenth century, and Thomas Mann. Young

Frisch too felt hemmed in by the harsh convention of a bourgeois society, more intact in Switzerland than elsewhere at that time and later. He began by asking the age-old question, raised so many times in German novels concerned with the self-definition of the individual, of how to realize oneself fully within the native society or, if that should prove impossible, in faraway places of splendid isolation (the names of these places are always rich in vowels). Frisch himself explained that his first novel, *Jürg Reinhart* (1934), was about the "mysterious growth of a young man's soul," which holds true for many subsequent works as well, including *Antwort aus der Stille* (1937; *Answer out of Silence*) and *J'adore ce qui me brûle, oder Die Schwierigen* (1943; *J'adore ce qui me brûle, or Difficult People*), which is largely a reworking of his first novel, but of wider range. We easily recognize the epic personnel: the pensive young man, an amateur in many arts but an expert in feelings; sensitive and mysterious women who either die prematurely or are surprisingly resilient; and a Swiss Parsifal who wants to find himself by scaling an Alpine peak nobody has ever conquered before. When young Frisch was asked by Kurt Hirschfeld, the émigré dramaturge of the local theater, to write for the stage, Frisch submitted *Santa Cruz* [1946], a sweet little play that retains some of its lyrical charms even today.

POSTWAR EXPERIENCES AND WORK IN THE LATE FORTIES AND FIFTIES

I shall simplify somewhat, but only to stress an essential strain of feeling and imagination that, after 1945, increasingly clashes and combines, in often complex and occasionally self-defeating ways, with Frisch's active attention to the social and political problems emerging in postwar Europe. Frisch had been close, in the mid-1930s, to a German Jewish fellow student whom he wanted to marry, and from her, as well as from a few trips to Nazi Germany, he learned a good deal about the realities of the "Third Reich." When, after fighting had ceased, Swiss citizens were again allowed to travel abroad, he was anxious to end his "captivity," as he called it, and so went to Germany, Italy, Czechoslovakia, and Poland, where he attended the Wroclaw Peace Congress in 1948. Frisch's *Tagebuch: 1946–1949* (1950;

Sketchbook 1946–1949), rightly rescued from oblivion by a late American translation (1977), offers substantial and illuminating views of his fine sensibility, which was shocked by experiences in devastated Germany, by cripples and hungry children among the ruins, by "the grass growing in the houses, and the dandelions in the churches," but also by the political vicissitudes of his new friends in Prague, and by the Stalinists' crude manipulation of peace-loving European liberals at the Wroclaw gathering, where Frisch wisely absented himself before the final resolution was voted.

For a considerable time from 1945 on, Frisch spoke with a "private" and a "public" voice, the one often strengthening the other. Prompted by experiences in occupied Germany and elsewhere, Frisch wrote "public" problem plays, among them the skeptical and artful farce *Die chinesische Mauer* [1946] (*The Chinese Wall*, 1961), suggesting that Nietzsche was basically right in his view of human history as a movement of recurrences. In the early 1950s Frisch turned to more private issues, haplessly in *Graf Öderland* [1951] (*Count Oederland*, 1962), a melodrama about a state prosecutor who changes into a romantic anarchist (a play revised many times before the real terrorists pushed it from the scene), and with superb success in *Don Juan: oder, Die Liebe zur Geometrie* [1953] (*Don Juan: or, The Love of Geometry*, 1967). In the late 1950s and early 1960s Frisch again preferred a public theater and concentrated on dramatic parables and allegories, including *Biedermann und die Brandstifter* [1958] (*The Firebugs*, 1959), the darling of American college theaters, and *Andorra* [1961; 1962], which was far more successful on the European than the American stage. *Andorra* is a play against the crimes of anti-Semitism but without a real Jew, since the protagonist merely acts out a role or an image; the scenic abstractions, at least according to Robert Brustein, merely provided "wet whips for a Germany repellingly eager to flagellate itself."

Frisch's *Don Juan; or, The Love of Geometry* (written in 1952–53, mostly in New York, and revised in 1961) admirably succeeds in using the issue of pernicious image-making in an effective way. Frisch's Don Juan knows only too well that he is forced into playing a particular role by the expectations of others, and rightly fears that the "myth," or what people say or believe about him, will undo his spontaneity. Everybody, including the ladies at court and those in Celestina's famous brothel, expects him to be a hero, a master of the saber, and a passionate seducer. He has an uneasy time systematically disappointing these expectations, reading Arabic books on mathematics or playing chess in Celestina's establishment, where young Miranda sentimentally pines for his embraces. Frisch's Don Juan is an intellectual and, whether his author knows it or not, something of a chauvinist prig. He does submit occasionally to his instinctive urges and to women in general, but he tells everybody, in discourse neatly balancing wit and the appropriate imagery, that women are mere passing episodes and that he longs for the timeless realm of geometric truth, untouched by emotion, change, or the mind of the individual. Since the image-makers, in the comely shapes of thirteen ladies seduced, not to mention their bloodthirsty cousins and fathers, are upon him, there seems no other way out of playing his role but to arrange a theatrical exit to hell before astonished witnesses (anticipating Mozart's *Don Giovanni*), and secretly to seek refuge in the distant and splendid castle owned by the Duchess of Ronda, none other than the onetime prostitute Miranda, still very much in love with him. There Don Juan has a serene life studying geometry, and the Duchess expects his child. While Spanish and other hack writers are busy spreading the myth that Don Juan has gone to hell, he will not fail to be a good husband and father, the last image he ever wanted to incarnate.

In his novels of the mid-1950s, *Stiller* (1954; *I'm Not Stiller*, 1958) and *Homo Faber* (1957; 1959), Frisch for the first time uses his mature energy as an artist to concentrate on essential issues in sober and ironic language finally freed of all misplaced preciosity. *I'm Not Stiller* made him suddenly well known beyond Switzerland and Germany (though *Homo Faber* was the more popular success), and it is regrettable that the American version has been considerably cut, omitting a good deal of the episodic material, which is as important to the plot, if there is one, as the interpolated tales are to the quest of Don Quixote, whom Frisch very much admires. *I'm Not Stiller* is another story of a man who does not want to be defined by the perceptions of others but rather wishes to be true to his own self. A middle-aged man who is arrested at the Swiss border with a false U.S. passport keeps insisting, "I'm not Stiller," but the authorities put him in prison and urge him to admit that he is the Zürich sculptor Anatol Ludwig Stiller, a rather dubious character who fought in Spain in the International Brigade and later left his fragile wife Julika, a ballerina, when she was almost dying of tuberculosis. What we are reading are seven notebooks filled, at the suggestion of the state prosecutor, with the prisoner's observations about the judicial procedure, including confrontations with Julika (who now runs a ballet school in Paris), comments on his friends, memories, tall tales about his sojourn in Mexico and the United States, and a lengthy postscript by the state prosecutor himself. The latter, married to one of Stiller's former girlfriends, understands him better than anybody else and ultimately watches Julika and Stiller withdraw to the countryside to make a new beginning of love and marriage—too late, for she dies of her illness at last, whereupon Stiller, firmly accepting his imperfect self, goes on living in self-chosen isolation, poverty, and silence. *I'm Not Stiller* is a miracle of a novel, particularly in the context of German literature, because it carries its late existentialism with the lightest and most disciplined touch. The issues and themes of Frisch's early narratives—the quest for the self, the problem of marriage, the making of false images—which were once handled as if emerging from behind a romantic fog, are gathered here in a novel that is paradoxically rich, playful, and intense.

Homo Faber wants to tell the story of false and repressive self-images shattered by experience that comes too late. The fifty-year-old Swiss engineer Faber works as a technical expert for UNESCO overseas and has become estranged from what he thinks is real life. He lives according to schedules and deadlines, and hates to feel, perspire, or be unshaven; his razor, his clean shirts, and his camera are his fetishes of distancing and sterility. Yet the disorderly powers of life and death lie in wait for him: on a trip to a forlorn Mexican hacienda, he finds an old friend dead by suicide, and when, divided against himself, he falls in love with a twenty-year-old girl, she proves to be his daughter, who, after a night of incestuous love on the shores of the Greek sea, suddenly dies of an undiagnosed hemorrhage. On a trip to pre-Castro Havana he is ready to "praise life," but recurrent stomach pains require his hospitalization, and his report breaks off as he is being prepared for surgery: his awakening to life and his dying are one, as in Thomas Mann's *Death in Venice*. Frisch curiously succeeds, I believe, in suggesting the changes of perception in the changes of language in which Faber writes about his experiences, but the story tends at times to turn into a test case or rather an allegory in which typical figures, if not symbolic puppets, function in a prescribed way: engineers, managers, and technologists are ranged on one side of life (the empty one), and musicians, archaeologists, and handsome Cuban shoeshine boys on the other. There is little to restrain the sentimental reader from interpreting *Homo Faber* as yet another German story about the sterility of the intellect and the virtues of deep feeling.

THE TRANSFORMATIONS OF THE SIXTIES

In the early 1960s Frisch found himself a middle-aged writer, and it would be legitimate to speak about his midlife crisis, had he not turned the years of crisis into a new moment of magnificent and creative transformation affecting everything he wrote—prose, plays, and occasional political essays. Anticipating the restlessness of the student revolt, Frisch energetically seized on the radical options long present in his writings and gave them full dominance. He began to rely on the discontinuities of narrative collage, assembling, weighing, and setting against each other facts and fictions, documents and fantasies. In his rare plays he totally discarded memories of Bertolt Brecht and experiments with a new dramaturgy of "variance" and "reduction" to move suddenly closer to Beckett and a stage of the private symbol, rather than public and instructive truth to be shared by many.

European and American critics often deplore the fact that it is easier to characterize Frisch's *Mein Name sei Gantenbein* (1964; *A Wilderness of Mirrors*, 1965, *Gantenbein*, 1982) in negative rather than in positive terms. It is certainly true that a critical vocabulary mainly derived from discussions of the nineteenth-century novel blocks rather than opens our way to knowing what the book is about and how its author operates. There is no cohesive story to retell, though there are many stories, episodes, and anecdotes told by various voices, more or less reliable. The characters are mostly of a disturbingly exchangeable kind, and our usual suspension of disbelief does not seem to serve any useful purpose, because we are constantly reminded by the narrator himself that everything is fiction anyway, though fiction in a functioning urban world that we recognize without effort as our own, with its cabs, cocktail parties, airports, ophthalmologists, and an occasional professor who receives an offer from Harvard. Instead of disappearing behind events and characters (as in the realistic novel), the ego of the author again and again asserts its imaginative privileges and projective presence by delineating characters, building situations, and analyzing itself while doing so, in order to communicate with us obliquely. The author does not communicate easily. He (for it is definitely a man's voice) first toys with the idea of haphazardly creating a fictional character, combining a body in Paris with a Manhattan face. Then, however, he immediately begins a more or less coherent story about himself as a patient in a hospital, where he bares his body to the nurse in order to return to the innocence of Adam and Eve (or so he tells himself), then runs out naked into the city traffic and hides in the darkness of an empty theater before being gently returned by the doctors to the hospital—a study of loss, of being vulnerable, of needing a place to hide, of needing clothes. It is the central image of the narrative procedure, for the narrator insists that he wants to try on stories like clothes in a tailor's shop. He proceeds by creating charades of four major characters circling and mirroring each other: Lila, a famous and (at least for long stretches of the book) capricious actress; her second husband, Gantenbein, who pretends that he is blind in order to see better what people do; Enderlin, a professor and one of Lila's reluctant lovers; and the bearlike architect Svoboda, her first husband, who feels as jealous of Gantenbein as Gantenbein himself later feels of Enderlin. Yet in an epilogue the characters disappear as easily as they once emerged, and the narrating ego reasserts its expansive presence and, for a finale, taunts us with an image of grotesque death that leaves no trace, exactly corresponding to the image of death that had appeared on page one, and a sudden and paradoxical suggestion of glorious life fully accepted—thirst, hunger, and all.

By playing blind and assuming a self-invented role, Gantenbein emancipates himself from the possible roles imposed on him by others and begins enjoying life as if it were a theatrical performance; he hopes to free people from feeling anxiety lest others see their lies, and consoles himself with the belief that people will not camouflage their lives. He may yet find out, he hopes, who they truly are: "A new and more truthful relationship emerges, and (while one even accepts their untruths) a more intimate relationship." At other times Gantenbein sadly knows that he is, as Lila's husband, a prisoner of his self-chosen blindness, for as soon as he insists on seeing, he sees more of her disloyalties than he can bear. "What I see, and what I don't see," he confesses, "is a question of tact." Marriage itself is shown to be perhaps nothing but "a question of tact."

Frisch's *Gantenbein* is certainly a novel about fictions, but I do not think that it is sufficient to rest the defense there and to stress the avant-garde qualities of a purely methodological exercise, or the virtues of another "book about nothing" of which Flaubert dreamed more than a hundred years ago. Frisch has never been content with technical exercises alone; the real question, I think, is how his fictional exercise functions emotionally and what kind of communication it establishes between author and reader. We are not uncertain about what compels the narrator to construct his stories; he tells us, more in the manner of a true confession at the beginning of the novel, that he finds himself sitting in an empty apartment in which, just some time ago, two people, a man and a woman, lived together. Frisch uses a game of fiction to cope with a traumatic shock of jealously, despair, and loneliness so as to purify a surfeit of destructive feelings. It is a witty exercise but also a cathartic one, and the narrator's final words, about accepting the fullness of the world again, are spoken by Frisch himself outside and behind all the turns of the game; they cease to be fiction.

Frisch was long concerned with how actual events determine the course of an individual's life, whether just for particular moments or irrevocably. *Gantenbein* is only one of his attempts to restore to the self, hungry for a life free of inevitable consequences, the realm of true potentiality. He would like us, as human beings caught in irreversible material affairs, to move back and forth in our experience and revise our actions as freely as we do in our imaginative consciousness, with its power to project possibilities. Frisch develops a polemical dramaturgy of potentiality or, as he himself suggested, "variability," radically opposed to the theater of the past, including above all his own plays of parable or allegory such as *The Firebugs, Andorra*, and others. He argues against all kinds of theater of fate and consequentiality (*Fügung*) in which one event inevitably functions as the cause of another and so on ad infinitum at least as long as an individual human life lasts. He does not spare the tragedy of the ancients, modern psychological drama, or the plays of Brecht, who still reveals "consequentiality within a social system" and presents fables made of strings of causes and effects; for Frisch, Brecht derides one chain of consequentiality but assumes another, a changed social system within which events are linked to each other again as causes and effects. Frisch proposes a dramaturgy that takes its cue from the earliest rehearsals of a play (which he finds truly fascinating) rather than from the performances of the finished product. He wants a theater kept alive by the aleatory: "We know," he writes in his correspondence (1969) with the critic Walter Höllerer, "that things happen only when they are possible, but thousands of things that are equally possible do not happen at all, and everything could happen in a different way, always." The new theater would offer a way of counteracting "the double continuity of time," which does not allow for freely toying with the possibilities and variants of life.

The theory of the "variant" theater is one thing and a play another, and the failure of *Biografie* [1967] (*Biography: A Game*, 1969), which was to exemplify the idea, increased Frisch's aversion to the contemporary stage. Frisch had to ask for special allowances to present his argument theatrically, and critics were quick to remark that the technical conditions of the stage adjust more easily to one set of prescriptive concepts than to another. In his play Frisch confronts us with the intellectual Kürman, who in spite of his allegorical name, "the man of choices," and his professorship, is very much an autobiographical hero. While Kürman makes and corrects his choices at important turning points of his life, he is accompanied by the Chronicler, another allegorical figure who dictates procedures, reads from Kürman's life file, and risks making the play as didactic as Frisch's earlier theatrical parables. Kürman's particular problem is to avoid falling in love with Antoinette, a smart young woman who translates Theodor W. Adorno and wants to own a small gallery in Paris; but however the Chronicler turns and twists the events of the fateful party on May 26, 1960, at which Kürman first meets

Antoinette, the professor is always bent on making the wrong choice, being the individual he is, and Antoinette always has a chance to stay the night with him, to his housekeeper's dismay. The Chronicler insists that things do not have to be this way or that, but the range of existential "variants" does not seem very extensive, and our hopes for extending them are dashed by Kürman's terminal illness, and the Chronicler's announcement that he has only seven more years to make his choices anyway. The play is not much helped by Frisch's awkward attempt to attach public relevance to Kürman's private experience by having the Chronicler read lists of important historical dates from the life file. Worse still is the resistance of stage events to the metaphorical categories of actuality and potentiality, since whatever happens on the stage affects the audience, and the distinctions between ontological potentiality and reality do not work neatly on the boards.

Yet Frisch does not give up easily. He felt hurt when *Biography* did not survive for long on the stage, but the question of what it means to act had long disturbed him, and he stubbornly returned to it ten years later in *Triptychon* [1981] (*Triptych*, 1981), a loose and puzzling sequence of "three scenic images" that would not be performed for long, he insisted, on the fickle contemporary stage. *Triptych* offers counterimages to *Biography*: if Kürman and his chronicler rehearsed for us what might have been, *Triptych* shows us what in the play itself is called "the validity" of living; once we have acted thus or thus, we have done something that will never change but will endure, unaffected by time, in a kind of "eternity" of its own. But the vantage point has changed, for in *Triptych* Frisch reveals a universe in which the borderline between the "living" and the "dead" has been obliterated; the dead, who dominate the middle part of the play, constantly return to the invariant experiences of their lives and unknowingly reveal what blissful opportunities they have missed. Dramatic tension is totally absent: the dead muse about their past like characters in a Chekhov play, and a wonderful aura of spiritual peace pervades these immobile scenes, as if the play were really a sad ballad or rather an elegy about the chances we have missed in our lives. Whether he knows it or not, Frisch is in full and paradoxically productive regression as a playwright. He may allude to Beckett here and there, but the fundamental design of these scenes again reflects, as did so many of his early plays, Thornton Wilder's *Our Town* (Frisch's pre-Brechtian source), while the songlike quality of the text, sustained by recurrence and quotation, cannot but remind us of his plays of forty years ago.

THE MASTER

Tagebuch 1966–1971 (1972; *Sketchbook 1966–1971,* 1974) suggests in its own way that the mid-1960s, when Frisch moved from Rome to the old stone house in the Ticino, was a troubled time of more than geographical dislocations. The new diaries, if compared with those of the immediate postwar period, look and read differently. Strikingly divergent texts, printed in four different kinds of typography, are gathered uneasily, and the principle of collage, suddenly so dominant here, will be used by Frisch in many of his subsequent narrative pieces. The texts include short paragraphs separated from each other by a good deal of glaring white space; ontologically different materials, factual or fictional or both; challenging parables; and fragments pushing the reader on to more intense reflections. In the early diaries a young writer, responding to a productive shock, energetically analyzed the past and projected expectations into the future. But in the new diaries, I suspect, an aging consciousness that is physiologically weary no longer indulges in useful illusions about what can be understood and narrated; rather, we are staring at raw materials that the diarist, skeptical and perhaps exhausted, balances on the brink of silence and self-effacement. He can do so because the artist, in his stead, develops a distinct pattern of recurrent formal elements that structure the reluctant assembly of discordant materials. There are "Questionnaires" in which a kind of Everyman responds to questions about the fundamentals of modern living, including love, suffering, and marriage; "Interrogations" in which somebody called B offers evasive responses about contemporary events, as for instance the Paris May Day revolt or German terrorism, to somebody called A, who is eager for firm commitments and clear definitions; "Notes from the Suicide Club Membership Handbook"; and newspaper clippings about the Vietnam war and the economic situation from the Swiss, West

German, and American press. All these are interrupted at regular intervals by sequences of private notes recounting Frisch's trips to Berlin, Prague, Moscow, and Washington (lunch with Secretary of State Henry Kissinger) and his discussions with Brecht in Zürich and with young Grass (a rather awkward fellow), as well as sketches of stories that Frisch may or may not use at another time.

Certainly this diary does not disdain the aesthetic ploys of a work of art, and yet, beyond the diversity of materials and Frisch's efforts to create an aesthetic structure (with which he was totally unconcerned in his immediate postwar diaries), there is a new motif or rather issue in which Frisch, in his midfifties, finds himself for the first time inescapably involved: the physiological and psychological process of aging, which he observes and analyzes in unsentimental detail. The signals are visible in the first pages of the diary, for Questionnaire #1, about happiness, is immediately followed by a newspaper clipping about the growing number of aged people in industrial societies and a somber story about an old craftsman withering away in a Zürich tavern. Notes about a medical cure in the old Swiss spa of Tarasp-Vulpera trigger Frisch's bitter and playful idea to establish a "Club for the Rejuvenation of Occidental Society," the members of which are bound to commit suicide at a certain point so as to ease their own burdens and those of society. Old age is an issue about which German writing, at the time of the youth revolt, was noticeably silent. In spite of some *longueurs* (because Frisch measures old age solely in erotic and sexual terms), his restless notes yield fascinating observations about how younger people change in their behavior toward aging men, and how aging men change in their feelings about younger fellow citizens.

Frisch's *Montauk* (1975; 1976) has troubled critics and readers in Europe and the United States. It may be useful to keep in mind the leitmotivs of aging and the theoretical disquisitions of the diarist, before joining those who are quick to dismiss the book as merely self-indulgent, or those who innocently praise it as an exemplary narrative of unalloyed sincerity. *Montauk* is a journal about a brief encounter: sixty-year-old Frisch spends a weekend with thirty-one-year-old Lynn, and they later part on a street corner, never to meet again (a somewhat literary assumption, for they lived together later in Greenwich Village).

Without intending to be cynical, I would call *Montauk* an artful exercise in which Frisch explores how far self-revelation, appropriately introduced by a quotation from Montaigne, can go. Frisch is compelled to think of other voyages, other days, and he looks deeper and more honestly into his past than ever before. Lynn, shadowy at best, quickly disappears from our ken, and other people emerge much more vividly than the gray-eyed, carrot-haired American woman in jeans running on the sand. They are more vivid because Frisch feels more torturing pain upon thinking of them: W., Frisch's brilliant rich friend who paid for his studies; a girlfriend who was later paralyzed and whom he refused to see again; his first and second wives; and the poet Ingeborg Bachmann and his uneasy three years with her in Rome. He also recalls "four abortions for three women" whom he loved; the last moments of his dying mother, who thought she was back in old Russia; and guilt, failures, sins of commission and omission. "Lynn," he adds hopefully, "is not a name for guilt."

American reviewers have read *Montauk* with the care it fully deserves, but I think they have underrated Frisch's insistence on using, if not toying with, different narrative attitudes, each of which may serve a specific function. As soon as we admit that he employs a sophisticated combination of narrative ploys, we cannot easily or exclusively stress the documentary or rather autobiographical value of the text alone. It is true that Frisch wants to work here with purely "factual" materials, "without inventing anything," but he has so long argued against the pure facticity of the factual, both in theoretical comments and in practice, that I would take his sudden documentary urge with a grain of skepticism. Actually, he uses three narrative stances, the "I," the "thou" (especially when addressing his second wife rather than the reader), and the "he/she" of narrative tradition. I do not believe at all that Frisch uses the third person singular, as a German critic has suggested, to characterize his relationship with Lynn as distant or superficial; rather it is used by way of testing "the role of the innocent (*einfältig*) narrator," who wants to be as close as possible to what really happened on the weekend and, as the notes in the diaries indicate, to exploit the "confessional potential" of the "he/she" stance. The other possibility, the attitude of the probing "I," is used in coping with the past, and it is not surprising that the heavy and bloody mass of the past, swelling and oozing, quickly pushes aside Lynn's guiltless but "thin presence"—more than sixty years of experience against a few days.

Frisch's *Der Mensch erscheint im Holozän* (1979; *Man in the Holocene*, 1980), which was more readily praised by the critics than any other of his publications of the 1970s, belongs to the laconic narratives that are fully anticipated, in method and concern, by the diaries, yet the mood has changed again, suggesting resilience more than bitterness or melancholy. We have to decode, as it were, the movement of the story from the implications of a text arranged in fragments and interspersed with little illustrations from an encyclopedia, and if we want to search for meaning, we have to rely, uneasily, on a few dispersed clues. An earlier story that Frisch abandoned was called "Climate," and the title would still be appropriate for this new narrative in which a lonely old man confronts the timeless powers of geology, vegetation, and the atmosphere shaping the earth rather than (as in so many of his other stories) the social pressures of a cosmopolitan city. Seventy-four-year-old Herr Geiser, having had a successful life in Basel, has retired to a comfortable old stone house in the Onsernone valley in the Swiss Ticino (as it happens, Frisch's own place of residence) and settled down there, in his solitude, to a quiet routine of thinking, walking, cooking, and reading. He has learned how to be attentive to the signals of nature, and when one day, after an uncanny moment of silence, heavy rains and thunderstorms roll over the valley, he instinctively fears that a landslide may endanger the village and his house. When the bad weather continues, he plans to escape over the mountain pass to another valley, laboriously ascends the difficult flanks of the mountains, and yet decides, when he sees the other valley from above, to return. At home he suffers a minor stroke, or so it seems, and shuts himself in; while his perceptions dim and his energy ebbs away, he clearly remembers how in his youth once he climbed the Matterhorn with his brother, who on those heights courageously protected him against the dangerous elements all around.

In presenting Herr Geiser's encounter with impassive nature, Frisch works with the collage technique developed in the diaries. The white space on the pages suggests gaps of memory, and the individual blocks of text are even leaner than before—often a single sentence. Frisch combines fragments of Geiser's inner monologue; sober comments by the narrator or rather an imperturbable chronicler; and the reproduction of everything that Geiser excerpts and cuts out of his books: occasional paragraphs from the Bible (though Geiser does not believe in the Flood), sections from a patriotic history of the Ticino, entries from the Brockhaus dictionary, information about the Holocene (our own time, going back to the ice age), and later, pictures of dinosaurs and other prehistoric creatures. The few cohesive pages of text are of fundamental importance, as for instance Geiser's memories of his Matterhorn tour (possibly the last moment of his consciousness before it totally deteriorates), and the last pages in the present tense, which assert the unimpaired continuity of daily life in the valley (passages that in themselves form a collage, bringing together sentences that appeared earlier in isolation from each other). I do not believe that Frisch simply handles nature as a convenient prop, but assume that he wants to suggest the disparities between "timeless" nature and the time of people who are prisoners of flesh and death, that he views time not in a melodramatic and sentimental way but as something to be borne with serenity, being constitutive of human existence.

The recent tale *Blaubart* (1982; *Bluebeard: A Tale*, 1983) has pleased most American reviewers, who finally have come to accept Frisch as a major European writer. Frisch's Bluebeard lacks most of the vicious energies usually ascribed to a killer of women; his middle-aged Zürich physician, whose name is Felix Schaad (etymologically combining "happiness" and "harm"), strikes me much more as a Swiss Casper Milquetoast embodying the metaphysical burdens and hidden guilt feelings of us all. Now in his seventh marriage (falling apart because his wife, on an African safari, has taken up with a TV producer), he is accused of murdering his sixth wife, Rosalind, who had chosen to earn her living as a high-class call girl and has died in a particularly nasty way. The authorities, however, are unable to gather sufficient evidence, and after a trial during which many witnesses are heard (including former wives who assure the jury that Felix would not hurt a fly), the accused is acquitted and even paid, according to Swiss law, a handsome sum to recompense him for his time in prison during the investigation. His alibi may be a bit shaky, but it is also made clear during the trial that his jealousy of Rosalind (while he was married to her) had changed into friendship after the divorce, when she allowed him to watch her in bed with customers by video, since he recognized that "the bed was not a particularly personal place to her." His problem is to go on living after the acquittal: his patients stay away and he wastes time playing billiards while still hearing what the witnesses said, and then new voices, among them those of his mother and father from the realm of the dead, who insist on making depositions about his life. The acquittal triggers in him the most hidden feelings of guilt: he thinks of the cruelties he committed in his boyhood games and then, compelled by the rising pressure of emotions, drives to the village where his mother was born, informs the local police that he did indeed murder his sixth wife (he is turned away), and, while returning home, runs his car at high speed against a tree. In the hospital he is told that the real murderer, a Greek student, has confessed, but he cannot answer any questions about himself because his power of speech is ebbing away and with it, perhaps, his life.

As a storyteller Frisch rarely starts from scratch; the Bluebeard story has its clear links to earlier texts. Some elements of the plot (the call girl, the murder, and the trial) have been anticipated in Gantenbein's visit to his willing manicurist Camilla and her violent death. He has already used the terse if not cryptic way of presenting narrative materials in *Man in the Holocene*, in which, however, the diversity of extracts (including documents and dictionary items) imbues the sparse text with surprising riches. In *Bluebeard* Frisch reduces further, until the white space predominates over the laconic articulation (which could be reproduced very effectively in a radio play). The sharp suspense of the whodunit inherent in the story suffers from questions that cannot be answered with any degree of certainty. We are compelled to watch the disintegration of a human being who might have done what he did not do and, by being acquitted, has to face a deeper truth about himself. Schaad may not have committed the crime, yet he feels overwhelmed by his lack of innocence and the onrushing recognition that he could easily have been the killer. Guilt turns into an existential burden that defies a neat legal definition.

Young Swiss writers today do not like the idea of a Swiss literature, because they think it old-fashioned and provincial, but it would be difficult to describe Max Frisch's career without talking about his Helvetian, or rather Zürich, origins. He grew up and wrote his first narratives and plays in a democracy ready to defend itself, and he enjoyed (precisely because Switzerland is so small) a geographical and intellectual mobility that we occasionally miss in the life and work of Günter Grass, and in particular that of Heinrich Böll. I would be inclined to say that Frisch's imaginative gifts have unfolded, rather than developed in a striking way. Although abrupt changes occur in his awareness of the self, the social world, and literature immediately after 1945 and again twenty years later, he never really discarded what he thought and wrote; with the one exception of the new leitmotiv of aging, which emerges from the second diary, he holds on to the central issues of false image-making, time, repetition, and marriage, quoting the Romantics in his early work, and Kierkegaard (rather than Freud) somewhat later. He is disturbed by the resilience of the strong Swiss middle-class society and its mouthpiece, the *Neue Zürcher Zeitung*, to which he himself contributed in younger years, but, unlike many of his German colleagues, in his fiction he does not easily move outside an environment of lawyers, architects, physicians, and professors, with attendant actors, writers, and sculptors, as if Thomas Mann's world of 1912 still existed. Frisch has never published a volume of poetry, but the attitude of the "I" that expresses feelings and thoughts is basic to his plays and prose pieces, and he does not always have an easy time suppressing and disciplining the lyrical intonation of his idiom, distinctly prominent in his early pieces and present, in a more sublimated way, everywhere else in his later work. Looking back, I would say that he has moved from the precious style of his early years to the spoken idiom of his novels of middle age, and from there to the sparse, laconic mode of his recent tales.

European and American critics cherish different views of Frisch but in the long run, I suspect, the American view of Frisch will prevail. Most European critics still see Frisch above all as a playwright, and perhaps even as Brecht's disciple, the author of political parables like *The Firebugs* or *Andorra* and a few psychological or experimental novels of dubious distinction. American critics are skeptical about the few plays that they know (abstract *Andorra*, for instance, rather than the brilliant comedy *Don Juan*) and tend to see Frisch's true achievement in his prose masterpieces from *Stiller* to *Gantenbein*, and from his earlier diaries to *Montauk, Man in the Holocene*, and *Bluebeard*. American critics do not know much about Frisch's political writings, including his speech at the 1977 party conference of the German Social Democrats stressing "innovation by criticism," but it is also true that Frisch views his own activist utterances (far less essential to the body of his writing than in the case of Böll) with ever-present self-doubt. He always thought more highly of Brecht's theatrical genius than of his politics and in the mid-1960s warned West German intellectuals against overrating the political potential of the theater at large. "The Left," he said, "is simply more gifted for the wooden boards of the theater, the boards that are *not* those of the world." Frisch deplores his failure to join the Spanish International Brigade as a young man but continues to speak of "the work of art," believes in social commitment by irritation and indirection, and defines successful art as something apt to disintegrate foolish abstractions and ossifying ideologies; no wonder Brecht thought that Frisch was "not expert enough" to function as a real partner in political discussions. Frisch's expertise is certainly elsewhere. "I do not write to teach," he said recently, "but to explore and to show the conditions of myself." It is an essential confession, for as a compassionate observer of the sensitive self and its painful consciousness of social pressures of both the intimate and the public kind, he has no equal among his fellow writers in German.

15

A PANORAMA OF FICTION

The war, the liberation by the Allies, and the first years of peace did not, and could not, quickly create a new German novel. The first books haphazardly published (often by houses having good contacts with a paper-dispensing officer in the military government) were written by established authors, including Kasimir Edschmid (1890–1966), the expressionist patriarch, and Ernst Wiechert (1887–1950), a conservative Protestant once briefly held at Buchenwald concentration camp. Younger writers, whether or not they knew of Hermann Broch's radical questioning of art in the age of the gas chambers, had ceased to believe in complex forms of writing, especially if they belonged to Group 47; instead they preferred reportage, the diary, or at most an "American" kind of short story, thought to be in contrast to the well-wrought German novella of the past. In the late 1940s and 1950s, formal options were largely a matter of the writer's age: the issue was whether it was still possible to encompass and interpret recent German history in the large-scale novel of Hegelian totality, surveying an entire society, or whether the narrative had to be content with less, either by trying to universalize the particular in an allegorical way (Kafka misunderstood) or by offering splinters of disjointed experiences not "beautiful" but alive, contemporary, and intense (Hemingway misread). The older writers of the Weimar Republic, returning from exile or the war, overwhelmed their readers with large novels in which they gathered their thoughts of a decade. Thus Theodor Plievier (1892–1955), who came back from exile in the Soviet Union, published his war novel *Stalingrad* (1945), rough but compassionate, pitting giant armies against each other, while Thomas Mann, who later left the United States for Switzerland, completed his highly personal *Doktor Faustus* (1947), incarnating the perversions of German history in the life and death of a demonic composer often reminding us of Nietzsche. In *Die Toten bleiben jung* (1949; *The Dead Stay Young*, 1950), Anna Seghers (1900–83) sketched from her Marxist and realistic point of view twenty-five years of German history, from the Spartacus rising of 1919 to the destruction of the Hitler regime; and the Austrian Heimito von Doderer (1896–1966), in *Die Dämonen* (1956; *The Demons*, 1961), the ultimate of the "total" novels, uncovered, in a piercing analysis of Viennese life in the 1920s, the vicious forces ready to take over his homeland, and more. These novels were widely discussed, praised, or despised, but not imitated, by a younger generation of writers.

The innovative writers of the Weimar Republic did not have an easy time restoring their readership and influence; the frustrations and lonely death of Alfred Döblin (1878–1957) disclose the force of historical discontinuity. In the 1920s and early 1930s Döblin, a neurologist, left-wing critic, and materialist philosopher of nature, had been the most intelligent defender of the experimental narrative. In *Berge Meere und Giganten* (1924; *Mountains Oceans and Giants*) technology and nature inexorably collided, while his world-famous *Berlin Alexanderplatz* (1929; 1931) articulated the rhythm of the modern city in a prose montage using techniques often reminiscent of the futurists and Dos Passos. In 1933 Döblin went to Paris, where he worked with Jean Giraudoux in the French ministry of information. Later, via the usual Lisbon route of German refugees, he left Europe, eventually reaching Hollywood, where he was briefly employed by the studios and later lived on the dole. (Meanwhile his son, who had joined the French army, killed himself rather than surrender to the Germans.) Döblin was among the first exiles to return to Germany, but it turned out that he was totally isolated among ideologies and generations: his older friends never forgave him for converting to Catholicism in Hollywood, and the younger generation had no particular interest in an aging writer employed by the French occupation forces and, occasionally at least, appearing in French uniform. With French support Döblin edited the periodical *Das goldene Tor* (*The Golden Gate*), whose announced goal was to consider new German writing and acquaint German readers with new writing in France and elsewhere, but he did not find a German publisher for his novel *Hamlet; oder, Die lange Nacht nimmt ein Ende* (*Hamlet, or the Long Night Ends*), later published in the GDR (1956), nor was he ever invited by Group 47. In 1953 he left Germany again, writing to American friends that Hitler had gone but nothing else had really changed. His ferocious attacks on Thomas Mann made it even more difficult for his loyal friends to defend his true achievements. When he died, half blind and paralyzed, in a German sanitarium in 1957, he was remembered by few. It was the ultimate irony of his life that he was rediscovered, as the master of the modern novel, only a few years after his death by a new generation of writers, among them Günter Grass, who considers him his first teacher in the art of writing.

In the early and mid-1950s readers of literary inclinations often discussed the novels of Gerd Gaiser (1908–76) and Wolfgang Koeppen (b. 1906), and, if genuinely concerned with experimental fiction, the prose texts by the loner Arno Schmidt (1914–79). Middle-aged readers and schoolteachers to the right of center were particularly attentive to Gaiser, who combined the Hermann Hesse tradition of German *Innerlichkeit* and the romantic ideas of the youth movement of the late 1920s with exacting craftsmanship; he often preferred the interior monologue and the narrative segmented into rapid scenes or vignettes, yet did not ultimately undermine conservative assumptions of what literature should do, structurally or ideologically. Gaiser's epic approach was that of the thoughtful German patriot unable to forgive the Nazis for how easily they had manipulated his ideal aspirations and those of his contemporaries in their struggle for power. In *Die sterbende Jagd* (1953; *The Last Squadron*, 1956), a pastel-colored war novel without gore, he closely observes the agonies of the Luftwaffe, which first is deprived by the Nazis of its old chivalric code, respectful of the gallant enemy, and then is destroyed by flying fortresses; in a classical language skillfully fused with the technical idiom of the pilots, he provokes searching questions about art and war.

Readers to the left of center were more closely attracted to Wolfgang Koeppen who, after surviving the Reich in odd jobs in the film industry, courageously analyzed contemporary issues of political power and individual sensibility in a nervous mode continuing the traditions of the avant-garde, the expressionists, and James Joyce. In *Tauben im Grass* (1951; *Pigeons in the Grass*) he describes, as a melancholy historian, what happens to some Germans and Americans during a single day in a Munich just recuperating from the hungry years. *Das Treibhaus* (1953; *The Hothouse*) tells about the suicide of a young member of the Bonn parliament who wants to realize his own self rather than serve political institutions. In *Der Tod in Rom* (1954; *Death in Rome*), a melodrama occasionally parodying Thomas Mann, he pits against each other sensitive sons and brutal Nazi fathers who go on hurting and killing people. As if exhausted by these explosive novels, Koeppen later fell silent for many years. His *Jugend* (1979; *Youth*), a tense and exhilarating volume of memories, was welcomed by nearly everybody as a sign that more important novels were perhaps waiting for publication.

Denounced as an atheist and later revered as the patriarch of experimental prose, Arno Schmidt (1914–79) belonged to a generation whose intellectual development was blocked for many years by the Nazi state and the war. Born in Hamburg of Silesian parents, he wanted to study astronomy and mathematics in Breslau, but had to give it up because his sister married a Jew. He served in the artillery during the war, and returned from a POW camp resolved to start from scratch and make literature of his own kind his only concern. He went hungry rather than disperse his interests, and while his sister kept him alive for some time by sending Care packages from Baltimore, he looked for an ascetic refuge in little villages so as to be alone and undisturbed. Finally, in 1958 he settled in forlorn Bargfeld/Celle on the Lüneburg heath, keeping away in the congenial moors from all literary coteries and creating his own legend of the stubborn sage. His texts of the 1950s were above all radical attempts to articulate his piercing consciousness of a disordered world. In *Brand's Haide* (*Brand's Heath*) and *Schwarze Spiegel* (*Black Mirrors*), both published in 1951, he looks at the modern apocalypse through the eyes of a returning soldier who wants only to read eighteenth-century literature, a kind of Robinson Crusoe who, after an atomic war, experiences a few days of happiness with a woman survivor yet is left alone again when she decides to roam through the empty world rather than to stay on as his *Hausfrau*. In the late 1950s and 1960s Schmidt began to translate systematically from English (mostly William Faulkner, James Fenimore Cooper, Stanislaus Joyce, Edward Bulwer-Lytton, and Edgar Allan Poe) and involved himself in studies of James Joyce and Freud. He tried to develop his own theory of writing, in which the generic concepts of the "photo album" used to recuperate memory, the "fragmentary present," the "extended play of thought," and his idea of "ethyms" (primal words emerging from the subconscious to sustain conscious articulation with elemental energy) were of essential importance.

Schmidt never renounced his belief in the essential importance of the thinking, speaking, and creating self, much to the dissatisfaction of some of his later structuralist readers. But many of his texts of the 1960s and 1970s, full of quirky erudition, intellectual wit, and increasingly conservative ideas about life, tended to substitute, for the earlier articulations of obsessive self-consciousness, "scripts" about the talks and walks of writers, translators, and intellectuals congregating for a day or two in the heath to consider his pet theories, however camouflaged. In *Kaff auch Mare Crisium* (1960; *The Boondocks, Also Mare Crisium*) two lovers visit an aunt, think about an American republic on the moon, and offer the narrator ample opportunity to cultivate Joycean puns like those in *Finnegans Wake*. In *Zettels Traum* (1970; *Zettel's Dream*)—usually described as the most monstrous publication of new German writing, seventeen pounds to carry and, potentially, five thousand pages long if printed in the traditional way—two Poe translators visit a learned scholar (alias Arno Schmidt) and consider, among many other things, the possibility of a psychoanalytical reading of Poe based on ethyms or primal words, surely of high interest to students of Marie Bonaparte and Jacques Lacan. In *Abend mit Goldrand* (1975; *Evening Edged in Gold*, 1980), perhaps most appropriately characterized as the script of a melancholy comedy (available to American and British readers in the miraculous translation by John E. Woods), Schmidt's personal thought and art, insisting on phonetic spelling and an ingenious spatial arrangement of the text, culminate in a witty and serene farewell to his readers and the world. Glowing memories of his early days are told in meticulous detail and, far more important, literature itself, after a heath village has been raided by a barbarian band of dropouts, is rescued for the future by a young writer who again resembles none other but young Arno Schmidt. German provincialism, the pedantry of a vast antiquarian knowledge, and the literate genius for innovation have never been combined in a more provocative achievement.

The fictions of the fifties were dominated, in West and East, by writers who had published in the Weimar Republic and afterward, and the new generation came of define its own experiences and views slowly and hesitatingly. At the early meetings of Group 47, Heinrich Böll (1917–85), Wolfdietrich Schnurre (b. 1920), Walter Jens (b. 1923; later a professor of classical philology at Tübingen), and Ilse Aichinger (b. 1921) read remarkable narratives, close to an unsparing realism or to Kafka, but it was not until the late 1950s, at least in the Federal Republic, that the writers of the first postwar generation published important books and established their own contemporary novel. Gabriele Wohmann (b. 1932) published an early novel in 1958, but the miraculous year of new fiction was 1959: Böll published his intricately constructed *Billard um Halbzehn* (1959; *Billiards at Half-Past Nine*, 1961); Günter Grass (b. 1927), his picaresque *Die Blechtrommel* (1959; *The Tin Drum*, 1962); and Uwe Johnson (1934–84), his difficult *Mutmassungen über Jakob* (1959; *Speculations about Jacob*, 1963). One year later Martin Walser (b. 1927) showed his rich linguistic gifts in *Halbzeit* (1960; *Halftime*). Writers of the new age group, born between 1927 and 1934, shared early experiences and many literary attitudes; during the war they had been in school and joined the *Flakhelfer* (the antiaircraft corps of students who manned guns after school hours), the Reich Labor Service, and the army in the last years of Nazi rule. They all had radical doubts about the ideals of the older humanists and about the possibility of continuing nineteenth-century narrative traditions. All experimented with styles and strategies preceding or following traditional realism, trying their hand at the picaresque, the interior monologue, or Faulkner's multiple narrative perspectives; yet they never pushed their experiments to an extreme, and were always eager to preserve a story of sorts and to pronounce a message of social criticism.

In the German Democratic Republic the articulate emergence of a younger generation was slowed for other reasons. More incisively than in the West, postwar fiction, powerfully represented by Anna Seghers (1900–83), Arnold Zweig (1887–1968), Bodo Uhse (1904–63), and Willi Bredel (1901–64), continued the Weimar novel of left-wing social criticism, while the authorities, especially after the early 1950s, pushed the principles of Socialist Realism and the Bitterfeld movement, demanding the grand industrial novel. Erwin Strittmatter (b. 1912), folksy and strongly plebeian, published his first tales about class conflicts on the farms in the early fifties, but it was only in the early and mid-sixties that a compact generation corresponding to that of Grass, Johnson, and Wohmann in the West made itself heard in the GDR, and the novels of Christa Wolf (b. 1929) and Hermann Kant (b. 1926) were widely read inside and outside their country.

Mainstream fiction in the West continued close to traditional realism, tending to the timely short story (the preference of the media); Siegfried Lenz and Marie Luise Kaschnitz were particularly successful in satisfying loyal readers of the professional middle classes, respectful of the past and a well-tempered modernism. Lenz, born in 1926 in the small town of Lyck/Masuren in East Prussia, served in the navy before turning to journalism at least for a while, and established himself as a free-lance writer who tended to locate his characters in North German, East Prussian, or Scandinavian scenes. His early novels, allegories of resistance to totalitarian regimes more symbolic than real, were far less successful than *So zärtlich war Suleyken* (1955; *So Tender Was Suleyken*), a collection of entertaining stories restoring his native Masurian lake region in East Prussia to its ancient, modest, and intensely humane glories. Lenz's later novel *Die Deutschstunde* (1968; *The German Lesson*, 1971) was a best-seller in the Federal Republic and a remarkable international success; while the didactic interests, as so often in his sober writings, are strongly visible, the story about a village policeman obsessed by doing his duty, Nazis or no Nazis, raises essential questions about recent history. The policeman, as ordered by the authorities, even tries to prevent his friendly neighbor (who resembles the expressionist painter Emil Nolde) from painting his disturbing pictures, and the obsessions of the father are reciprocated by the obsessions of the son, who rescues the pictures against his father's will. After the war the son goes on "rescuing" pictures and, arrested as an art thief, is sent to a reformatory, where he tries to cope with his own past and that of his country. Marie Luise Kaschnitz (1901–74), who came from the gentry of the Wilhelmine empire, liberated herself early from social tradition and worked in bookshops in Weimar and in Rome, where she met her future husband, an eminent Austrian archaeologist. For a long time after the war she wrote poetry and essays before turning to her short stories or rather novellas about the vicissitudes of ugly children, uncanny events overwhelming the daily order of things, or death in many disguises. I particularly like her last book, *Orte* (1973; *Places*), a collection of short lyrical prose pieces triggered by memories of the many towns and country houses in Germany, Italy, and other countries where she had lived a rich and glowing life as wife, mother, writer, and a strikingly sensitive enthusiast of the ancient and modern arts.

In the 1960s most younger writers, as well as some older novelists, no longer hid their increased suspicion of fiction at large, whether nineteenth-century realism or the prerealist picaresque. Peter Weiss (1916–82), in his earliest prose piece published in German (1960), insisted on ruthlessly microscopic description, while others began asking radical questions about the self, consciousness, fiction, and language far beyond Arno Schmidt's unquestioned assumptions. Once all forms of fiction were suspect, attention concentrated on the capability of language to refer to something outside itself (not to speak of "reality"). Authors closely observed consciousness operating, or being operated by, language itself. The writing of novels was increasingly challenged by experimental exercises testing the possibility of reference or trying to seize experience in inchoate consciousness. In *Schlachtbeschreibungen* (1964; *The Battle*, 1967), Alexander Kluge (b. 1932), one of the fathers of the New German Cinema, gathered authentic documents concerning the battle of Stalingrad, including the daily Wehrmacht communiqués of the time, in order to "demonstrate" the realities of the war without the interference of art (which was still present, however, in his selection and arrangement of documents). His work signaled the new demand for nonfictional materials, which at first were attractive for epistemological reasons and somewhat later became of essential importance to the new industrial writers, the social criticism of the student revolt, and the new feminists.

The other option for contradicting mere fiction was to concentrate on the workings of consciousness itself. Jürgen Becker (b. 1932), in *Felder* (1964; *Fields*) and *Ränder* (1968; *Margins*), confronted everyday experience as conscious perception, without being able *not* to create literature—consisting, in his case, of selected words asyntactically arranged in ingenious texts in close analogy to concrete poetry and Helmut Heissenbüttel's prose. Challenged by these exercises, the novel of the sixties tended to be as self-conscious as possible, and some of the older writers, long in search of an appropriate mode of articulating their particular interests, published remarkable novels about the possibility, or impossibility, of writing prose. Among them were Franz Tumler (b. 1912) with his *Aufschreibung aus Trient* (1965; *Trient Protocol*), and Wolfgang Hildesheimer (b. 1916) with his *Tynset* (1965), which revealed a creative self burdened by terrible memories of past dangers and persecution, in a liberating cycle of tentative stories and projections of dreams.

Among the younger people of the late sixties (for he would loathe being called a writer), Herbert Achternbusch (b. 1938) has gone furthest in his "narratives," as well as in his movies, which never fail to provoke the authorities while pitting the consciousness of his chaotic self against an ordered world of traditions, habits, and conventions. As writer and filmmaker, Achternbusch strikes me as a Bavarian peasant anarchist of deeply rooted regional loyalties; although, like any good romantic, he always wants to be somewhere else in order to find himself completely, he is loyal to Bavarian forests, towns, and inns, from which he sets out simply to astonish his contemporaries. (Upon receiving the Petrarca Award in Tuscany, he publicly burned the check for twenty thousand marks.) In *Die Alexanderschlacht* (1971; *Alexander's Battle*) he shows what is going on in his consciousness, which, to his disgust, is caught in the daily rites of provincial family life. He explores the past of his forefathers, small peasants and poachers; tells stories about a (Jewish?) girl who was involved in the student protests and died in prison; and invents images of a free life in vineyards on the slopes of Mount Vesuvius, that central symbol of eruptive revolt, or in the empty wastes of Greenland, once inhabited by sturdy Vikings. Yet in his writings he refuses to cultivate a form that could be called a novel (usually putting together a few people to lead a "formally administered life"), and makes fun of his colleagues Bernhard and Hildesheimer, the toast of publishers' cocktail parties. He wants to reveal the immediacy of his perceptions and yet, as he well knows, he cannot but fail in his fundamental intention since he cannot present consciousness itself, or rather his report about it, without using language, syntax, and print. He at least undermines the use of rule-governed language by mobilizing a repertory of devices long rehearsed in the history of the novel from Sterne to Joyce, and magnificently succeeds in creating a funny, moving, and occasionally self-pitying book full of poetic moments and memories of an ancient Bavarian peasant life now withering away. He works with the power of accumulation and, using language against language, brings together fictions and "facts," speculations and confessions, satire and longings for an unfettered life, fighting not so much against the rules of traditional novels (which he calls "totalitarian forms") but against the requirements of narration as such. In his writing, it is the exhilarating intensity that counts.

The independent intellectual Dieter Wellershoff (b.1925) wants to explore how people live in industrial societies, and how writing could contribute to changing their lives, sadly ritualized in listless routines. Like Heinrich Böll, Wellershoff comes from the Rhineland but, unlike his compatriot, he does not write about the historical burdens of the Germans or the disturbing fate of Cologne before and after the Nazi regime. Wellershoff's Cologne, where he and most of his fictional characters reside, stands for the anonymous structures of the big city; if it were not Cologne, it would be Duisburg or Hamburg, with fast-food places, *Autobahnen*, traffic jams, and the gray and barracklike apartment blocks built in the Adenauer era.

In Wellershoff's essential ideas there is a distinct continuity of psychological concerns and rational, if not scientific, commitment that sustains his critical essays, his novels, and his many features for the mass media. At Bonn University Wellershoff read Gottfried Benn, whose sonorous aversion to history made him suddenly attractive to young German readers (even while the Allies were blacklisting him). Writing his 1952 dissertation on Benn's philosophy and style, Wellershoff also began to study and admire the conservative anthropologist Arnold Gehlen and, rare among German students of that particular time, the writings of Freud, above all the essays about the id, repression, and culture. Wellershoff's contemporaries were just about to indulge in the mush of popularized existentialism, but he was set on a systematic study of Erikson, Breuer, and Horney, and early widened his literary studies to include Hemingway, Camus, and Beckett.

In some contrast to German tradition, the critic Wellershoff does not want to see our thinking burdened with metaphysical concepts, yet when he wishes to describe the function of literature he asks large questions. The sequence of his essays, collected in *Literatur und Veränderung* (1969; *Literature and Change*), *Literatur und Lustprinzip* (1973; *Literature and the Libido*), *Die Auflösung des Kunstbegriffs* (1976; *The Dissolution of the Concept of Art*), and *Das Verschwinden im Bild* (1980; *Disappearing in the Picture*), suggests something of his insistent anthropological interests but also his stubborn refusal, as a professional writer, to sacrifice his literary concerns to the psychotherapist, however erudite. People, he believes, are surrounded by an incessant chaos of stimuli and, wanting to live, cannot but tame, order, and reduce this challenging chaos by developing responding schemes, or useful habits, of perceptions, thoughts, and actions that create a world of meanings. (Wellershoff follows the anthropologist Gehlen, who in turn sounds like Nietzsche.) When people want to exert their energies, they have no other choice but to simplify changing situations into a few basic, constantly recurring patterns. "Reality" is but a habit of behaving, and these routines become an inescapable part of living because life in society is impossible without some mechanization of perception and the reduction of potentialities.

In terms close to Freud's, Wellershoff suggests that all people "in a suppressed element of their lives" are enemies of culture, which offers security but demands denials, negations, and a discipline foreign to the elementary drives. In such a situation, it is the essential function of fiction to widen the author's and the reader's spontaneity. In a world of practical actions narrowly defined by specific aims and therefore by an inclination to stabilize operational concepts, fiction, surging against the reality principle, fulfills the pressing desires for a more untrammeled life, because it does not hesitate to probe intentions, wishes, and daydreams hitherto inarticulate or pushed aside. Wellershoff has a tendency to combine psychological and technological images; though on occasion he describes the writing of fiction as "symbolic strategies to create an *Ersatz* for the lost objects of primal desire," he also speaks about fiction in terms of space engineering, as a field of simulation or a space of playful exercise in which writers and readers together "transcend the narrow experiences and routines, without running real risks." Wellershoff has written excellent essays on the compensatory functions of the thriller, which allows us to exercise our desires for security and our wish to destroy them, and also pornography, those "dreams of unchaining, dreamt by people in bondage." Pleading for narratives about criminals, psychopaths, and near catatonics, he tells us that, dialectically, these images of extreme "unfreedom" (*Unfreiheit*) imply to the reader "translucent proto-images of freedom" itself.

In his novel *Die Schattengrenze* (1969; *The Shadow Line*), Wellershoff shows us the rapid disintegration of a bleak mind from the inside, wanting to compel us to understand the haunted, splintered, diffuse experiences of a middle-aged salesman whose minor criminal offenses express rather than cause his subconscious drive to annihilate himself in a world that has never ceased to threaten him. (He always remembers how in the war, hiding once in a barn, he pressed his body ever deeper in the warm hay while Soviet tanks rolled by.) It is a story of failure and flight beyond the frontier, in a geographical as well as a psychological sense: the Rhenish salesman, a superfluous man in the tradition of the nineteenth-century Russian novel, never succeeds in his checkered career because he always falls ill when confronted with the possibility of succeeding. At a time when his friends and bosses build new supermarkets and gorge themselves at the gargantuan PR cocktail parties of the West German economic miracle, he shacks up with an actress who has failed on the stage; sells a few stolen cars with false papers; cheats on his income tax; and after a desperate attempt to grasp what he feels is real in the embraces of a tired cinema cashier and a meretricious bar girl, crosses the border into Holland. We last see him sitting in a shabby little hotel room, a hiding place, a trap, without any hopes or feelings: "He observed the chairs, sitting on the edge of the bed, with fear, yes there are chairs, on which he always sits: with his eyes to the window, with his eyes to the door." The narrator locates himself within the decaying senses of the central figure and identifies more or less with the protagonist's dislocated perspectives of the world, neither confirming nor denying what he seems to see. It is certainly a tough and brooding text, regurgitating disturbing images of spectral cities in bluish floodlights, of women and men holding each other in the combative embraces of withering flesh.

In his novel *Die Schönheit des Schimpansen* (1977; *The Beauty of the Chimpanzee*), Wellershoff works in a lucid narrative mode that corresponds to the analytical aim of enlightening rather than mystifying. The strange title refers to a number of allusions and leitmotivs, including a passage in Gustav Mahler's *Song of the Earth*, and the ancient emblem of the ape looking into the mirror (with suggestions of human mortality), but the story does not remove us to transcendental realms. Once again, against the gritty horizon of plebeian life between Cologne and North Germany, we are confronted with the terrifying experiences of a salesman close to middle age who cannot find his proper place among his fellow citizens because, wherever he turns, he feels overwhelmed, threatened, and exploited. Claus Junghans fails as a student (he plagiarized his examination paper), does a stint as a periodicals salesman among a group of people nearly outlawed by the community, and finds a young woman who takes him for a long vacation to Tenerife, paid for from her savings, only to discover that she is using him as a convenient companion while eyeing the men of the smarter set on the beaches and in the hotel bars. Yet when the two return to Cologne they marry, though she lives her own life in their dilapidating apartment, while he works installing and checking game machines in lunchrooms. Knowing that in his absence his wife sleeps with other men, he spends a weekend with a woman whom he has picked up in a lonely-hearts café, then brutally kills her when suddenly she seems no different from his wife and all the other people "who are dragging him along and dismembering him." The narrator does not identify with his central figure, as he did in

The Shadow Line, but firmly watches him from a critical distance. We are spared nothing of pain and nausea, but it is precisely the narrator's close if not clinical attention to the fragile and brutal mind of the killer that enables us to learn something from his fate. Wellershoff has long argued against the mechanization of human experiences in narrowing habits, and I wonder whether he has not established, at least in the early 1970s, his own set ways of unsettling our sensibilities.

Though Wellershoff has long clung to the naturalist assumption that the sober writer of scientific inclination should not interfere with his characters or speak from outside, in his novel *The Beauty of the Chimpanzee* and his novella *Die Sirene* (1980) he no longer attempts to hide from us his fine reflective intelligence, does not bore us with inarticulate characters and, discarding his earlier experiments in the mode of the *nouveau roman*, moves closer to storytelling, which is not wholly unwelcome in narratives of psychological developments. His narratives, which show the dangers of total submission to the social code, and the perils of an irreducible incapacity to cope with the denials demanded by civilization, yield harsh and disturbing insights. His satellite cities, stuffy apartments, and streetcar rides through industrial suburbs have a hallucinatory presence, and his disturbed people, or psychopaths on their way to madness, are human beings of full corporeality with recurrent headaches, nosebleeds, and sudden sweat in their armpits, infecting the cracking world in which they live lonely lives, kill, and die. The radicals of the late sixties disliked Wellershoff for many reasons, but many young people today have rediscovered the social and political significance of analysis and psychotherapy of the most varied orientations. It is not impossible that Wellershoff in his intellectual isolation has anticipated a major current of contemporary German intellectual life, now more visible than ever.

By the early and mid-1970s the documentary and experimental impulses, directly or obliquely related to the ideological quests of the student movement, had spent their force, and prose writers again returned to narrative fictions, or to traditional forms that made it possible to examine intimate experiences with renewed attention. Yet the prose of the New Subjectivity did not emerge suddenly or in absolute opposition to the collective temper of the late 1960s. Frisch, Bernhard, and Handke had long anticipated the new interests, and if, during the stormiest days of the student revolt, the muses marched in the streets shouting and singing, the claims of silence and privacy were sustained by many movies of the New Cinema (especially those directed by Werner Herzog), by Austrian poets, and by GDR writers who in the early 1960s had begun to define the desire for intimacy in poems and prose. Younger and older authors looked intently into their own past and the history of their countries again. The younger, for instance Bernward Vesper (1938–71), Peter Rühmkorf (b. 1929), and the Austrian Peter Henisch (b. 1943), described their involvement in the student movement, or rather their frustrations after the movement had withered away, while renowned writers of the older generation, among them Wolfgang Koeppen, Jakov Lind (b. 1927), Stephan Hermlin (b. 1915), Manès Sperber (b. 1905), and Elias Canetti (1905), published thoughtful accounts of their lives and of the social and intellectual experiences that had shaped them, in the context of European history at large. Walter Kempowski (b. 1929) and Horst Bienek (b. 1930), who had once been political prisoners in the GDR or in Siberian camps, wrote massive "historical" trilogies about the lives of their families in Rostock and Upper Silesia respectively, closely watching speech habits and the daily rites of surviving in the age of war and Nazi power. The seventies were also the time of rediscovering and rescuing the fathers, in one's own family and in literary history in general. Imaginative biographies of great poets, revolutionary or not, almost developed into a genre of their own, and sons and daughters, among them Peter Härtling (b. 1933) and Jutta Schutting (b. 1937), sketched composite portraits of their fathers, trying to do justice to their uneasy lives in a difficult time.

Die erdabgewandte Seite der Geschichte (1976; *The Far Side of History*) by Nicholas Born (b. 1937) was widely acclaimed as a novel almost emblematic of changing sensibilities and the turn from collective engagements to private desires. Born himself was not exactly, by age and training, a member of the revolting student generation, but he had long sympathized with many of their ideas and shared their way of living, talking, writing, and demonstrating in West Berlin. In his novel, rich in images of particular Berlin streets and *S-Bahn* stations, he discloses his feelings for a few people whom he loves, rather than his experiences with groups or political factions. Ultimately, he reverts to his solitude because all those close to him insist on their own way of living (or dying): a young woman who works for a recording firm prefers absolute autonomy, professionally and otherwise; his young daughter from a shattered earlier marriage is growing up rapidly; and one day his only friend, an intellectual and activist, is found dead in his apartment. The writer takes part, without real involvement, in the Berlin demonstrations against the Shah of Iran, noting that "everything was serious but not really," and marches in radical May Day parades, horrified by his own indifference and aware that he has very few answers to problems and disdains those who believe they have. His trouble is not with women or politics but with the principle of reality itself, or rather the impossibility of getting closer to the real in the act of writing: he is paralyzed "by a balance of escape and attachment" and unable to see more in the world than a void, "colors and shapes" being mere "reflexes of libraries" or "archives in motion." There is a glowing moment of intimacy when father and daughter spend a few vacation days in the Bavarian forests, but the child has to return to her mother, and the lonely father to Berlin, where he at least can find comfort in going to the movies, feeling "protected" by "enveloping warmth" as people in the audience slowly take off their coats.

Among the many autobiographies of the 1970s, Elias Canetti's *Die gerettete Zunge* (1977; *The Tongue Set Free: Remembrance of a European Childhood*, 1979), *Die Fackel im Ohr* (1980; *The Torch in My Ear*, 1982), and *Das Augenspiel* (1985; *The Play of the Eyes*, 1985) have a special place, illuminating as they do the life and unusual achievement of an eminent writer and psychologist who was rediscovered by German readers only decades after the war. Written in unhurried and pellucid language and with an almost visionary power of resuscitating places, people, and encounters in the past, Canetti's memoirs have the supreme virtue of cosmopolitan range in the full meaning of the term, and of intellectual loyalty to those writers and thinkers who (among them the Viennese satirist Karl Kraus and his contemporary Sigmund Freud) provoked him into admiring submission or independent response. Canetti, who received the Nobel prize in 1981, quietly tells the story of his childhood in Rustchuk, a Bulgarian port at the mouth of the Danube that was "wonderful . . . for children," and in stern Manchester, where his father suddenly died. He tells of his school years in Zürich, the real paradise of his youth, and in chapters particularly rich in sharply etched portraits, describes Brecht, Isaac Babel, and other contemporaries and his studies in Vienna, Frankfurt, and Berlin, where, in opposition to Freud, he developed his ideas about mass psychology, and conceived his (later famous) novel *Die Blendung* (1935; *Auto-da-Fé*, 1964), compared by many critics to Kafka's or George Grosz's work. Born into a clan of Sephardic Jews whose first language was an older Spanish loyally preserved, Canetti recalls how he learned German, the language in which he came to write, "late and tortuously." His mother and father had both studied in Vienna and had kept German as their idiom of trust and marriage, excluding young Elias (who repeated what he overheard in "precise intonation like magic formulas") from intimate conversations; only after the father died did his mother instruct him in the German language of love and introduce him to German readings. Without his mother and the German language (which, to him, were fundamentally one), Canetti writes, all his later life would have been "meaningless and incomprehensible."

In spite of years of attrition after the student revolt, the novel emerged again in the early 1980s as the dominant genre in the minds of readers, publishers of literature, and reviewers. In the virtual absence of great poetry, and at a time when innovative producers still outnumber provocative playwrights, fiction, though never far from daily experience, represents literature at large, and three or four generations, Ernst Jünger (b. 1895) being among the oldest, continue writing with and against each other. Among the older writers, Hermann Lenz (b. 1913, Stuttgart) had been writing steadily for more than thirty years before being discovered by a younger generation; his quiet prose, often wavering between fiction and autobiographical narratives, is now appreciated by a widening group of readers, including Peter Handke. In his trilogy *Der innere Bezirk* (1980; *The Inner Sphere*) Lenz tells the story of Margot, the daughter of a diplomat and military attaché, from the early 1930s to the first postwar years. Not surprisingly, the Margot trilogy was long ignored by the new West German literary establishment, which is suspicious of anybody wearing a tie. (Lenz's insistence on dealing calmly with the political dilemma of conservative officers and diplomats on the fringes of Nazi power did not endear him to critics more used to Böll's or Grass's petits bourgeois than to white-gloved lieutenants who, when in Berlin, always stayed at the old Hotel Adlon.) Young Margot von Sy enjoys early independence: her mother has committed suicide, her father Franz (whom she deeply admires) has been posted to Belgrade, and she is being educated, if this is the word, in a Heidelberg finishing school where she has many friends, including a Jewish girl from France. In Munich, where she feels happy in a little inn owned by simple people strongly opposed to the Hitler regime, she has an affair with an elegant young man whom she suspects of pretending to be a Nazi in order to spy on the powerful Nazi organizations. After having a miscarriage, she returns to Stuttgart, her hometown, and in her loneliness tries to kill herself, as her mother had done. She is saved, and her father applies for a leave of absence to stay with her. It turns out, however, that both daughter and father have been under Gestapo surveillance for some time: the elegant young man has escaped abroad, while Franz von Sy and his friends have been involved, somewhat half-heartedly, in a military conspiracy against Hitler. Yet Franz von Sy's case is handled by a weary Gestapo functionary who begins to think about his own future after the war; after trying in vain to become Margot's lover, he has her father released, hoping that his favor will be returned after the war, if necessary. Franz von Sy is ordered to Nancy as city commandant and against his will has to round up French citizens; when France is liberated, he is imprisoned by the French authorities for some time as a potential war criminal. When we see them last, father and daughter are on a little excursion to the mountains and forests on the Bavarian-Bohemian border, happily resuscitating their old loyalties to each other.

The Margot von Sy trilogy, seemingly so melodramatic and compact in its political events, suggests little of the actual texture of Lenz's narratives. Lenz speaks of historical and social issues against his fundamental intentions. As a German writer of his generation he is forced, like it or not, to see his characters and himself within a close context of political pressures. Left to his own narrative instincts, however, he would be more than happy simply to register what sensitive people perceive in particular moments of their experience, and to offer us nuances of colors and sounds isolated from each other, rather than a narration of coherent actions. Lenz's prudent men and women are almost afraid of abstract thoughts or big words, preferring to translate abstract issues into personal experiences that can be grasped in more humane, relative, and perhaps even earthy terms. The narrator is not averse to using local dialect, Swabian or Viennese, to counteract or explode "big" statements made by somebody totally out of tune with a universe of sensual perception.

Lenz is a snob, I suspect, but of a particular kind, secretly proud of being inconspicuous, withdrawn, and provincial; yet his novels, social and political in spite of themselves, distinctly suggest that there is legitimate engagement not only to the left of center. Lenz combines a deep respect for unheroic people who have to survive in unpropitious times, with a striking disinclination to search for the abstract or absolute. In his world there is nothing more unfortunate than to arrive at inflexible conclusions; the really happy people view, from a distance, "how love and hate fuse . . . and the water turns lighter and darker." Lenz's protagonists, students or generals, refugees or artists, are difficult characters who thrive only in a universe of skepticism, sympathy, and self-reflection; the noblest among them are the stoics who believe that people should be left in peace and "in harmony with themselves."

In some contrast to media interests elsewhere, writers in German, East or West, young or old, cannot really complain that the electronic or print media ignore what they are doing. But it is also true that close media attention and market pressures compel writers to seize what they believe to be timely issues and to produce novels in waves, on children and fathers one year, on ecology the next, and on the obligatory frustrations of the lonely heart for the coming Frankfurt Book Fair. In spite of all TV discussions about intellectual nonconformity, the authentic nonconformists have become rare; there are four or five authors whom I read with particular enthusiasm because they have been more successful than many of their contemporaries in resisting pressures and doing what they alone can do. Among these are Hubert Fichte (1935–86), who, classifying himself as a half-Jew born out of wedlock and a homosexual, first wrote experimental narratives about his early experiences and later turned to imaginative and documentary studies on voodoo religions in Haiti, Trinidad, and Brazil, and Elisabeth Plessen (b. 1944), the first among those capable of looking at the generation of the fathers clearly and soberly. There is also Hans Jürgen Fröhlich (b. 1932), a biographer of Schubert and one of the few authors of German novels of marital manners untainted by self-pity; Eckardt Henscheid, who has elevated the Rabelaisian stream of gossip to the rank of artful provocation; and last but not least, Erich Loest (b. 1926), once much favored by the GDR authorities and now thoughtfully recalling what happened to him and his contemporaries on that side of the wall, without rage or exaggeration. We may be closer to a marvelous summer of German fiction than we think.

UWE JOHNSON: THE NOVELIST AS HISTORIAN

Among postwar German writers, none was more honest, serious, and exacting than Uwe Johnson in his commitment to discover and tell the truth about how people lived through recent history or died in its snares. Johnson (1934–84) was involved early in German vicissitudes. As the son of a Pomeranian civil servant, he was trained for some years in a Nazi school in occupied Poland; returned in a trek of refugees to Mecklenburg, which became part of the GDR; studied English and German at the University of Leipzig, where Hans Mayer and Ernst Bloch taught in the early 1950s; and after completing his studies found himself, in the socialist republic that guaranteed a job to everybody, unemployed because his personal file was not conducive to employment in state-controlled institutions. When his first novel, *Ingrid Babendererde* (published posthumously in West Germany in 1985), was rejected by GDR publishing houses, he decided to go west but, averse to melodramatic expressions of any kind, insisted that he did not "escape," but merely moved to West Berlin by leaving the train at the appropriate railway station.

In the late 1950s and early 1960s Johnson published three novels and established himself as one of the major writers of his generation by combining a strong interest in new methods of storytelling with a quiet belief that a more human way of living continued to survive, unperceived by most Western observers, behind the disfiguring slogans and economic regimentation engineered by GDR functionaries. In his difficult novel *Mutmassungen über Jakob* (1959; *Speculations about Jacob*, 1963), he investigated the death of a taciturn East German railway dispatcher who had briefly joined his girlfriend in the West, only to die on the tracks when returning home (accident, suicide, or a liquidation arranged by the state security service?). In *Das dritte Buch über Achim* (1961; *The Third Book about Achim*, 1967), he made another attempt to overcome the almost ontological difficulties of knowing life "over there." In contrast to these remarkable novels, *Zwei Ansichten* (1965; *Two Views*, 1966) strikes me as of a lesser kind: this story of two lovers in the year of the Berlin Wall, a soulful nurse from the East and a rather vacuous young photographer from the West, clearly discloses its schematic construction, and the lovers are so listless that they cannot engage our interest for long.

In the early 1960s Johnson participated fully, with Günter Grass and his lively crew, in Berlin literary life, more exhilarating at that time than twenty years later. He also spent a year in Rome and, clad in his notorious black leather jacket, embroiled himself eagerly in public discussions of his ideas, not to be misinterpreted by anyone. As a new generation of radical students converged on Berlin, Johnson traveled a good deal, then in the mid-1960s settled for two years in New York, first in a nine-to-five publisher's job to compile a textbook anthology of German literature for high school use, with an advance from his American publisher. Later he received a Rockefeller Foundation grant that enabled him to work on his novel *Jahrestage* (1970–84; *Anniversaries*, first part 1975, remainder due 1987), which, originally planned as one volume but expanding into a massive tetralogy, brought together the German past and the American age of racial disturbances and Vietnam. The first three volumes appeared in rapid succession (1970, 1971, 1973), but after he had moved with his family to the little English port of Sheerness in 1974, possibly to re-create for himself the lost Mecklenburg of cold winds, marshes, and the sea, he felt suddenly paralyzed by the discovery, or his belief, that his wife of many years had betrayed him with a member of the Czech secret service. There is not much sense in trying to elucidate these events, long discussed in the German media, as it might well be impossible to separate the obsessions of a near recluse (from whose fictions the secret services of the superpowers are rarely absent) from what really happened in a marriage that his few friends thought to be close and exemplary. Johnson himself, shattered and confused, did not hesitate to speak about his wounded feelings in his Frankfurt University lectures and to write a short and disturbing narrative, transposing his experiences into a 1940s tale about an exiled antifascist writer who kills his wife because she has deceived him "from the beginning" with an agent of the Reich. In the late 1970s Johnson slowly began writing again, a few lines a day; the last volume of *Anniversaries* (1984) appeared just a month before his untimely death. Because he lived alone, he was found only three weeks after he had died from a heart attack in a cold and inhospitable house. A piece of paper discovered in his wallet stipulated, in four languages, that he wanted to be cremated without hymns, preachers, or music.

The Third Book about Achim, a cryptic but extremely rewarding novel, represents Johnson's early writing at its best. Speculations about the life and death of a railway dispatcher are followed by conjectures about Achim, a famous cycling champion and member of the People's Parliament of the German Democratic Republic, but instead of collecting the reports of many friends and witnesses, Johnson uses a relatively central sensibility to pursue the search. He tells the story of Karsch, a West German journalist who travels from Hamburg to the East to meet the actress Karin, once his mistress. Through Karin, Karsch meets Achim, who fascinates him because he seems to reap the benefits of both spontaneous popular enthusiasm from below and political approval from above. Two books have already been written about Achim, but Karsch signs a contract with the state publishing house to write a third and more relevant book to show Achim in his total involvement with society, then immediately encounters growing quandaries about knowledge, politics, and art. One day Karsch receives an anonymous letter with a snapshot showing Achim marching with the rebellious workers on June 17, 1953. Karsch realizes that he has failed in his search for Achim's true image, for not even Karin was aware of Achim's involvement with the protesters. Achim himself shies away from admitting the evidence of the photograph. The end is a new beginning: Karsch returns to Hamburg, tells a close friend (who poses searching questions) about his failure, and thus turns his provincial search for a true life story into an all-embracing metaphor for the impossibilities of literary narration as such.

Johnson's *The Third Book about Achim* turns against rash ideological conclusions formulated in either East or West, but the author seems less tense than in his first novel. As narrator he closely and slowly follows the journalist Karsch, who wants to write a book about a representative hero of the GDR; although the narrator does not claim omniscience, he keeps both Karsch and Achim at a half-ironical, half-compassionate distance and sometimes comments on Karsch's desperate fight to see his man as he really is. (André Gide arranged a similar exercise in his novel *The Counterfeiters*.) Karsch first tries to write a traditional realistic biography by selecting the main railroad station as a place emblematic of historical changes; ironically, he discovers only much later that Achim's mother and sister were killed there in an Allied bombing raid. But his difficulties increase when delegates of the state publishing house try to impose upon his search the official prescription for Socialist Realism and then oppose his work completely, while the champion himself has long accepted his public image as a genuine self-portrait.

Johnson's early attention to "things" relates to his peasant-and-worker myth of a simple and warm community, but his things are far from being analogous to the objects of the *nouveau roman*. Alain Robbe-Grillet either isolates his things (like the tomato in *The Erasers*) in the stark nakedness of absolute being or, in other instances, involves them in frenzied subjective vision; they are either absolutely "cold" or unbearably "hot." Johnson's old pieces of furniture are close to Rilke's *Dinge*, hallowed by long human use; even his telegraphs, telephones, bicycles, and typewriter have the virtue of being involved in daily human work that endows them with a permanent dignity. Johnson includes the manufactured and the technical in the blessed realm of Rilkean *Dinge* only if they are part of a working process; he reserves his bitter antipathies for things that are either emblems of prestige (like a sports car) or objects of mere commercial, i.e. meretricious, exchange. Jean Baudrillard rightly indicates that, at least in his early writings, Johnson, in his attention to things and "serving" things, comes close to a *marxisme artisanal* or rather, as I would put it, to a belief in a closed society in which workingmen and their things dwell happily (if unthinkingly) together. Robbe-Grillet may have experimented with viewpoint and structure, but Johnson, at least in his beginnings, pressed his search for the "existing" much further than his French ally did, and did not spare his reader astonishing peculiarities of narrative structure, syntax, and vocabulary. Johnson's early writings not only deal with East and West but actually thrive on their own East-West tensions; some elements of Socialist Realism, including characters unfolding in their professional milieu, stubbornly survive and yet are constantly modified by experiment.

In the late 1960s and 1970s Johnson was more a mythical figure than a living writer to many of his readers. He lived most of the time in New York and England in self-chosen isolation, in order to concentrate on his proliferating *Anniversaries*. In his early writings Johnson did not hide his skepticism about Balzac's choice of the omniscient narrator; in most of his novels the author as narrator certainly does not claim many more privileges than the knowing characters (perhaps fewer). In his later writings, however, Johnson does accept Balzac's technique of recurring characters. Going back to his early narratives, he resuscitates many of his principal figures, building from epic strength and changing his early work into a prologue to the later. In *Anniversaries* he energetically counteracts the attractive dangers of provincialism by moving his Gesine Cresspahl (from *Speculations about Jacob*, where Jacob, the dispatcher, was her first love) and her ten-year-old daughter Marie (Jacob's child) to New York, where she settles near many earlier emigrants on Riverside Drive. There she tries to educate her daughter (when not being educated by her) and works in a midtown bank, where the management increasingly appreciates her knowledge of central European affairs.

From the massive accumulation of materials, an epic structure emerges that juxtaposes reports about Gesine's experiences in New York from August 1967 almost day by day to August 1968, with an interpolated Mecklenburg novel about the marriage of her parents and her own life in the northeast German provinces, commencing around 1922 and ranging far into the 1950s and even later. The textures differ: in the American composition

Johnson often works with a Dos Passos–like montage of dialogues, letters, and extensive quotations from the *New York Times*, which speaks like "an aunt from a distinguished family" about Vietnam and racial unrest, while in the Mecklenburg narrative he relies on a quiet, circumstantial, often ironic tone reminiscent of Theodor Fontane and other nineteenth-century classics of the German novel. The Mecklenburg core has so much strength and energy that he would not really need a more timely frame of press clippings, were it not for his firm intention to show political events and documents of 1967–68 so as to direct our attention, through analogies and contrasts, to the persistent question whether people can survive without guilt in culpable societies. I confess that I find myself far more involved with Gesine's mother Lisbeth than with her frigid daughter who, especially in the last volume, turns into a narrative apparatus that absorbs and regurgitates the contents of the *New York Times*. In Nazi Germany her mother's life exhausted itself in a helpless attempt to expiate guilt—the guilt of having compelled her husband to return from England to Mecklenburg when the Nazis came to power, the guilt of her family (both her brothers are active Nazis), and the guilt of her fellow citizens. Feeling a mystical desire to sacrifice her life in atonement for the sins of others, she strikes the town mayor in the face in public, then dies a horrible death by setting fire to her husband's workshop and suffocating in the flames—"the murder of herself to atone for murder," as the minister says at her funeral before the Gestapo takes him away. Gesine too wants a life of purity but, some twenty-five years later, evil has become more diffuse. She does not want to simplify, desires peace (though she does not participate in pro-Vietcong demonstrations), helps her friend Anita bring over GDR citizens on false papers, and learns Czech to find out what is going on over there in the nascent Prague socialism with a human face. She knows that decisions have to be made within an uncertain compass: "Should we give up shopping because shopping produces taxes, and we don't know anything about the ultimate use of these taxes?"

Uwe Johnson's books would be among the first classics of Socialist Realism, if such realism existed without capital letters, created by gifted writers spontaneously and without coercion. Like his Gesine, Johnson began to think and write in the GDR, and the traumatic experience of the disturbing gap between public speeches and private awareness, between façade and meaning, marked him deeply (as was the case later with Christa Wolf and others). So it happened, Johnson said in his 1980 Frankfurt lectures, that he "found himself involved in a personal conflict with the Republic, his dispute with the world about the question of when something was to be the truth"; and since, he added, he was not permitted "to settle his dispute publicly, he wanted to do so in writing." Johnson is a master of microscopic mediation, showing without subterfuge and with careful precision how individuals reflect and act in their particular place in time and society. Inquisitive and patient readers who want to know what really happened at the time of the Nazis and later, when the Socialist Unity Party took over, will find many more illuminating insights in Johnson's *Anniversaries* than in abstract sociological and historical monographs. Johnson knows exactly what happens when the regiments of one occupying power (Western) leave a small German town and the others (Eastern) enter; how high school demonstrations are organized by GDR authorities, relying on the skill of a school choir conductor who, a few years earlier, organized the sing-alongs of the Hitler Youth; or what happens when a student (Gesine) is being cross-examined by the state security police (Christa Wolf, who tells us a good deal about the GDR university elite, never mentions such mundane events). Perhaps it is also true that the historian Johnson feels increasingly inclined, in the last volume perhaps more visibly than in earlier ones, to dissolve the compact Mecklenburg tale into a collection of individual biographies of Gesine's friends and small-town contemporaries. Each individual life now emerges as its own little novel, as for instance Gesine's English teacher, who remains a loyal friend for decades; a man named Johnny who spontaneously establishes an agricultural commune in which everybody works, eats, and makes merry, until the Party of Socialist Unity has him sentenced to prison for fifteen years; and D.E. who, born a barber's son in the Soviet zone of occupation, later becomes a physicist and apparently works in New Jersey for a Dew Line subcontractor. D.E. always wanted to marry Gesine, who is on the verge of accepting him when she learns that he has died under strange circumstances on one of his mysterious trips.

In all his writings, early or late, Johnson turns against a reduced image of history and experience, as it is forced upon us by the competing mass media and highly organized ideologies, and tries, as fairly and stubbornly as he can, to discover what is out there in the world. He has his own personal myth of human affairs corresponding, in many ways, to the ritualized, neighborly, and perhaps almost preindustrial life that he knew during his youth in the small towns of Pomerania and Mecklenburg; wherever he went later, he always looked for such an "eastern" landscape (in an older meaning) and for such a way of life, totally opposed to capitalist consumerism. Johnson did not like to speak about his literary forebears and usually stressed that he had used some of their strategies in his own way. He mentioned William Faulkner, important for his early work, but was reluctant to discuss the legacy of the conservative German regional tradition reaching from Hermann Löns (1866–1914) to Ernst Wiechert (1877–1950), whose peaceful visions of serene provincial life he secretly shared. He certainly liked old-fashioned German(ic) names, and some of his early reviewers reacted negatively to his sentimental landscape descriptions, the usual staple of blood-and-soil kitsch. (In *Anniversaries* he mocks himself for these "green" propensities.) In his universe of deep souls and wise silences, the cards are stacked against quick thinkers, intellectuals, and physicists who work with papers and numbers. His explicit sympathies are with children, the taciturn cabinetmaker Cresspahl, the nearly silent but efficient dispatcher Jacob, the sports champion who is almost mystically one with his perfectly functioning bicycle, and Gesine, who is fond of inquiry and loyal to her job (however dubious it may seem at times). Work, dedication, and reticent loyalty count, not the self-centered prattle of the intellectuals (for instance, his colleague Hans Magnus Enzensberger). In the German Romantic tradition, Johnson prefers, to an abstract, mobile, and fabricated society, an earthly *Gemeinschaft*. It is a question of where and how people can establish a "moral Switzerland" (as the critic Manfred Durzak has suggested) in our historical world and solve the insoluble difficulties of living in innocence again. Even those of the most tender consciousness, like Gesine, cannot do more than "learn" about the world and "live with the knowledge" offered by the writings of incorruptible observers. It is Uwe Johnson's distinction that he was foremost among them, elevating the art of the novel once again to the dignity and abundance of a great history of our age.

GABRIELE WOHMANN: IRONY AND COMPASSION

Gabriele Wohmann's corrosive, ironic, and occasionally compassionate stories and novels about the frustrations of living in a competitive society were initially read as radical criticism. But as time goes on, younger Marxists and feminists insist that she is really a more or less conservative writer who voices her disgust with contemporary life because it has ceased to reflect the lost paradise of her experience of having once been, blissfully, a child among children. Wohmann was born in 1932 in Darmstadt (Hesse), one year before Hitler came to power, and started to write in the 1950s, when Adenauer dominated the West German scene. Her father was a prominent Protestant minister and director of a nursing home for the chronically ill (founded, in turn, by his father), a charitable institution definitely not favored by the Nazis in the city administration. She clearly remembers how her older brother was chased from the *Gymnasium* because of his father's religious loyalty, and how she and her sister were expelled from the Nazi youth organization for similar reasons. After 1945 her father, who chose to retire early to his literary and theological studies, was asked by the new authorities to help screen his colleagues in other parishes being denazified. Memoirs of her early life sound like excerpts from novellas by Thomas Mann: the impeccable tastes of the patriciate, her father's large library (including his beloved three editions of James Joyce), old furniture and antiques, and an intense awareness of family rituals and intimate traditions. For a few terms Wohmann studied German literature, French, music, and philosophy at the University of Frankfurt, then taught German to foreigners and married a teacher who became her first reader and loyal critic. In the 1960s she attended the meetings of Group 47, though she did not share many of the group's initial ideas. She spent a year (1967–68) on a writing fellowship at the Villa Massimo, a kind of German academy in Rome, away from the restive students and the political upheaval. Unlike many of her contemporaries, she insists on concealing her private life from her readers, but since she writes mostly about herself, she has a difficult time hiding and yet revealing what has happened to her—like, for instance, finding herself, in the late 1960s, in a German clinic (different books offer different explanations), and in the early 1970s experiencing the loss of her father, whom she deeply loved. In her writing she may appear as a tomboy of rapidly changing moods and emotions, but as a writer she is admittedly driven by an incessant thirst for experience and a distinct graphomania that knows almost no bounds. She goes on writing as other people breathe or read.

Wohmann's earlier stories, written from the late 1950s to the early 1970s, suggest many of her central interests: everyday relations among family members are closely if not mercilessly analyzed; a cold eye is cast on the sweet habits of togetherness, bisexual or lesbian; while passion is reserved for the plight of loveless children mistreated by wrong pedagogical attitudes or ignored, battered, or even killed. Wanting to be truthful to experience, she writes from a woman's point of view, without, however, being sentimental about either women or men. As she more and more relinquishes the role of the distant narrator without gender or intimate involvement, she offers, at least in her most effective stories, inside reports on the consciousness of many women who all seem to resemble Wohmann herself. Reinhard Baumgart, a critic who usually wishes her well, speaks of her method of "*wohmannisieren*," absorbing and reproducing the world in fragments of interior monologue. In "Ein unwiderstehlicher Mann" (1966; "An Irresistible Man"), a middle-aged French professor tells the story of her infatuation with a friend in California who himself does not know whether to stay with his middle-aged wife, recently pregnant, or to run away with a "flower child" expecting his baby. When he asks the professor's advice, she tells him half-jokingly to kill himself, which he promptly does, so that later she consoles herself with the idea that she did have her paradoxical share in his life by "being responsible for his death."

As a teacher, Wohmann took an early stand against German traditions of education by stern authority, whether masked or not by progressive terminology. In her short novel *Die Bütows* (1967) she ridicules the law-and-order obsessions of German parents of the older generation, while her novel *Paulinchen war allein zu Haus* (1974; *Little Paula Stayed at Home Alone*) excoriates those progressive mothers who, following the *Zeitgeist* of the late 1960s, unthinkingly and dogmatically ram their emancipatory ideas down the throats of their helpless kids. (These short novels or long stories are in themselves far too didactic to convince anybody but the converted.) Her gruesome short stories about children silently rebelling, or neglected or murdered, are far more tense and revealing. In "Konrad und was übrig bleibt" (1968; "Conrad and What Was Left") the family of an honest butcher mourns neglected and retarded Conrad, who was murdered by a perverted killer, but also rejoices that at least his imitation leather jacket was left intact, "while everything else was destroyed, even his shoes, poor Conrad." The story "Ländliches Fest" (1968; "A Rustic Party"), central to the collection of the same title, strikes me as the most complex of these sober *Kindertotenlieder* in prose. At a fashionable garden party, possibly in Rome, writers and artists try their best conversational ploys to entertain the hostess, who, obsessed by the newspaper snapshot of a dead child lying near some forlorn railway tracks, tries to reconstruct the short life and wretched death of that little girl, possibly killed by having been thrown from the window of a passing train. The usual tidbits are served, and the hostess dances with one of her admirers, yet in her mind the corpse has long turned into an emblem of the world in which she moves so eagerly. It is easy to see why Wohmann early acquired a reputation for setting out to destroy the complacency of the new German middle classes, bent on forgetting as rapidly as possible the vicissitudes of the recent past.

In her novel *Ernste Absicht* (1970; *Serious Intent*) Wohmann energetically establishes a narrative procedure that works exceedingly well because it allows her to speak exclusively of herself, however complex the camouflage, and to rely on an inner monologue organized by associations, memories, and obsessions rather than on the exigencies of the usual plot. A young woman writer has to undergo a serious operation in a German clinic, and we are confronted with her "consciousness report" telling us day by day, if not hour by hour, what she feels in and about the present and her past (her future is left nearly blank). The text abruptly shifts backward and forward from perception to memory and waking dreams, and there are at least six strains of her experience that slowly begin to form a discernible pattern: the present medical experience, including the many nurses, the surgeon, the preparation for the operation, and its aftermath (her terrible thirst); memories of her family life in a crowded apartment and her recent divorce from her scholarly husband, who has chosen early retirement (he is an image of her father); the involvement with her friend and lover Rubin and his own complicated ménage; memories of traveling in West Germany to read from her books to provincial audiences; working at the Writers' Institute in Rome; and last but not least, excursions to California and New York. We encounter a crowded scene, a feverish sensibility on the edge of despair and dying—and yet, contrary to the reader's early expectations, little progress and few cathartic effects. There is nothing to suggest that she will return with a firm resolve to join her husband again or to stay with the other man. All possible experience is suspended in a void.

Serious Intent constitutes Wohmann's first attempt to reassert her solitude by an exterior circumstance suspending what she calls, with Peter Handke, the terror of the daily, and to offer, while trying to hide, a view of her bare self in a recurrent act of self-examination as woman, artist, and our contemporary. Her first attempt differs from later prose pieces of a similar kind by the searing, bitter, and cutting tone used in speaking about herself and the people around her. In the clinic the woman is very much concerned with maintaining her integrity as an individual, and records anxiously and with masochistic precision how she is adjusting or succumbing to the institutional, or occasionally genuine, friendliness of the nurses. In her terrible moments of anxiety, she relives her suffocating experiences in the "emergency apartment," a small flat given to her family after the early retirement of her husband, and her constitutional inability to stay away from him and his in-laws, including a middle-aged and retarded sister-in-law who falls out of bed and urinates on the floor at night. Her trouble is that her scattered moments with Rubin, on trips in Germany or abroad, yield little consolation. Rubin is "a melancholy and infantile" artist, manipulated by his maliciously tolerant wife, who is not interested in his emotions but hates high telephone bills (he calls his love too often) and, for the rest, blackmails him with her gallbladder spasms; the lovers, if such they are, cling to each other nevertheless because they know that they have put together "their best instincts." It is characteristic for Wohmann, who was never afraid of repeating herself, that she used the raw materials of the novel, occasionally right down to identical dialogues, in her remarkable TV movie *Die Entziehung* (1974; *The Cure*), in which a youngish woman stays in a clinic to dry out from drugs and alcohol; and since she played the woman herself, she had a magnificent chance to indulge in her games of hiding yet revealing herself in front of four million viewers. In public comments on her TV movie she repeatedly stressed that she is not at all identical with Laura, the reticent woman who undergoes the cure, but few viewers were convinced.

Wohmann's novels of the early 1970s are remarkable for a change of narrative tone that reveals something of her shifting attitudes, or rather her rising desire to see herself and other people in a mellower light. She is now accepting the ambivalence of experience, and her irony takes on a distinct tinge of compassion. In *Schönes Gehege* (1975; *Beautiful Preserve*) Wohmann, after having had so many men pushed around or killed in her early narratives, makes her job both easier and more difficult by assuming a male self as central and exclusive sensibility. Robert Plath, fortyish, a famous writer with a distinctly (Wohmannesque) cynical attitude toward love and life, has been asked to coproduce with a television crew a movie about his past and present, which is burdened, so the script assumes, by crisis and crying despair. While we begin listening to his thoughts and conversations, the crew and the producer travel in eager search of a pictorially satisfying backdrop for scenes from a life that is to be somber, romantically adrift, and totally unfulfilled. But Plath (whose name suggests Wohmann's deep sympathies for Sylvia Plath) increasingly feels that the projected film falsifies his life; it may correspond to moments of his past from which he wishes to escape, but certainly not to his present or to his hopes for the future. He feels guilty for "collaborating" with the crew and tries to convince the director and himself that he is actually a different human being. He confesses that he has "victimized" the people closest to him and, to the disenchantment of the TV crew, promises "to work continually toward something that is good, right, and beautiful." Paradoxically—as it may seem, at least, to more experienced Wohmann readers—he records happy moments of reading Goethe and listening to Schubert, and he even looks forward, while continually confusing James Stewart and Stewart Granger, to watching one of those old-fashioned East German movies in which young nurses predictably fall in love with the new physician.

Robert Plath's arguments against false TV image-making sound like a chapter from one of Max Frisch's novels of the late fifties, but while Frisch and Wohmann certainly share an outspoken commitment to exploring their own private lives, Wohmann (as Plath) has a sharper bite, since she does not shirk from confronting herself with contempt. In a 1968 autobiographical narrative about her father, the first "affirmative prose" piece she ever wrote (as she has said herself), she recalls her admiration and love for her father so intensely as to leave some of her left-wing critics almost speechless. It would not be too farfetched, I suspect, to describe *Beautiful Preserve* as an attempt to come to terms with terrible loss. In Plath's thoughts the date of his father's death, September 19, recurs as an important signal, and Plath assures himself and his readers that his turn toward a new affirmation has been triggered by new experiences: "I have to say that death after September 19th is not a borderline for me any more, it does not sit as a foreign object in my larynx, and I don't feel that I will suffocate while I am chewing it." A midlife crisis initiated by the father's death creates its own resolution through the emerging awareness that one "cannot think beyond terrible beauty," yet we are far from a Teutonic novel of existential gloom (though gloom may linger under the surface). In Wohmann's view Plath turns out to be—in spite of, or precisely because of, his wish to be open about himself—an occasionally funny character, without particularly pressing his point or taking a stand against all the sacred cows of the seventies. Attending, for instance, a conference at a Westphalian academy, Plath discovers in himself religious yearnings of the most basic kind, complains about the functional chapel afraid to reveal its theological message, partakes of holy communion by putting the host in his left hip pocket, and feels himself to be the center of God's attention. Plath is a master of sophisticated self-delusions, but he knows it and encourages his contemporaries, including his readers, to be as frank with themselves as they possibly can be.

It is difficult to read much of Wohmann without ambivalent feelings, for even when she bores one with her unrelieved nastiness, she does so with intensity and intelligence. I would not hesitate to say, resolutely dissenting from German critics, that her novel *Frühherbst in Badenweiler* (1978; *Early Autumn in Badenweiler*) is her first true masterpiece and a book of real distinction. Repeating herself fearlessly once again, she seizes on the formula situation that she developed earlier, while sustaining her repetitions with elegant irony. And if, in earlier novels, important moments of sympathy alternated with habitual Wohmannesque butcherings of nearly everybody not living up to her norms of excellence, here compassion triumphantly carries the novel into the realm of a sophisticated comedy of intellectual manners, as rare in Germany today as a hundred years ago. We immediately grasp the elements of the situation: a moment of abeyance outside everyday life with its disturbing and insoluble problems; the exhausting importance of tense family bonds; a marriage more or less suspended, at least for the time being; and a creative intelligence, male again, trying to come to terms with failures, indecision, and pretense. Here Wohmann has picked up one of Robert Plath's acquaintances and elevated him to the role of the self-conscious, vain, and funny protagonist: Hubert Frey, a composer in his forties, is staying for a few weeks in an expensive hotel in Badenweiler Spa so as to have a nervous breakdown, thinking this an excellent way to regain some of his creative drives, sadly in remission recently. He happily settles in room 247 to realize his somewhat morbid project ("Hubert's crisis"); establishes his daily ritual in the dining room and on prescribed walks that are not too strenuous; builds himself a little cinema around his TV in a corner of the room; and closely watches his bodily functions and intellectual conditions with foreboding. His wife Selma, an efficient career woman in TV, comes for brief visits to discuss matters of mutual concern, including a possible divorce, and his sister and brother-in-law drop in for an exhausting weekend. Yet he has to tell himself that he never felt better in his life, which he attributes to relaxing, gaining weight, and metaphysical reasons.

There is not much of a plot here, but a good deal of wit in dealing with the narcissism of a contemporary intellectual who more than once resembles Goncharov's Oblomov on his bed of sweet self-torture. The morning hours are particularly difficult, but toward evening Hubert usually feels as though a new play were being given for the first time in the elegant hotel; besides, he thinks it is totally "legitimate if a burdened man, painfully aware of the difficulty of living when he awakes in the morning . . . takes a vacation for himself in the evening." A lovable neurotic, "he energetically resolves to be passive," and though he formulates in his mind innumerable friendly letters to the waiters, the marvelous concierge, his sister, students, and colleagues, and constantly rehearses telephone calls to his friends, he never writes or phones anybody, then pities himself because the world has passed him by (nowadays the newspapers rarely mention his name). Hubert takes care to offer a complex image of himself to the hotel guests, but they mostly ignore him; he regularly wears his corduroy pants (the sign of the leftist intellectual), yet asks the concierge pointedly for the *Frankfurter Allgemeine Zeitung*, preferred by the corporate set and the more intelligent members of the CDU/CSU. While he daily announces his coming breakdown, we are distinctly aware that Hubert is having a nice time feeling lonely and play-acting, and that nothing will change when he returns to his wife, his desk, and his students feeling amply invigorated by a prolonged and pleasant intimacy with himself.

Wohmann occasionally pretends to detest literary theory, but she has defined her relevant ideas in many interviews and hundreds of book reviews (mostly about American, British, and younger German writers), as well as in a whimsical obituary for herself written to correct mistaken views of her work. Published in 1966, before her major novels, the obituary alludes half-grudgingly to the consensus of the critics that she concentrated on "middlish little events taking place among middlish little people," and defends her choice by saying that she is simply uninterested in fashionable pornography or in producing "cosmically unfolding supernovels" (clearly a dig at Günter Grass). In speaking of her obsession with significant detail, strikingly present in her stories, she likes to refer to James Joyce's "epiphanies" or, more often, to William Carlos Williams's "glimpses," those "short and rapid insights, from the corner of the eyes as it were, fleeting and yet capable of producing extracts, snapshots which result in suddenly arresting emotion," showing "the essence of things." Wohmann has been an efficient and intelligent reviewer of modern prose for more than two decades and, whether she knows it or not, increasingly likes to discuss her own inclinations and narrative methods in the texts of others. Writing about new editions of Italo Svevo or Virginia Woolf, or new books by John Updike, Mary McCarthy, Philip Roth, Susan Sontag, Joyce Carol Oates, or Sylvia Plath, she adds characteristic shades and colors to a self-portrait as practicing author. It may well be that she learned a good deal from, or at least felt sustained in her attitudes by Virginia Woolf, whom she praises for accepting "reality" solely as reflected in consciousness, and for attaching herself to "splinters of perception" (*Wahrnehmungssprenkel*). In the writings of Philip Roth, whom she early defended against the indifference of her fellow German reviewers, and in those of Mary McCarthy, she finds a consonant loyalty to truth shown by "intense precision" and by writing about the self whom the author knows best. Wohmann has long been attracted to Sylvia Plath, about whom she has written many reviews and brief essays examining her close feeling for the American poet, "a climate of consent, of a professional and really almost of a private kind." In 1980, after trying to answer the question whether Sylvia Plath would have drawn sustenance from a supporting women's group, she confessed that she would have liked to "mobilize" Sylvia "against men and women," against everything that smells of fellow traveling (in the widest sense) or of "tamely adjusting" to society.

Wohmann's insistence on exploring a self totally unwilling to adjust or conform to predominant social codes or to the demands of alternative pressure groups in public life—or rather, her old-fashioned individualism expressing itself in cryptic fictions—has been challenged by the Left and by feminists, who have a difficult time finding an appropriate place for her. Critics close to the women's movement respond ambivalently to Wohmann's indecisions; though among the first in the 1950s to explore the thinking of contemporary women, she does not seem to have an overwhelming following in the feminist community. Ingeborg Drewitz, herself a writer of note, suggests much of the unease in psychological terms. Basically, she accuses Wohmann of writing rather than living, of indulging in her predilections "to wound without being wounded herself," or rather in "her unwillingness to give up the privileges of a young girl," sexually overstimulated and yet strangely unfulfilled. Wohmann, she says, has the girlish distaste for strong and firm relationships, tolerates partners only as guests and visitors, and knows nothing at all about the intoxication of the savage animal or the euphoria of young mothers. The argument is articulated even more sharply in a finely nuanced 1979 essay by Dagmar Barnouw, who finds herself particularly irritated by Wohmann's "fiction of an honest self-analysis," in contrast to younger women writers less arrested in the role of the beautiful daughter.

Gabriele Wohmann, now in her fifties, published her first tentative stories when Günter Grass and Uwe Johnson were establishing themselves on the literary scene, and we easily forget her tenacious ways of exploring literary possibilities, admittedly within tightly circumscribed borders, at a time of rapid and substantial changes in political and literary preferences. If in the 1980s many young writers, women and men alike, have turned away from collective issues to such questions as how to live with each other inside and outside of marriage, they tread a road on which Wohmann preceded them long ago. Her earlier stories, usually praised by West German critics of social inclinations, as for instance *The Bütows*, will possibly survive in anthologies of literature as social criticism; other stories and essays, including "A Rustic Party," are masterpieces of narrative prose not easily forgotten. But it is high time that readers and critics stop clinging to her short stories, as they do in West Germany, and confront her important novels of the 1970s as central to her growing achievement of finely balancing irony and compassion. From a writer who published *Early Autumn in Badenweiler* in midcareer, much is still to be expected, even if she were not producing her habitual eight pages a day between six and eleven in the morning.

MARTIN WALSER: ANALYZING EVERYMAN

There are many labels used in dealing with Martin Walser, who was once among the angry young men and is now approaching his early sixties. Critics speak about the radical, if occasionally loquacious, intellectual of the independent Left, the regional writer loyally attentive to the lives of simple people on the shores of his native Lake Constance, or the sharp-eyed analyst of the way in which industrial society deforms and paralyzes those drawn into competition for money and power. Other issues are perhaps less frequently considered, as for instance whether or not it was the early loss of his Catholic beliefs that turned Walser into a restless seeker of general truth. Also worth noting are his quick and curious shifts from one genre to the other, and the disturbing sequence, or rather coexistence, of successful and unsuccessful books, revealing a rather insecure judgment of his own literary possibilities.

Walser was born in 1927, the son of a rustic innkeeper (and coal merchant on the side) in the small town of Wasserburg on Lake Constance. His father died early and his mother, unaffected by the Nazis because of her strong Catholic upbringing, kept the family together. Martin was sent to the Lindau *Gymnasium*, and later in the war served in the student antiaircraft artillery (as did Günter Grass), the Reich Labor Service, and the army. After the Allies occupied southern Germany, he found himself in a POW camp in Garmisch-Partenkirchen, where he spent his time working and reading in the library of Radio Munich, which had been moved to this Bavarian resort at the time of the air raids.

Walser's story is that of the highly gifted student who, after many years in the editorial offices of state-supported radio stations, resolved that the time had come to concentrate on his own plays and novels. Immediately after the war, Walser first studied German literature and history at the University of Regensburg, and later at Tübingen, where he wrote a first-rate dissertation on Kafka's narrative habits. By 1949 he had settled in Stuttgart, again working for the regional broadcasting corporation, together with his colleagues Helmut Heissenbüttel and Alfred Andersch. His first reading for Group 47 was not exactly a success, but in 1955 he received the group's literary award for one of his short stories, which, taken as a whole, demonstrate his difficulties in emancipating himself from Kafka's example. German critics, I suspect, somewhat underrate the importance of his first stay in the United States, in 1958. He was invited by Henry Kissinger to attend the Harvard International Seminar, lingered many hours on the steps of Widener Library, studied the structure of the American advertising industry, and, upon returning home, immediately wrote the first two volumes of his trilogy about corporate life. In the early 1960s Walser shifted to writing a spate of plays exploring the recent German past; their success made it possible for him to leave his small city apartment and move with his family to his own house at Nussdorf on Lake

Constance, where he lives today. The political restlessness of the late sixties affected him deeply in a kind of ideological midlife crisis. For a brief time he nourished illusions about the German Communist Party as a viable alternative to the Social Democracy he had supported earlier. He turned against the traditional theater by insisting on abortive theatrical experiments and published cryptic texts about the function of the intellectual in contemporary society. Only in the mid-1970s did he complete his corporate trilogy and write a series of more relaxed narratives and novels confronting the pains and middling hopes of his fellow citizens caught in crippling jobs and subjected to demanding social hierarchies. Walser recently said that he was enjoying a new kind of success as a novelist, and it may be fair to say that he has become the favorite of the younger and not-so-young West German urban professionals, who all share his nostalgia for the late sixties and early seventies.

In his compact first novel, *Ehen in Philippsburg* (1957; *Marriage in Philippsburg*, 1961), which was little praised by American reviewers, Walser explored the attitudes of the new German professional classes. His trilogy, *Halbzeit* (1960; *Halftime*), *Das Einhorn* (1966; *The Unicorn*, 1971), and *Der Sturz* (1973; *The Fall*), consists, at least at first sight, of the rambling confessions, revelations, and disordered thoughts of one Anselm Kristlein, who pursues a picaresque career as a traveling salesman, an advertising expert in the rapidly expanding West German mass media, and a moderately successful second-rate writer who frequents fashionable parties and ends up as a corporation employee. The volumes of the trilogy are different in tone and yet intimately linked by a recurrent pattern of events. The earlier volume shows Kristlein (who as a philosophy student had married the daughter of his professor) trying to find a place in the sales and advertising jungle, drawing on the spiel of his business colleagues and his secondhand knowledge of Madison Avenue jargon. In the second volume Kristlein, who has moved from Stuttgart to Munich, operates on the higher level of sales campaigns and publishers' advance contracts, and now offers his confessions in a more literary language, sustained by Joycean allusions and intricate pastiche.

Der Sturz (1973; *The Fall*), the long-delayed final volume of the trilogy, published nearly ten years after the second, marks

Walser's turn to social and Marxist thought. The adventurous Kristlein, more tired, shabby, and vulnerable than ever, lacks much of his earlier verve; even in his ingenious ploy of separating his usual ramblings into three distinct sections (retrospective, concurrent, and anticipatory), he again reveals his compulsion for repeating his experiences. Once more, after losing the family savings in a dubious investment, he has left the family in order to escape, an inspired vagrant, to Bavarian and Allgäu landscapes; and once more—after going through assorted picaresque experiences in a factory, a nature commune, and the embraces of fat or anorexic damsels—he finds himself back home, confessing all his sins to his understanding wife Alissa. Again there is hope: husband and wife are employed as house parents in a vacation home for the employees of a small corporation, but Kristlein of course has trouble adjusting to the job, nor is it particularly helpful to his career that he invites a literary friend who drinks a good deal and plans to fabricate a Soviet samizdat manuscript, to be sold either to Helen Wolff of Harcourt Brace Jovanovich or to Mondadori Publishers. Unfortunately, the German corporation is bought by Nabisco and the house parents are immediately fired. In the final section, Kristlein plans to cross the Alps via the dangerous Splügen Pass with his old sailboat in tow, and clearly envisions how car and boat will go crashing down the mountainside, burying him and Alissa in the burning wreckage. But Kristlein speaks about his "happiness and his end" in the future tense and Walser, in an ironic coda published separately, assures us that Kristlein has visited him to say good-bye and to look, after so many loquacious volumes, for bliss in utter silence. While the author expresses doubts that Kristlein was ever a critic of society as some commentators assumed (he rather saw him as a tragicomic figure of total conformity), he consoles us with the news that Kristlein, when last seen, was sitting on a stone bench in a little village not far from the Grande Chartreuse, that old monastic refuge of those who have chosen silence as the ultimate good.

Throughout the trilogy, Walser depends exclusively on the expanding consciousness of the one character whom he knows as well as himself, yet he insists that he avoids narrative solipsism. He does not present the traditional lonely hero "held together by a skin," but maintains that Anselm Kristlein has many existences and is right in considering himself a "parliament of personal pronouns" in which the first person represents the married, professional, eager salesman, while the second fondly and slavishly submits to the unicorn's sexual desires, and the third meanwhile is checking up on both and possibly on other selves emerging from Anselm's ego. Present experience and the language of the moment (in whose power Walser fervently believes) are closely related, but an immense abyss opens up between *past* life and *present* language; Anselm's recurrent elegy on the "pastness" of things reveals that all the exuberant richness of his language is but a desperate attempt to do the impossible and make the past a *now*. In the final conjuration of love, Kristlein combines his ultimate passion with the archetypical force of amorous words of all ages, yielding a finesse of verbal intelligence unparalleled among Walser's contemporaries.

As if wanting to convince himself of the range of his literary potentialities, Walser in the early and mid-1960s wrote a number of plays that were usually welcomed by warm applause and demonstrative whistling (the German way of protesting in the theater), while reviewers insisted with a certain regularity that the playwright showed considerable promise and that the best was yet to come. His first play, *Der Abstecher* [1961] (*The Detour*, 1963), in which two men band together against a woman, should be rediscovered by the feminists because it tells, in spite of its "absurd arabesques," the story of a woman who learns how husband and lover resemble each other in their thoughtless brutality. *Die Zimmerschlacht* [1967] (*Home Front*) takes a long look at a middle-aged couple and articulates what the marriage partners have hidden from each other for so long. The only trouble with the living-room battle is that we look at a *Hausfrau* and a pedant who, in the long run, exhaust our interest; since the German professional classes abound in such people, it is not quite clear why the playwright insists on duplicating their problems on the stage.

In his more political plays of the sixties, Walser had a difficult time extricating himself from what the critic Clara Merck called his "exact eclecticism." His use of Brecht, absurdist theater, and traditional farce did not necessarily strengthen his historical examination of moral failures past and present and his attempts to teach us something about ossifying capitalism. In *Eiche und Angora* [1962] (*The Rabbit Race*, 1963) theatrical method and polemical questions work at cross-purposes. Wanting to show us a panorama of German history since May 1945, Walser assembles a motley crew of average Nazis, a castrated and brainwashed concentration camp survivor who from time to time relapses into his radical ideas, schoolteachers still imbued with nationalist ideas, and numerous frustrated women; yet he fails to fuse the separate conventions of the literary and nonliterary theater. (It is symptomatic of the play that, in a printed version, the abstract figure of a Jew in search of his lost children had to be cut.) Walser's *Der schwarze Schwan* [1964] (*The Black Swan*) was the most ambitious and thoughtful of all his plays of the 1960s, but its opaque language and complex structure left some audiences and critics confused. For once, Walser moves away from inappropriate farce and thin allegory toward a renewed realism and sets against each other a Nazi father involved in the mass killings, and his son who discovers documentary evidence about his father's crimes and asks himself how *he* would have acted, had he been born earlier. Memory itself is being explored in all its recent German varieties, but the son who, like Hamlet, puts on a play to force the guilty to make a public confession, fails in his efforts and kills himself. Walser succeeds in holding up a scenic mirror to the fictions of remorse rampant in German contemporary life.

By inclination sympathetic to the aims of Social Democracy, in 1961 Walser was the spokesman of a group of younger writers eager to persuade their fellow citizens to vote Socialist. Later, appalled by what he considered the soft attitude of the SPD toward U.S. intervention in Vietnam, he moved closer to the Extraparliamentary Opposition and, after it had withered away, for two years (1972–74) expressed his active sympathy with the German Communist Party (DKP), which he hoped would offer an alternative home to restive Socialists. (He had sufficient common sense, however, to notice that the DKP was directed from the GDR, and that it did not protest against the persecution of writers and artists there.) Only in the mid-1970s did Walser feel new respect for the grand old SPD for upholding "democracy in practice" in an age of terrorists and blatant irrationalism to left and right. Many of his irritations, with both his fellow citizens and himself, show in his hostile plays of the time and in forbiddingly cryptic prose pieces exploring the chances of intellectuals in a post-1968 society. In *Wir werden schon noch handeln* [1968] (*We Are Going to Act, Just Wait*) he tested the fictions of the theater in left-wing Pirandello imitations, and in *Ein Kinderspiel* [1971] (*Children's Play*), an arid work about young radicals and conformists, sorely strained the patience of his critics, even the friendly ones. Three years later he returned to German history in *Sauspiel* [1975] (*Sow Game*), though not necessarily to discuss the past. He suggested that he was concerned with present issues in the image of past events and, stubbornly undeterred by the dangers of historical analogies, presented, in a sequence of loosely related scenes, a view of the proud city of Nuremberg immediately after the defeat of the peasant (i.e., student) revolt of 1525 (i.e., 1968). Concentrating on a group of illustrious magistrates, artists, and intellectuals, he demonstrates that all they do is provide arguments to strengthen ossifying power, while murdered peasants rot in the fields and radical Anabaptists rot in prison; but the play is too diffuse to be of service to its own ideological intent.

The prose pieces of Walser's wintry discontent are no less questionable. In *Fiction* (1970) a somewhat disembodied voice offers an internal monologue in five parts, being paradoxically attracted and repulsed by experiences in the city streets and by any attempt to speak about them. In *Die Gallistl'sche Krankheit* (1972; *Gallistl's Disease*) Walser exorcises his devastating uncertainties in a hapless narrative in which, by way of self-therapy, a middle-aged citizen speaks of leaving his old circle of friends, in hopes that he might find more sympathy and perhaps a glimpse of the historical future among a group of friendly Communists. Gallistl's sincerity is not entirely balanced by acumen; he would be a perfect character in one of R. W. Fassbinder's minor movies about the dull Bavarian provinces.

Though Walser's final demise as writer and playwright has time and again been announced by his critics, he has his own way of recouping his losses. He passed through his ideological late-sixties crisis with undiminished courage to continue what he had begun twenty years before. If, in the beginning, the traditionalists usually disliked and the progressives adored whatever he did, there has been a recent shift in his critics' responses, which now range from the complaints of aging experimentalists deploring what they call his flat language and new traditionalism, to unexpected praise from traditionalists who like his recent novellas and novels, which are closer to an acceptable diction and characterization. With renewed energy Walser confronts the question of narrative proportion, explores possibilities of disciplining his linguistic exuberance (which tempted some observers to quote Heidegger and say that language speaks Walser rather than the other way around), and alternates between a Balzacian solution of separate narratives sustained by recurring sets of characters, and the sharply delineated novella of classical tradition. In *Jenseits der Liebe* (1976; *Beyond All Love*) and *Brief an Lord Liszt* (1982; *Letter to Lord Liszt*) he again uses a middle-management character to show how competition and the power of corporate hierarchies deform and paralyze people born to realize their full potential of spontaneity. Taking on the burdens "of most people," as he defined his intentions in an open letter to the Soviet writer Uri Trifonov, he also has to solve his recurrent problem of how not to bore us, the average readers, with stories about ourselves. In *Beyond All Love* he closely watches the growing frustrations of Franz Horn, a sales manager who has long marketed dentures produced by Chemnitzer Zähne, Inc., a firm originally located in the Soviet zone. He tells us about Horn's ambivalent relationship with his boss; his resolution to leave his wife and children; his inability to outsmart his colleague Horst Liszt, once his subordinate and more recently his superior; a sales trip to England that utterly fails; and Horn's unsuccessful attempt at suicide. The second part of the story, published six years later, turns into an epistolary novel consisting of a very long letter and nineteen postscripts in which Horn regurgitates his boss hate (which may be but love unreciprocated), his disappointments, and the entire history of his departmental degradations and office sufferings. The cathartic letter is not mailed, of course, and Horn returns from a holiday to his office, still loyal to the marketing department (now selling a line of surfboards) and with all his repressions intact. Walser often complains that his bourgeois critics do not sufficiently consider his political point of view. He prefers Brecht-trained readers—those who do not want to follow Horn's example and now, warned by his fate, more clearly recognize their own role in offices and factories and actively wish to help change social hierarchies.

Walser's novella *Ein fliehendes Pferd* (1978; *Runaway Horse*, 1980) was immediately welcomed by nearly everybody on the (moderate) left and the right as a witty, wise, and well-constructed story of deeper significance. It is a subdued comedy of seventies manners sustained by gentle melancholy rather than aggressive bitterness and, unusual for Walser, successfully explores the social attitudes of the professional classes without ranting about the vices of dying capitalism. Helmut Halm, a somewhat morose teacher in advancing middle age, and his rather passive wife Sabine spend their summer vacations, as they have for years, in a small town on the shores of Lake Constance, where by chance they encounter Klaus Buch, Helmut's high school buddy of twenty years before, with his much younger second wife Helga. Klaus immediately insists that they all go dining, walking, swimming, and sailing together. But the two couples have different ideas about how to spend their time. Helmut, an introvert, likes to take it easy, drink red wine, and read Kierkegaard's diaries (though he never proceeds beyond one sentence), whereas the trendy Klaus and Helga jog, talk of their successes on TV, demonstratively stick to their health diet of steaks and mineral water, and constantly irritate their more sedate friends by being beautifully *sportif.* On a walk through the countryside, Klaus shows his energy when he skillfully stops a runaway horse (knowing, to everybody's surprise, that you have to do it sideways), but when the two men go sailing and Klaus exhibits his virile daring in a sudden storm, Helmut unexpectedly pushes the tiller out of his hand and Klaus is immediately washed overboard. Believing him drowned, his wife reveals that his stories about his successes are untrue. Yet Klaus comes back, the couples part quietly, and we never hear how they are going to live in the future.

Working meticulously with details of gesture, funny idiomatic conversations, and minute irritations at the dinner table and during nature walks, the narrator avoids melodrama. The episode of the runaway horse cannot easily hide its symbolic function, but Helmut's sudden and murderous revolt against Klaus is perfectly plausible. Helmut, an introspective man who has come to terms with being a failure, refuses to indulge, as does Klaus, in memories of past hopes, adventures, and expectations. It is Klaus (reminding us of the loquacious Anselm Kristlein) who is in real trouble; in spite of all his talk about his TV appearances and the high print orders for his popular ecology books, he cannot afford the vacation. Walser certainly tells an interesting story for middle-aged professionals of a certain standard of living, and it sold nearly two hundred thousand copies within a few months in Germany.

Once Walser develops a character successfully, he does not let go easily. In *Brandung* (1985; *Breakers*, due 1987) he sends Helmut Halm (with his wife and one of their daughters) to California, where Halm teaches for a term at a large university easily recognized as Berkeley, the scene of many academic novels showing a European intellectual confronting an alien civilization. Walser compassionately watches how Halm, under the strong sun of San Francisco Bay, himself comes close to changing into a kind of Klaus Buch, or rather (to the enjoyment of the reader) an Anselm Kristlein. He buys a flashy new suit, begins to jog, and falls in love with a blonde student who regularly wants his advice about her literary essays for another course. The ritual of departmental parties, emotional confusions at the student cafeteria, and the plight of frustrated faculty wives may be more surprising to German than to American readers, yet Walser prefers his comedy of academic manners distinctly on the melancholy side. The middle-aged teacher, in spite of Anselm Kristlein's blessed self-irony, has a difficult time resisting his rising emotions, even if only expressed in office-hour conversations about Shakespeare, Rilke, and Faulkner. After he has returned to Stuttgart he receives a newspaper clipping saying that the young woman died in a landslide, trapped in a car parked on the edge of a cliff above the surging waves of the sea. For the rest of his life he will have to cope with his burden of guilt, because he knows that she was still on crutches after hurting her ankle at his farewell party, where he and she danced with abandon and crashed to the floor. Walser's *Breakers* differs from the American academic novel by virtue of its quiet sympathy for fallible people (including a departmental chairman) on the ironic scene of bittersweet romance. Perhaps without wanting to do so, Walser delivered to his readers a successful campus novel (or rather an example of its subgenre about the German visitor on an American campus)—a genre first attempted by the critic Hans Egon Holthusen in his novel *Das Schiff* (1965; *The Ship*), little appreciated in its time, which firmly established the essential characters of the charmed European intellectual and the financially independent femme fatale in the guise of an American undergraduate who drives an expensive car barefoot.

In *Seelenarbeit* (1979; *The Inner Man*, 1984) and *Das Schwanenhaus* (1980; *The Swan Villa*, 1982), Walser once more turns to his Lake Constance schlemiels, trapped by oppressive jobs, family pressures, and the burdens of industrial society. The protagonists of the two novels are both members of the Zürn clan (*zürnen* means "to be angry"), and while Xaver Zürn in the first novel works as a chauffeur for a local industrialist, his cousin Gottlieb in the other narrative earns his income as an independent real estate agent meeting cutthroat competition. In Walser's world the boss and the driver have always been contemporary versions of Hegel's *Herr* and *Knecht*; now, in *The Inner Man*, we witness the psychosomatic and other difficulties of the honest Xaver, who suffers silently whenever he chauffeurs his boss around. Walser always had his populist sympathies for truck drivers (Xaver reads books about the German peasant revolt, Christian mystics, and whodunits in English and French), but *The Swan Villa*, the novel about Gottfried Zürn, is far more interesting, since it involves the reader in the complexities of community politics and the real estate business. Far from being content with a diagnosis of psychosomatic gastritis, the narrative looks in moving, funny, and grotesque detail at the daily experience of a lawyer and real estate agent of romantic inclinations. Gottlieb finds himself imprisoned by the incessant necessity of making more money to fulfill the demands of his family (four daughters, like Walser), to keep up with the Joneses of provincial Stuttgart and Lake Constance, and to impress his inventive competitors, who have few if any scruples, with his energy and the number of wretched condos sold. He dreams of acquiring the exclusive listing for the Swan Villa, a neo-Gothic monster with stained-glass windows and Lohengrin frescoes, which he admired when he was a poor boy, but his competitors, allying themselves with local political interests, are far more successful. When he arrives at the villa to pursue negotiations, he comes just in time to see it blown up and the park trees cut down by a consortium of real estate operators who plan to build luxury apartments on the site. Again, as in many other Walser novels, it is the faithful wife, seemingly colorless and introverted, who has the quiet strength to save the protagonist from utter despair.

Walser likes to speak about a kind of contemporary life that sociologists, statisticians, and demographers would find interesting; in his own way, he continues the work of Siegfried Kracauer, who in the Weimar Republic was the first to describe how white-collar employees actually lived. Friedrich Schiller, in the age of the French Revolution, clearly anticipated the emergence of "people who are but copies of their business," and Walser translates Schiller's idealist concepts into the idiom of market research, public relations, and corporate structures (via Marx and, recently, Kierkegaard). For a long time Walser has consistently avoided speaking in a language of his own making. In the early Kristlein trilogy, the archaic exuberance of the German language, in many dialects and historical idioms, asserted itself against events and individual characters. In the later narratives the author attaches himself, like a leech, to one of the central figures (usually professional, and frustrated or a failure), impersonally reporting his thoughts, sensations, and sayings without ever claiming the privilege of looking at him from a distance in order to judge whether he is right or wrong. Perhaps it is easier to hear Walser's own voice in the radio features and essays that he has gathered in many collections, including *Erfahrungen und Leseerfahrungen* (1965; *Experiences and Reading Experiences*), *Heimatkunde* (1968; *Local History*), *Wie und wovon handelt Literatur?* (1973; *Manners and Themes of Literature*), and *Liebeserklärungen* (1983; *Confessions of Love*). Writing, he says, comes from the experience of dearth: the writer responds in his fictions to inimical realities, and the reader then responds to the writer's response by activating his own energies of protest, criticism, and desire. Walser freely confesses that he feels closest to Hölderlin, Kafka, and the Swiss author Robert Walser; writes with perception and particular insight about Proust, Swift, and Heine; and conducts a protracted argument for and against Goethe, the "department store" of literature, crammed full of dubious goods. He is at his best when he writes about German history and the German language, which, as he suggests, may have been affected by the Nazis on its periphery but must never be "disqualified" in its totality for that reason. Walser is a more engaging writer when he does not strain to be a dutiful intellectual. The second volume of the Kristlein trilogy, *The Unicorn* (with its marvelous language associations), his probing play *The Black Swan*, and the later narratives, including *Runaway Horse* and *The Swan Villa*, are first-rate achievements that reveal a fragile sensitivity and an ironic intelligence in a continuing search for self-realization, as elusive as ever.

16

GÜNTER GRASS: THE POWER OF IMAGINATION

Günter Grass is the only postwar German writer who has been on the cover of *Time* magazine (April 13, 1970). "The old mullers and brooders, the old definers of crisis, are heard no more in the novel," the cover story said, suggesting that Grass, "an odd figure with a loser's accent and a bizarre past," was the only successor to the grand old men who died, fell silent, or became ministers of culture. *Time* told us that Grass, "dutch-comic soup-strained moustache" and all, did not look like "the world's or Germany's greatest novelist," but that he was possibly both. Much has changed in German life since 1970, but overseas readers like to think of him as the burly man of the people who exudes a Renaissance, or rather a horse trader's, vitality and indisputably dominates the German literary scene. Such an image may have been appropriate some years ago but is no longer entirely fitting. Precisely because Grass has been a writer of self-doubt, irony, and common sense, and because in political life he has defended a pragmatic view to the left of center, both the conservatives and the radical students of the late sixties and early seventies repudiated him openly. It is not impossible that his more recent turn to the ideas of the peace movement and to radical opposition to American foreign policy reflects an instinctive urge never to feel isolated again from readers of his own or the younger generation. Grass is not a writer who wants to be alone.

There is nothing "bizarre" in Grass's early life, as the *Time* reporters believed; rather, I would say that his experiences are emblematic of an entire generation of young people who were sent from the school benches to the crumbling front lines of the "Third Reich." Grass was born in 1927 of German and Kashubian (Slavic) parents in Danzig when it was still a "free city" under the mandate of the League of Nations, and was five years old when the Nazis took over in Germany. His father ran a little grocery in a suburb, and his mother had Kashubian relatives on small farm plots near the city. Grass has never freed himself of obsessive childhood memories of teachers, grocers, Jews, Poles, and plebeian Nazis in an age-old community in which many cultures met, merged, or clashed with one another. He was fourteen when he was inducted into the Hitler Youth, fifteen when he served in the local antiaircraft batteries, and at seventeen was called to army duty in the Panzer infantry. Wounded in the last months of the war, he spent time in a Marienbad hospital and later as an American POW in Bavaria. He did not want to finish school, worked on a farm and in a mine, then apprenticed himself to a Rhenish stonecutter and learned how to letter tombstones. Contemporary snapshots show him vulnerable and hungry, with eyes as sad as those of young Brecht. He wanted to become a sculptor; studied at the art academies of Düsseldorf and Berlin; wrote a good deal of poetry and a few short plays, neither particularly successful; and with his wife Anna, a Swiss dancer, moved to Paris, where he lived for four years (1956-60), selling his drawings and writing about his childhood near the Baltic and the Vistula.

The turning point of his career came in 1958–59. In 1958 Grass read a chapter from his manuscript of *Die Blechtrommel* (*The Tin Drum*) to Group 47 and was awarded the group's prize; the complete novel was published in 1959, to the shrieks of the prudes and conservatives. He awoke one morning and, amid scandal and protest, found himself famous, hailed as the representative of a changing German literature now being newly discussed in Paris, London, and even New York. Returning from Paris in 1960, he settled in West Berlin and increasingly committed himself in local and national campaigns to independent support of the Social Democrats and his personal friend Willy Brandt (he joined the party only much later). To many he symbolized, at least in the 1960s, the indomitable Berlin spirit, sober, witty, and cosmopolitan. Golo Mann, the son of Thomas, nominated him as a candidate for mayor of Berlin at a time when the police were beginning to battle students in the streets. Then in the late 1970s Grass divorced his wife, moved from Berlin to Wewelsfleth in northern Germany, married an organist, and published *Der Butt* (1977; *The Flounder*, 1978) to mixed reviews and excellent sales. He now lives in Hamburg while keeping another residence in Berlin, where he presides over the Academy of the Arts, publicly speaking his mind about German problems of West and East, American politics, and the affairs of the Third World. For all practical purposes he has come to function as a West German minister of culture, perhaps of another Socialist government yet to come.

Richly gifted as a graphic artist and writer, not to mention his culinary talents, Grass needed time to discover and develop his real strength as a skillful narrator of complicated fictions. He always wanted to do too many things at once and provokes us, often intentionally, by the imbalance of a disorderly imagination and the exigencies of form. I read Grass's early poetry as a chronicle of his productive turn from a surrealist repertory of highly personal images (perhaps secondhand Jacques Prévert rather than firsthand André Breton) to a relaxed, irritated, and revealing way of speaking about his intimate feelings as husband, artist, and citizen living at a particular moment of history in the city of West Berlin, a place of rubble and anxieties. In his early volumes strange birds, insects, dolls, fruits, and deck chairs tend to crowd out people, unless they are nuns, brutal butchers, or wicked cooks, but his later volume *Ausgefragt* (1967; *New Poems*, 1968) constitutes a diary in which he asks himself how well or badly he has lived up to his best intentions. He recalls many scenes of his Danzig childhood and in some of his best reflective poems, among them "Love" and "Marriage," speaks, in the sober, everyday speech characterizing his poems in general, of his disillusions and rare moments of intimacy (". . . and sometimes, distrait, we are tender"). As a citizen, he impatiently protests against "impotent protests," defending his creative spontaneity against those radical sons and daughters of good families whose righteousness, on the left, makes it so difficult for him to breathe. In later years Grass has usually absorbed his poems into the textures of all-encompassing narratives, as is consonant with his changing view of writing, and rarely publishes, as he did in 1974, a separate volume of verse.

As a young playwright Grass relied on his Paris experiences of Alfred Jarry, Ionesco, and Beckett to create absurdist plays that, in the public's mind, had to compete with Brecht's epic theater and its far less tentative messages. *Die bösen Köche* [1961] (*The Wicked Cooks*) [1967] offers a good example of Grass's involvement with the theater of the absurd, dominated, in his case, by the strange power of things (here: trumpets, kitchen pots, and recipes) and a gathering of white-clad characters well known from his poems and narratives. Absurdist plays do not want to yield stories or meaning, but Grass does not push too far. A crew of wicked cooks pursues a young man named Herbert who knows the wondrous recipe for a "gray soup," which may or may not suggest the secret of poetry or Life; while Herbert and his beloved Martha, a nurse in appealing white, refuse to submit to the cooks and serenely commit suicide, the young and dreamy cook Vasco, whom Herbert has befriended, will go on keeping the secret, which cannot be written down anyway, and the cooks will pursue Vasco in turn. The play was performed a few times off Broadway (1967), with Jára Kohout, a famous Czech émigré comic, in the role of senior cook, but what the performance revealed to a sparse New York audience was, of course, a Grass anachronism going back in its intentions to the early 1950s, rather than the imaginative splendor of his narratives.

We are fortunate that the West German theater of the fifties, by not eagerly responding to his early plays, compelled Grass to turn from his theatrical toys to an exploratory narrative of unbounded invention. *Die Blechtrommel* (1959; *The Tin Drum*, 1962), *Katz und Maus* (1961; *Cat and Mouse*, 1963), and *Hundejahre* (1963; *Dog Years*, 1965), which made him the favorite author of the younger West German intelligentsia challenging the Adenauer establishment, were later characterized by Grass himself as a Danzig trilogy. Substantial or lean, these novels and stories are fiercely sustained by his memories and stubborn attempts to probe, though by somewhat unorthodox means, the past of the place and the petty bourgeois whom he knows best. In this claustrophobic world we confront strangely attractive characters who walk from one book into the next (as for instance the bony preteen Tulla Pokriefke, who likes to watch boys masturbate), and learn about the exact topography of Danzig life, including the number of streetcars and the location of movie houses. But Danzig is never totally absent from any of Grass's important writings, early or late. Perhaps a better way of describing how the individual books of the trilogy hang together would be to say that, in opposing the traditions of nineteenth-century realism, they often go back to the prerealist attitudes of the picaro who tells his adventures one after another, or that they skip forward to surrealist games with poetic imagery. It is most essential that the moralist Grass in these early novels delegates narrative authority to speakers of dubious veracity.

In his novella *Cat and Mouse* Grass masterfully checks his epic force and creates an intense, rich work of art that competes successfully with some of the most perfect stories of the nineteenth century. A striking chip off the Danzig block, *Cat and Mouse* unfolds the story of Great Mahlke, a boy of curious obsessions and notable achievements, as told many years after the events, by his reluctant admirer Pilenz, who is trying to clarify for himself what happened on a half-sunken Polish minesweeper in the Gulf of Danzig near Neufahrwasser back in 1944 or so. The boy Mahlke has to take great care to cover his large Adam's apple, which resembles a nervous mouse. He collects all sorts of things, including a screwdriver, religious medals, a can opener, and fashionable tassels, to be worn as "counterweights" around his neck in order to hide his abnormal feature. But when a famous submarine commander, with the Knights' Cross of the Iron Cross around his neck, addresses the boys in school, Mahlke realizes that this is what he has to have; he steals the cross and wears it under his tie, but does not enjoy it for long because the theft is investigated and Mahlke is transferred to a less prestigious school. Yet Mahlke cannot forget the "thingamajig," and when he joins the army he feels personally inspired by the Virgin Mary, who enables him to destroy many Russian tanks, for which he is finally awarded the "thingamajig" himself. On leave, he hastens back to his old school, hoping to give a lecture like the submarine commander's to the students, but school director Klohse, reminding him of his theft, refuses permission, and Klohse's obedient colleagues agree. Deprived of his triumph, Mahlke does not want to return to the front, deliberately misses his train, rows out to the old minesweeper where he had built himself a hideout in the watertight radio cabin, and dives down, never to come up again.

As narrator, Mahlke's friend Pilenz is driven by feelings of involvement, responsibility, and guilt that emerge more clearly as the story advances. His confession does not come out easily because he was raised a believing Catholic and formulates his story in a constant dialogue with his parish priest, who, sensing the therapeutic value of the text, urges Pilenz to cultivate his God-given artistic gifts. As a boy, Pilenz was among those who admired Mahlke boundlessly. Yet he inadvertently admits (if often by mere implication) that he longed to free himself from Mahlke. He keeps silent, however, about those last moments when his friend, the cross and two cans of food around his neck, went down into the deep; he does not say why he did not return to the boat at night as he had promised. Only Pilenz's ambivalent view can penetrate into Mahlke's deepest secret: Pilenz knows that Mahlke was driven by the urge to be like his father who, while working for the Polish railroads, died a hero's death averting a dangerous accident. Pilenz is able to grasp Mahlke's grotesque determination to go his own way and pays hesitant homage to a man who demonstrated unusual resilience in the cat-and-mouse game that fate plays with everybody.

Günter Grass's second full-length novel, *Dog Years*, is an extraordinary ragbag of wild yarns, clever parodies, tragic insights, piercing satire, and Rabelaisian gags. Grass leaves the job of narrator to three other men who, being from Danzig or nearby, are all supremely qualified to compete with him in knowledge of local detail. He continues to discuss, with piety and pedantry, the differences between Danzig-Langfuhr's two movie theaters a generation ago. But one of the narrators, Herr Brauchsel or Brauxel (alias Goldmäulchen alias Haseloff alias Eddi Amsel), seems particularly interested in editing the substantial manuscript. As an introspective man of considerable means (he owns a kind of scarecrow factory in an old mine near Hildesheim), he retains the literary services of his collaborators, Harry Liebenau and Walter Matern, discusses their writings, suggests modifications, and combines his own contributions, entitled *Early Morning*

Shifts, with Harry Liebenau's more epistolary part and the 103 irregularly numbered Materniads of the somewhat picaresque third contributor, his lifelong friend and enemy. Herr Brauchsel, relying partly on an old diary, writes of his own childhood, of "sunsets, blood, earth, and ashes"; dreaming of the rolling waters of the Vistula and the wide marshes, he remembers the days when he was fat and freckled Eduard Amsel, built his first scarecrows, and fought with his friend Walter Matern, who threw away the penknife that the boys had used in the rite of blood brotherhood. He recalls windmills, peasants, birds, and later the smell of chalk and classrooms in a landscape of boys. He also recalls Eddi Amsel, beaten by others because he was helpless, sensitive, and half-Jewish, and Walter, his protector who handled his early business affairs (selling his scarecrows to eager peasants), always wearing Eddi's new clothes, gnashing his teeth, and abusing his friend in fits of theatrical rage.

In Harry Liebenau's contribution, consisting of love letters to his cousin Tulla Pokriefke and a concluding fairy tale, the circle widens: Eddi and Walter appear among a crowd of students, teachers, petits bourgeois, Nazi storm troopers, and local artists. The real dog years have begun: the National Socialists dominate Danzig and most of Europe, and those who resist are tortured and killed. In the concluding Materniads Walter, in his own disorderly way, reports on the first years after the war. Released from a POW camp as an antifascist, he sets out on a picaresque tour of revenge to punish those functionaries, officers, military policemen, and judges who have made his life miserable and, while enjoying their hospitality, sleeps with their wives and daughters, kills their chickens and canaries, and infects everybody with his gonorrhea (while curing himself in a fashion not recorded in medical literature). When in danger of becoming a bourgeois, he fortunately meets Harry Liebenau, who arranges a roundtable radio discussion about German guilt (the star speaker: Matern). Then in Berlin he encounters Eddi Amsel, who again begins to cling to him and takes him, in a descent worthy of a true epic, to his mine to show him his scarecrows; they are together, and alone, again.

Grass anticipated the ambivalent relationship of Eddi and Walter in Pilenz's terse loyalty to Great Mahlke in *Cat and Mouse*, but in *Dog Years* the ambivalence of feelings combines almost lethally with the political situation. Matern protects his friend Eddi against belligerent boys and cruel fellow students, but loyalty has its own burdens: after Matern has caught Eddi donning a Nazi uniform, he personally leads a group of Nazi bullies to the house and almost kills his friend, who loses all his teeth in the struggle, collapses in the snow, and suffers for the rest of his life from the consequences of the freezing cold. But as soon as Eddi has left Danzig, the lonely Matern begins to drink, steals SA funds for his schnapps, tries to make a living as an actor, gets into trouble with the political authorities again, saves his skin by volunteering for the army in 1939, and is finally transferred to a punitive battalion because he has abused the regime's highest functionaries. Matern lies constantly about his responsibility for hurting Eddi. Yet when they meet again and Eddie half-ironically confesses that he continues to be fascinated by Germany, the land of forgetfulness and primeval scarecrows, and offers Matern the old penknife of blood brotherhood, miraculously retrieved from the sands of the Vistula, Grass comes close to suggesting the idea of an almost mystical, recurrent communion between Germans and sons of Jewish fathers, destined to hate and love each other eternally.

A READING OF THE TIN DRUM

In Grass's novel *The Tin Drum*, a hunchback named Oskar, approaching his thirtieth birthday and haunted by memories and anxieties, tells of his picaresque life, his particular vantage point being the cozy white bed of a West German mental institution to which he was transferred after being tried for the murder of a nurse. His precise memory roams with ease through past experience, and whenever memory does not suffice, his intense imagination, aided by his little child's drum, produces streams of images, smells, and colors: brown potato fields near the mouth of the Vistula River; the Danzig suburb of Langfuhr with its shops, churches, barracks, schools, and streetcars; eels, sea gulls, and herrings; coco matting in bathhouses; and after the war, the industrial landscape of the Rhine, the city of Düsseldorf, and yellow fields of rye between the coal mines. He did not want to be an adult or a grocer like the others, Oskar asserts, therefore he decided to remain a permanent three-year-old who, though maturing in mind, sensitivity, and virile reserves, continues to haunt the adult world with his piercing and glass-shattering voice. Only after the death of the grocer Matzerath, his archenemy (who also happened to be his father), did Oskar decide to grow again, but he did not entirely succeed: he remains deformed, but proudly cherishes his fine hair, expressive eyes, and sensitive hands. The story of his life, as Oskar tells it, centers on the women to whom he has been stubbornly and sometimes perversely loyal: his sensuous mother Agnes, who was not sure whether she loved her sentimental Polish cousin Jan Bronski or the Rhinelander Matzerath, whom she married; during the war years, Maria, who liked fizz powder, smelled of vanilla and mushrooms, and finally decided to marry Matzerath senior; and in the Rhineland, the nurse Dorothea, whom Oskar pursued with cunning, endless curiosity, and (as a ribald episode demonstrates) impotent fury. Yet Oskar's experiences are not merely private ones; unlike the picaro of the old Spanish novel, he cannot live outside history and constantly finds himself confronted with political events of growing importance. In search of his drum, he witnesses the burning of the Danzig synagogue on the *Kristallnacht* of November 9, 1938, and finds his Jewish friend Markus (who had always provided drums at reduced prices) dead in his shop, which has been destroyed by Nazi storm troopers. On September 1, 1939, he happens to be among the hapless Polish defenders of the Danzig post office, and in his own way lives through the historic beginning of World War II. Later, traveling with a troupe of acrobats to perform before German Wehrmacht audiences in Normandy, he has to pack his little bags rather quickly on June 6, 1944, when the Canadians arrive on the beaches. Being a man—or rather a dwarf—of his age, he cannot speak of himself without implying something about the rise and fall of Hitler's Reich, and the ensuing days of the merely economic "miracle."

The trouble is that we have to accept whatever Oskar says. Although a few parts of his confessions, true or false, are provided by his friendly male nurse Bruno (book 2, chapter 17) and his friend Vittlar (book 3, chapter 11), theirs are not "objective" voices, for they are manipulated by Oskar and say only what he wants them to say. Being the most unreliable of narrators, he is also one of the most challenging, erratic, and ambivalent characters in recent German fiction, a moral monster with aesthetic talents and metaphysical anxieties who calmly observes a morbid world. He protects himself against adults by withdrawing into a fake childhood, yet his path is strewn with people offended, wounded, and dead. He is responsible for the death of Jan Bronski because he drags him, against his will, to the Polish post office, but when the Nazi victors take the Poles away to shoot them, Oskar pretends to be a helpless little boy whom the Poles have kidnapped. He tries twice to abort Maria's child when she is pregnant by Matzerath senior (until he decides that he himself was responsible). He refuses to help his lilliputian mistress Roswitha Raguna and forces her out into an open yard, where she is killed by a grenade. He leads the Duster Gang with a swagger, but promptly betrays the young people when they are tried by the authorities. And while Matzerath senior stubbornly refuses to sign a document turning Oskar over to the health authorities (who want to do away with him in accordance with their theories of racial "health"), Oskar does not hesitate to cause Matzerath's ugly death when the first Russian soldiers arrive. He has never killed with his own hands, but he is nevertheless a vicious killer.

Yet Oskar also embodies, as Henry Hatfield has suggested, the gifts of the artist in a dull society of grocers, functionaries, and squares. He has gathered a "little learning of wide scope," usually relies on Goethe and Rasputin or, like any good post-Nietzschean intellectual, on Apollo and Dionysus. His drum turns into his instrument of revolt, dream, and metamorphosis. For good reason he constantly reminds us of the toy's red-and-white-colored fringe: the colors suggest the Polish flag (associated, in turn, with abstract heroism); his grandfather's life of arson, close escapes, and revolt; and an aura of fire, fierce feeling, and strange innocence. Things of the past, implacable revolt, and a powerful transformation of feelings become one in the suggestive rhythm of his drumming, as behind this hunchbacked cousin of Thomas Mann's talented outsiders, an archetypal troll full of ambivalent magic powers appears. It is his infinite self-assertion and his concern for his art that define the limits of his stance in the epoch of rising Nazi power. He does not revolt against the Brown Shirts but against the adult world; he joins the Poles at the post office because he wants to have his drum repaired; and he clearly separates his own gang from the more politically oriented sabotage groups of the Communist-led apprentices on the docks. He disrupts well-organized Nazi demonstrations by drumming a waltz or "Jimmy the Tiger," because he cannot stand their competing fanfares or, for that matter, those played by the bands of other political groups, including the Socialists and the Nationalist Young Poles. In the particular constellation of his native Danzig, he comes close to being a virtual ally of the Nazis and yet occasionally functions as an antifascist, if only for wholly inappropriate reasons.

Yet Oskar's deepest secrets may well be religious or ontological. Negating all philosophy except that of his ego, he feels strongly attracted to the Church of the Sacred Heart and considers the figure of the Christ child his most radical challenge, since Jesus is the "most perfect Oskar." Unbelieving and nevertheless expecting a miracle (and little Jesus does drum, when Oskar puts the toy in his wooden hands), Oskar constantly returns to the church, mobilizes his gang, has the Christ child sawed off Mary's lap, and installs himself there to be adorned by his friends, all well-trained Catholics perfectly able to say a (Black) Mass with the correct Latin texts. He is one of those atheists who cannot live without intensely hating God; even the most satanically clever curses that he hurls at Christ confirm an inescapable bond. The vicious little artist Oskar essentially longs for salvation from existence—against, not with, time. His early decision to remain a three-year-old constitutes only one of his strategies of regression to the protective womb; others include his constant desire to hide under his grandmother's five skirts (he playfully imagines how pleasant life would be *inside* her body), and his urge to hide under tables, behind closed doors, or, at certain crucial moments, in a wardrobe, in order to spy on his enemies or to indulge in drumming and sexual self-gratification (closely related) in a sphere of warmth and protection. Obsessed by white-clad nurses *d'ogni forma* because they remind him of his mother, who was a nurse before she married Matzerath, Oskar turns into a compulsive repeater who, in his urge to stop time, constantly relives and rearranges past experiences in protest against present and future. But as time goes on he is forced closer to his inveterate enemy Death, the "Black Witch" who is waiting to ambush him; in growing agony, he desperately tries to avoid the final often-anticipated encounter. Like Pirandello's Henry IV, who would rather be mad than face time, Oskar for his own reasons sits in his white bed, reminiscent of the neat womb of motherly nurses, drums up his protective past on his white-and-red toy, and senses in fear and trembling the coming of the inescapable witch.

THE SIXTIES: NEW POLITICAL AND LITERARY COMMITMENTS

In the course of the 1960s the belated surrealist and teller of disorderly tales developed firm political commitments. Perhaps the building of the Wall convinced him that he should participate in the public discussions of the Federal Republic. His open letter in 1961 to Anna Seghers, the dean of GDR writers, asking her to protest against the builders of the Wall (just as he would fight the traditionalists in his own country), was followed by many other open letters, statements, and speeches to voters, members of parliament, SPD gatherings, trade union conferences, and audiences in Athens, Belgrade, New Delhi, New York, and elsewhere. In the federal elections of 1965 Grass, in his role of a "Berliner who couldn't vote" (according to Allied statutes), declared his support for the Social Democrats and in the name of Walt Whitman, "the Lincoln of language," traveled all over the republic to give his basic speech in favor of the Socialists, only to be terribly disappointed by the *Realpolitik* of his friends, who agreed to form the Grand Coalition with the conservatives. In the campaign of 1969, Grass joined with other intellectuals to organize a network of "electoral initiatives," groups of volunteers working in support of the SPD, and found himself, after the Socialist/Liberal government had been formed, in the eminently visible role of being a trusted friend of Willy Brandt, the new chancellor of the republic and 1971 laureate of the Nobel Peace prize, and yet not strictly bound by party discipline. In the years of the Brandt government, Grass was politically more active than ever: he traveled with the chancellor to Warsaw and Israel; castigated the intellectual pride of the radical students and the violence of the terrorists; and in a regular column appearing in the *Süddeutsche Zeitung*, discussed the gritty details of national politics. He respected Brandt's successor Helmut Schmidt, "the effective pragmatist," but that resourceful economist (who preferred Siegfried Lenz to Grass anyway) did not really fire his imagination. Dissatisfied with what he believed was a far too submissive attitude toward U.S. foreign policy, which he viewed as undermining the spirit of détente, Grass turned from fully supporting the SPD to criticizing its viewpoints from within and to organizing peace conferences with fellow writers, including colleagues from Hungary and the GDR.

There is a strongly populist, antielitist, if not antibookish strand in his political sensibilities, characteristic more of the British than of the German Left. Grass has never been particularly patient with those of his fellow intellectuals who preferred the pure realm of theory or concentrated their energies on fighting geographically distant adversaries. Enraged by the Socialist losses in the mid-1960s, he bitterly complained about what he thought was the political abstinence of Heinrich Böll (who was rarely excited about party politics) and others who merely uttered "finely chiseled cries of distress." He was particularly outspoken about H. M. Enzensberger, who, he suggested, would rather write a heroic epic on Fidel Castro than use his pen for daily affairs at home. Grass is well versed in the history of socialism; he always had great praise for the "revisionist" Eduard Bernstein, who wanted to go the slow parliamentary way. Unlike many of his romantic colleagues, Grass systematically accentuated the libertarian element in the socialist tradition, which to his mind was most clearly defined by Rosa Luxemburg with her ideas about the necessary spontaneity of the working people. He cannot easily forget the battle of Kronstadt, where the Soviet sailors fought against the dictatorship of the Communist Party in 1921, for it was repeated when Soviet tanks were ranged against East German workers in 1953 and against the Czechoslovak comrades in 1968, and again when the Polish militia fired on striking dock workers in the Gdansk shipyard in 1970. As a Socialist and Liberal, Grass was harshly treated by the students in revolt. He was among the first to protest publicly when the Berlin police hunted down student demonstrators, but he could not stand the manipulation of young people by a middle-class elite and, as he termed them, scholastic theorists. Accusing the radicals of offering nothing but "revolutionary gestures," he confessed freely that he felt disturbed by "symptoms of fascism" reminiscent of Mussolini's Italy among the students. In the early 1970s he was virtually proscribed by the radicals; one evening in 1971, when he attended a performance at the Berlin Schaubühne am Halleschen Tor, the performance was interrupted, and the actors demanded that Grass leave the house. He refused to do so, and after a few courageous remarks about the "Stalinist methods" by which the audience was being manipulated, he and his wife stayed on until the end of the performance.

His own play *Die Plebejer proben den Aufstand* [1966] (*The Plebeians Rehearse the Uprising*, 1966), and his narrative *Aus dem Tagebuch einer Schnecke* (1972; *From the Diary of a Snail*, 1973), are closely related to the political commitments and activities of the late 1960s. In his play, anticipated by a rather disorganized 1964 academy speech about Shakespeare's *Coriolanus*, Brecht, and his own writing projects, Grass took up the question of the intellectual and the revolution in recent German history. He defines the issue theatrically by a confrontation between the "boss" of a theater subsidized by the Ulbricht government and working people in East Berlin and other GDR cities who are revolting against the Party dictatorship over the proletariat (shades of Kronstadt). In his academy speech Grass called the "boss," meaning Brecht, an "unspoiled theatrical nature," but in the play he grants some ambivalence to Brecht's response to the revolting workers. It is June 1953: a delegation of working men comes to the theater (where the boss happens to be rehearsing his adaptation of Shakespeare's *Coriolanus*), in hopes that the renowned socialist author will formulate a statement on their behalf. While they state the case of the people marching in the street, he coolly studies their voices and gestures in order to enhance his production with authentic plebeian detail. A young girl brings in a worker grievously wounded in the incipient fighting, and the boss, quoting from his early poetry, feels tempted for a sweet nostalgic moment to join the workers outside. But it is too late—Soviet tanks are intervening against the working people. So the boss composes an ambivalent statement that he knows the government will use to prove that he is in sympathy with the repressive measures of the future. Conscious of his failure, he contemplates the blessings of pastoral solitude in his government-donated country house. Grass has called his play a "German tragedy," not to express his loyalties to the Aristotelian genre, but to point far beyond the play itself to German history. He had high aims, but twenty years later the play strikes me as yet another *Bildungsstück*, curiously static in its construction and as didactic as some of the "boss's" minor plays.

It is more difficult to describe *From the Diary of a Snail* as a book related to questions of political experience past and present, because Grass plays against each other, in a text addressed to his children, the fictional and the documentary, the openly autobiographical and the didactic. Grass reports about his experiences as an SDP campaign speaker from March 3 to September 28, 1969, when the Social Democrats increased their vote to 42.7 percent and, for the first time since World War II, established a Socialist/Liberal government headed by a Socialist chancellor. Looking at himself with a good deal of self-irony, he jots down lively observations about small towns and big cities from Westphalia to Bavaria; admits (in a kind of personal platform) that his belief in utopia is tempered by an utter melancholy not at all popular among young conservatives and radicals; and, as a graphic artist, substitutes for the rooster crowing from a manure heap (his own onetime image of the pragmatic Socialist) the far less provocative but resilient snail that slowly winds its way through the landscape of history. There also emerge, in contrapuntal arrangement, the life stories of two German contemporaries who incarnate chapters of social anthropology. One story is a true account of a middle-aged man (a former National Socialist with idealist leanings) who commits suicide during a protest rally, because he cannot revive his feelings of community, lost in the destruction of the Reich. The other story concerns an only half-fictional Danzig teacher who prefers to work in a Jewish school (before the Jews of Danzig are forced into exile or murdered) and later hides in the cellar of a Kashubian bicycle mechanic, as did the critic Marcel Reich-Ranicki in real life after the destruction of the Warsaw ghetto. Grass of course cannot resist the temptation of playing with his leitmotivs, which function here as hinges that bring together the many elements of the text. Snails abound, even as an organic *dildo* used by the teacher to awaken the sensibilities of a Kashubian girl. We may feel disturbed, at least in our first reading, by the grotesque collage combining serious discussions of Willy Brandt's electoral strategies with the adventures of the picayune if antifascist Danzig snail collector, but we should be aware that Grass is radically disengaging himself from his older ways of storytelling, and experimenting with narrative strategies that he is proud to have learned from Alfred Döblin.

Grass the self-made author always learned his literary lessons in the actual process of writing, and his academy address "Teacher Döblin" (1967) strikes me as being of essential importance for any understanding of his attitude as storyteller. Grass's relationship to Alfred Döblin, the pioneer of prose experiment in the Weimar Republic, is a rather bookish affair: Grass never met Döblin personally, and many of the formulations of the academy speech derive, I think, from the Döblin edition of 1963, largely ignored in Germany, or to be more precise, from the volume gathering Döblin's theories of narrative, developed by him between 1912 and 1919 under the impact of the Italian futurists. What attracts Grass to Döblin, and through Döblin to the pre–World War I avant-garde, is their belligerent attitude toward the limitations of realist narrations, that is, toward inherited psychology, the reductive monotony of established forms, and the linear plot that falsifies the explosive fullness of the world. When Grass praises Döblin for setting people and natural forces in motion in his epic novels, he sounds exactly like Döblin, who once praised F. T. Marinetti for an early novel in which he moved mountains and masses as lightly as feathers. Döblin demanded a narrative that would not "talk about" the world but make it present in its cosmological flux. Deriding the French preference for a thin and clear *récit*, he called for a *Kinostil* of rapid montage, the use of the "Fantastic, the Epic, the Enhanced, the Fairy Tale, the Burlesque," and a mode of "stratifying, pushing, and shoving" rather than of satisfying foolish demands for a unified plot. He wanted a narration that above all made a deliberate attempt to cancel sequential time—one that, by "tectonically" combining sequences with juxtapositions, would realize the principle of synchrony, the futurist *simultaneità* that alone reveals the fullness of the world.

Unlike some of his contemporaries, Grass may for a while have been an amateur in literary theory, but in coming to terms with Döblin he lost his theoretical innocence. I would recommend his paper "Der lesende Arbeiter" (1974; "The Reading Worker"), written for the centennial of the socialist Gutenberg Book Club, as his most advanced, thoughtful, and articulate theoretical statement, one well worth considering in its substantial implications for his own work. It is a polemical piece addressed to those who believe that working people can read only the simplest kind of literature. Grass defines his argument by a striking futurist analogy between the complexities of the technological process of industrial production and the complications of modern writing. Using Döblin's, if not Marinetti's, terms, he suggests that people in factories are better qualified than others to read difficult narratives, because they know their assumptions from their own daily experience, "that synchrony of what goes on, consciousness overlapping in many patches, the chorus of unarticulated inner monologues." The aesthetic of new writing, he insists, closely corresponds to what happens on the production floor: it explodes all linearities and chronologies, and reflects the structure of technological processes in its "thrusts, blockages, and discharges." Analogies of industrial technology and literary experimentations may have their own history by now, from the Italian futurists to Döblin and to Walter Benjamin, but I know of no other statement by Grass more useful to our critical understanding of what he wants to do in his writings of the sixties, the seventies, and later, including *Örtlich betäubt* (1969; *Local Anaesthetic*, 1970), *Der Butt* (1977; *The Flounder*, 1978), and *Kopfgeburten; oder, Die Deutschen sterben aus* (1980; *Headbirths; or, The Germans Are Dying Out*, 1982).

In *Local Anaesthetic* (perhaps more successful overseas than in Germany, where readers expected a tale of the old brand), Grass moves, as in *From the Diary of a Snail*, from his early narrative procedures to testing new techniques, yet not at once or totally. Eberhard Starusch, the narrator, comes of course from Danzig, where he was the daredevil leader of the Duster Gang of juveniles, who robbed church collection boxes and fought the uniformed Hitler Youth, and now lives in Berlin as a somewhat mediocre teacher of German and history. He is always eager to talk about his experiences (those of Grass himself) in the war and as a POW, but his real problems are those of the city of Berlin *anno* 1968, when students and the Establishment confront each other about educational policies, Vietnam, and the expected visit of the Shah of Iran. Patiently suffering in the chair of his dentist, who usually quotes Seneca's precepts of equanimity, Starusch, his teeth hurting, fights the good fight for the soul of his talented student Philipp, who in protest against his elders in general, wants to burn his beloved dachshund in front of the famous Kempinski Café, where ladies of the Establishment gorge themselves on cakes topped with a lot of whipped cream. Starusch is afraid that the enraged Berliners (who, he suspects, love dogs more than students) would lynch the young man on the spot. With the help of the dentist and a young girl who likes to quote Mao's warnings against "motley intellectuals," he tries to convince Philipp to devote his energies to a more useful project, perhaps editing a student newspaper. Philipp finally agrees to abandon the dachshund auto-da-fé, but for his own reasons: he does not want to fulfill the expectations of the "beautiful people" on the left, or one day to resemble his fatherly friend who, he feels, has nothing left in his middle age but to tell heroic stories about the Duster Gang. We are not just moving from historical Danzig to contemporary Berlin; the two different worlds are continually present. Starusch, the teller of tales, is not only a character with a distinct function in the sequence of events but also, perhaps more important, an epic label for a rapidly expanding consciousness in which Seneca and Marx, past and present, soldiers and dentists, liberals and radicals have a nervous and disturbing copresence in suspended time. Nietzsche is often alluded to, half ironically, half seriously, and for good reason, since we are approaching a kind of history that has come to a stop and is beginning to repeat itself. Starusch, a left-of-center educator, may still believe in step-by-step social progress, but he cannot rid himself of an instinctive perception of history as cycle: the melancholy conflict between what he thinks as a politically conscious citizen and what he feels in his bones remains totally unresolved.

IN DEFENSE OF THE FLOUNDER

Grass himself has said in an American interview that he first conceived the idea for *The Flounder* when, traveling as a campaign speaker, he felt the urge to get away from it all. He needed more than five years to complete this much-disputed novel, which was an immediate best-seller in West Germany and elsewhere. I would like to suggest that he initially intended to write a prose epic about the primary role of food in world history, but that at a later stage, coming to grips with an irrepressible crew of formidable women, some fictional and some real, who did the world's important cooking, he confronted recent feminist ideas about women in culture at large. *The Flounder* is an ample, exuberant, and skillfully structured narrative about eating, cooking, procreating, women, men, and a cunning fish who represents the male principle and offers philosophical advice of a dubious kind. Grass manages all these interests by working with three strains, each with many ramifications: the narrator talks excitedly to his wife Ilsebill, who is expecting his child; he tells the individual stories of nine or eleven cooks (the number depends on the method of counting) who have creatively excelled in culinary expertise, though of a particular kind, throughout the ages; and, last but not least, he offers a report of how the cunning Flounder, who once advocated the emancipation of men from matriarchy and later offered his services to women, was put on trial by a group of German feminists. The time narrated spans millennia from the Stone Age down to our own century, but in the storyteller's consciousness "past, present, and future happen simultaneously," as Grass assured an American critic, and we have to accept his authorial claim that all major figures of the narrative have a recurrent life and are incarnated in different periods. Our contemporary, the storyteller, identifies for instance with rustic Edek, an exemplary if somewhat slow-witted Stone Age male, and with almost any other male in history, while his Ilsebill of the blessed womb is none other than the Stone Age goddess Awa of the triple bosom, as well as the president of the feminist tribunal examining the historical crimes of the philosopher-fish.

On page 1 of chapter 1, the narrator and his Ilsebill decide to have a child, enjoy an energizing dish of shoulder of mutton with pears and beans, and make love. The subsequent nine months of Ilsebill's pregnancy give the narrator his chance to talk about all the admirable women cooks from the Stone Age down to the present, all living and toiling, it so happens, in the Danzig region, old or new. In analogy to the individual chapters of

Joyce's *Ulysses*, each narrated in a particular mode and using a central symbol, we move here in a similar if more diffuse way from cook to cook, from period to period, and from one preferred dish to another. Awa, Wigga, and Mestwina (who killed the Christian missionary Adalbert of Prague with a wooden spoon) are the three goddesses of the earliest time, cooking from about 2300 B.C. to A.D. 997; their essential nourishments offered to the yet docile males of the tribe are primal milk pap, fish, and a kind of ancient yogurt, respectively. The High Gothic of ecstasies and lean spires is represented by the cold mystic Dorothea von Montau (1340–94), responsible for a complex menu of spiritual Lenten fare, while the contrasting age of the Reformation is amply incarnated in the abbess Margarete Rusch (of expansive appetites in bed and at the table), who wants her geese fat and her farts to roll like thunder (she is Grass's particular pet). Subsequent ages tend to more fragile, tender, and politically conscious women. Agnes Kurbiella serves two aging Baroque artists, warming their beds with her own body and preparing a fine repertory of wholesome diet dishes before she is burned at the stake as a witch. Amanda Woyke, who represents the enlightened age of Frederick the Great, seizes on the newly imported potato, exchanges letters with Count Rumford of the famous soup, and delights in preparing all kinds of potato dishes for underprivileged farm workers. Sophie Rotzoll, a secret Jacobin of the Napoleonic age, specializes in mushrooms and nearly succeeds in poisoning the French governor of Danzig, who continues to keep her lover, a onetime student radical, rotting in prison. And Lena Stubbe, a kind of Mother Courage of the old German Social Democracy in the age of August Bebel, believes in hearty soups for the working masses and dreams of a proletarian cookbook but dies, over eighty years old, in the Nazi concentration camp of Stutthoff near Danzig. Women numbers ten and eleven are personally very close to the narrator and make appearances of a somewhat different kind. Billy, a young woman, is raped and murdered by a group of motorcycle thugs in 1962 (we hear little about her cooking), while Maria Kuczorra, the narrator's distant Polish cousin, works as an efficient canteen manager in the shipyards of Gdansk, feeding pork chops and cabbage to the restive workers who rise against the government in December 1970 (her lover Jan is shot in the stomach by the militia and dies).

Grass's contribution to a history of cooking is clearly of a populist kind; he once alludes to Claude Lévi-Strauss but prefers his own brand of binary oppositions, clearly implied in his stories. On the negative if not wicked side are the male cooks who work for emperors, Hilton chains, and three-star restaurants and are responsible for the haute cuisine that flourishes in feudal societies. On the more glorious side are ranged ethnic and peasant women cooks of eastern and northern Europe, close to the earth and the sea, who watch over their steaming pots (never mind the beneficial garlic) and provide for the tribe, the large family, the workers in factory canteens, the crowds of poor relatives at a groaning board. In our age of culinary democracy it is precisely Grass's binary opposition that, I suspect, challenged many of his feminist readers, and legitimately so.

Grass has long been obsessed by ichthyological myths (sustained by childhood memories of the Baltic shore and his reading of Herman Melville), and by an aversion to German or rather Hegelian attempts to discover meaning in progressing history. The talking Flounder, who keeps the ideological arguments going throughout all history and nine months of pregnancy, comes close to being a kind of Moby Dick in reduced if not provincial circumstances, oozing dialectics from every fin. He (in German, "Der *Butt*") is terribly loquacious and on occasion enriches his Hegelian discourse with pedantic snatches from the later Thomas Mann and learned allusions to Freud, Heidegger, and the philosophical Marxist Ernst Bloch. But his wit, though dampened by historical experience, does not inevitably endear him to the feminists, who cannot forgive him his first literary appearance, in a Grimm fairy tale in which a fisherman is superior to his wife, who is greedy, irritable, and generally unbearable. (He insists that in an original version it is the other way around.) As a Mephistophelian mentor, he teaches his Kashubian Faust (who takes his time to wean himself away from the comfortable bosom of nature) how to count, how to deal with abstract concepts, and how to engineer world history. The fish allows himself to be caught by a trio of vacationing Berlin feminists and, switching allegiance, offers his services as philosophical adviser to the movement. The feminists, however, put him on trial, and in a speech of great rhetorical splendor he just barely succeeds in appealing at least to the moderates among his judges. After a meal to celebrate the symbolic annihilation of the male fish, he is returned to the watery element, in spite of all the attempts by the more radical feminists to do away with him entirely.

Critics on both sides of the Atlantic have been at odds in dealing with this novel that so adamantly refuses to be one. Grass's chaos of seemingly unkempt inventions hides rather than reveals any principle of order. His pastiches and parodies come in avalanches that overwhelm by their mass, but we would be wrong to underrate the marvelous precision of his language collages. Grass himself ironically characterizes something of his own procedures when he describes Margarete Rusch's table conversations or rather monologues as "subliminal nibblings with subplots as intricate as the politics of her time," and when he praises her, Gargantua's German sister, for her wondrous ability to "reel off several stories—and instructive disquisitions—at once without dropping a thread." Whether or not *The Flounder* is an efficiently ordered narrative can be decided, if at all, only in terms of Döblin's futurist theory of the new novel.

Grass has never avoided controversy, but I wonder whether he expected that his populist commitment to heroic women cooks would provoke the feminists to question the novel's ideology and its author's civic virtues. The narrator does not explicitly say that women *have* to cook, make love to men loyally or not, and/or give birth to children, but in his epic universe that is what they ultimately do whenever they are truly admirable. Even if a woman happens to be a saint of the faith (Dorothea von Montau was canonized by the Church a few weeks after the novel was published) or, as is the case with Lena Stubbe, a saint of the Social Democracy, we are constantly prompted to look closely at her culinary expertise as totally expressive of her experience, while the men scurry around in history organizing civilization—or, as the Flounder says, tongue in gills, in his first speech to the tribunal: "The oppressed male terminated many thousands of years of historyless female domination by resisting the servitude of nature, by establishing principles of order, replacing incestuous and therefore chaotic matriarchy, with the discipline of patriarchy, by introducing Apollonian reason, by beginning to think up Utopias, to take action, and to make history." There is little evidence in the text that the narrator would basically disagree with the Flounder's proclamation that women embody life in an ontological sense, and that men, biologically underdeveloped because they cannot give birth, have to be busy with ersatz creations like the Strasbourg cathedral, the diesel engine, the theory of relativity, the gas mask, Watergate, and a semiotic universe of mere signs devoid of all substance. The question is whether these ideas imply a desire for restored matriarchy, or the latent frustrations of a narrator longing to return to the Great Kashubian Womb.

In chapter 8, structurally isolated from the context of the narrative and of particular importance, Grass reveals more fully than elsewhere what he thinks has changed in the relationship of the sexes and why he feels at a loss. While I concede that one may well detect the voice of the frustrated macho, I am also convinced that he tells the story with such power, precision of language, and melancholy energy that his warnings cannot easily be dismissed. Chapter 8 is about nature violently defiled in many ways. The four young Berlin women who on Father's Day 1962 decide to go on an excursion to the suburban Grunewald Forest (then teeming with hordes of males) were once, as the narrator says, "intelligent and normally high-strung girls, who fled to their own sex after too much experience with idiotic boys and boring men." Now they affect the most vulgar habits of their masculine adversaries and decide to love each other rather than men of the narrator's kind. The four women camp near a lake and try to outdo the male groups all around, drinking hard and showing off their muscular strength. They also test each other: there is fierce emotional tension, and Siggi, who was once the narrator's fiancée, is violated by the other three, who want to celebrate a "surreal act of procreation that requests only the barest imitation of nature." When Siggi staggers away from the campsite, she runs into a group of motorcyclists in black leather jackets who gang-rape and finally kill her, running their motorcycles over her prostrate body. I know of no other prose chapter in Grass's writings that has similar force; we of either sex would be insensitive not to feel the elemental sadness articulated here in a surprisingly harsh way. Ideas about what is "natural" to men and women are open to ideological discussion, but it would be difficult to argue against the suggestion of the chapter itself that something important may have been lost in a world in which the sexes "crawl into themselves"—understanding, closeness, compassion, charity, call it what you will.

GRASS IN THE EIGHTIES

After concentrating on *The Flounder*, Grass returned to the political scene again, but at some distance from the mainstream Social Democrats and closer to citizen's groups concerned with questions of the environment and protesting the construction of atomic reactors, the placement of cruise missiles on West German soil, and U.S. foreign policy endangering the spirit of détente. He affirmed his commitment to a democratic socialism, but unfortunately began questioning the legacy of the Enlightenment, identifying it too quickly with the pernicious advances of technology; more resolutely than in earlier years, he warned the federal government, then headed by his fellow Socialist Helmut Schmidt, not to be drawn by the United States, long deprived of its privilege to appeal to morality, into a course of action that "could result in the destruction of all life on the planet." In *Das Treffen in Telgte* (1979; *The Meeting at Telgte*, 1981) he loyally celebrated the literary importance of Group 47. But in *Kopfgeburten* (1980; *Headbirths*, 1982) he turned to matters less literary. Going back to structural principles first tested in the 1960s, he used a personal and fictional strain of narratives to consider the social and political issues of the moment, combining, toying, reporting, and freely imagining. Grass travels with the film producer Volker Schlöndorff (who made the movie of *The Tin Drum*) in the Far East, and invents two young people, married teachers who intensely remember the days of the student revolt. He sends them to India, Bali, and Singapore, listens to their conversations, replete with the terminology of '68, and with loving irony participates in their ongoing dialogue about having or not having a child these days. (The two are not bright enough to interest me for long, however; for once, Grass's intimate memories of recent events, among them his meetings with the dying poet Nicolas Born, are far more rewarding than the slapdash fiction.) In his political statements of the early eighties, Grass has gone far beyond his ideas of the seventies and those suggested in *Headbirths*. In earlier years he spoke about the gap between the spirit and the realities of the federal constitution, to be bridged by patient reform. More recently, however, he has come to take an angrier, if not apocalyptic stand, asking young citizens to refuse to serve in the Bundeswehr because, after the stationing of cruise missiles in West Germany in submission to U.S. strategies, the West German army has become an instrument of aggression, violating the federal constitution. He advocates an attitude of equidistance from the "infantile" superpowers who "want to be loved," compares the Polish Solidarity movement to the Nicaraguan Sandinistas (a particular piece of surrealist fiction), and has little to say about the GDR peace movement, unprotected by constitutional guarantees.

Grass articulates his new political concerns, intensified by an overwhelming anxiety about the future of Germany in a nuclear conflict between the superpowers, in his recent novel *Die Rättin* (1985; *The Rat*, due 1987), published after a longish writing pause in which he renewed his creative interest in sculpture and printmaking. Four or possibly five stories are presented synchronically in a broad panorama (again following Döblin). Grass binds them all closely together by his vision of a nuclear explosion triggered by the impersonal computers of West and East, destroying all human life as we have known it: the earth is given over to the tribes of more resilient rats who, sole heirs to humanity, continue history without history. In spite of the cosmic range of events, Grass does not really move away from his Danzig home ground and the Baltic Sea. If, in the Danzig trilogy proper (*The Tin Drum*, *Cat and Mouse*, and *Dog Years*), he delineated the presence of the city in the period of the Nazi dictatorship and World War II, and in *The Flounder* went far into the past of the Danzig region (matriarchy, the Stone Age, Gothic spires, and all that), he now turns to the terrifying future, starting with sudden and ominous lightning on the horizon, mushroom clouds over the sea, storms of fire and radioactive dust changing humanity into heaps of "dejuiced" stiffs, the brief appearance of mutants, and their annihilation by the triumphant rats competing for food and territories. Grass ultimately leaves in abeyance the question whether it is the narrator who tells us his nightmares about what is going to happen, or the clever and articulate Rat who, dreaming about the narrator Grass, recounts the last chapter, our own *Menschendämmerung*. The philosophical Flounder still had rational reasons to believe that it would make a difference to mankind if the sterile dominance of males gave way to gynocracy, but now the mood has totally darkened: the Rat has no illusions about people anymore, male or female—gone, *perdu, Schluss, Aus!*

The dialogues proceed between the irritated and defensive author, clinging to human realities by listening to German *Kultur* broadcasts (if not, in his nightmare, floating in a space capsule over the devastated earth), and the self-assured Rat who (occasionally falling back on her primal language, which sounds like an ingenious mixture of North German *Platt* and Hebrew) proudly recounts the vicissitudes of the rats. Their dialogues constitute a central field of narrative energy, creating the basic configuration of other epic elements. As elsewhere in Grass's novels, these plots and stories struggle for their own autonomy. In one important strain of the narrative, a group of five bold women set out on a refurbished ship ostensibly to do marine research. Urged on by their captain (who may or may not consult the famous Flounder swimming close to the ship), they are really seeking the mystical city of Vineta in order to establish their "Feminal City," the ultimate community of free women. However, the women feel increasingly frustrated by group tensions developing in their close quarters and are, perhaps, even a little bored by the monotony of their life between heaven and the sea—a skeptical view of their group experience certain to challenge the feminist critics who will be provoked, anyway, by the usual macho insistence of the narrator that he has slept with most of them.

In other playful sections, and much to the enjoyment of the reader (especially the Grass connoisseur who recalls his other novels), Oskar Matzerath makes his reappearance, sixtyish, balding, sans tin drum but plagued by prostate troubles and very much concerned with the sins of his past, about which he does not want to speak unduly. He too, of course, cannot rid himself of his Danzig obsessions. He travels in his Mercedes (for he is now the successful boss of an outfit producing video movies) to his old Kashubian haunts to attend the 107th birthday of his grandmother Anna Koljaiczek (once of the ample skirts). There he meets members of the Koljaiczek clan recently dispersed all over the world, and untiringly discusses, with his old friend the narrator, two video treatments incorporated into the book more or less in full. The one, rather extensive, sketches in a kind of grotesque music-hall *revue* of many surprising reversals and gags, the re-greening of Germany by the concerted action of all the personae of the Grimm fairy tales and others, including Rumpelstiltskin, Little Red Ridinghood, the Witch, and the Brothers Grimm themselves as new ministers of the environment in the Bonn government. The other one tells us about the career of a North German artist named Lothar Malskat who in the 1950s successfully forged early Gothic church paintings but then, unable to bear the thought of deceiving people, gave himself up to the police and confessed.

Much of the astonishing vitality of the book again springs from the surreal coexistence of people and animals; from the montage of time perspectives (in one episode we are told how, at the insistence of the parents, the Pied Piper rid the town of Hamelin of their punk children, who had taken up with the rats); from the literary collage of fictions (Brothers Grimm and Grass); and, as elsewhere in his novels, from individual characters who insist on their independence from the novel's overall context. Yet I feel that the novelist's art—for all its skill in developing surprising situations, including the sad and marvelous appearance of the "Watsoncrick" rat/people mutants of curiously Social Democratic habits—prefers, formally, to consolidate narrative structures and achievements well tested in Grass's works of the seventies and before, rather than to challenge the reader by striking out into radically new ventures of idiomatic and epic arrangement. In his most somber mood, Grass wants to warn his reader about the dangers of the future. The message prevails, and I am struck by the paradoxically conservative quality of the book, which clearly avoids the provocations (sexual and otherwise) that so often irritated traditionalist readers in the past (the fairy-tale "Greens' " use of witches' piss in their car when driving to Bonn will raise few eyebrows today). As *praeceptor Germaniae*, Grass for once holds his imaginative powers on a short if not too short leash, in order to communicate his message to a middle group of readers who have to be told it with a certain straightforwardness and almost folksy clarity. He spins out his phantasmata of black humor with a sure hand, and his usual lists and catalogues (mobilizing all the forces of the idiom) have inventive wit, yet the central figures are not often allowed to play their games against the ideological intentions of the author (as they often do in *The Flounder*). The exuberance of his Big Bang baroque, of people and rats, is counteracted every so often by the gestures of the schoolmaster who, constantly protesting against the didactic temper of his human and zoological characters, explains much of what happens in terms of an allegory of definite political meanings—meanings largely coinciding with the ideas of the 1980s peace movement, pushing its visions of a serene German *Heimatland* that is free of submission to the United States and the Soviet Union, so indistinguishable from each other. Even the painter Malskat, one of the most interesting and "realistic" figures of the narrative, ultimately appears to be a contemporary of the mendacious politicians Konrad Adenauer and Walter Ulbricht (though as an artist he has the courage to tell the truth). As readers, we do not always enjoy the wide range of interpretive privileges granted us in the earlier novels.

We are all fond of Grass's moustached trade image (in the sixties, nearly identical with the bear in the Berlin city escutcheon), but I would not underrate the unresolved contradictions of his sensibilities and social commitments. He is an extremely vulnerable artist possessed by an inchoate imagination that expresses itself in entire image syndromes: nurses, fish, cooks, teeth, and more recently rats. His fundamental problem as a writer lies in the tendency of the rich and linguistically innovative force of his creative appetites to run wild and cultivate disparities, gags, and puns in improvised but inconsequential fireworks. From his younger years on, in his poems and perhaps in his graphic art as well, as a late surrealist he rejected the nineteenth-century conventions of realism, yet did not want to give up his sober probing of the German or rather Danzig past that he knows best. For some time he tended toward a narrative technique close to the picaresque novel, perhaps with a few surrealist interpolations, eager to observe the petty bourgeois at close range, and by using dubious narrators all burdened with terrible responsibilities, he kept his own perspective cool and firm. Being a realist in temper but not in method, he never demonized the Nazis, as Thomas Mann did in *Doktor Faustus*, nor did he put them in neat theoretical pigeonholes, as did Brecht; rather, he revealed the true face of small-town evil, the daily betrayal, the shabby drive for murderous power, the unadulterated greed.

Grass belongs to the generation of returning young soldiers whose instinctive ideology it was to oppose all ideologies, but when the Social Democrats redefined their program in populist terms and the Wall went up in Berlin, he committed himself to working for a pragmatic socialism, inevitably alienating himself from the radical students and the APO intelligentsia. In the 1970s and early 1980s he moved closer to the ideas of the peace movement and to a radical critique of U.S. foreign policy. It is another of his paradoxes that as a concerned citizen Grass has committed himself to step-by-step reform of society, while as an artist he has come to believe that utopia and melancholy belong together, and that history moves in recurrences, with oppressors and slaves merely changing names. For reasons perhaps not yet clear to himself, in the 1960s Grass was eager to follow Alfred Döblin's creative example and his theory of the experimental novel as a welcome instrument for defining his own changing views. The principle of simultaneity counteracting linear motion was eminently useful in articulating a frozen if not tragic vision of history, and Döblin's idea of the antipsychological and tectonic novel of many linguistic levels strengthened Grass's hand in dealing with disparate materials in *Local Anaesthetic*, *The Flounder*, *Headbirths*, and *The Rat*. Few writers of his age in Germany are as magnificently gifted as Grass; if he has blood brothers at all, they are Julio Cortázar and Gabriel García Márquez, to be found in the volcanic literatures of Latin America.

Postscript

After a survey of so many books, trends, and events of literary importance, the moment has come to conclude and summarize, but I shall keep my summary brief and submit to the reader a personal reading list accompanied by a selective catalogue of translations.

I am, in literary and other matters, a nominalist by instinct and ideological persuasion, inclined to believe that generalities or summaries covering four literatures over many uneasy years might be too reductive or boring, or both. I will simply say that, in the first twenty years after the war, writers of both East and West were busy restoring lost continuities and traditional genres that, in the mid-sixties, explosively yielded to wider concepts of literature, including systematic experimentation (long anticipated by Arno Schmidt), the documentary mode, and the intimate confession, which were to be of fundamental importance in the seventies and later. Yet if I were to raise questions of achievement and value, I would have to say that the most remarkable genre of the 1950s was poetry, that of the 1960s drama, and that of the 1970s and early 1980s the prose narrative with its many shapes and aims.

Gertrude Stein once suggested that memory, with its particular pressures of involvement, stands in the way of creating true masterpieces, but postwar German writers of two generations were convinced in their guts that it was far less important to create instant masterpieces than to explore memory, however terrifying; to look back in pity and anger and sometimes silence; and after the floods and fires, to ask questions more radical and unsparing than any generation before them had had to ask. From such a tortuous process of questioning, the books of many authors emerged—from Günter Grass to Uwe Johnson, from Paul Celan to Christa Wolf, from Hermann Lenz to Peter Weiss—books providing the ground on which future generations of writers will stand. In the mid-sixties, writing in German turned into a magnificent battlefield on which the energies of the collective and the individual, in many shapes and guises, engaged each other fiercely. In the liberal West, young writers of the restless student generation again disputed the privileges of the individual, while their colleagues in the GDR rediscovered, after many years of prescribed collective orientations, the importance of the imaginative individual—until, in the mid-seventies and beyond, these chiastic patterns of conflict suddenly dissolved into a new kind of subjective, psychological, and frequently anti-intellectual writing often shared on both sides of the Elbe.

It would be difficult to understand the postwar renascence of the poem in German without reading the aging Benn and later Brecht, Ingeborg Bachmann, Wilhelm Lehmann (grievously underrated), and those who developed the tradition of nature poetry in different ways, including Karl Krolow and Peter Huchel. For the time being, Michael Hamburger's bilingual edition of Paul Celan's poetry will serve magnificently (the reader untrained in Celan should start at the beginning and proceed chronologically). My later favorites are Sarah Kirsch, Nicolas Born, Jutta Schutting, and Volker Braun (the poet); instances of their poetry, in German and English, can be conveniently found in Michael Hamburger's anthology, *German Poetry 1910–1975* (1976); the recent collection *Contemporary East German Poetry*, edited by Richard Zipser (1980); and the new anthology *Austrian Poetry Today*, edited by Milne Holton and Herbert Kuhner (1985). A wide-ranging anthology of recent poetry is still missing; for inquisitive readers I mention Karin Kiwus and Michael Buselmeier, who hold great promise for the future.

Most German plays, especially of the last twenty years or so, do not fulfill commercial Broadway expectations, and translations of plays performed by small professional groups and university theaters are rare. Peter Weiss's terrifying work *The Investigation* and Rolf Hochhuth's *The Deputy* (as a play, on the traditional side) should be reread by anybody concerned with what happened in Auschwitz and other concentration camps. My choices among more recent plays would include F. X. Kroetz's *Men's Business* and *Farmyard*, intense and compassionate despite appearances, and Botho Strauss's *Big and Little*, which reveals much of his imaginative gifts and the questions burdening the younger professionals in contemporary Western society. We are fortunate that Michael Roloff, Gitta Honegger, and Carl Weber often combine their work as innovative directors with translating Handke, Bernhard, and Heiner Müller. I confess that I consider Müller's *Philoctetes* the most remarkable play of the new German theater. It was translated by Oscar Mandel (1981), and a collection of Müller's other "texts for the stage," many of which I have discussed, has been translated by Carl Weber (1984).

New German, Austrian, and sometimes Swiss novels and stories are more readily available in translation. My list of the twelve best (from 1945 until recently) includes Heimito von Doderer's *The Demons*, a massive narrative about the emergence of murderous ideologies in Vienna; Theodor Plievier's *Stalingrad*; Gerd Gaiser's *The Last Squadron*; and Elisabeth Langgässer's *The Quest*—all novels about World War II or the summer after the liberation. My list also includes four novels about growing up in Nazi Germany and the Federal Republic: Günter Grass's "classic" *The Tin Drum*; Uwe Johnson's *Anniversaries*, combining exact views of North Germany under Nazi and SED rule and New York in the late 1960s; Heinrich Böll's *Group Portrait with Lady*, particularly rich in illuminating details about daily life on the home front; and Hermann Lenz's *Im innern Bezirk (In the Inner Sphere)*, which has yet to be translated. More intimate in their concerns are three novels about the search for identity: Max Frisch's *Gantenbein*, Christa Wolf's *The Quest for Christa T.*, and Thomas Bernhard's *The Correction*. Finally, Gabriele Wohmann's *Frühherbst in Badenweiler* (*Early Fall in Badenweiler*), also untranslated, is one of the rare sophisticated comedies of intellectual manners to come out of Germany. Those readers interested in new writing in German may wish to read or subscribe to *Dimension*, a periodical edited by A. Leslie Wilson (University of Texas Press), loyally serving the cause of younger and older writers of the German language overseas.

Selected Bibliography of Translations

COLLECTIONS

Hamburger, Michael. *German Poetry 1910–1975: An Anthology*. New York, 1976.
———. *Modern German Poetry, 1910–1960*. London, 1962.
Holton, Milne, and Herbert Kuhner. *Austrian Poetry Today*. New York, 1975.
Zipser, Richard A. *Contemporary East German Poetry*. Oberlin, Ohio, 1980. Special issue of *Field*.

AICHINGER, ILSE

Herod's Children. Trans. Cornelia Schaeffer. New York, 1963.

ANDERSCH, ALFRED

The Cherries of Freedom. In *My Disappearance in Providence, and Other Stories*. Trans. Ralph Manheim. Garden City, N.Y., 1978.
Efraim's Book. Trans. Ralph Manheim. Garden City, N.Y., 1970; New York, 1984.
Flight to Afar. Trans. Michael Bullock. New York, 1958.
The Redhead. Trans. Michael Bullock. New York, 1961.
Winterspelt. Trans. Richard and Clara Winston. Garden City, N.Y., 1978.

APITZ, BRUNO

Naked among Wolves. Trans. Edith Anderson. Berlin, 1978.

BACHMANN, INGEBORG

The Thirtieth Year. Trans. Michael Bullock. New York, 1964.

BECKER, JUREK

Jacob the Liar. Trans. Melvin Kornfield. New York, 1975.
Sleepless Days. Trans. Leila Vennewitz. New York, 1979.

BERNHARD, THOMAS

Correction. Trans. Sophie Wilkins. New York, 1978.
Eve of Retirement: A Comedy of the German Soul. In *The President and Eve of Retirement.* Trans. Gitta Honegger. New York, 1982.
Gargoyles. Trans. Richard and Clara Winston. New York, 1970.
Gathering Evidence. Trans. David McLintock. New York, 1985.
The Lime Works. Trans. Sophie Wilkins. New York, 1973.
The President. In *The President and Eve of Retirement.* Trans. Gitta Honegger. New York, 1982.

BIERMANN, WOLF

The Wire Harp. Trans. Eric Bentley. New York, 1968.
Wolf Biermann: Poems and Ballads. Trans. Steve Gooch. London, 1977.

BÖLL, HEINRICH

Absent without Leave. Trans. Leila Vennewitz. London, 1966.
And Never Said a Word. Trans. Leila Vennewitz. New York, 1978.
Billiards at Half-Past Nine. Trans. Patrick Bowles. London, 1961.
The Bread of Those Early Years. Trans. Leila Vennewitz. New York, 1976.
The Clown. Trans. Leila Vennewitz. New York, 1965.
The End of a Mission. Trans. Leila Vennewitz. New York, 1967.
Group Portrait with Lady. Trans. Leila Vennewitz. New York, 1973.
Irish Journal. Trans. Leila Vennewitz. New York, 1967.
The Lost Honor of Katharina Blum. Trans. Leila Vennewitz. New York, 1975.
The Safety Net. Trans. Leila Vennewitz. New York, 1982.
Tomorrow and Yesterday. Trans. not given. New York, Criterion Books, 1957.
The Train Was on Time. Trans. Richard Graves. New York, 1956.

BORN, NICOLAS

The Deception. Trans. Leila Vennewitz. Boston, 1983.

BRUYN, GÜNTER DE

Buridan's Ass. Trans. John Peet. Berlin, 1973.

CANETTI, ELIAS

Auto-da-Fé. Trans. C. V. Wedgewood. New York, 1964.
The Conscience of Words. Trans. Joachim Neugroschel. New York, 1979.
Earwitness: Fifty Characters. Trans. Joachim Neugroschel. New York, 1979.
The Human Province. Trans. Joachim Neugroschel. New York, 1978.
The Play of the Eyes. Trans. Ralph Manheim. New York, 1985.
The Plays of Elias Canetti. Trans. Gitta Honegger. New York, 1984.
The Tongue Set Free: Remembrance of a European Childhood. Trans. Joachim Neugroschel. New York, 1979.
The Torch in My Ear. Trans. Joachim Neugroschel. New York, 1982.

The Voices of Marrakesh: A Record of a Visit. Trans. J. A. Underwood. New York, 1978.

CELAN, PAUL

Paul Celan: Poems. Trans. Michael Hamburger. New York, 1980.
Selected Poems. Trans. Michael Hamburger and Christopher Middleton. Harmondsworth, 1972.
Speech-Grille and Selected Poems. Trans. Joachim Neugroschel. New York, 1971.

DODERER, HEIMITO VON

The Demons. Trans. Richard and Clara Winston. New York, 1961.

ENZENSBERGER, HANS MAGNUS

The Havana Inquiry. Trans. Peter Mayer. New York, 1974.
Poems for People Who Don't Read Poems. Trans. Michael Hamburger, Jerome Rothenberg, and the author. New York, 1967.
The Sinking of the Titanic. Trans. the author. Boston, 1980.

FRIED, ERICH

Last Honours. Trans. Georg Rapp. London, 1968.
One Hundred Poems without a Country. Trans. Stuart Hood. New York, 1980.
On Pain of Seeing. Trans. Georg Rapp. Chicago, 1969.

FRIES, FRITZ RUDOLF

The Road to Oobliadooh. Trans. Leila Vennewitz. New York, 1968.

FRISCH, MAX

Andorra. In *Three Plays.* Trans. Michael Bullock. London, 1962.
Biography: A Game. Trans. Michael Bullock, New York, 1969.
Bluebeard: A Tale. Trans. Geoffrey Skelton. New York, 1983.
Count Oederland. In *Three Plays.* Trans. Michael Bullock, London, 1962.
Don Juan, or the Love of Geometry. In *Three Plays.* Trans. James L. Rosenberg. New York, 1967.
The Firebugs: A Learning-Play without a Lesson. Trans. Mordecai Gorelik. New York, 1959.
Gantenbein. Trans. Michael Bullock. New York, 1982.
The Great Fury of Philipp Hotz. In *Postwar German Theatre: An Anthology of Plays.* Trans. Michael Benedikt and George E. Wellwarth. New York, 1967.
The Chinese Wall. Trans. James L. Rosenberg. New York, 1961. Also in *Four Plays.* Trans. Michael Bullock. London, 1969.
Homo Faber. Trans. Michael Bullock. New York, 1959.
I'm Not Stiller. Trans. Michael Bullock. New York, 1958.
Man in the Holocene. Trans. Geoffrey Skelton. New York, 1980.
Montauk. Trans. Geoffrey Skelton, New York, 1976.
Now They Sing Again. In *The Contemporary German Theater.* Trans. Michael Roloff. New York, 1972.
Sketchbook 1946–1949. Trans. Geoffrey Skelton. New York, 1977.
Sketchbook 1966–1971. Trans. Geoffrey Skelton. New York, 1974.

Triptych. Trans. Geoffrey Skelton. New York, 1981.
When the War Was Over. In *Three Plays.* Trans. James L. Rosenberg. New York, 1967.

FÜHMANN, FRANZ

The Car with the Yellow Star: Fourteen Days out of Two Decades. Trans. not given. Berlin, 1968.

GAISER, GERD

The Final Ball. Trans. Marguerite Waldman. New York, 1960.
The Last Squadron. Trans. Paul Findlay. New York, 1956.

GRASS, GÜNTER

Cat and Mouse. Trans. Ralph Manheim. New York, 1963.
Dog Years. Trans. Ralph Manheim. New York, 1965.
The Flounder. Trans. Ralph Manheim. New York, 1978.
From the Diary of a Snail. Trans. Ralph Manheim. New York, 1973.
Headbirths, or the Germans Are Dying Out. Trans. Ralph Manheim. New York, 1982.
New Poems. Trans. Michael Hamburger. New York, 1968.
Local Anaesthetic. Trans. Ralph Manheim. New York, 1970.
The Meeting at Telgte. Trans. Ralph Manheim. New York, 1981.
On Writing and Politics. Trans. Ralph Manheim. New York, 1985.
The Plebeians Rehearse the Uprising: a German Tragedy. Trans. Ralph Manheim. New York, 1966.
The Rat. Trans. Ralph Manheim. New York, due 1987.
Rocking Back and Forth. In *Postwar German Theatre: An Anthology of Plays.* Trans. Michael Benedikt and George E. Wellwarth. New York, 1967.
The Tin Drum. Trans. Ralph Manheim. New York, 1962.
The Wicked Cooks. In *Four Plays.* Trans. A. Leslie Wilson. New York, 1967.

HANDKE, PETER

Childstory. In *Slow Homecoming.* Trans. Ralph Manheim. New York, 1985.
The Goalie's Anxiety at the Penalty Kick. Trans. Michael Roloff. New York, 1972.
The Innerworld of the Outerworld of the Innerworld. Trans. Michael Roloff. New York, 1974.
Kaspar. In *Kaspar and Other Plays.* Trans. Michael Roloff. New York, 1969.
The Left-Handed Woman. Trans. Ralph Manheim. New York, 1978.
The Lesson of Mont-Sainte-Victoire. In *Slow Homecoming.* Trans. Ralph Manheim. New York, 1985.
A Moment of True Feeling. Trans. Ralph Manheim. New York, 1977.
My Foot My Tutor. In *Shakespeare the Sadist.* Ed. Renata and Martin Esslin. Trans. Michael Roloff. London, 1977.
Nonsense and Happiness. Trans. Michael Roloff. New York, 1976.
Offending the Audience. In *Kaspar and Other Plays.* Trans. Michael Roloff. New York, 1969.
The Ride across Lake Constance. In *The Contemporary German Theater.* Ed. Michael Roloff. New York, 1972.

Self-Accusation. In *Kaspar and Other Plays*. Trans. Michael Roloff. New York, 1969.
Short Letter, Long Farewell. Trans. Ralph Manheim. New York, 1974.
Slow Homecoming. In *Slow Homecoming*. Trans. Ralph Manheim. New York, 1985.
A Sorrow beyond Dreams. Trans. Ralph Manheim. New York, 1975.
They Are Dying Out. Trans. Michael Roloff. London, 1974.
The Weight of the World. Trans. Ralph Manheim. New York, 1984.

HEISSENBÜTTEL, HELMUT

Texts. (Selections.) Trans. Michael Hamburger. London, 1977.

HEYM, STEFAN [original texts in English, written by the author]

Collin. Secaucus, N.J., 1980.
The King David Report. New York, 1973.
Uncertain Friend [*Lassalle*]. London, 1969.
The Wandering Jew. New York, 1984.

HILDESHEIMER, WOLFGANG

Nightpiece. In *Postwar German Theatre: An Anthology of Plays*. Trans. Michael Benedikt and George E. Wellwarth. New York, 1967.

HOCHHUTH, ROLF

The Deputy. Trans. Richard and Clara Winston. New York, 1964.
A German Love Story. Trans. John Brownjohn. Boston, 1980.
Soldiers: An Obituary for Geneva. Trans. Robert David MacDonald. New York, 1968.

HUCHEL, PETER

The Garden of Theophrastus and Other Poems. Trans. Michael Hamburger. Manchester, 1983.
Selected Poems. Trans. Michael Hamburger. Cheadle, England, 1974.

INNERHOFER, FRANZ

Beautiful Days. Trans. Anselm Hollo. New York, 1976.

JOHNSON, UWE

An Absence. Trans. Richard and Clara Winston. London, 1969.
Anniversaries: From the Life of Gesine Cresspahl. Trans. Leila Vennewitz. New York, 1975. (Translation of vol. 1 and part of vol. 2 of *Jahrestage*; the remainder, trans. Leila Vennewitz and Walter Arndt, due 1987.)
Speculations about Jacob. Trans. Ursule Molinaro. New York, 1963.
The Third Book about Achim. Trans. not given. New York, 1967.
Two Views. Trans. Richard and Clara Winston, 1966.

KASCHNITZ, MARIE LUISE

Long Shadows. In *German Women Writers of the Twentieth Century*. Trans. Elisabeth Rütschi and Edna Huttenmaier Spitz. New York, 1978.

Selected Later Poems of Marie Luise Kaschnitz. Trans. Lisel Mueller. Princeton, N.J., 1980.
Whether or Not. Trans. Lisel Mueller. La Crosse, Wis., 1984.

KIPPHARDT, HEINAR

In the Matter of J. Robert Oppenheimer. Trans. Ruth Speirs. New York, 1968.

KIRSCH, SARAH

Conjurations: The Poems of Sarah Kirsch. Trans. Wayne Kuam. Athens, Ohio, 1984.

KLUGE, ALEXANDER

Attendance List for a Funeral. Trans. Leila Vennewitz. New York, 1966.
The Battle. Trans. Leila Vennewitz. New York, 1967.

KROETZ, FRANZ XAVER

Farmyard. [*Stallerhof*]. In *Farmyard, and Four Other Plays*. Trans. Michael Roloff and Jack Gelber. New York, 1976.
A Man, a Dictionary. In *Farmyard, and Four Other Plays*. Trans. Michael Roloff and Carl Weber. New York, 1976.
Men's Business. In *Farmyard, and Four Other Plays*. Trans. Michael Roloff and Carl Weber. New York, 1976.
Michi's Blood. In *Farmyard, and Four Other Plays*. Trans. Michael Roloff and Denis Gordon. New York, 1976.
Request Concert. In *Farmyard, and Four Other Plays*. Trans. Peter Sonder. New York, 1976.

KOGON, EUGEN

The Theory and Practice of Hell: The German Concentration Camps and the System behind Them. Trans. Heinz Norden. New York, 1973.

KROLOW, KARL

Foreign Bodies: Poems. Trans. Michael Bullock. Athens, Ohio, 1969.
Invisible Hands. Trans. Michael Bullock. London, 1969.
Poems against Death. Trans. Herman Salinger. Washington, 1969.

LANGGÄSSER, ELISABETH

The Quest. Trans. Jane Bannard Greene. New York, 1953.

LENZ, SIEGFRIED

The German Lesson. Trans. Ernst Kaiser and Eithne Wilkins. New York, 1971.
The Lightship. Trans. Michael Bullock. New York, 1962.
The Survivor. Trans. Michael Bullock. New York, 1965.

MÜLLER, HEINER

The Correction. In *Hamletmachine and Other Texts for the Stage*. Trans. Carl Weber. New York, 1984.

Hamletmachine. In *Hamletmachine and Other Texts for the Stage*. Trans. Carl Weber. New York, 1984.
Gundling's Life Frederick of Prussia Lessing's Sleep Dream Scream. In *Hamletmachine and Other Texts for the Stage*. Trans. Carl Weber. New York, 1984.
Philoctetes. In *Philoctetes and the Fall of Troy*. Trans. Oscar Mandel. Lincoln, Nebr., 1981.
Quartet. In *Hamletmachine and Other Texts for the Stage*. Trans. Carl Weber. New York, 1984.

MUSCHG, ADOLF

The Blue Man and Other Stories. Trans. Marlis Zeller Cambon and Michael Hamburger. New York, 1985. Also Manchester, 1983.

PEDRETTI, ERICA

Stones, or the Destruction of the Child Karl and Other Characters. Trans. Judith L. Black. New York, 1982.

PLIEVIER, THEODOR

Stalingrad. Trans. Richard and Clara Winston. New York, 1948.

REINIG, CHRISTA

Vocational Counselling. In *German Women Writers of the Twentieth Century*. Trans. Elisabeth Rütschi and Edna Huttenmaier Spitz. New York, 1978.

SCHMIDT, ARNO

The Egghead Republic. Trans. Michael Horowitz. London, 1979.
Evening Edged in Gold. Trans. John E. Woods. New York, 1980.
Scenes from the Life of a Faun. Trans. John E. Woods. New York, 1983.

SEGHERS, ANNA

The Dead Stay Young. Boston, 1950.
The Excursion of the Dead Girls. In *German Woman Writers of the Twentieth Century*. Trans. Elisabeth Rütschi and Edna Huttenmaier Spitz. New York, 1978.
The Seventh Cross. Trans. James A. Galston. Boston, 1942.

SPEER, MARTIN

Hunting Scenes from Lower Bavaria. In *The Contemporary German Theater*. Ed. Michael Roloff. Trans. Christopher Holme. New York, 1972.

STEFAN, VERENA

Shedding. Trans. Johanna Moore and Beth Weckmueller. New York, 1978. The introduction to *Shedding* has been translated in *German Feminism: Readings in Politics and Literature*. Ed. Edith H. Altbach et al. Albany, 1984.

STRAUSS, BOTHO

Big and Little. Trans. Anne Cattaneo. New York, 1979.
Devotion. Trans. Sophie Wilkins. New York, 1979.
Tumult. Trans. Michael Hulse. Manchester, 1984.

WALSER, MARTIN

Breakers. Trans. Leila Vennewitz. New York, due 1987.
The Detour. In *Plays*. Trans. Richard Grunberger. London, 1963.
Home Front. In *The Contemporary German Theater*. Ed. Michael Roloff. New York, 1972.
The Inner Man. Trans. Leila Vennewitz. New York, 1984.
The Rabbit Race. In *Plays*. Adapted by Ronald Duncan. London, 1963.
Runaway Horse. Trans. Leila Vennewitz. New York, 1980.
The Swan Villa. Trans. Leila Vennewitz. New York, 1982.
The Unicorn. Trans. Barrie Ellis-Jones. London, 1971.

WEISS, PETER

Bodies and Shadows. Trans. E. B. Garside and Rosemarie Waldrop. New York, 1969. Later translated as *The Conversation of the Three Walkers and the Shadow of the Coachman's Body*. Trans. S. M. Cupitt. London, 1972.
Discourse on Vietnam. Trans. Geoffrey Skelton. London, 1970.
How Mister Mockingpott Was Cured of his Sufferings. In *The Contemporary German Theater*. Ed. Michael Roloff. New York, 1972.
The Investigation. Trans. Jon Swan and Ulu Grosbard. New York, 1966.
The Leavetaking. Trans. Christopher Levenson. New York, 1962.
Marat/Sade. Trans. Geoffrey Skelton. New York, 1965.
Song of the Lusitanian Bogey. In *Two Plays*. Trans. Lee Baxandall. New York, 1970.
The Tower. In *Postwar German Theatre: An Anthology of Plays*. Trans. Michael Benedikt and George E. Wellwarth. New York, 1967.
Trotsky in Exile. Trans. Geoffrey Skelton. New York, 1971.
Vanishing Point. In *Leavetaking and Vanishing Point*. Trans. Christopher Levenson. New York, 1966.

WOHMANN, GABRIELE

Return Indefinite. Trans. James Hawkes. 1985.
The Sisters. In *German Women Writers of the Twentieth Century*. Trans. Elisabeth Rütschi and Edna Huttenmaier Spitz. New York, 1978.

WOLF, CHRISTA

Cassandra. Trans. Jan van Heurck. New York, 1984.
Change of Perspective. In *German Women Writers of the Twentieth Century*. Trans. Elisabeth Rütschi and Edna Huttenmaier Spitz. New York, 1978.
Divided Heaven: A Novel of Germany Today. Trans. Joan Becker, Berlin, 1965.
A Model Childhood. Trans. Ursule Molinaro and Hedwig Rappolt. New York, 1980.

No Place on Earth. Trans. Jan van Heurck. New York, 1982.
The Quest for Christa T. Trans. Christopher Middleton. New York, 1970.

ZORN, FRITZ

Mars. Trans. Robert and Rita Kimber. New York, 1981.

Recommended Readings

GENERAL/HISTORICAL

Craig, Gordon. *The Germans*. New York, 1982.
Dahrendorf, Ralf. *Society and Democracy in Germany*. Garden City, N.Y., 1967.
Dawidowicz, Lucy L. *The War against the Jews*. New York, 1975.
Friedländer, Saul. *Reflections of Nazism: An Essay on Kitsch and Death*. New York, 1984.
Gay, Peter. *Weimar Culture: The Outsider as Insider*. New York, 1968.
Gray, Ronald Douglas. *The German Tradition in Literature: 1871–1945*. Cambridge, 1965.
Hatfield, Henry C. *Modern German Literature: The Major Figures in Context*. New York, 1967.
Laqueur, Walter. *Germany Today: A General Report*. Boston, 1985.
Mosse, George L. *The Crisis of German Ideology: Intellectual Origins of the Third Reich*. New York, 1964.
Stern, Fritz. *The Politics of Cultural Despair: A Study in the Rise of German Ideology*. Berkeley, 1961.

GROUP 47

Lettau, Reinhard, ed. *Die Gruppe 47: Ein Handbuch*. Neuwied and Berlin, 1967.
Schwab-Felisch, Hans, ed. *Der Ruf: Eine deutsche Nachkriegszeitschrift*. Munich, 1962.
Wehdeking, Volker. *Der Nullpunkt*. Stuttgart, 1971.
Widmer, Urs. *1945 oder die "Neue Sprache."* Düsseldorf, 1966.

Schütz, Erhard. *Alfred Andersch*. Munich, 1980.
Wehdeking, Volker, ed. *Zu Alfred Andersch*. Stuttgart, 1983.
Wittmann, Livia Z. *Alfred Andersch*. Stuttgart, 1971.

ON AUSCHWITZ, AND ON GERMAN WRITING

Améry, Jean. *At the Mind's Limit. Contemplations by a Survivor on Auschwitz and Its Realities.* Translated by S. and S. P. Rosenfeld. Bloomington, Ind., 1980.

Anders, Günther. *Besuch im Hades: Auschwitz und Breslau 1966: Nach "Holocaust" 1979.* Munich, 1979.

Bauer, Yehuda. *A History of the Holocaust.* New York, 1982.

Bier, Jean-Paul. *Auschwitz et les nouvelles littératures allemandes.* Brussels, 1979.

New German Critique. An interdisciplinary journal of German Studies. Special issues on "Germans and Jews" 1 and 2, Winter and Spring 1980. Includes indispensable essays by Martin Jay, Andreas Huyssen, Jeffrey Herf, Jack Zipes, and others, mostly from a self-critical neo-Marxist point of view.

H. G. Adler: Buch der Freunde. Edited by W. P. Eckert and W. Ungar. Cologne, 1975. Includes remarks by Böll, Canetti, Doderer, and others.

Lanz, Alfred Otto. *"Panorama" von H. G. Adler—ein "moderner Roman."* Bern, 1984.

Reich-Ranicki, Marcel. "Das Prinzip Radio." *Die Zeit,* Nov. 19, 1970.

Vormweg, Heinrich. "Ein zerbrochenes Leben" [Becker's *Der Boxer*]. *Süddeutsche Zeitung,* Sept. 25, 1976.

PAUL CELAN

Burger, Hermann. *Auf der Suche nach der verlorenen Sprache.* Zürich, 1974.

Chalfen, Israel. *Paul Celan: Eine Biographie seiner Jugend.* Frankfurt, 1979.

Colin, Amy. "Nonsensgedichte und hermetische Poesie: Ein Vergleich am Beispiel der Gedichte Paul Celans." *Literatur und Kritik* 142 (1980): 90–97.

Felstiner, John. "The Biography of a Poem." *The New Republic,* April 2, 1984, pp.27–31.

———. "Paul Celan: The Strain of Jewishness." *Commentary* 79/4 (1985): 44–55.

Glenn, Jerry. *Paul Celan.* New York, 1973.

Hommage à Paul Celan: Etudes Germaniques 25 (1970). Includes essays by Beda Allemann, Bernhard Böschenstein, Claude David, Jean Starobinski, and others.

Lyon, James K. "The Poetry of Paul Celan: An Approach." *Germanic Review* 39 (1964): 50–67.

Meinecke, Dietlind. *Wort und Name bei Paul Celan.* Bad Homburg, 1970.

Menzel, Wolfgang. "Celans Gedicht 'Todesfuge': Das Paradoxon einer Fuge über den Tod in Auschwitz." *Germanisch-Romanische Monatsschrift* 18 (1968): 431–47.

Neumann, Peter H. *Zur Lyrik Paul Celans.* Göttingen, 1968.

Prawer, Siegbert. "Paul Celan." In *Essays on Contemporary German Literature,* edited by Brian Keith-Smith, pp. 161–84. German Men of Letters 4. London, 1966.

Schocken, Gershom. "Paul Celan in Tel-Aviv." *Neue Rundschau* 91 (1980): 256–59.

Schulze, Joachim. *Celan und die Mystiker.* Bern, 1967.

Szondi, Peter. *Celan-Studien.* Edited by Jean Bollack et al. Frankfurt, 1972.

Weissenberger, Klaus. *Die Elegie bei Paul Celan.* Bern, 1969.

PETER WEISS

Best, Otto Ferdinand. *Peter Weiss*. New York, 1976.
Canaris, Volker, ed. *Über Peter Weiss*. Frankfurt, 1970.
Carmichael, Joel. "German Reaction to a New Play about Auschwitz." *American-German Review* 32 (1966): 30–31.
Götze, K. E., and K. R. Scherpe, eds. *Die "Aesthetik des Widerstandes" lesen*. Berlin, 1981.
Hilton, Ian. *Peter Weiss: A Search for Affinities*. London, 1970.
Marcuse, Ludwig. "Was ermittelte Peter Weiss?" *Kürbiskern* 2 (1966): 84–89.
Milfull, John. "From Kafka to Brecht: Peter Weiss' Development toward Marxism." *German Life and Letters* 20 (1966): 61–71.
Roloff, Michael. "An Interview with Peter Weiss." *Partisan Review* 32 (1965): 220–32.
Salloch, Erika. *Peter Weiss' Die Ermittlung*. Frankfurt, 1972.
Sontag, Susan. "Marat/Sade/Artaud." *Partisan Review* 32 (1965): 210–19.
Vormweg, Heinrich. *Peter Weiss*. Munich, 1981.
Waldrop, Rosmarie. "Marat/Sade: A Ritual of the Intellect." *Bucknell Review* 18 (1970): 52–68.
Wendt, Ernst. "Peter Weiss zwischen den Ideologien." *Akzente* 12 (1965): 415–25.

FEDERAL REPUBLIC OF GERMANY

Balfour, Michael. *West Germany*. London, 1968.
Brand, K. W., D. Büsser, and D. Rucht. *Aufbruch in eine andere Gesellschaft: Neue soziale Bewegungen in der Bundesrepublik*. Frankfurt, 1984.
Capra, F., and C. Spretnak. *Green Politics*. New York, 1984.
Dahrendorf, Ralf. *Society and Democracy in Germany*. 2nd ed. Garden City, N.Y., 1969.
Hartrich, Edwin. *The Fourth and Richest Reich*. New York and London, 1980.
Jaeggi, Urs. *Macht und Herrschaft in der Bundesrepublik*. Frankfurt, 1969.
Otto, Karl A. *Vom Ostermarsch zur APO*. Frankfurt, 1977.
Wallich, H. C. *Mainsprings of the German Revival*. New Haven, 1955.

WEST GERMAN WRITING

Arnold, Heinz Ludwig, ed. *Literaturbetrieb in Deutschland*. Munich, 1971.
Bullivant, Keith, and Richard Hinton Thomas. *Literature in Upheaval: West German Writers and the Challenge of the 1960s*. Manchester and New York, 1974.
Durzak, Manfred, ed. *Die deutsche Literatur der Gegenwart*. Stuttgart, 1971.
Hüser, Fritz. *Von der Arbeiterdichtung zur neuen Industriedichtung der Dortmunder Gruppe 61: Abriss und Bibliographie*. Dortmund, 1967.
Kühne, Peter. *Arbeiterklasse und Literatur: Dortmunder Gruppe 61/Werkkreis Literatur der Arbeitswelt*. Frankfurt, 1972.
Lattmann, Dieter. "Stationen einer literarischen Republik." In *Kindlers Literaturgeschichte der Gegenwart*, vol. 1, pp. 3–164. Frankfurt, 1980.
Lützeler, P. M., and E. Schwarz, eds. *Deutsche Literatur in der Bundesrepublik seit 1965*. Königstein/Taunus, 1980.

Matthaei, Renate. *Grenzverschiebung: Neue Tendenzen in der deutschen Literatur der 60er Jahre*. Cologne, 1970.
Wiesand, A. J., and Karla Forbeck. *Literature and the Public in the Federal Republic of Germany*. Munich, 1976.

THE STUDENT REVOLT

Baum, Gerhard. *Die Studentenbewegung der Sechzigerjahre in der Bundesrepublik und Westberlin*. Cologne, 1977.
Behr, Wolfgang. *Jugendkrise und Jugendprotest*. Stuttgart, 1982.
Cohn-Bendit, Daniel. *Le grand bazar*. Paris, 1975.
Dutschke, Rudi. *Geschichte ist machbar: Wurzeln und Spuren eines Aufbruchs*. Edited by Gretchen Dutschke-Klotz, J. Niermeister, and J. Treulieb. Reinbek/Hamburg, 1983.
Habermas, Jürgen. *Protestbewegung und Hochschulreform*. Frankfurt, 1969.
Herrmann, Kai. *Die Revolte der Studenten*. Hamburg, 1967.
Lüdke, Werner Martin, ed. *Nach dem Protest: Literatur im Umbruch*. Frankfurt, 1979.
Mosler, Peter, ed. *Was wir wollten—Was wir wurden: Studentenrevolte zehn Jahre danach*. Reinbek/Hamburg, 1977.
Wolff, F., and E. Windaus, eds. *Studentenbewegung 1967–1969: Protokolle und Materialien*. Basel and Frankfurt, 1979.

TERRORISM

Becker, Jillian. *Hitler's Children: The Story of the Baader-Meinhof Terrorist Gang*. Philadelphia, 1977.
Dornberg, John. "West Germany's Embattled Democracy: The Antiterrorist Menace from the Right." *Saturday Review* 5 (1978): 18–21.
Fetscher, Irving. *Terrorismus und Reaktion*. Cologne, 1977.
Holthusen, Hans Egon. *Sartre in Stammheim*. Stuttgart, 1982.
Kramer, Jane. "A Reporter in Europe: Hamburg." *New Yorker*, March 20, 1978.
Lasky, Melvin I. "Ulrike Meinhof and the Baader-Meinhof Gang." *Encounter* 45 (1975): 9–16.
Mehnert, Klaus. *Twilight of the Young: The Radical Movements of the 1960s and Their Legacy*. New York, 1976.

THE WOMEN'S MOVEMENT

Borenschen, Sylvia. *Die imaginierte Weiblichkeit*. Frankfurt, 1979.
Doormann, Lottemi. *Keiner schiebt uns weg: Zwischenbilanz der Frauenbewegung in der Bundesrepublik*. Weinheim and Basel, 1979.
Drewitz, Ingeborg, ed. *Die deutsche Frauenbewegung*. Bonn, 1983.
Evans, Richard J. *The Feminist Movement in Germany, 1896–1933*. London, 1976.
Havé, Florence. *Brot und Rosen: Geschichte und Perspektiven der demokratischen Frauenbewegung*. Frankfurt, 1979.
Herzog, Marianne. *Von der Hand in den Mund: Frauen im Akkord*. Berlin, 1976.
Krechel, Ursula. *Selbsterfahrung und Fremdbestimmung: Bericht aus der neuen Frauenbewegung*. Darmstadt and Neuwied, 1975.
Pusch, Luise F. *Feminismus: Inspektion der Herrenkultur*. Frankfurt, 1982.
Schenk, Herrad. *Die feministische Herausforderung*. Munich, 1980.

HEINRICH BÖLL

Bronsen, David. "Böll's Women: Patterns in Male-Female Relationships." *Monatshefte* 57 (1965): 291–300.
Conrad, C. Robert. *Heinrich Böll.* New York, 1981.
Friedrichsmeyer, Erhard. *The Major Works of Heinrich Böll.* New York, 1974.
Ley, Ralph. "Compassion, Catholicism, and Communism: Reflections on Böll's *Gruppenbild mit Dame.*" *University of Dayton Review* 10 (1973): 25–40.
Nägele, Rainer. *Heinrich Böll: Einführung in das Werk und die Forschung.* Frankfurt, 1976.
Reich-Ranicki, Marcel, ed. *In Sachen Böll: Ansichten und Aussichten.* Cologne, 1968. Essays by various critics.
Reid, James Henderson. *Heinrich Böll: Withdrawal and Re-emergence.* London, 1973.
Schwartz, Wilhelm J. *Der Erzähler Heinrich Böll: Seine Werke und Gestalten.* Bern, 1967.
Sokel, Walter. "Perspective and Dualism in the Works of Heinrich Böll." In *The Contemporary Novel of Germany: A Symposium*, edited by Robert R. Heitner, pp. 111–38. Austin, Texas, 1967.
Ziolkowski, Theodore. "Albert Camus and Heinrich Böll." *Modern Language Notes* 77 (1962): 282–91.
———. "The Author as *Advocatus Dei* in Heinrich Böll's *Group Portrait with Lady.*" *University of Dayton Review* 12 (1976): 7–18.
———. "Heinrich Böll: Conscience and Craft." *Books Abroad* 34 (1960): 213–22.

GERMAN DEMOCRATIC REPUBLIC

Baylis, Thomas A. *The Technical Intelligentsia and the East German Elite.* Berkeley, 1974.
Doernberg, Stefan. *Kurze Geschichte der DDR.* Berlin, 1968. The official point of view.
Dornberg, John. *The Other Germany.* Garden City, N.Y., 1968.
———. *The New Germans.* New York, 1976.
Ludz, Peter Christian. *The German Democratic Republic from the Sixties to the Seventies.* Cambridge, Mass., 1970.
———. *Mechanismen der Herrschaftssicherung.* Munich, 1980.
McCauley, Martin. *The German Democratic Republic since 1945.* London, 1983.
Mellor, Roy A. *The Two Germanies.* New York, 1978. Useful on economic conditions.
Das System der sozialistischen Gesellschafts- und Staatsordnung in der Deutschen Demokratischen Republik. Berlin, Deutsche Akademie für Staats- und Rechtswissenschaft "Walter Ulbricht," 1970.

GDR WRITING

Emmerich, Wolfgang. *Kleine Literaturgeschichte der DDR.* Darmstadt and Neuwied, 1981.
Franke, Konrad. "Die Kulturpolitik der DDR und ihr Einfluss auf die Literatur." In *Kindlers Literaturgeschichte der Gegenwart*, vol. 3, pp. 5–230. Frankfurt, 1980.

Hohendahl, P.U., and Patricia Herminghouse. *Literatur und Literaturtheorie in der DDR*. Frankfurt, 1976.
Mayer, Hans. *Zur deutschen Literatur der Zeit*, pp. 374–94. Reinbek/Hamburg, 1967.
New German Critique. Special issue on GDR economic reforms and literary life, Spring 1974. Contains articles by Jutta Kneissel, Hanns Eisler, David Bathrick, and others.
Püschel, Ursula. *Mit allen Sinnen. Frauen in der Literatur*. Halle/Saale, 1980.
Raddatz, Fritz J. *Traditionen und Tendenzen: Materialien zur Literatur der DDR*. Frankfurt, 1972.
Sander, Hans Dietrich. *Geschichte der schönen Literatur der DDR*. Freiburg/Breisgau, 1972.
Schonauer, Franz. "DDR auf Bitterfelder Weg." *Neue Deutsche Hefte* 13 (1966): 91–117.
Silberman, Mark D. *Literature of the Working World*. Bern and Frankfurt, 1976.
Studies in German Democratic Republic Culture and Society. Edited by Margy Gerber et al. Washington, D.C., 1981– . Contains papers from a yearly symposium on the GDR.

Frank, Ted E. "Günter de Bruyn's *Preisverleihung*: A Novel with a Mission." *University of Dayton Review* 13/2 (1978): 83–91.
Petr, Pavel. "Stefan Heym and the Concept of Misunderstanding." *Journal of the Australasian Universities Language and Literature Association* 48 (1977): 212–21.

CHRISTA WOLF

Behn, Manfred, ed. *Wirkungsgeschichte von Christa Wolfs "Nachdenken über Christa T."* Königstein/Taunus, 1978.
Cicora, Mary A. "Language, Identity and the Woman in *Nachdenken über Christa T*." *Germanic Review* 57 (1982): 16–22.
Ezergailis, Inta. *Women Writers: The Divided Self*. Bonn, 1982.
Fries, Marilyn S. "Christa Wolf's Use of Image and Vision in the Narrative Structure of Experience." In *Studies in GDR Culture and Society*, vol. 2, pp. 59–74. Washington, D.C., 1982.
Hill, Linda. "Loyalism in Christa Wolf's *Nachdenken über Christa T*." *Michigan German Studies* 7/2 (1981): 249–61.
McPherson, Karin. "In Search of the New Prose: Christa Wolf's Reflections on Writing and the Writers in the 1960s and 1970s." *New German Studies* 9/1 (1981): 1–13.
Reso, Martin. *"Der geteilte Himmel" und seine Kritiker: Dokumentation*. Halle/Saale, 1965.
Sauer, Klaus, ed. *Christa Wolf: Materialienbuch*. Darmstadt and Neuwied, 1979.
Stephan, Alexander. *Christa Wolf*. Munich, 1976.
Wohmann, Gabriele. "Frau mit Eigenschaften." *Christ und Welt*, Dec. 5, 1969.

SHAPES OF POETRY

Bormann, Alexander von. "Politische Lyrik in den sechziger Jahren: Vom Protest zur Agitation." In *Die deutsche Literatur der Gegenwart*, edited by M. Durzak, pp. 170–91. Stuttgart, 1971.

Büttner, Ludwig. *Von Benn zu Enzensberger: Eine Einführung in die zeitgenössische Lyrik 1945–1970*. Nuremberg, 1971.

Endler, A. "Sarah Kirsch und ihre Kritiker." *Sinn und Form* 27 (1975): 142–70.

Flores, John. *Poetry in East Germany: Adjustments, Visions and Provocations*. New Haven, 1971.

Franke, Konrad. "Lyrik." (In the GDR.) In *Kindlers Literaturgeschichte der Gegenwart*, vol. 3, pp. 231–325. Frankfurt, 1980.

Grimm, Reinhold. *Texturen*. (On H. M. Enzensberger.) Bern and Frankfurt, 1984.

Gumpel, Liselotte. *"Concrete Poetry" from East and West Germany*. New Haven, 1976.

Hinderer, Walter. "Komm ins Offene, Freund: Tendenzen der westdeutschen Lyrik nach 1965." In *Deutsche Literatur in der Bundesrepublik seit 1965*, edited by P. M. Lützeler and E. Schwarz. Königstein/Taunus, 1980.

———. "Sprache und Methode: Bemerkungen zur politischen Lyrik der sechziger Jahre." *Revolte und Experiment* (5th Amherst Colloquium), pp. 98–143. Heidelberg, 1972.

Holzner, J. "Gegennachrichten: Zu den Gedichten von Erich Fried." *Literatur und Kritik* 152 (1981): 113–26.

Klinger, Kurt. "Lyrik in Österreich seit 1945." In *Kindlers Literaturgeschichte der Gegenwart*, vol. 6, pp. 291–476. Frankfurt, 1980.

Krolow, Karl. *Aspekte zeitgenössischer deutscher Lyrik*. Gütersloh, West Germany, 1961.

Laschen, Gregor. *Lyrik in der DDR*. Frankfurt, 1971.

Rothschild, Thomas. *Liedermacher: 23 Portraits*. Frankfurt, 1980.

Schäfer, H. D. "Zusammenhänge der deutschen Gegenwartslyrik." In *Die deutsche Literatur der Gegenwart*, 4th ed., edited by M. Durzak, pp. 166–203. Stuttgart, 1981.

Weissenberger, Klaus, ed. *Die deutsche Lyrik 1945–1975*. Düsseldorf, 1981. Includes an essay on Sarah Kirsch by Wolfgang Wittkowski; on Jürgen Theobaldy by Fritz Martini; on Hans Magnus Enzensberger by Hans Egon Holthusen; on Wilhelm Lehmann by Manfred Hoppe; and a panorama of the 1950s by James Rolleston.

AUSTRIA

Andics, Hellmut. *Die Insel der Seligen: Österreich von der Moskauer Deklaration bis zur Gegenwart*. Vienna, 1968.

Arndt, Sven W. *The Political Economy of Austria*. Washington, D.C., 1982.

Bader, William B. *Austria between East and West*. Stanford, Calif., 1966.

Goldner, Franz. *Die österreichische Emigration: 1938–1945*. Vienna, 1972.

Johnston, William M. *The Austrian Mind*. Berkeley, 1972.

Mayer, Klaus Wolfgang. *Die Sozialstruktur Österreichs*. Vienna, 1970.

Rosenmayr, Leopold, ed. *Politische Beteiligung und Wertwandel in Österreich*. Vienna, 1980.

Steiner, Kurt. *Politics in Austria*. Boston, 1972.

———, ed. *Tradition and Innovation in Contemporary Austria*. Palo Alto, Calif., 1982. Includes articles on politics, economics, and culture.

Sully, Melanie. *Political Parties and Elections in Austria*. London, 1981.

Vodopivec, Alexander. *Die Balkanisierung Österreichs*. Vienna, 1966.

———. *Der verspielte Ballhausplatz: Vom schwarzen zum roten Österreich.* Vienna, 1970.

AUSTRIAN WRITING

Bartsch, K., D. Goltschnigg, and G. Melzer, eds. *Für und Wider eine österreichische Literatur.* Königstein/Taunus, 1982.
Breicha, Otto. "Zur Wiener Gruppe." *Literatur und Kritik* 4 (1969): 492–94.
Greiner, Ulrich. *Der Tod des Nachsommers.* Munich, 1979.
Kraus, Wolfgang. *Der fünfte Stand: Aufbruch der Intellektuellen in West und Ost.* 3rd ed. Bern, 1966.
Magris, Claudio. *Il mito absburgico nella letteratura austriaca moderna.* Turin, 1963.
Pfoser, Alfred. *Literatur und Austro-Marxismus.* Vienna, 1970.
Rühm, Gerhard, ed. *Die Wiener Gruppe.* Reinbek and Hamburg, 1967. An anthology.
Ruiss, G., and J. A. Vyoral. *Zur Situation junger österreichischer Autoren.* Vienna, 1978.
Schmidt-Dengler, Wendelin. "Contemporary Literature in Austria." In *Modern Austria,* edited by Kurt Steiner. Palo Alto, Calif., 1981.
Schorske, Carl J. *Fin-de-siècle Vienna.* 2nd ed. New York, 1979.
Spiel, Hilde. "Die österreichische Literatur nach 1945: Eine Einführung." In *Kindlers Literaturgeschichte der Gegenwart,* vol. 5, pp. 3–136. Frankfurt, 1980.
Weiss, Walter. "Die Literatur der Gegenwart in Österreich." In *Deutsche. Literatur der Gegenwart,* edited by M. Durzak, pp. 386–99. Stuttgart, 1971.

THOMAS BERNHARD

Bartsch, K., D. Goltschnigg, and G. Melzer, eds. *In Sachen Thomas Bernhard.* Königstein/Taunus, 1983.
Botond, Anneliese, ed. *Über Thomas Bernhard.* Frankfurt, 1970.
Craig, D. A. "The Novels of Thomas Bernhard." *German Life and Letters* 25 (1972): 343–53.
Dierick, A. P. "Thomas Bernhard's Austria." *Modern Austrian Literature* 12 (1979): 73–91.
Dittmar, Jens, ed. *Thomas Bernhard: Werkgeschichte.* Frankfurt, 1981.
Donnenberg, Josef. "Thomas Bernhard und Österreich: Dokumentation und Kommentar." *Österreich in Geschichte und Literatur* 14 (1970): 237–51.
Höller, Hans. *Kritik einer literarischen Form: Versuch über Thomas Bernhard.* Stuttgart, 1979.
Jurgensen, Manfred. *Thomas Bernhard.* Bern, 1981.
Sorg, Bernhard. *Thomas Bernhard.* Munich, 1977.
Steiner, George. "Conic sections. Thomas Bernhard: *Korrektur.*" *Times Literary Supplement,* Feb. 13, 1976.
Text und Kritik 43. Munich, 1973. Special issue on Bernhard, edited by H. L. Arnold.

PETER HANDKE

Buselmeier, Michael. "Peter Handkes Entdeckungen." *Merkur* 21/236 (1967): 1090–94.

Dixon, Christa K. "Peter Handke: *Die Angst des Tormanns beim Elfmeter:* Ein Beitrag zur Interpretation." *Sprachkunst* 3 (1972): 95–97.
Durzak, Manfred. *Peter Handke und die deutsche Gegenwartsliteratur*. Stuttgart, 1982.
Gilman, Richard. *The Making of Modern Drama*. New York, 1974. A chapter on Handke.
Hern, Nicholas. *Peter Handke*. New York, 1972.
Hill, Linda. "Obscurantism and Verbal Resistance." *The Germanic Review* 52/4 (1977): 304–15.
Kermode, Frank. "The Model of a Modern Modernist." *New York Review of Books*, May 1, 1975, pp. 20–23.
Klinkowitz, Jerome, and James Knowlton. *Peter Handke and the Postmodern Transformation*. Columbia, Mo., 1983.
Lederer, Otto. "Über Peter Handkes Sprachspiele." *Literatur und Kritik* 58 (1971): 478–582.
Nägele, Rainer. "Peter Handke: The Staging of Language." *Modern Drama* 23/4 (1981): 327–38.
Pütz, Peter. *Peter Handke*. Frankfurt, 1982.
Scharang, Michael, ed. *Über Peter Handke*. Frankfurt, 1972.
Schlueter, June. *The Plays and Novels of Peter Handke*. Pittsburgh and London, 1981.
Taëni, Rainer. "Handke und das politische Theater." *Neue Rundschau* 81 (1970): 158–69.
Text und Kritik 24. Munich, 1969. Special issue on Handke. Essays by Hans Mayer, Klaus Stiller, Peter Schumann, and others.

DRAMA

Böhm, Gotthard. "Dramatik in Österreich seit 1945." In *Kindlers Literaturgeschichte der Gegenwart*, vol. 6, pp. 295–506. Frankfurt, 1980.
Daiber, Hans. *Deutsches Theater seit 1945*. Stuttgart, 1976.
Esslin, Martin. *The Theater of the Absurd*, pp. 191–95. Garden City, N.Y., 1961.
Hinck, Walter. *Das moderne Drama in Deutschland*. Göttingen, 1973.
Hoover, Marjorie L. "Revolution und Ritual: Das deutsche Drama der sechziger Jahre." *Revolte und Experiment* (5th Amherst Colloquium), pp. 73–97. Heidelberg, 1972.
Huettich, Gunnar. *Theater in the Planned Society*. Chapel Hill, N.C., 1978.
Kesting, Marianne. "Das deutsche Drama seit Ende des Zweiten Weltkriegs." In *Die Deutsche Literatur der Gegenwart*, edited by M. Durzak, pp. 76–98. Stuttgart, 1971.
Klarmann, Adolf D. "German Documentary Drama." *Yale German Review* 2 (1966): 13–19.
Patterson, Michael. *Post-War Theatre in West and East Germany, Austria, and Northern Switzerland*. London, 1976.
Schivelbusch, Wolfgang. *Sozialistisches Drama und Brecht: Drei Modelle; Hacks, Müller, Lange*. Darmstadt and Neuwied, 1974.
Taëni, Rainer. *Drama nach Brecht*. Basel, 1968.
Zipes, Jack D. "Documentary Drama in Germany: Mending the Circuit." *Germanic Review* 42 (1967): 49–62.

KROETZ, MÜLLER, STRAUSS

Adelson, Leslie. "Subjectivity Reconsidered: Botho Strauss and Contemporary German Prose." *New German Critique* 30 (1983): 3–59.
Blevins, Richard W. *F. X. Kroetz.* New York, 1983.
Carl, Rolf-Peter. *F. X. Kroetz.* Munich, 1978.
Hoffmeister, Donna L. *The Theater of Confinement.* (On Fleisser and Kroetz.) Camden, S.C., 1983.
Kafitz, Dieter. "Die Problematisierung des individualistischen Menschenbildes im deutschsprachigen Drama der Gegenwart." (On Kroetz, Bernhard, Strauss.) *Basis* 10 (1980): 93–126.
Müller, Heiner. *Rotwelsch.* Munich, 1981. Interviews.
Schulz, Genia. *Heiner Müller.* Stuttgart, 1980. Scholarly materials.
Silberman, Marc. *Heiner Müller.* Amsterdam, 1980.
Wieghaus, Georg. *Heiner Müller.* Munich, 1981.

SWITZERLAND

Chopard, Theo. *Switzerland: Present and Future.* Bern, 1963.
Dürrenmatt, Peter. *Schweizer Geschichte.* Zürich, 1963.
Glaus, Beat. *Die Nationale Front. Eine Schweizer faschistische Bewegung.* Zürich, 1969.
Gretler, Armin, and Pierre-Emeric Mandl. *Values, Trends and Alternatives in Swiss Society.* New York, 1973.
Hauser, Albrecht. *Schweizerische Wirtschafts- und Sozialgeschichte.* Erlenbach and Zürich, 1961.
Hughes, Christopher. *Switzerland.* New York, 1975.
Ich hab im Traum die Schweiz gesehen: 35 Schriftsteller aus der Schweiz schreiben über ihr Land. Salzburg and Vienna, 1980.
Schmid, Carol L. *Conflict and Consensus in Switzerland.* Berkeley, 1981.
Schmidt, Max. *Eine Stadt in Bewegung: Materialien zu den Zürcher Unruhen.* Zürich, 1980. Social Democratic point of view.
Sorell, Walter. *The Swiss.* New York, 1972.
Steinberg, Jonathan. *Why Switzerland?* New York, 1976.

SWISS WRITING

Bohnen, Klaus, and Conny Bauer, eds. *Themenheft: Deutschsprachige Literatur der Schweiz nach 1945.* Copenhagen and Munich, 1983. Includes important essays by Rolf Kieser, Hans Wysling, and others.
Burkhard, Marianne. "Gauging Existential Space: The Emergence of Women Writers in Switzerland." *World Literature Today* 20 (1981): 607–12.
Calgari, Guido. *The Four Literatures of Switzerland.* London, 1963.
Fringeli, Dieter. *Dichter im Abseits: Schweizer Autoren von Glauser bis Hohl.* Zürich, 1974.
Fringeli, Dieter, and Paul Nizon, eds. *Taschenbuch der Gruppe Olten.* Bern, 1970.
Gsteiger, Manfred, ed. "Die zeitgenössische Literatur der Schweiz." In *Kindlers Literaturgeschichte der Gegenwart,* vol. 7. Frankfurt, 1980. Includes a panoramic essay by the editor and a survey of German-Swiss writing by Elsbeth Pulver.

Kieser, Rolf. *Erzwungene Symbiose: Th. Mann, R. Musil, und B. Brecht im Schweizer Exil.* Bern, 1984.
Nizon, Paul. *Diskurs in der Enge.* Bern, 1970.
Weber, Werner. *Tagebuch eines Lesers*, pp. 267–90. Olten, 1965.
Zbinden, Hans. "Zur Situation der Literatur in der Schweiz." *Welt und Wort* 24 (1969): 308–11.
Zeltner-Neukomm, Gerda. *Das Ich ohne Gewähr: Gegenwartsautoren aus der Schweiz.* Zürich, 1980.

ADOLF MUSCHG

Fringeli, Dieter. *Von Spitteler zu Muschg: Literatur der deutschen Schweiz seit 1900.* Basel, 1975.
Kieser, Rolf. "Interview mit Adolf Muschg." *Basis* 9 (1979): 61–70.
Ricker-Abderhalden, Judith, ed. *Über Adolf Muschg.* Munich, 1984.
Voris, Renate. *Adolf Muschg.* Munich, 1984.

MAX FRISCH

Bänziger, Hans. *Frisch und Dürrenmatt.* Bern, 1976.
Beckermann, Thomas, ed. *Über Max Frisch.* Frankfurt, 1971.
Begegnungen: Eine Festschrift für Max Frisch zum siebzigsten Geburtstag. Frankfurt, 1981.
Butler, Michael. *The Novels of Max Frisch.* London, 1976.
Hage, Volker. *Max Frisch (Bildbiographie).* Reinbek/Hamburg, 1983.
Kieser, Rolf. *Max Frisch: Das literarische Tagebuch.* Frauenfeld, 1975.
Merrifield, Doris F. *Das Bild der Frau bei Max Frisch.* Freiburg/Breisgau, 1971.
Petersen, Carol. *Max Frisch.* New York, 1972.
Probst, G. F., and Jay F. Bodine, eds. *Perspectives of Max Frisch.* Lexington, Ky., 1982.
Stephan, Alexander. *Max Frisch.* Munich, 1983.
Weisstein, Ulrich. *Max Frisch.* New York, 1967.

PROBLEMS OF THE NOVEL

Ball, Kurt. *Die Exekution des Erzählers.* Frankfurt, 1974. From a sophisticated GDR perspective.
Baumgart, Reinhard. *Aussichten des Romans oder Hat Literatur Zukunft?* Neuwied and Berlin, 1968.
Boa, Elizabeth, and J. H. Reid. *Critical Strategies: German Fiction in the Twentieth Century.* London, 1972.
Dietze, Gabriele. *Die Überwindung der Sprachlosigkeit: Texte aus der neuen Frauenbewegung.* Darmstadt, 1979.
Durzak, Manfred. *Der deutsche Roman der Gegenwart.* 3rd ed. Stuttgart, 1979. Eminently useful.
Hahn, Ulla. *Literatur in Aktion. Zur Entwicklung operativer Literaturformen in der Bundesrepublik.* Wiesbaden, 1978.
Hatfield, Henry. *Crisis and Continuity in Modern German Fiction.* Ithaca, N.Y., 1969.

Heimann, Bodo. "Experimentelle Prosa." In *Die deutsche Literatur der Gegenwart*, edited by M. Durzak, pp. 230–55. Stuttgart, 1971.
Reich-Ranicki, Marcel. *Deutsche Literatur in West und Ost*. Munich, 1963.
———. *Entgegnung: Zur Literatur der siebziger Jahre*. Stuttgart, 1979.
Thomas, Richard Hinton, and Wilfried van der Will. *The German Novel and the Affluent Society*. Toronto, 1968.
Trommler, Frank. "Von Stalin zu Hölderlin: Über den Entwicklungsroman in der DDR." *Basis* 2 (1971): 141–90.
Waidson, H. M. *The Modern German Novel*. London, 1960.
Ziolkowski, Theodore. *Dimensions of the Modern Novel*. Princeton, 1969.

JOHNSON, LENZ (HERMANN), WALSER, WELLERSHOFF, WOHMANN

Baudrillard, Jean. "Uwe Johnson: La frontière." *Les temps modernes* 18 (1962): 1094–1107.
Detweiler, Robert. "Speculations about Jacob: The Truth of Ambiguity." *Monatshefte* 58 (1966): 25–32.
Diller, Edward. "Uwe Johnson's Karsch: Language as a Reflection of the Two Germanies." *Monatshefte* 60 (1968): 34–39.
Michaelis, Rolf. *Kleines Adressbuch für Jerichow und New York: Ein Register zu Uwe Johnsons Roman "Jahrestage."* Frankfurt, 1983.
Migner, Karl. *Uwe Johnson: "Das dritte Buch über Achim": Interpretation*. Munich, 1966.
Zehm, Günther. "Ausruhen bei den Dingen: Notiz über Uwe Johnsons Methode." *Der Monat* 14 (1961/62): 69–73.

Handke, Peter. "Jemand anderer—Hermann Lenz." In *Als das Wünschen noch geholfen hat*, pp. 81–100. Frankfurt, 1974.
Kreuzer, Ingrid and Helmuth, eds. *Über Hermann Lenz: Dokumente seiner Rezeption (1949–1979)*. Munich, 1979. With excellent bibliography.
Schäfer, Hans Dieter. "Hinweis auf Hermann Lenz." *Neue Rundschau* 86 (1975): 513–18.

Andrews, C. "Comedy and Satire in Martin Walser's *Halbzeit*." *Modern Language Notes* 50 (1969): 6–10.
Beckerman, Thomas, ed. *Über Martin Walser*. Frankfurt, 1970.
Enzensberger, Hans Magnus. *Einzelheiten*, pp. 240–45. Frankfurt, 1962.
Nelson, Donald F. "The Depersonalized World of Martin Walser." *German Quarterly* 42 (1969): 204–16.
Parkes, K. S. "Crisis and New Ways: The Recent Development of Martin Walser." *New German Studies* 1 (1973): 95–98.
Pickar, Gertrud B. "Martin Walser: The Hero of Accommodation." *Monatshefte* 62 (1970): 357–66.
Siblewski, Klaus. *Martin Walser*. Frankfurt, 1981. Important essays by Rainer Nägele, Volker Bohn, and others.
Trommler, Frank. "Demonstration eines Scheiterns. Zu Martin Walsers Theaterarbeit." *Basis* 10 (1980): 127–41.
Waine, A. E. *Martin Walser*. Munich, 1980.

Helmreich, Hans. *Dieter Wellershoff.* Munich, 1982.
Thomas, Hinton R., ed. *Der Schriftsteller Dieter Wellershoff.* Cologne, 1975. Essays by members of the Dept. of Germanic Studies, Warwick, England.
Vollmuth, Eike H. *Dieter Wellershoff. Romanproduktion und anthropologische Literaturtheorie.* Munich, 1979.
Vormweg, Heinrich. "Ein soziologischer Realismus." (On Wellershoff.) *Merkur* 20 (1966): 991–94.

Ferchl, Irene. *Die Rolle des Alltäglichen in der Kurzprosa von Gabriele Wohmann.* Bonn, 1980.
Häntzschel, Günter, et al. *Gabriele Wohmann.* Munich, 1982.
Holbeche, Yvonne. "The Early Novels of Gabriele Wohmann." *Journal of Australasian Universities Language and Literature Association* 52 (1979): 241–52.
Knapp, Gerhard Peter and Mona. *Gabriele Wohmann.* Königstein/Taunus, 1981.
Scheuffelen, Thomas, ed. *Gabriele Wohmann: Materialienbuch.* Darmstadt, 1977.
Waidson, H. M. "The Short Stories and Novels of Gabriele Wohmann." *German Life and Letters* 26 (1972/73): 214–27.

GÜNTER GRASS

Brode, Hanspeter. *Günter Grass.* Munich, 1979.
Cepl-Kaufmann, Gertrude. *Günter Grass: Eine Analyse des Gesamtwerkes unter dem Aspekt von Literatur und Politik.* Königstein/Taunus, 1975.
Cunliffe, W. Gordon. *Günter Grass.* New York, 1969.
Görtz, Franz Josef. *Günter Grass: Zur Pathogenese eines Markenbilds.* Meisenheim an der Glan, 1978.
A Günter Grass Symposium, edited by A. Leslie Willson. Austin, Texas, 1971.
Günter Grass's "The Flounder" in Critical Perspective, edited by Siegfried Mews. New York, 1983.
Hollington, Michael. *Günter Grass: The Writer in a Pluralist Society.* London and Boston, 1980. Particularly illuminating.
Holthusen, Hans Egon. "Günter Grass als politischer Autor." *Monat* 18 (1966): 66–81.
Leonard, Irène. *Günter Grass.* Edinburgh, 1974.
Miles, Keith. *Günter Grass.* New York, 1975.
Reddick, John. *The "Danzig Trilogy" of Günter Grass.* London and New York, 1975. Useful.
Schlöndorff, Volker, and Günter Grass. *"Die Blechtrommel" als Film.* Frankfurt, 1979.
Steiner, George. "A Note on Grass." In *Language and Silence*, pp. 110–17. London, 1969.
Text und Kritik. 1/1a, edited by H. L. Arnold. Munich, 1978. 5th ed. Special issue on Grass.

Index to Authors and Books